Democracy's Privileged Few

JOSH CHAFETZ

Democracy's Privileged Few

LEGISLATIVE PRIVILEGE AND
DEMOCRATIC NORMS IN THE
BRITISH AND AMERICAN
CONSTITUTIONS

Yale University Press
New Haven &
London

Published with assistance from the Louis Stern Memorial Fund.

Set in Sabon by Keystone Typesetting, Inc.
Printed in the United States of America.

Library of Congress Cataloging-in-Publication Data
Chafetz, Joshua A. (Joshua Aaron), 1979–
Democracy's privileged few : legislative privilege and democratic norms in the British and American constitutions / Josh Chafetz.
p. cm.
Includes bibliographical references and index.
ISBN-13: 978-0-300-11325-9 (cloth : alk. paper)
ISBN-10: 0-300-11325-0
1. United States. Congress — Privileges and immunities. 2. Constitutional law — United States. 3. Great Britain. Parliament — Privileges and immunities. 4. Constitutional law — Great Britain. I. Title.
K3324.C47 2006
328.41'074 — dc22   2006014036

A catalogue record for this book is available from the British Library.

10 9 8 7 6 5 4 3 2 1

To mom and dad,
with love and thanks
for everything

Contents

Acknowledgments

This project began its life as a master's thesis, continued as a doctoral dissertation, and has come to completion in the book in front of you. Along the way, I have been blessed with friends and colleagues who have contributed immeasurably to the work's progress and the author's well-being. This note merely acknowledges my debt to them; I am under no delusion that it repays it.

The time spent and advice proffered by my advisers, Nick Barber and Vernon Bogdanor, went far above and beyond the call of duty, and their generosity is greatly appreciated. Akhil Amar has been a teacher, mentor, and friend since I was an undergraduate, and his advice and encouragement have been invaluable throughout this project. Nigel Bowles and Diana Woodhouse were my dissertation examiners, and their comments have proven most helpful, as have those of two anonymous reviewers for Yale University Press. Michael O'Malley, Steve Colca, and Otto Bohlmann at the Press have been helpful at every turn, and I am truly grateful.

I would also like to thank David Adesnik, Erin Ashwell, Patrick Belton, Jennifer Bennett, Joey Fishkin, Kristin Javaras, Rachel Kleinfeld, Marin Levy, Brett Marston, Brook McKinney, Stephen Sachs, Guglielmo Verdirame, Stuart White, Lindsey Worth, and Paul Yowell for helping to keep the book on track and its author sane.

The Rhodes Trust very generously funded my graduate studies, and the

Institute for Humane Studies funded an additional summer's worth of work on this book. Merton College, Oxford, and the Yale Law School have provided hospitable and stimulating environments in which to work. I owe a special debt of gratitude to the librarians at Oxford and Yale — their craft is a vital but underappreciated one.

Finally, Catherine Roach's love and patience have sustained me, and her brilliance has enriched my life, and this book, immeasurably. And my parents have never stopped teaching me — always by example — what it is to be a good scholar, a good citizen, and a good person. This book is for them.

Democracy's Privileged Few

Introduction

    Few things are more important to the collective political life of a modern state than that state's constitution. Yet in two of the states that are considered exemplars of modern democratic constitutionalism — Britain and America — the very word "constitution" means radically different things. In the mother country, the Constitution is an amorphous thing, without sharp edges or a clearly defined status. The British Constitution cannot be distinguished from institutional interpretations of it: the actual, current structure of institutions is constitutive of the Constitution itself. When Albert Venn Dicey and later Vernon Bogdanor described the British Constitution as "historic" — that is, as "the product, not of deliberate design, but of historical development"[1] — they were situating themselves within a long line of constitutional scholarship. In discussing the origins of civil society in 1767, Adam Ferguson wrote of institutions whose development is "indeed the result of human action, but not the execution of any human design."[2] In the twentieth century, Friedrich Hayek would make this wording central to his definition of the concept of spontaneous order, of which he thought the common law was a prime example.[3] And J. R. Pole, noting the flexibility and fluidity of the British Constitution, wrote that it "may be thought of as an organism, but not as a machine."[4]

    What accounts for this fluidity? The first thing that occurs to modern minds is what is commonly called the unwrittenness of the British Constitution.

Although much of the British Constitution is indeed written (the Magna Carta [1215], the Bill of Rights [1689], the Articles of Union [1706], and so on), no person or group of people ever sat down to write the British Constitution (perhaps, then, "uncodified" would be a better description than "unwritten"). At the margins, there can even be debate as to which written documents have constitutional status and which do not. Although the doctrine of parliamentary sovereignty means that there is no constitutional norm that cannot be overturned by a new statute, there are plenty of constitutional norms that do not have a statutory basis. They result from either ancient practice or judge-made common law, yet they are legally binding, just like norms arising from statutes. Moreover, when statutes are ambiguous, judges will interpret them so as not to disturb constitutional norms. The result is that the British Constitution is in a constant state of flux, and the interaction among new statutes, old norms, and changing circumstances is constantly being negotiated by the courts, Parliament, and the voting public. The resulting uncertainty led Sidney Low to remark that the British government is based upon "a system of tacit understandings. But the understandings themselves are not always understood."[5]

Yet, as Adam Ferguson appreciated, out of such hectic processes arises a complex and subtle order. Principles that animate and have long animated the British polity can be traced over the course of centuries. But historical analysis of the British Constitution is a complicated dialectic: from specific events, decisions, and laws, we induce general animating principles, and using these principles, we analyze and critique those same events, decisions, and laws. Out of this dialectic arises a better understanding of both what the British Constitution is and what it should be.

The Americans, like all rebellious children, rejected the outward forms of their parents' way of (political) life. They reconstituted themselves as a national people, and they used a single, explicit document to do so. The document has, of course, changed over the years — it has been amended twenty-seven times — and interpretations of it have changed continuously. But they are precisely that — interpretations *of it,* a short document (of fewer than five thousand words at the Founding, and even today fewer than eight thousand), read in high schools throughout the country. Not even the most highly trained lawyer could fail to distinguish between the Constitution itself and interpretations of it by the three branches of government.[6]

Yet, for all the differences between the two, an understanding of the British Constitution is absolutely crucial to an understanding of the American. The American Constitution was, after all, written by men who had only recently ceased to be British subjects. Their background constitutional assumptions were British, and they knew which parts they wanted to keep (for example, the writ of habeas corpus, a bicameral legislature, a unitary executive) and which they did not (for example, bills of attainder, titles of nobility, the monarchy). Most important of all, the Americans declared with their opening words that "We the People of the United States" were to be sovereign in the new nation.

Although the British Constitution has never fully warmed to popular sovereignty, it certainly should not be thought of as undemocratic. Indeed, one of the animating spirits of British constitutional history has undoubtedly been the drive toward greater democracy. The democratic element of the Constitution has grown stronger, while the monarchical element has been reduced to a figurehead and the aristocratic element has been both reduced in power and made more responsive to the democratic element.[7] As democracy has put down deeper roots in the Constitution, the understanding of what constitutes democracy has grown broader — one might say that the understanding of democracy ingrained in the Constitution has grown from democracy *simpliciter* (that is, the existence of an elected, representative body constitutes democracy) to *liberal* democracy (that is, democracy involves certain checks, even on elected bodies, and seeks to promote a tighter nexus between the wishes of the people and the actions of the government). In short, while the Americans can be said to have designed a democracy, the British stumbled into one.

This book aims to throw light on the British and American constitutions, separately, but also on the relationship between them. That, however, is a lot of territory to cover, a broad vista that would encompass many of the most significant constitutional developments in human history. The book will not attempt to survey the entire field but rather will try to provide a window onto it. I have chosen legislative privilege — those special rights that individual Members or Houses of the legislature possess in order to facilitate their legislative duties — to serve as our portal because privilege gives us a particularly clear view of important institutional cleavages. Much of the history of British parliamentary privilege is the history of clashes among the House of Commons, the House of Lords, the monarch, and the courts. Likewise, much of the history of American congressional privilege is the history of clashes among the House or Senate, the president, and the courts. These conflicts provide a uniquely valuable perspective on the way power dynamics among those institutions work and have worked in the past. This perspective, in turn, will help us get at many of the fundamental values and ideas lying at the heart of these constitutions.

Moreover, the field has received surprisingly little attention — the last book-length treatment of British parliamentary privilege was published in 1921.[8] A survey of parliamentary privilege in the American colonies was published in the 1940s.[9] Shorter studies of individual aspects of privilege have been spo-radically published and will be cited throughout this work. However, there has been no attempt to consider under a single head (and therefore under a single analytic framework) the various privileges of Congress guaranteed by the American Constitution. Of course, this means that there has also been no systematic comparative study of legislative privilege in the British and American constitutions. This book aims to remedy these deficits.

Two British Conceptions of the Function of Privilege

I shall argue that there are two basic paradigms of the role of parliamentary privilege in the British Constitution. For ease of reference, I shall dub them the Blackstonian and the Millian paradigms, although I am not making the exegetical claim that William Blackstone or John Stuart Mill would necessarily have agreed with everything I say under their labels. Broadly speaking, the Blackstonian conception is that, because the House of Commons is the democratic element of the Constitution, the function of privilege must be to protect the House at all costs from outside interference. The Millian conception recognizes that democracy has come to have deeper roots in the Constitution than simply the House of Commons, and it allows room for constituents and the courts when determining the scope of privilege. My purpose is not to argue that one of these conceptions is right and another wrong; rather, I am positing that each was appropriate in its own historical circumstances. When the democratic element of the Constitution was struggling, it made sense to do whatever possible to strengthen the House of Commons, even if one of the side effects was to keep the connection between Members and their constituents a loose one. This was the Blackstonian view. But as the democratic element grew broader and deeper, this need to strengthen the House at any cost began to dissipate, and the focus of privilege rightfully shifted to allow for checks on the House and a tighter nexus between Members and their constituents. This is the Millian view. Blackstonian interpretations of privilege are only inappropriate when made in Millian political climates. It should, however, be noted that these two paradigms are at opposite ends of a continuum: there is no bright line of division between them, and there are plenty of cases that fall somewhere in the middle. With that in mind, let us turn to a more detailed examination of what the Blackstonian and Millian conceptions entail.

THE BLACKSTONIAN PARADIGM

William Blackstone, the famous eighteenth-century English legal academic, treatise writer, and judge, wrote:

Privilege of parliament was principally established, in order to protect it's [*sic*] members not only from being molested by their fellow-subjects, but also more especially from being oppressed by the power of the crown. If therefore all the privileges of parliament were once to be set down and ascertained, and no privilege to be allowed but what was so defined and determined, it were easy for the executive power to devise some new case, not within the line of privilege, and under pretence thereof to harass any refractory member and violate the freedom of parliament. The dignity and independence of the two houses are therefore in great measure preserved by keeping their privileges indefinite.[10]

As a thinker — and, for a while, a jurist — who sought "to reconcile not just in theory but in detail the principles of liberal political theory and the practices of English common law,"[11] Blackstone adopted this view of privilege because he thought it the best way to protect the democratic institution of the House of Commons while it was still in a fragile stage of its development. In order to ensure that the Commons would not fall prey to the manipulations of other powerful actors — most notably, the monarch and the nobility (and therefore the courts, which were royally controlled and whose highest court of appeals was the House of Lords) — Blackstone sought to erect a legal wall around the House. In the chapters that follow, it will frequently be noted that the Blackstonian view often expresses itself as a *geographical* view of privilege: it focuses on absolutely protecting from interference by any outside power actions that take place within the physical confines of the House. In the Blackstonian paradigm, the promotion of democratic values requires an absolute commitment to bolstering the power of the House of Commons, the only democratic institution in the state. On this view, anything threatening the power of the House constitutes a threat to those democratic values. The function of privilege, then, is to protect those values by protecting the power of the House, at almost any cost.

This intense focus on the powers of the House means that the Blackstonian conception of the role of privilege has almost nothing to say about ordinary subjects (that is, constituents). Indeed, if anything, the Blackstonian paradigm views the public and the press as potential threats, rather than as essential components of the democratic system. Because they are so thoroughly left out of the equation, Blackstone's formula has the potential to cause them great mischief. One of the functions of law is to provide for stability of expectations. By arguing that the outlines of parliamentary privilege ought to remain indefinite, Blackstone is, effectively, denying protection of the law to citizens in any case in which Parliament might choose to assert privilege. It ought, then, to come as no surprise that the passage quoted above comes just a few short pages after Blackstone's insistence that Locke was wrong to assert that ultimate sovereignty remains in the people.[12] Instead, Blackstone tells us, Parliament alone

> hath sovereign and uncontrolable authority in making, confirming, enlarging, restraining, abrogating, repealing, reviving, and expounding of laws, concerning matters of all possible denominations, ecclesiastical, or temporal, civil, military, maritime, or criminal: this being the place where that absolute despotic power, which must in all governments reside somewhere, is entrusted by the constitution of these kingdoms.[13]

In a time in which the power of Parliament is precarious, the function of privilege must be to do everything possible to shore up that power and to ensure that the other great powers in the state—the monarch and the nobility—cannot invade it. For a liberal in such times, the first imperative is protecting the Commons, as the only democratic organ in the state. Ensuring a tight nexus between the actions of the Commons and the wishes of its constituents was an afterthought, if it was a thought at all. Indeed, Blackstone seems at times simply to have assumed that protecting the House of Commons was tantamount to protecting the rights of citizens.[14] For Blackstone, then, the primary function of parliamentary privilege was the defense of a sovereign legislature against encroachments by a jealous monarch or nobility. This view of the function of privilege, which appears both in Blackstone's theoretical writings and in his writings from the bench, led to the conclusion that its protection justified significant impositions on the rights of British subjects, as well as an insulated attitude that largely neglected any role for constituents.

THE MILLIAN PARADIGM

As Carl Wittke has noted, during the nineteenth century

> the House of Commons became more and more a truly representative body, the organ of the people, and the real power in the state. As such, its position became more and more secure, and sweeping claims of privilege were no longer so necessary to protect it in the exercise of its legislative activities, and to guard it against encroachments from Crown, Lords, and courts.[15]

It is perhaps unsurprising, then, that it was a nineteenth-century liberal theorist, John Stuart Mill, who best articulated the democratic theory underlying the new conception of privilege. In a chapter of *Considerations on Representative Government* titled "The Ideally Best Polity," Mill wrote that "the only government which can fully satisfy all the exigencies of the social state is one in which the whole people participate."[16] He went on to clarify what degree of participation he had in mind: "[T]he electors are entitled to know how [their representative] means to act; what opinions, on all things which concern his public duty, he intends should guide his conduct."[17] On this view, the function of privilege is to facilitate something approaching popular sovereignty — that is, to promote the convergence of the will of the public with the actions of the state. Mill was far from alone among nineteenth-century thinkers in adopting this view. Walter Bagehot — hardly a radical — wrote matter-of-factly about "the nation, which is the present sovereign."[18] Indeed, even Dicey, insistent though he was on the absolute legal sovereignty of Parliament, wrote that "the fundamental dogma of modern constitutionalism" is that "the legal sovereignty of Parliament is subordinate to the political sovereignty of the nation."[19] Moreover, "the conduct of the different parts of the legislature should be determined by rules meant to secure harmony between the action of the legislative sovereign and the wishes of the political sovereign."[20]

The application of this theory of the proper role of Parliament to the specific area of privilege does not require much imagination. The citizenry benefits from living under representative government, and the effective functioning of an independent representative legislature requires that its Members be able to attend Parliament, speak freely in pursuance of their duties as Members, consult with their constituents, and vote without undue interference. These are the functions that privilege is meant to secure in the Millian paradigm. Justice Littledale found that privilege exists to protect

> what is necessary for the transaction of the business [in Parliament], to protect individual members so as that they may always be able to attend their duties, and to punish persons who are guilty of contempts to the House, or against the orders and proceedings or other matters relating to the House, or to individual members in discharge of their duties to the House, and to such other matters and things as are necessary to carry on their Parliamentary functions; and to print documents for the use of the members.[21]

Note the continual focus on the "business" of Parliament, the "duties" of Members, "matters relating to the House," and matters "necessary to carry on their Parliamentary functions." And, as Justice Littledale makes clear in the next sentence, when an issue becomes "no longer any matter of the House,"[22] then privilege no longer applies. In contrast to the Blackstonian geographical conception of privilege, the Millian view could be called *functional* — it focuses on protecting those — and only those — functions that are essential to a Member of Parliament (MP) in carrying out his public duty. Because the Commons is no longer under significant threat from other powerful actors, it can afford a more precise defense of its constitutional role, one that focuses on fine-tuning, rather than merely increasing, its power. Instead of a rigid legal wall surrounding the House floor, privilege is now seen more as a semipermeable membrane surrounding a fluid organism: it can stretch in various directions to protect important functions that take place away from the floor, and it can also allow the vital "nutrients" of constituent communication to pass through unhindered, all while continuing to protect the essential functions of Parliament. Patricia Leopold expresses this understanding of privilege when she writes (citing a parliamentary committee report) that privilege "exists not as a prerogative of a Member in his personal capacity, but as an aid to enable him to fully discharge his parliamentary duties, and is 'in truth the privilege of (his) constituents.' "[23] As we shall see in the chapters ahead, this shift will involve allowing the courts to determine whether privilege applies in a given situation, extending privilege to cover the dealings of MPs with their constituents (including through the press), limiting MPs' freedom from arrest and civil process, giving the courts jurisdiction over disputed parliamentary elections, and sharply limiting the use of breach of privilege and contempt of Parliament proceedings.

INSTITUTIONAL ROLES

Another way of thinking about the transition from the Blackstonian to the Millian framework would be to think of it as a transition from a classical understanding of the powers in a constitution to a modern one.[24] In the classical understanding, the polity was composed of three powers: the royal, the aristocratic, and the democratic. For many classical theorists, the best constitution was one in which these three elements balanced one another.[25] In this classical understanding, the way one strengthens the democratic part of a constitution is by recognizing the democratic institutions in the state and helping those institutions assert their power against their royal and aristocratic rivals. Loosely speaking, this view could be identified with the Blackstonian paradigm. It recognizes the House of Commons as the democratic part of the Constitution,[26] and it provides the House with tools—a legal wall, as I have described it above—to protect it against anything external. Democracy, on this view, is identified with the House of Commons. That which strengthens the House, strengthens democracy.

However, as democracy was continually strengthened, the classical view gave way to a new view, which saw the state as essentially democratic. When "democratic" became how one thought of the whole state, rather than simply one faction within it, then it was no longer necessarily the case that strengthening one institution at the expense of others was the way to promote democracy.[27] If the ancient division of powers can be thought of as running between classes, then the modern division can be thought of as running between institutions, each (ideally) representing all classes. One can thus see the transition as one from the ancient division of the Constitution into monarchical, aristo-cratic, and democratic parts to a modern division into executive, legislative, and judicial parts, all of which serve democratic governance in different ways.[28] As I noted above, this realization can be thought of as the beginning of ideas of liberal democracy. It can also be thought of as the idea underlying the Millian paradigm outlined above. The Millian paradigm thus recognizes that allowing the courts to check certain actions of the House of Commons need not be antidemocratic. Indeed, judicial checks can further the cause of liberal demo-cratic government (understood as government that facilitates a tight nexus between the will of the people and the actions of the government) by preventing legislative self-dealing. That is, the courts can serve as a check on MPs who might use their power to pursue their own interests rather than those of the nation. The Millian paradigm also recognizes that threats to democracy are no longer as acute as they were when the Blackstonian model was appropriate; hence, the legal wall around the House can be lowered. Rules that were de-signed to prevent the House from *any* attacks that might lower its prestige or power can be changed to allow certain attacks — for example, attacks from constituents, who take a much more prominent role under the Millian concep-tion. Under the modern view, the House, the courts, and the public all play important democratic roles, and democracy is served by allowing them to check one another, not by indiscriminately privileging the House of Commons.

DEMOCRATIC CONCEPTIONS

It is, however, important to reiterate that both the Blackstonian and the Millian conceptions of privilege are essentially democratic conceptions — that is, they attempt to strengthen democracy in the Constitution. The different focuses of the two conceptions serve to illustrate and clarify the ways in which the Constitution has changed as it has become more broadly democratic. As the House of Commons has become the dominant power in the state, it has been able to adopt a less defensive posture. As the most democratic institution became the most powerful, the focus of a doctrine, like privilege, which is meant to promote democracy, could shift from the protection of the Com-mons at any cost to the more nuanced protection of the Commons in such a way as to strengthen its responsiveness to its constituents. The result is a move from what I have described as a geographical to a functional view of the role of privilege, and it also represents a move from a political theory in which it was believed that "all members of the community were present in Parliament, either in person or by proxy, and therefore were 'privy and parties' to its decisions,"[29] to one which recognizes that institutions must be structured so as to encourage legislators truly to act as proxies for their constituents.

It must also be remembered that these are dynamic conceptions: there is no bright-line point in history at which Parliament, the monarch, and the courts suddenly dropped the Blackstonian view and adopted the Millian view. Indeed, it will become apparent that there were still decisions that could be described as Blackstonian well after there had been decisions best described as Millian. It will also be apparent that many decisions fall in the middle: as noted above, these two paradigms exist at opposite ends of a continuum, and actual examples will fall everywhere in between. Moreover, it should be remembered that the Blackstonian and Millian views are interpretive constructs projected backward onto historical events. The historical actors themselves were conscious of these paradigms to a greater or lesser extent. Interpretive issues such as these necessitate a degree of caution—a topic that will arise again soon when we turn to methodological concerns.

The American Conception of the Function of Privilege
AMERICAN POPULAR SOVEREIGNTY

If the Millian paradigm of British constitutionalism promoted a mild form of popular control over the state, the dominant theme of American constitutionalism can be thought of as a more muscular Millianism. Indeed, the American Constitution is fully framed by the notion of popular sovereignty.[30] It begins with the radical notion that, in America, "We the People"[31]—and not some external higher power—are the lawgivers. The original Constitution ends by telling the sovereign people how they can ratify the document and make it the "supreme Law of the Land."[32] After the first set of amendments, the Constitution ended by telling them that the "enumeration in the Constitution of certain rights shall not be construed to deny or disparage others retained by the people," and that the "powers not delegated to the United States by the Constitution, nor prohibited by it to the states, are reserved to the States respectively, or to the people."[33] The language here is crucial: rights and powers are *retained* by and *reserved* to the people. The meaning is clear—these rights and powers lay with the people before the Constitution was formed. The American people have delegated derivatives of their sovereignty to the national and state governments, but these delegated powers remain fundamentally derivative, and the Ninth and Tenth Amendments state "but a truism that all is retained which has not been surrendered."[34] Indeed, even today's Constitution ends with a ringing endorsement of popular sovereignty, telling national legislators that they cannot give themselves a pay raise until the people have had time to consider the matter and vote them out of office if they do not think their public servants deserve it.[35] The Constitution thus was and is fully framed by the notion of popular sovereignty, with the Preamble at the beginning and

Article VII, the Ninth and Tenth Amendments, and the Twenty-seventh Amendment variously at the end.

"In free Governments the rulers are the servants, and the people their superiors & sovereigns,"[36] said Benjamin Franklin at the Philadelphia Convention, and this spirit seems to have carried the day. The original report from the Committee of Detail contained a preamble reading, "We The People of the States of New-Hampshire &C do ordain declare and establish the following Frame of Govt as the Constitution of the . . . United States."[37] The suggestion in this draft version that the new government was founded on a compact between states (within which the people were sovereign) was closer in spirit to the Articles of Confederation (which spoke of a "Confederation and perpetual Union between the States"[38]) than to the finished version of the Constitution (which clearly speaks of a *national* people). By the end of the Convention, without any recorded debate on the topic, the Preamble had shifted dramatically to its present form.

After the Philadelphia document became public and was sent to the people, the debate over popular sovereignty became much louder. The debate was carried on in two main venues: the press and the states' ratifying conventions. Both indicate an overwhelming belief that the Constitution was premised on popular sovereignty. Of course, the most famous of the commentators in the press on the proposed Constitution was Publius, the pseudonymous author of *The Federalist Papers.* Madison seemingly argued that sovereignty could be divided and that this division was to be between the people of America and the people of each state. In his words,

> it appears, on one hand, that the Constitution is to be founded on the assent and ratification of the people of America, given by deputies elected for the special purpose; but, on the other, that this assent and ratification is to be given by the people, not as individuals composing one entire nation, but as composing the distinct and independent States to which they respectively belong.[39]

In this respect, Madison seems to have tried to chart a middle course between the principles of the Articles of Confederation and those that almost every other observer found in the Constitution. Indeed, as Akhil Reed Amar has pointed out, on this point, Madison "was uncharacteristically without followers. Almost every other major figure thought that ultimate sovereignty was indivisible and therefore had to reside solely in either a state or a continental People."[40] Gordon Wood explains why: during colonial debates,

> [e]very new institution and new idea sooner or later had to be reconciled with this powerfully persuasive assumption that there could be but one final, indivisible, and incontestable supreme authority in every state to which all other

authorities must be ultimately subordinate; "for otherwise, there could be no supremacy, or subordination, that is no government at all." The theory of sovereignty pervaded the arguments of the whole Revolutionary generation from the moment in the 1760's when it was first raised through the adoption of the federal Constitution in 1787.[41]

In fact, it seems likely that Madison was not speaking literally in *Federalist No. 39*. In the Philadelphia Convention, he remarked,

> [w]e are vague in our Expressions — we speak of the sovereignty of the States — they are not sovereign — there is a regular gradation from the lowest Corporation, such as the incorporation of mechanicks to the most perft. Sovereignty — The last is the true and only Sovereignty — the states are not in that high degree Sovereign — they are Corporations with power of Bye Laws.[42]

In *Federalist No. 39*, Madison himself was simply guilty of this imprecision. In any event, he made it clear that the locus of sovereignty was in the people, regardless of whether it was in their capacity as state citizens or in their capacity as federal citizens: "[U]ltimate authority, *wherever the derivative may be found*, resides in the people alone."[43] The people, for Madison, "are the only legitimate fountain of power," and they have the unconditional right to "enlarge, diminish, or new-model the powers of government."[44]

Madison's principal coauthor was, if anything, more emphatic on the point. "It has not a little contributed to the infirmities of the existing federal system that it never had a ratification by the PEOPLE. . . . The fabric of American empire ought to rest on the solid basis of THE CONSENT OF THE PEOPLE."[45] Indeed, Hamilton rested a strong argument for judicial review on the fact that the Constitution was undergirded by popular sovereignty:

> No legislative act, therefore, contrary to the Constitution, can be valid. To deny this would be to affirm that the deputy is greater than his principal; that the servant is above his master; that the representatives of the people are superior to the people themselves.[46]

Publius clearly thought that the Constitution for which he was advocating rested on a firm basis — indeed, the only legitimate basis for a government — of popular sovereignty.

And Publius was not alone. Pennsylvania Federalist Timothy Pickering wrote that, "as all power resides originally in the *people*, they have a right to make such a distribution of it as they judge their true interests require."[47] Popular sovereignty means that all governmental authority is derivative; the people have the right to organize their government however they see fit precisely because *they* are the ones doing the organizing. "The powers vested in

Congress are little more than *nominal*; nay *real* power cannot be vested in them, nor in any body, but in the *people*,"[48] wrote Noah Webster in the same vein. That premise formed the baseline of thought for those who supported the Constitution,[49] and even those who opposed the Constitution did not deny that it was founded upon popular sovereignty, although some did deny that popular sovereignty — as opposed to state sovereignty — was a solid grounding for the legitimacy of the government.

This debate was clearest in the states' ratifying conventions, especially in Virginia, where Patrick Henry attacked national popular sovereignty with a vengeance.

> [G]ive me leave to demand, What right had they to say, *We, the people*? My political curiosity, exclusive of my anxious solicitude for the public welfare, leads me to ask, Who authorized them to speak the language of, *We, the people*, instead of, *We, the states*? States are the characteristics and the soul of a confederation. If the states be not the agents of this compact, it must be one great, consolidated, national government, of the people of all the states.[50]

Thus, even the opponents of the proposed Constitution recognized its foundation as one of popular sovereignty. Edmund Pendleton, the president of the Virginia Convention, offered a vigorous defense of popular sovereignty, asking, "[W]ho but the people can delegate powers? Who but the people have a right to form government? . . . If the objection be, that the Union ought to be not of the people, but of the state governments, then I think the choice of the former very happy and proper."[51] Indeed, even Governor Randolph, who, as a delegate to the Philadelphia Convention had refused to sign the document, responded to Henry: "The gentleman then proceeds, and inquires why we assumed the language of 'We, the people.' I ask, Why not? The government is for the people; and the misfortune was, that the people had no agency in the government before."[52] Thus, in Virginia, federalists (like Pendleton), anti-federalists (like Henry), and those in the middle (like Randolph) all agreed — whether they liked it or not — that popular sovereignty was fundamental to the proposed Constitution. Other state ratifying conventions saw similar debates.[53]

But in order to determine whether the Constitution's lofty words were sincere, we have to look at its actions — we have to see how it went about *constituti*ng a nation. That is, we have to examine the method of its adoption. Article VII provides, "The Ratification of the Conventions of nine States, shall be sufficient for the Establishment of this Constitution between the States so ratifying the Same."[54] The ratification conventions were unlike anything the world had ever seen. For the first time in history, the people were being given the chance to vote on the very foundations of their government. The Framers were quite cognizant of — and took great pride in — this innovation. In a 1788 oration, James Wilson gloated:

> You have heard of Sparta, of Athens, and of Rome; you have heard of their admired constitutions, and of their high-prized freedom. In fancied right of these, they conceived themselves to be elevated above the rest of the human race, whom they marked with the degrading title of barbarians. But did they, in all their pomp and pride of liberty, ever furnish, to the astonished world, an exhibition similar to that which we now contemplate? Were their constitutions framed by those, who were appointed for that purpose, by the people? After they were framed, were they submitted to the consideration of the people? Had the people an opportunity of expressing their sentiments concerning them? Were they to stand or fall by the people's approving or rejecting vote? To all these questions, attentive and impartial history obliges us to answer in the negative. The people were either unfit to be trusted, or their lawgivers were too ambitious to trust them.[55]

When the issue of submitting the Constitution to the people for ratification was first raised at the Philadelphia Convention, Madison announced that he thought this provision "essential" and that he found the Articles of Confederation "defective in this respect."[56] Fellow Virginian George Mason thought that the resolution to let the people in special conventions ratify the Constitution was "one of the most important and essential of the Resolutions."[57] His reasons were twofold: first, the state legislatures, as mere instruments of derivative sovereignty, had no authority to ratify a document that claimed to speak for the whole people. Second, in some states — like his own Virginia — "Some of the best & wisest citizens considered the [state] Constitution as established by an assumed authority," rather than by the consent of the people. "A National Constitution derived from such a source would be exposed to the severest criticisms," he argued.[58] Such arguments carried the day in the Convention, with only the Delaware delegation voting to submit the document to the state legislatures rather than to special conventions.[59]

Perhaps the finest example of reasoning from the principle of popular sovereignty inherent in the method of ratification comes in Chief Justice Marshall's opinion for the Court in *McCulloch v. Maryland*.[60] The counsel for Maryland insisted that the Constitution was merely "a compact between the States,"[61] and therefore that the federal government did not have supremacy over the states. "It would be difficult to sustain this proposition," the chief justice wryly noted.[62] Marshall asserts that it is the people, not the states, who are the agents of the Constitution, and his reasoning relies explicitly and extensively on the method of ratification. His logic is sufficiently powerful to be worth quoting at length:

[T]he instrument was submitted to the people. They acted upon it in the only manner in which they can act safely, effectively, and wisely, on such a subject, by assembling in Convention. It is true, they assembled in their several States — and where else should they have assembled? . . . Of consequence, when they act, they act in their States. But the measures they adopt do not, on that account, cease to be the measures of the people themselves, or become the measures of the State governments. From these Conventions, the constitution derives its whole authority. The government proceeds directly from the people; is "ordained and established" in the name of the people; and is declared to be ordained, "in order to form a more perfect union, establish justice, ensure domestic tranquility, and secure the blessings of liberty to themselves and to their posterity." . . . [T]he people were at perfect liberty to accept or reject it; and their act was final. . . . [W]hen, "in order to form a more perfect union," it was deemed necessary to change this alliance [the Confederation] into an effective government, possessing great and sovereign powers, and acting directly on the people, the necessity of referring it to the people, and of deriving its powers directly from them, was felt and acknowledged by all. The government of the Union, then, . . . is, emphatically, and truly, a government of the people.[63]

This passage is breathtaking in its insight into the fundamental structure of the Constitution. Marshall's blending of quotations from the Preamble with a discussion of popular ratification indicates an understanding on his part that there is a fundamental unity between these first and last passages of the original Constitution. Article VII, by sending the document to the people, who were, as Marshall notes, "at perfect liberty to accept or reject it," fulfills the promise of the Preamble, which tells the people that this new government is their creation. The Preamble announces that popular sovereignty is the foundation of American government. Simply saying this, however, does not make it so. The Constitution, in Marshall's words, "derives its whole authority" from the states' ratifying conventions because they constituted "*at the time* the most democratic and inclusive act in world history."[64] In other words, the states' ratifying conventions were the first realization of the promise of the Preamble. If it was something of an exaggeration to claim that the necessity of submitting the Constitution to popular ratifying conventions "was felt and acknowledged by all," the basic insight was nonetheless sound. No one who truly thought about and approved of what the Preamble meant could possibly wish to see its promise betrayed in Article VII.

Of course, it cannot be ignored that the Constitution had, and continues to have, serious democracy deficits. The most striking was the protection of chattel slavery — the exclusion of millions of persons from "We the People." And there were other lapses of popular sovereignty — everything from the widespread disfranchisement of women and free blacks to the indirect election of senators and the electoral college. How, then, can it be claimed that the document issues from "We the People?" This is an oft-repeated attack on the democratic mandate of the Constitution, and with good reason—it is quite powerful.[65] But I shall offer two responses to this critique, both intended to demonstrate that the Constitution's popular-sovereignty basis remains firmly intact. The first response addresses the historical situatedness of the Founding; the second demonstrates that the Constitution transcends that situatedness as an organic text.

The first response to this critique is simply that, as noted above, the Constitution embodied a degree of popular sovereignty never before seen in the world. Those who were excluded here—and many who were included—had never been included anywhere else. Women, slaves, the poor, and resident aliens had all been excluded from participation in the famous Athenian and Spartan democracies. Even those who did participate in public affairs had no part in shaping the constitution. Solon, for instance, "fram[ed] his laws *for* the Athenians" and stipulated that they were to remain unchanged for one hundred years.[66] Solon and Lycurgus surrounded themselves with the myth of divine inspiration, which "helps to explain why the Greeks were reluctant to change their laws."[67] What God (or the gods) giveth, only he (or they) taketh away. Americans remain free to alter their most fundamental laws because they collectively are the Creator. For the Greeks, to do so would be the height of hubris—it would be claiming the authority to alter what the gods had instituted. The most celebrated democracies of antiquity thus refused to allow the citizenry to lay down the basic ground rules of their government. The British Constitution—even the increasingly Millian British Constitution of the 1780s—did not provide a more inspiring example, with its hereditary monarch and House of Lords, its rotten boroughs, and its ideas of virtual representation. In America, by contrast, not only did the people have the final say in these ground rules, the American people also included a higher percentage of the persons living within the geographical boundaries of the country than any previous democracy had.

However, the critic is also confounding two concepts that it is absolutely crucial to keep separate: the Founders and the Constitution. Simply put, *the Founders are not the Constitution.* Moreover, even *the Founders' Constitution is not the Constitution.* The Constitution is an organic document; its original structure has been substantially modified by twenty-seven subsequent amendments, almost all of which have significantly decreased the document's democracy deficit. If the critics want to critique the *Founders* based on today's standards of justice and morality, they are free to do so. If, however, they want to critique the *Constitution* based on today's standards, then they must critique *today's* Constitution. Through what Bruce Ackerman has termed "multigenerational synthesis,"[68] the meaning of the document changes with each amendment. Ackerman describes the process thus: interpreters after Reconstruction "would first have to identify which aspects of the earlier Constitution had survived Republican reconstruction. Having isolated the surviving fragments, they would have to synthesize them into a new doctrinal whole that gave expression to the new ideals affirmed by the Republicans in the name of the People."[69] Interpretation requires bearing in mind that the Constitution "is the joint product of eighteenth-, nineteenth-, and twentieth-century exercises in popular sovereignty."[70] I propose that the best way to read this synthesis is the following: subsequent amendments can be seen as significant steps towards fulfilling the promise of the Preamble.

What allows us to be sure that popular sovereignty, and not what I have been referring to as the "exceptions," is the dominant theme of the Constitution is the unity of what the document *says*, what it *does*, and how it has *progressed*. What it *says* is that it comes from "We the People of the United States," and for that reason is the "supreme Law of the Land." What it *does* is allow more people than ever before to participate in the affairs of government. From its very inception, it allowed more participation than had any other government in the history of humanity. Moreover, it allowed that participation on a more fundamental level: nowhere had the citizens ever voted on their constitution before. Finally, it has *progressed* toward an increasingly inclusive view of the people. Reading these factors together, it is more than apparent that popular sovereignty is the most fundamental principle of the Constitution, one in light of which the rest of the document must be read. The Framers set this up as an ideal, but they were unable to follow through. The subsequent two hundred-plus years of constitutional history have been the fulfillment of this ideal, and today the document, read through the lens of multigenerational synthesis, should be seen as embodying it more than ever.

POPULAR SOVEREIGNTY AND PRIVILEGE

The centrality of popular sovereignty to the American constitutional order suggests that our interpretations of congressional privilege ought to ensure, insofar as possible, that legislators are kept subordinate to the people, while still being able to carry out the political programs of the people. This idea will best be fleshed out by looking at specific cases in the chapters that follow, but a few general words may be said here. First, privilege must not be used in a way that shields legislators from the people. In a system of popular sovereignty, the people are the master of their legislative servants — the servants have no right to erect legal procedures to protect themselves from the displeasure of their master. But it must be noted that the people are sovereign only in their collective capacity — individual persons may interfere with the collective sovereignty of the people if those persons are allowed to distract legislators who are meant to be conducting the people's business. Responsibility and openness to the people militate against secrecy — as John Hart Ely put it, "[P]opular choice will mean relatively little if we don't know what our representatives are up to"[71] — and against treating legislators' public statements as if they were less intimately related to their job as legislators than are their statements to their colleagues or to the other branches of government. However, they do not militate against protecting legislators from certain kinds of harassment or distractions brought by individual persons.

Second, and relatedly, popular sovereignty suggests that there ought to be strong safeguards against legislative self-dealing. Self-dealing occurs when legislators act in pursuance of their own interests rather than those of the people. Privilege must not be interpreted so as to allow legislators to entrench themselves in office or unfairly aid their friends (or fellow partisans). For example, while privilege (as we shall see in chapter 4) provides strong protection to speech by incumbent legislators, it must not be interpreted so as to curtail the speech rights of challengers. Similarly, the right of each House of Congress to judge election disputes must not (as we shall see in chapter 8) turn into a weapon for excluding political enemies from the legislature.

Third, popular sovereignty requires full enfranchisement. As noted above, this ideal has taken a long time to realize — but with each amendment increasing the scope of the franchise, the logic of full enfranchisement grew stronger and stronger in the Constitution. While the Founders were unwilling or unable fully to understand the electoral implications of popular sovereignty, those implications have become clearer as direct election of senators has been instituted and as the vote has been extended to blacks, women, residents of the District of Columbia (partially), the poor, and eighteen-year-olds.[72] Majority disfranchisement of minorities may be majority rule, but it is not popular sovereignty, which presupposes free and equal participation by every member of the polity. As Ely noted,

> Extension of the franchise to groups previously excluded has therefore been the dominant theme of our constitutional development since the Fourteenth Amendment, and it pursues both of the broad constitutional themes we have observed from the beginning: the achievement of a political process open to all on an equal basis and a consequent enforcement of the representative's duty of equal concern and respect to minorities and majorities alike.[73]

Congressional privilege should be interpreted so as to guarantee as fully as possible the right to participation in the political process.

Finally, the American Founders made the judgment that popular sovereignty was best served by (among other mechanisms) a separation of powers among the three branches of the national government. As Madison put it, "The accumulation of all powers, legislative, executive, and judiciary, in the same hands, whether of one, a few, or many, and whether hereditary, self-appointed, or elective, may justly be pronounced the very definition of tyranny."[74] But, of course, the separation neither can nor should be total: "[U]nless these departments be so far connected and blended as to give to each a constitutional control over the others, the degree of separation which the maxim requires, as essential to a free government, can never in practice be duly maintained."[75] Congressional privilege must be structured in such a way as to preserve the fine equilibrium between separation of powers and checks and balances.[76] As we shall see in chapter 2, this means that the other branches must not be able to control the Houses of Congress in areas in which they are privileged, but it also means that the Houses must not be free to define the scope of their own privileges.

Interpretive Methodologies

The interpretive methodologies that will be used throughout this book are already partially on display in the preceding sections. They should, however, be made more explicit. The methodological issues relevant to this study fall into three broad camps: (1) generally applicable notes on the kinds of text under analysis; (2) interpretive problems specific to the British Constitution; and (3) interpretive problems specific to the American Constitution. I shall address each in turn.

GENERALLY APPLICABLE NOTES

The primary documents that I shall be analyzing are judicial decisions, legislative debates, convention debates, and legislation. These types of texts necessitate caution on two fronts. First, it must be borne in mind that these texts arise out of specific conflicts. Legislative debates, committee reports, convention debates, and legislation arise when legislators think that there is a problem that must be solved; judicial decisions are issued when two parties take a conflict to court. Such texts therefore have at least two levels of meaning. One is the solution to the specific problem at hand, and the other is the principle according to which the actors dealt with the circumstances confronting them. For example, in judicial decisions, the job of judges is to settle the conflict in front of them. But they must do so in accordance with the general principles of the law. Discussion of the general principle is necessarily intertwined with discussion of the specifics of the case at hand. Moreover, judges will typically delve no deeper into the general principle than is absolutely necessary for coming to a determinate conclusion — in this way, they ensure that the law's progress is measured and deliberate. However, for the purposes of understanding what the law is and should be, it is precisely the general principles that interest us. It is thus necessary to attempt to tease the principles away from their specific situation. This project can only be undertaken once we are fully familiar with that situation. Because the underlying principles are never fully explicit, they must be reconstructed. We can think of political and judicial decision-making as involving three elements: an input (the specific facts and conflict at hand), a process (the general principles that are brought to bear on the conflict and the way those principles are applied), and an output (the decision/report/law produced).[77] As interpreters, we begin with the output and seek to understand the process. This can only be done by becoming familiar with the input — only once we know the initial conditions can we understand what process would have led to the result with which we are faced. In other words, we seek to understand how a problem was solved, but in order to do so, we must first understand the problem. It is thus imperative that judicial decisions be looked at in light of the facts of the case and that legislative reports and legislation be looked at in light of the conflicts that gave rise to them. Meaning does not exist in a vacuum.[78]

These types of texts require caution on another front as well. The authors of these texts are political actors — in fact, they are often committees or panels of political actors. They are contending with one another for both personal and institutional advantage. Indeed, the struggle for institutional advantage is one of the prime subjects of interest here: institutional conflict is central to any discussion of privilege. But the personal and institutional motivations of political actors must be borne in mind throughout. For example, when considering the vigor with which Parliament presses its claim to be the sole judge of its own privileges, one must consider the possibility that Parliament will be less vigorous when the MP alleging a breach of privilege is a member of the opposition party than when he or she is a member of the governing party. Thus, in reading these texts, attention must be paid to the possibility that the actors are governed by personal and institutional advantage either instead of or in addition to principle.

READING THE BRITISH CONSTITUTION

The central challenge in interpreting the British Constitution is, of course, its unwrittenness. It is more a canon than a text, and, like any canon, it generates its own peculiar dialectic. What is included in the canon? That which fits with the general tenor of the canon. What is rejected as unconstitutional (the apocrypha of the Constitution)? That which does not fit. How do we know what the general tenor is? By looking at what is included and what is rejected. Because of this dialectic, a project, such as this one, that seeks to work on both sides of the line separating legal analysis from political theory — that is, which seeks to integrate a discussion of what the law is with a discussion of what fundamental principles underlie it — can only address the British Constitution via a distinctly common-law type of reasoning. In other words, the interpreter must seek to derive the general principles from the positive analysis. And by understanding those general principles that animate the British Constitution as a whole — principles that can only be seen by looking at the statutes, decisions, and norms which compose the Constitution — we can evaluate how well individual pieces of the Constitution jell with the whole.[79] Such is the peculiar dialectic of common-law constitutionalism — small changes or additions are tentatively proposed, evaluated by the various constitutional actors to see how compatible they are with general constitutional norms, and then either adopted or rejected on that basis. The Constitution itself is then altered, which affects how the next proposed change is evaluated.

This process is similar to what philosophers have called the "hermeneutic circle" — that is, the interdependent relationship between the whole and its parts.[80] As Hans-Georg Gadamer described it, the circle consists of this: we can only understand a text in light of the tradition out of which it arises, and yet we can only understand a tradition in terms of the individual texts which make up that tradition.[81] British constitutionalism must be understood as such a tradition, composed of numerous overlapping strands. These strands are uniform neither as to type — some are traditional, some statutory, some judicial — nor as to purpose: they are sometimes mutually reinforcing and sometimes in tension. And yet from these disparate strands arises a tradition whose broad outlines and animating principles can be sketched. (I have begun such a sketch with my analysis above of the Blackstonian and Millian paradigms; the sketch will continue to grow more detailed as we progress through the study.) The individual strands can then be examined to see how well they comport with the broader principles. As with any circular venture, there is the potential pitfall of taking away no more than what one has put in. However, if one remains on guard against such question begging, this process can produce substantively new insights.

READING THE AMERICAN CONSTITUTION

Reading the American Constitution is, of course, a very different exercise. As a single written document, it allows for a degree of originalism in our interpretative methodology that simply is not possible in a constitution in which many of the doctrines result from ancient custom or are slowly defined by judicial precedent. No one is quite sure when the privilege of free speech on the floor of Parliament came into being (in 1399, freedom of speech was already considered a traditional liberty of the House of Commons), and it is therefore impossible to talk about the context in which it was originally intended to operate, or the problems it was originally intended to solve. In contrast, one can very easily trace the origin and development of the American Constitution's provision in Article I, Section 6, that "for any speech or debate in either house, [senators and representatives] shall not be questioned in any other place."[82]

But the fact that the origins of the clause can be traced raises at least two important interpretive questions. First, if the original meaning is relevant, to *whose* understanding of the original meaning should we look? Second, *how* should we make use of that original understanding? On the first question: there is no single, authoritative interpreter of the Founding meaning of the Constitution. Although, as we have seen, there was widespread agreement at the Founding that the Constitution was to be democratic and grounded in popular sovereignty, there were strong disagreements about many of the specifics. Indeed, at the time of the Founding, there was intense interest in politics, and a great many voices contributing to a very vibrant public discourse. However, for someone who interprets the Constitution as being founded on principles of popular sovereignty, it is important to emphasize that *publicly accessible* meanings are to be given the most weight. That is, the debates in the press and in the states' ratifying conventions ought to be taken very seriously as authorities, for it was these debates that were open to ordinary citizens trying to decide whether or not they wanted the proposed Constitution to take effect. This is not, however, to denigrate the value of the Philadelphia Convention debates — the thoroughness of those debates will often help us to understand what problems the Constitution was thought of as solving, and what particular words and phrases meant to late eighteenth-century ears.

And this suggests an answer to our second question of *how* we should make use of our originalist sources. The brand of originalism employed here is a very particular one, and it is crucial for the reader to understand the difference between this approach and a simple "Framers' intent" approach. The essential question to ask, on this view, is *not* "What would the Framers have done if faced with this decision?" The question is, instead, "What *problems* was the Constitution trying to solve, and what are the modern *analogues* to those problems?" That is, the way to understand the Constitution is to understand what evils it was trying to combat. Unlike the strict Framers' intent approach, this does not suggest that interpretations of the text ought to be limited to the ways in which it was understood in 1789. Facts and circumstances change, and governmental responses to them must keep pace. However, if the Constitution is to have any coherent and enduring meaning, its basic philosophy of governance must not be subject to the facts and circumstances of the day. Insofar as the text itself is not changed — that is, amended — it must be seen to embody a constant understanding of the basic objectives of government. To deny the document this stable ground is to deny the fundamental basis of written constitutionalism. An example may prove helpful. There is a strong case to be made that one of the central problems that the First Amendment was meant to solve was the British government's occasional silencing of its political enemies.[83] That is, it was meant primarily to protect *political* speech. The Framers would have been aghast to see the Free Speech Clause used to protect pornography. On a Framers' intent mode of interpretation, this settles the question; on my mode of interpretation, it does not.[84] The question then becomes this: is pornography, in today's society, political? That is, can it be shown that pornography plays a role in debates over the meaning and scope of sexuality in modern society, debates that are undeniably political? If the answer is yes, then pornography deserves First Amendment protection, regardless of the scandal it would have caused Hamilton and Madison.

Understanding the problems that the Constitution is intended to solve also entails an understanding of the conceptual and legal resources available to the Founders. The Founders were all familiar with British constitutional law, and it provided much of the background for their project. As noted above, some elements of British constitutionalism were rejected outright; others were incorporated outright; still others were modified to fit the New World. But whichever option was chosen for any given piece of constitutional text, a careful observer must always see the British Constitution hovering in the background of the American, and it is precisely this historical perspective that provides much of the impetus for such a study as this one. Both the Articles of Confederation and the preexisting state constitutions provided additional background both to the Founders who met in Philadelphia and to the American people who met in ratifying conventions in the states, and those documents must be kept in view as well.

Of course, original understandings, even in this loose sense, are by no means determinate. People at the Founding had very different ideas of what problems they were trying to solve and how to go about solving them. Thus, much of the interpretive work will still have to be done using the same techniques that I use to interpret the British Constitution: judicial precedent, the avoidance of interpretations that could potentially lead to legal absurdities, and the attempt to make the interpretation of the particular law fit with the general sense of the legal system. No single rule will ever provide a complete, satisfactory legal hermeneutic.

It should be emphasized that my approaches to both the British Constitution and the American Constitution are historical in nature. Without some substantial conception of continuity over time, constitutionalism—and, indeed, self-government generally—is impossible.[85] Where the Constitution is grounded in a written text, the historical investigation has a clear, easily identifiable starting point (an *analytic* starting point, that is—as I noted above, good historical analysis of a document must inquire into the *pre*history of the document). In that case, the focus of the historical investigation is to understand how the Constitution works—what problems it was meant to solve and how it solves them. Where the Constitution is unwritten, however, the historical investigation must take a different focus. It must seek to understand the principles animating the tradition and use those principles to critique the specific elements that make up the tradition itself.

Structure of the Argument

THE CHAPTERS

This book is divided into five pairs of chapters. The first chapter in each pair discusses one of the main issues in British parliamentary privilege; the second chapter discusses the similar issue in American congressional privilege. By interspersing the British and American chapters in this way, I hope both to facilitate comparison of the two doctrines and to demonstrate how the American conceptions built upon and reacted to their British forebears. The first chapter pair addresses jurisdictional conflicts. Chapter 1 deals with conflict between *lex parliamenti* and *lex terrae*—the law of parliament and the law of the land. Such conflicts have arisen when a House of Parliament claims privileges that conflict with generally applicable laws. It has often taken the form of a conflict between an ordinary court and the House over whether the court has the jurisdiction to question orders of the House. Chapter 2 deals with that part of the American political-questions doctrine that addresses the relationship between the Houses of Congress and the courts. It looks at when and why the courts are forbidden from interfering in certain congressional actions. The second chapter pair looks at the privilege of freedom of speech. Chapter 3 examines the parliamentary privilege of free speech and debate, and it compares the liberty enjoyed by MPs to that enjoyed by ordinary citizens and the press. Chapter 4 considers the same issues for Members of Congress. Chapters 5 and 6 consider the freedom from civil arrest historically guaranteed to Members of Parliament and Congress. The fourth chapter pair takes up the issue of disputed elections. Chapter 7 looks at how the House of Commons has resolved disputed parliamentary elections as well as disputes over the qualifications of elected Members. It also considers how and why the House surrendered that role to the courts in the late nineteenth century. Chapter 8 looks at how the House of Representatives and the Senate have handled disputed election results and qualifications, along the way addressing whether it would not be best to hand over their role to the courts as well. The final chapter pair examines the internal discipline of the legislatures. Chapter 9 discusses contempt of Parliament and breach of privilege. Each House has the right to imprison or impose lesser punishments (on both Members and non-Members) for these offenses (although imprisonment is no longer used by either House). Examining how expansively the Houses have interpreted their right to punish (and to what degree the courts have been willing to intervene) tells us a great deal about how much of a "buffer zone" has been seen to be necessary to protect the House from outside interference. Likewise, Chapter 10 looks at the ability of the Houses of Congress to maintain discipline — over Members and non-Members alike.

THE STRUCTURE OF THE CHAPTERS

Each chapter aims both to give the relevant historical background and cases and to show how these cases fit into the broader analytical framework that I have begun to sketch out. The British chapters are divided into two main sections — one looking at the cases that fall under the Blackstonian heading, and the other looking at the cases that fall under the Millian. This structure follows from the method of reading the British Constitution discussed above — the analysis is mixed in with the case histories, as the relevant analytic criteria can arise from no source other than the constitutional tradition itself. The American chapters are structured differently. There, the discussion begins with constitutional text and history — we start with the document itself and with the investigation into what problems it was meant to solve and how it went about solving those problems. The next section looks at the analytic conclusions to be drawn from the text and history. After that, we consider the relevant case law, which is examined and evaluated with those analytic conclusions in mind. The final section of the American chapters compares the British and American doctrines and attempts to draw some general conclusions from this comparison.

The case histories cannot be — and do not aim to be — comprehensive. Rather, I aim to discuss all of the seminal cases and cases that signify important doctrinal turning points, as well as to provide a representative sample of cases that illustrate the prevailing doctrine at different times. The cases discussed should thus both give an accurate depiction of the historical development of privilege in Britain and America and allow us to evaluate the interpretive paradigm sketched above. Here, again, it will be noted that we run into the hermeneutic circle. And yet, as noted above, this circle is productive of meaning. Examining the specific cases will tell us whether the general interpretive schema is correct, and it will deepen our understanding of this schema by providing concrete examples; at the same time, we can use the schema to understand how the individual cases fit within a larger pattern. With those aims in mind, we now turn to the examination and analysis of these aspects of parliamentary privilege.

I

Lex Parliamenti vs. Lex Terrae

The nature of the relationship between *lex et consuetude parliamenti* ("lex parliamenti," for short) and *lex terrae* is central to any conception of privilege in Britain. Lex parliamenti is that body of law dealing with issues internal to Parliament — each House's composition, its organization, its procedures, its privileges, and so forth. Lex terrae — the law of the land — is the general law, applicable to all, and enforceable by the ordinary courts. The important question here is one of institutional power, and there are, broadly speaking, three possibilities: (1) the courts can say nothing at all about lex parliamenti and must simply accept a House of Parliament's assertions on the matter, (2) the courts can adjudicate on the extent but not the interpretation or application of lex parliamenti, and (3) the courts can review both the extent and (at least to some degree) the interpretation and application of lex parliamenti. Questions about which of these possible arrangements is best have recurred throughout Parliament's history.

I shall argue that the Blackstonian conception of privilege necessitates giving lex parliamenti primacy over lex terrae in cases of conflict (which includes denying to the ordinary courts the power to rule on questions of lex parliamenti) in order to prevent other powerful political actors from manipulating the House of Commons. This means accepting either 1 or a very weak version of 2, above. The Millian conception is not quite so straightforward. A tighter nexus between the wishes of the people and the actions of the government is best promoted by allowing the courts to adjudicate on lex parliamenti, but only where the courts are sufficiently independent that they can avoid being used as the pawns of some other powerful actor (the monarch or the Lords) to attack the Commons. Where that condition holds, popular control of the government is best served by allowing the courts to function as a check on potential self-dealing by the House while still ensuring sufficient parliamentary independence that MPs are free to carry out their public duties — a strong version of 2, or possibly even a weak version of 3, above. Where that condition does not hold, we are back in a Blackstonian world.

The Blackstonian Paradigm

Because the Blackstonian conception of privilege focuses on the absolute protection of the Houses of Parliament from external influence, it naturally demands that the Houses' assertions of privilege not be reviewable by the courts. Indeed, Blackstone was explicit on this point:

> It is declared by the records of parliament, that all weighty matters moved concerning the peers of the realm, ought to be determined, *adjudged* and discussed by the *course of parliament*, and not by the civil law, nor yet by the common laws of the land used in other courts of the realm.
>
> The same declaration, for the like reason, says lord Coke, respects the *commons*, for any thing done or moved in their house: And this is the reason, he adds, why the *judges ought not to give any opinion of a matter of parliament, because it is not to be decided by common law, but according to the law and custom of parliament, and so the judges* (he concludes) *in divers parliaments have confessed.*[1]

Moreover, from the decisions of a House of Parliament "there lies no appeal, and it is essential . . . to the preservation of public liberty, that no appeal should lie."[2] This was especially true so long as the courts were royally controlled, and so long as the whole House of Lords heard appeals, because the House of Commons was especially wary of threats to its independence from the monarchy and the upper house. However, under the Blackstonian paradigm, even a fully independent judiciary ought not to have been able to interfere with claims of privilege, as this paradigm focuses on the blunt protection of the functions of the House from all outside actors.

EARLY CASES

In 1545, the executors of the late John Skewys sued William Trewynard to recover a debt. Trewynard was therefore taken into custody by Richard Chamond, the sheriff of Cornwall. However, Chamond soon received a writ of privilege directed to be issued by the House of Commons claiming Trewynard as a burgess of Parliament. Chamond then released his prisoner, whereupon the executors sued Chamond to recover the debt. The King's Bench ruled that privilege was absolute, even if it resulted in a failure of justice, and thus exculpated the sheriff.[3] The plaintiffs could, however, take comfort in the fact that the court saved them their remedy: the court ruled that Trewynard's release was limited to the time of privilege, so that he could be rearrested forty days after the end of the next session. In *Chamond*, we can clearly see the "geographical" focus at the heart of the Blackstonian conception: privilege is absolute, and the resulting injustice to a subject is unfortunate, but unavoidable. At the same time, the MP is only free from arrest during the time of privilege (that is, while Parliament sits, plus forty days on either side). To return again to the geographical metaphor, once the Member steps away from the privileged confines of his role at Westminster, he is again ruled by lex terrae and not lex parliamenti.

In 1604, a committee of the House of Commons issued a report proclaiming that House a "Court of Record, and so ever esteemed,"[4] and, indeed, a higher court than any of the common-law courts. Lex parliamenti, on this view, was simply a higher law than lex terrae, and only the House was competent to judge according to lex parliamenti. The common-law opinions of judges do not "bring any prejudice to this High Court of Parliament, whose power being above the law, is not founded on the Common Law, but have their Rights and Privileges peculiar to themselves."[5]

The same year that saw this strong defense of the supremacy of lex parliamenti in theory also saw one of the strongest applications of this theory. On the opening day of the session in 1604, the House learned that Sir Thomas Shirley, MP for Steyning, was unable to attend because he had been arrested for debt. A warrant was issued to bring Shirley before the House, and, when he was not produced, the creditor and the arresting sergeant were committed to the Tower of London.[6] The Warden of the Fleet, who was holding Shirley, was concerned that he would be liable for the debt if he released his prisoner, so the Commons passed a bill relieving the warden of any liability. However, when the Lords were considering the bill, the Commons realized that, were it to pass, they would have surrendered the right to enforce their privileges to the King and Lord Chancellor, whose aid the bill invoked.[7] They therefore rejected a motion to request the King's assent to the bill and issued their own writ to have Shirley released. The warden refused, whereupon he was committed to the custody of the Sergeant of the House.[8] The warden offered to release the prisoner upon receipt of a writ directing him to bring Shirley before the Chancellor. The House sent the warden to the Tower.[9] Still unable to obtain Shirley, the House passed another bill absolving the warden of responsibility for Shirley's debt. This bill, however, did not make any appeal to the King or Chancellor, but rather provided for action by the House to secure Shirley's release.[10] The warden again refused to release Shirley, whereupon the Commons had the warden thrown into the "Little Ease" dungeon of the Tower.[11] After spending four days in the dungeon, the warden was served with another writ, which he accepted, and Shirley was released. The House allowed the warden to spend another four days in the dungeon before releasing him.[12]

The House had won an important victory. In effect, when the warden refused to comply with the Commons' order to release Shirley, he was declaring that greater obedience was due to the courts than to the House of Commons. For a House anxious to protect its role against other powerful institutions, this was intolerable. It is thus telling that the House declined to seek the King's assent on the bill relieving the warden of liability for releasing Shirley: had it done so, "the prisoner would have owed his liberty, not to the direct action of the house, but to the potent intervention of the chancery."[13] In other words, the Commons would have been an institutional loser. The same reason explains why the House refused the warden's offer to release Shirley upon receipt of writ directing him to bring Shirley before the Chancellor. To protect its role, the House needed to secure Shirley's release by itself, and, using its contempt power, that is precisely what it did.

In a similar case in 1675, a different Thomas Shirley — not an MP — won a suit against Sir John Fagg — who was a Member of the House of Commons — in the Court of Chancery. In the normal course of appeals, the case came before the House of Lords, and Fagg was served with an order to respond to Shirley's petition before that body. The Commons responded both by dispatching a message to the upper house warning it not to encroach upon the privileges of the Commons and by ordering Shirley to the bar to answer for a breach of privilege.[14] When the Commons' messenger appeared in the assembly hall of the Lords seeking to serve the Speaker's warrant on Shirley, Lord Mohoun seized the warrant from him. The Commons, outraged, issued another warrant for Shirley's arrest and demanded that the Lords punish Mohoun. The upper house responded by granting Shirley its protection.[15] Fagg, who had disregarded the order of his own House and filed a response to Shirley's appeal, was sent to the Tower for doing so, and at the same time the Commons imprisoned the attorneys in another appeal filed before the Lords against an MP.[16] The Lords instructed the Gentleman Usher of the Black Rod (its equivalent of the House of Commons' Sergeant) to liberate the attorneys, which "brought the two houses to the verge of using physical force in the struggle over their privilege."[17] Black Rod found the attorneys, who had not yet been taken into custody (a fact that so upset the Commons that it ordered its own Sergeant to be sent to the Tower).

The new Sergeant, under explicit order of the House, arrested the attorneys at the bar of the Court of Chancery.[18] The Lords ordered Black Rod to arrest the Sergeant and liberate his prisoners, but he was unable to do so. The Commons ordered the Lieutenant of the Tower to ignore writs of habeas corpus, as they were insufficient to liberate anyone imprisoned for breach of privilege (this will be further discussed shortly).[19] The Commons passed a resolution asserting that "whosoever shall solicit, plead, or prosecute any Appeal against any Commoner of *England*, from any Court of Equity, before the House of Lords, shall be deemed and taken a Betrayer of the Rights and Liberties of the Commons of *England*; and shall be proceeded against accordingly,"[20] an even stronger defense of the supremacy of lex parliamenti than the House committee's 1604 report had been. Shirley's appeal was not revived; this was, however, the last case in which the House of Commons pressed the claim that bringing an appeal against an MP before the Lords was a breach of privilege.[21] Note that, as in the *Shirley* case, the House of Commons in *Shirley v. Fagg* sought to protect itself against the Lords' appellate jurisdiction. The fear of an encroachment by the upper house into its power was sufficiently acute that the Commons actually imprisoned its own Member simply for defending himself in front of the Lords. The implication was clear: if Members of the House of Commons could be called upon to answer for their actions in the House of Lords, then the Lords had a strong institutional advantage over the lower house, and the Commons were prepared to use their contempt power to prevent the upper house from gaining the upper hand.

Jay v. Topham stood for the same principle in the lower courts. In 1689, the Sergeant of the House of Commons, John Topham, reported that he had suffered from King's Bench prosecutions arising from carrying out orders of the House against John Jay. The House resolved that these decisions were breaches of privilege, and it summoned the judges to the bar.[22] The House was unpersuaded by the judges' defense of their decisions and ordered them into custody, where they remained until Parliament was prorogued.[23] Here, as in *Shirley* and *Shirely v. Fagg*, the House was intent on demonstrating that it alone, using its own law, would determine the nature and extent of its own privileges.

Rolle's Case in 1629 vividly demonstrated the crucial role that assertions of the primacy of lex parliamenti could play in maintaining Parliament's independence. In the midst of Charles I's fights with his Parliaments over tonnage and poundage,[24] John Rolle, an MP and a merchant, had his goods seized by customs officials for nonpayment of taxes and duties.[25] He complained to the House, and, while it was discussing the issue, Charles sent it a message offering to drop the entire matter if the House would agree to grant him the old taxes of tonnage and poundage.[26] The House refused, and soon thereafter Rolle's warehouse was locked and he was served with a subpoena to appear in the Star Chamber. After extensive debate, Rolle's goods were granted privilege of Parliament.[27] Soon thereafter, Charles dissolved Parliament, partly on the grounds that he could not allow privilege to be extended to Members' goods, which would have the effect of exempting them from taxation during the sitting of Parliament.[28] The *Rolle* case clearly underscores the necessity of the Blackstonian view in the mid-seventeenth century. Charles I attempted to use his control over customs officials and the courts to extort funds from the House of Commons, even explicitly offering to drop charges against Rolle if the House would grant him the taxes he sought. It is precisely to prevent this sort of manipulation that the Blackstonian paradigm seeks to build an impregnable wall of privilege around the activities of the House. Maintaining the independence of the House, in this case, required granting privilege even to the Member's goods, thus removing power over the liberty and property of MPs from the royally controlled courts. A triumph of lex terrae over lex parliamenti in this case would have meant the triumph of the monarchical element of the Constitution over the democratic one.

HABEAS CORPUS CASES

As many of the cases of conflict between lex parliamenti and lex terrae involve imprisonments for contempt or breach of privilege (to be discussed in detail in chapter 9), the ability of the common-law courts to free those imprisoned by the House has always been contentious. In a 1642 resolution, the House of Commons emphatically denied that the common-law courts "hath any Cognizance or Jurisdiction touching the Commitment of any Person who stands committed by Order of both or either of the said Houses of Parliament."[29] A 1647 resolution was somewhat less confrontational, ordering the Sergeant to bring prisoners before the court and show the cause of their detention whenever he received a writ of habeas corpus, but the resolution also warned judges to give notice to the House before discharging or bailing prisoners that it had committed.[30]

A glance at early case law, however, suggests that the 1642 resolution was taken more seriously—by both the courts and the House itself—than the 1647 one. In 1653, Captain John Streater was imprisoned by order of the Commons for distributing seditious pamphlets, and the warrant stated that he was to remain imprisoned until freed by a subsequent order of the House. He applied for a writ of habeas corpus and was granted a hearing before the Upper Bench at Westminster (during the interregnum, the King's Bench was renamed the Upper Bench), where he argued that the return was too general, failed to specify the time and place of his alleged offense, and showed no lawful cause for his imprisonment.[31] He argued that the common-law courts have the obligation to enforce the lex terrae at all times, even against the Houses of Parliament. In a moving courtroom speech, Streater himself proclaimed that

> if it should be objected, That [my imprisonment is] grounded upon an Order of Parliament, and that the parliament are not bound to shew a cause; Truly, I am of opinion that the parliament would not own any one that should so argue, it being so perfectly repugnant to their honour; it being condemned in parliament within our memory, as unjust, illegal, unreasonable, and perfectly contrary to law; and law is the only sceptre of senates, parliaments, councils, empires, kings, princes, governors and magistrates.[32]

He continued by asking, "Who will question but that the warrant of a justice of Peace, shewing lawful cause of imprisonment, is of greater force in law, than an Order of Parliament shewing no cause of imprisonment? . . . Shall an Order of Parliament over-rule laws, statutes, customs, usages and reason? No, my lord."[33] The attorney-general barely deigned to offer a response. He merely informed the court that Streater was committed by an order of the House, "which is not to give an account to the court,"[34] and that the House did not wish him released. The judges sided with the attorney-general, holding that the House was judicially superior to the court, and that it was not the role of the court, as an inferior body, to question the validity of the orders of its superior.[35] Streater was therefore remanded to prison. Soon thereafter, Parliament was dissolved, and Streater applied for a new writ of habeas corpus. The attorney-general argued that "when Parliaments do dissolve, their acts do not cease. Besides, a parliament is the Supreme Court, and they do constitute other courts; and therefore it is not for other courts to question the proceedings of a parliament."[36] Streater's counsel emphasized the difference between an order of a House of Parliament and an act of Parliament, and argued that the former did indeed cease to be operative upon the dissolution of Parliament. The judges agreed, and Streater was released.[37]

A similar case arose out of the House of Lords in 1676. The Lords had committed the Earl of Shaftesbury to the Tower for "high contempt" of their House.[38] Shaftesbury applied to the King's Bench for a writ of habeas corpus. At the hearing, he argued that the form of commitment had a number of procedural flaws, and he argued strenuously that even the House of Lords must act within the bounds of the ordinary laws,

> for otherwise one may be imprisoned by the House of Peers unjustly, for a matter relievable here, and yet shall be out of all relief by such a return; for upon a supposition that this Court ought not to meddle where the person is

committed by the Peers, then any person, at any time, and for any cause, is to be subject to perpetual imprisonment at the pleasure of the Lords.[39]

Lex parliamenti had to be subordinated to lex terrae if it was not to be a grave threat to the liberties of the subject.[40] The Lords' main reply was that they were the highest court in the realm, and their procedure could not be controlled by the inferior court of the King's Bench.[41] "The Judges in no age have taken upon them the judgment of what is *lex et consuetudo Parliamenti*," the attorney-general argued for the House.[42] The judges agreed with the House, arguing that, although the return did indeed have serious defects, ordinary rules of procedure did not constrain the House of Lords.[43] Shaftesbury was remanded to the Tower, where he remained until he begged forgiveness of the House.

The courts' most explicit recognition that habeas corpus was unavailable to those committed by the House came in the 1705 case of *R. v. Paty*.[44] In the famous 1702–03 controversy over the Aylesbury elections (most notably in *Ashby v. White*), the House of Commons made clear its belief that it had the exclusive right to determine voter eligibility and that any suits against constables enforcing the House's eligibility requirements constituted breaches of privilege.[45] Shortly after the Lords' ruling in Ashby's favor (more on that in chapter 7), John Paty, who had also been denied the vote in Aylesbury, filed suit against the constables. The Commons immediately had Paty committed to Newgate for contempt and breach of privilege. He instituted habeas corpus proceedings in the Queen's Bench but was unsuccessful. Justice Gould argued, "We cannot judge of the privileges of the House of Commons, but they are to debate them among themselves. . . . [T]he privileges of Parliament are not to be determined by the common law."[46] Gould also said,

> As to the objection, that if this proceeding here were not allowed, it would make the people of England bondmen; I answer, that this commitment is a punishment used by them, and that it determines with the sessions. . . . [T]he House of Commons [is] intrusted with the liberty of the people, and . . . nobody could suppose they would make any invasions upon it.[47]

The argument that the House of Commons cannot deprive the people of their liberties because the House represents the people (the punishments doled out by the House are punishments "used by them" — that is, by the people themselves, acting through their agents in Parliament) speaks clearly to the contemporaneous (Blackstonian) understanding of democracy. Chief Justice Holt was the lone dissenter, arguing, "The privileges of the House of Commons are well known, and are founded upon the law of the land, and are nothing but the law."[48] In other words, lex parliamenti is part of lex terrae, and therefore the ordinary courts are competent to rule on questions of lex parliamenti. Holt thought that Paty's action clearly did not constitute a breach of privilege: "[T]his, which was only doing a legal act, could not be made illegal by a vote of the House of Commons."[49] That is, Holt presents claim 3 from the introductory section of this chapter. The ways in which Holt's understanding of lex parliamenti differed from that of his colleagues will prove instructive. Although Holt's ideas in general would later come to predominate, the courts would never hold that those imprisoned by the House could be freed by habeas corpus proceedings.[50]

In a 1771 case that will be discussed again in chapter 9, Brass Crosby, the Lord Mayor of London, had messengers of the House of Commons arrested as they were attempting to arrest a printer by order of the House.[51] The House imprisoned Crosby for breach of privilege, and he petitioned the Court of Common Pleas for a writ of habeas corpus. Crosby's attorneys asserted that the common-law courts were perfectly capable of navigating what they presented as a jurisdictional conflict between the Lord Mayor and the House of Commons:

> The question at present is, whether this Court has not power to examine into the jurisdiction of the House of Commons? I submit it, with deference to the Court, that you have lawful power to inquire, whether the House of Commons had any jurisdiction in this case, and that their privileges are not to be supposed so transcendent and mystical, as to exclude all inquiry. My Lord! I deny that the mayor's act is a breach of the privilege of the House of Commons, the lord-mayor was in full possession of jurisdiction in the case; he was obliged to decide upon the question before him; he was obliged to form an opinion upon a case within his jurisdiction: shall his opinion be adjudged a contempt? Is this the law of the land; that when different Courts, having jurisdiction of the same nature, differ in their decisions, they are guilty of contempts one against the other, and may be punished for such contempts?[52]

So far as the judges were concerned, the answer was yes — or at least the lower "court" (the Lord Mayor) is guilty of a contempt against the higher one (the House of Commons). Lord Chief Justice de Grey bluntly declared, "The laws can never be a prohibition to the Houses of Parliament; because, by law, there is nothing superior to them"[53] — claim 1 from above. Blackstone, then a justice on the Court of Common Pleas, concurred: "The House of Commons is a Supreme Court, and they are judges of their own privileges and contempts.... The sole adjudication of contempts, and the punishment thereof, in any manner, belongs exclusively, and without interfering, to each respective Court.... The House of Commons is the only judge of its own proceedings."[54]

The history of controversies over habeas corpus thus illustrates the Blackstonian view of privilege, although it might perhaps be thought that the Black-stonian view was rather too solicitous of parliamentary power in some of these cases. Defendant after defendant, from Streater to Shaftesbury to Paty to Crosby, argued that the privileging of lex parliamenti over lex terrae would result in an impermissible infringement on their rights. In none of the cases, however, were the judges convinced, and they frequently noted that the privileges of Parliament stood outside the purview of the common law. In *Paty*, as noted above, Justice Gould explicitly argued that the proceedings of the House of Commons could not be detrimental to the liberties of Englishmen because the penalties meted out by the House were, in fact, penalties meted out by the people themselves. It is important to note that he held this in a case in which the House found a subject in contempt for suing because he was denied the right to *vote*, a right that he undoubtedly possessed under lex terrae. However, the "siege mentality" of the Blackstonian conception of privilege is such that the actions of the House of Commons — the only democratic part of the Constitution — are seen as necessarily democratic — or at least as close to democratic as the actions of a constitutional actor could be. Hence, it was the role of privilege to protect the functioning of the House from outside interference, even if, as in *Paty*, that "interference" was from a subject seeking his voting rights. It is, of course, also worth noting that Blackstone himself, both speaking from the bench in *Brass Crosby's Case* and writing as an academic, affirmed this view of privilege, holding that only the House could judge the nature and extent of its own privileges.

The Millian Paradigm

It is somewhat harder to give a conclusive answer as to what the Millian view of privilege prescribes for navigating the clash between lex parliamenti and lex terrae. It is clearly insufficient to say simply that lex parliamenti must be subsumed by lex terrae, and therefore that judges must be given authority to determine the scope of the Houses' privileges. After all, the function of privilege on the Millian conception is to tighten the nexus between the will of the people and the actions of the government. In a situation in which the courts are subservient to a powerful political actor (the *Rolle* case comes to mind), allowing the courts to pass judgment on Parliament's privileges would serve to make the system less democratic, not more so. Thus, in determining the relationship between lex parliamenti and lex terrae, the nature of the institutions charged with interpreting and upholding each — the Houses of Parliament and the ordinary courts, respectively — must be taken into account. When the courts are independent, and thus able to make decisions based on the law without undue pressure from other political actors, then the Millian goal of promoting popular control over the government is best served by allowing those courts to check potentially self-dealing actions by the Houses of Parliament—that is, by adhering to a strong version of claim 2 or perhaps even some version of claim 3 from the introductory section of this chapter.

THE *KNOLLYS* CASE

The first Millian case was also one of the most extreme rulings in favor of the primacy of lex terrae over lex parliamenti—that is, a case in which conception 3 of the courts' role was adopted. After Charles Knollys was indicted for the murder of his brother-in-law in 1695, he petitioned the House of Lords for a trial by his peers, on the grounds that he was Earl of Banbury.[55] The Lords "dismissed his petition" and "disallowed his peerage."[56] When the murder case came before the King's Bench, Knollys demurred to the order of the Lords, and the judges sustained the demurrer. Chief Justice Holt held that peerage was a purely factual question, over which the House of Lords had no power other than that which the King gave it: "[A]s no peer can be created without the King's consent, who is the fountain of honour, no more can any be degraded without his consent. And an ordinance of the House of Peers cannot confer peerage."[57] As a purely factual question, peerage was well within the purview of the common-law courts.[58] Holt went on explicitly to subordinate lex parliamenti to lex terrae: "[I]t is the law which hath invested [the House of Lords] with such ample authority, and therefore it is no diminution to their power to say, that they ought to observe those limits which this law hath prescribed for them, which in other respects hath made them so great."[59] This ruling did not sit well with the Lords, who summoned Holt to the bar, but when Holt refused to explain his ruling "in so extrajudicial a manner," the Lords backed down,[60] giving lex terrae a rare total victory in one of its frequent skirmishes with lex parliamenti.

NINETEENTH-CENTURY CASES

A trio of nineteenth-century controversies, while moving toward the Millian conception of the relationship between lex parliamenti and lex terrae, tended to favor something closer to conception 2 above. The first of these controversies was the famous *Burdett* case. The genesis of this case will be discussed further in chapter 9; for now, it suffices to note that Sir Francis Burdett, MP, was arrested by order of the House of Commons in 1810 and that his arrest involved forcible entry into his house by police and soldiers.[61] Four days after Burdett was sent to the Tower, he notified Charles Abbott, the Speaker of the House, that he would bring suit against him in the King's Bench for trespass and false imprisonment.[62] In a break with precedent, the House directed Abbott and John Coleman (the Sergeant who had arrested Burdett) to plead in court, and it instructed the attorney-general to serve as their counsel.[63] Appearing in court, Abbott gave a detailed account of the facts of the case and claimed privilege, but withdrew without making a plea.[64] Burdett's counsel argued that to allow the Houses of Parliament to act outside the check of normal law was to give them arbitrary and despotic power. But in contrast,

> by laying the basis of Parliamentary privileges in the law of the land, and subjecting them to the examination and control of the Courts of Law, no arbitrary and despotic power can be exercised, and no person can be deprived of his liberty, without ultimate redress, except by a law made or recognized by the whole body of Parliament; whereby the one House may operate as a check upon the other.[65]

The attorney-general noted simply that the Commons had spoken on the matter, and that its decision should be taken as final by the judges.[66] The judges unanimously supported the House of Commons. Chief Justice Ellenborough asked,

> [C]ould it be expected that [the Houses of Parliament] should stand high in the estimation and reverence of the people, if, whenever they were insulted, they were obliged to wait the comparatively slow proceedings of the ordinary course of law for their redress? That the Speaker with his mace should be under the necessity of going before a grand jury to prefer a bill of indictment for the insult offered to the House? They certainly must have the power of self-vindication and self-protection in their own hands.[67]

However, Ellenborough also wrote that, if the House

> did not profess to commit for a contempt, but for some matter appearing on the return, which could by no reasonable intendment be considered as a contempt of the Court committing, but a ground of commitment palpably and evidently arbitrary, unjust, and contrary to every principle of positive law, or national justice; I say, that in the case of such a commitment, (if it ever should occur, but which I cannot possibly anticipate as ever likely to occur,) we must look at it and act upon it as justice may require from whatever Court it may profess to have proceeded.[68]

This claim could be read two ways. The less radical reading would be to view it as a claim that the common-law courts have the authority to police the boundaries between the two distinct systems of law, lex parliamenti and lex terrae, but they do not have the authority to intrude upon lex parliamenti (claim 2, above). An apt analogy might be Henry II's determination to reserve to the royal courts the right to draw the boundaries between canon law and common law, without ever claiming that canon law was somehow subsumed by common law.[69] The more radical reading involves a claim that lex parliamenti is simply a part of lex terrae, albeit a part in which judges should tread lightly, if at all (a weak version of claim 3, above). This more radical reading was, in fact, the one the Lords gave when affirming the ruling of the King's Bench: "[P]rivileges are part of the law of the land. . . . [B]y this judgment, it appears that it is the law which protects the just privileges of the House of Commons, as well as the rights of the subject."[70] But it is important to note that, under either reading, the ordinary courts do have some role to play in questions of lex parliamenti.

Stockdale v. Hansard[71] will be discussed in more detail in chapter 3. For our purposes here, it is enough to say that Stockdale sued the printer Hansard for libel. Hansard's defense was that he had published by order of the House of Commons and was therefore protected by privilege. The Court of Queen's Bench disagreed, with Chief Justice Denman writing:

> Where the subject matter falls within their jurisdiction, no doubt we cannot question their judgment; but we are now enquiring whether the subject matter does fall within the jurisdiction of the House of Commons. It is contended that they can bring it within their jurisdiction by declaring it so. . . . [I]t is perfectly clear that none of these Courts could give themselves jurisdiction by adjudging that they enjoy it.[72]

Carl Wittke interprets this as an explicit statement that the judges saw lex parliamenti as part of lex terrae,[73] but it seems that Denman's words are capable of sustaining either of the two meanings suggested above. The court could be claiming that lex parliamenti is a part of lex terrae (claim 3), but it could also be claiming that they are separate bodies of law with the courts as judges of the boundaries (claim 2). Indeed, a closer look at Denman's statement would seem to suggest that claim 2 is a better reading. But whichever of these interpretations is correct, the ruling was unacceptable to the House, which imprisoned the sheriffs who attempted to carry out the orders of the court. The sheriffs' application for habeas corpus was denied by the Queen's Bench on the strength of the case law discussed above.[74] Realizing that the judges were not going to come to their rescue, the sheriffs secured their own release by promising the House not to carry out the orders of the court. As a result, the judges promptly imprisoned them for contempt of court.[75] Within a year, Parliament passed the Parliamentary Papers Act, which effectively overruled *Stockdale*, thus allowing the House of Commons to maintain its substantive position without facing continual clashes with the courts.[76] Thus, this series of events left the relationship between lex parliamenti and lex terrae no clearer than it had found it.

The *Bradlaugh* controversy had similarly inconclusive results. Charles Bradlaugh was an outspoken atheist who was elected to Parliament in 1880. After several rounds of debate on the floor, it was decided that he could not take the oath of office, and therefore could not take his seat. In 1883, he sued Mr. Erskine, the deputy Sergeant of the House, for assault and for forcibly preventing him from entering the House to take his seat.[77] Erskine claimed privilege and that no other court had the right to interfere in parliamentary affairs. The Queen's Bench agreed. Undeterred, Bradlaugh filed another suit, this time against R. A. Gossett, the new Sergeant of the House, claiming that his exclusion violated the Parliamentary Oaths Act of 1866, which required Bradlaugh to take the oath.[78] The judges agreed that, as they understood the law, the House's exclusion of Bradlaugh violated it. However, they held that the House must be assumed to act in accordance with some interpretation of the law of which the judges were simply unaware.[79] This holding was limited to actions internal to Parliament,[80] but it was nonetheless a sweeping statement of judicial deference. Justice Stephen meekly noted that a contrary decision "should provoke a conflict between the House of Commons and this Court, which in itself would be a great evil."[81] Once again, it was left unclear what the exact contours of the relationship between lex parliamenti and lex terrae were.

In *Burdett*, *Stockdale*, and *Bradlaugh*, the courts seem to have moved closer to the Millian position, although they did not quite reach it. In *Burdett*, for example, even the House seemed to recognize the role of the courts in determining questions of privilege when it ordered its Speaker and Sergeant to plead their defense in court. Although the judges sided with the House, Chief Justice Ellenborough was quick to point out that the court's deference to the House was not infinite: if the House locked up an individual for something other than contempt, the courts would have a duty to intervene. Indeed, in Ellenborough's decision, the reason that the House has the power of imprisonment is not that the courts cannot understand or apply lex parliamenti, but rather that the House cannot be expected to wait around for the courts to do so. In other words, the court seems to be propounding a doctrine of extreme deference to the Houses of Parliament, but not unlimited deference, a position that they stuck to in *Bradlaugh*. In between *Burdett* and *Bradlaugh*, the courts seem to have taken a much more aggressive stance in *Stockdale*, in which the Queen's Bench actually ruled against the House. However, the House of Commons' strong reaction to *Stockdale*—both locking up the sheriffs who attempted to enforce the court's decision and overruling the decision by statute—may have convinced the courts to back off somewhat in subsequent cases.

TWENTIETH- AND TWENTY-FIRST-CENTURY CASES

Several more recent cases continued this trend of making the relationship between lex parliamenti and lex terrae more subtle and complex. The first two can be seen as almost complete victories for lex parliamenti. In the 1935 *Graham-Campbell* case,[82] the King's Bench Division held that the House of Commons' bar fell within parliamentary privilege, and thus the courts lacked jurisdiction to punish its operators for selling liquor without a license. Counsel for the bar's operators charmingly noted,

> The House sits for long periods and arrangements have to be made for heating the House when the weather is cold and the provision of refreshment for the mind in the library and refreshment for the body in suitable places. The regulation of those matters is clearly within the area of the internal affairs of the House and connected with the affairs of the House.[83]

Lord Chief Justice Hewart agreed, striking a surprisingly Blackstonian note: "To take the opposite course [and hold the bar subject to ordinary licensing laws] might conceivably be, in proceedings of a somewhat different character from these, after the various stages of those proceedings had been passed, to make the House of Lords the arbiter of the privileges of the House of Commons."[84] It was left unexplained why the operation of a bar was so intimately connected with Members' parliamentary duties that it fell within the privileges of the House. After all, the fact that the House of Lords might be the final judge of the legality of the House of Commons' refreshment operations hardly bespeaks great power on the Lords' part to interfere in the *legislative* workings of the Commons. The *Graham-Campbell* decision was anachronistically Blackstonian because it focused on the geographical consideration of whether the bar was within Westminster Palace rather than on the functional consideration of whether the bar was integral to Members' legislative duties.[85] After cases like *Burdett* and *Stockdale*, this focus would seem to be misplaced.

The second important twentieth-century case, the 1958 *Strauss* case,[86] can also be seen as an almost complete victory for lex parliamenti. George Strauss, an MP, had criticized the London Electricity Board in a letter to the paymaster-general, and the board threatened to sue for libel. The Committee on Privileges determined that the letter constituted a "proceeding in Parliament" and was therefore privileged under Article 9 of the Bill of Rights (more on that topic in chapter 3).[87] The committee, however, requested an advisory opinion from the Judicial Committee of the Privy Council as to whether it could, consistent with the Parliamentary Privilege Act of 1770, treat the institution of such a suit as a breach of privilege. The 1770 act provides that "any person . . . may at any time commence and prosecute any action or suit in any court" against any Member of either House of Parliament, "and no such action . . . shall at any time be impeached, stayed or delayed by or under colour or pretence of any privilege of Parliament."[88] The Privy Council determined that this language applied only to "Members of Parliament in respect of their debts and actions as individuals and not in respect of their conduct in Parliament as Members of Parliament."[89] Thus, the 1770 act did not prevent the House from treating the institution of a libel suit against an MP for words written in proceedings in Parliament as a breach of privilege. Lord Denning, in a dissent that remained unpublished for over a quarter of a century,[90] thought that privilege was a defense to be raised in court, rather than a bar preventing recourse to the courts in the first place. Article 9 of the Bill of Rights, he wrote, "did not prevent a plaintiff from *commencing* an action or laying an information. It only prevented him from *prosecuting* it in the court. . . . The article is a direction *to the courts of law* not to allow speeches or debates or proceedings in Parliament to be impeached or questioned."[91] In other words, while the Privy Council's decision adhered to conception 1 of the courts' role in questions of lex parliamenti, Lord Denning's dissent favored conception 2.[92]

But while the decisions in the *Graham-Campbell* and *Strauss* cases were strongly in favor of the primacy of lex parliamenti, several subsequent cases were more nuanced. In the 1972 case *Church of Scientology v. Johnson-Smith*,[93] the plaintiff in a libel action sought to introduce statements that the defendant, an MP, had made on the House floor in order to demonstrate that statements made by the defendant during a television interview were malicious. The Queen's Bench, however, refused to allow the floor statements to be introduced, holding that "what is said or done in the House in the course of proceedings there cannot be examined outside Parliament for the purpose of supporting a cause of action even though the cause of action itself arises out of something done outside the House."[94] The court's decision was based on functional considerations: "[A] member must have a complete right of free speech in the House without any fear that his motives or intentions or reasoning will be questioned or held against him thereafter,"[95] and such fear could certainly result from a decision allowing floor statements to be used against Members in actions for things said elsewhere. In 1993, the House of Lords, in *Pepper v. Hart*,[96] held that it did not violate privilege for courts to refer to parliamentary debates when seeking to interpret legislation. Lord Browne-Wilkinson held that the purpose of the Article 9 speech privilege

> was to ensure that Members of Parliament were not subjected to any penalty, civil or criminal for what they said and were able . . . to discuss what they, as opposed to the monarch, chose to have discussed. Relaxation of the rule [against referring to parliamentary debates] will not involve the courts in criticising what is said in Parliament. The purpose of looking at Hansard [the

official record of parliamentary debates] will not be to construe the words used by the Minister [in introducing the legislation] but to give effect to the words used so long as they are clear. Far from questioning the independence of Parliament and its debates, the courts would be giving effect to what is said and done there.[97]

Lord Browne-Wilkinson acknowledged that judges would have to be "astute to ensure that counsel does not in any way impugn or criticise the Minister's statements or his reasoning,"[98] but he concluded that judges were up to the task. He also noted that the decision in *Pepper* did not conflict with *Johnson-Smith*, because the plaintiffs in *Johnson-Smith* sought to use parliamentary debates as evidence "that the defendant acted improperly in Parliament in saying what he did in Parliament. That plainly would amount to questioning a member's behaviour in Parliament and infringe article 9."[99] In *Pepper*, on the other hand, the court was simply looking to the debates to get a better understanding of the law, not to question, criticize, or examine the lawmakers in any way.[100] Finally, in a supremely Millian passage, Lord Browne-Wilkinson defended the court's right to be deciding this issue at all:

> Although in the past the courts and the House of Commons both claimed the exclusive right to determine whether or not a privilege existed, it is now apparently accepted that it is for the courts to decide whether a privilege exists and for the House to decide whether such privilege has been infringed.[101]

It would be hard to find a more succinct statement of interpretation 2 of the relationship between lex parliamenti and lex terrae.

In 1995, the Privy Council was faced with a case reminiscent of *Johnson-Smith*, but with the parties reversed. In *Prebble*,[102] a New Zealand government minister sued a television station for defamation. The station tried to use statements made on the floor of the House of Representatives in its defense, and the plaintiff claimed that this was a violation of privilege. Lord Browne-Wilkinson held that Article 9 of the Bill of Rights protected two important values: (1) "the need to ensure so far as possible that a member of the legislature and witnesses before committees of the House can speak freely without fear that what they say will later be held against them in the courts," and (2) the prevention of institutional conflict between a house of the legislature and the courts.[103] Moreover, since parliamentary privilege is "the privilege of Parliament itself," and not of individual Members, a Member cannot waive privilege when he or she chooses to sue.[104] Based on this, the Privy Council held that privilege prevented the defense from bringing into question words spoken on the floor of Parliament. However, it also held that when "the exclusion of material on the grounds of Parliamentary privilege makes it quite impossible fairly to determine the issue between the parties," then the proceedings could be stayed.[105] Although the Privy Council did not believe that the facts of *Prebble* met that criterion, and therefore refused to grant a stay,[106] the case was cited later the same year in a similar (British) case, in which the Queen's Bench did grant a stay.[107]

The next year, 1996, the Defamation Act was enacted. That act provided, inter alia, that

> [w]here the conduct of a person in or in relation to proceedings in Parliament is in issue in defamation proceedings, he may waive for the purposes of those proceedings, so far as concerns him, the protection of any enactment or rule of law which prevents proceedings in Parliament being impeached or questioned in any court or place out of Parliament.[108]

The House of Lords relied upon the Defamation Act in the 2001 case *Hamilton v. Al Fayed*.[109] In a television program, Mohamed Al Fayed accused Neil Hamilton, then an MP, of requesting and accepting money from him in return for asking questions on his behalf in the House of Commons. After Hamilton lost his seat, he gave evidence before a committee of the House on the matter. Hamilton then sued Al Fayed for defamation, waiving his privilege pursuant to the Defamation Act. Al Fayed requested a stay, arguing that privilege precluded challenging evidence already heard before a parliamentary committee and that he therefore could not get a fair trial. Lord Browne-Wilkinson agreed that, were it not for the Defamation Act, a stay would be necessary, but he held that the waiver under the act allowed Al Fayed to challenge the statements made before the committee and therefore allowed him to make a defense.[110]

The relationship between lex parliamenti and lex terrae was thus complicated in three ways. First, the combination of *Johnson-Smith* and *Pepper* allowed courts to refer to parliamentary debates in order to clarify the meaning of legislation but not in order to inquire into the behavior of legislators. This was a functional turn — instead of focusing simply on the question of whether anything said within the geographical confines of the House floor could ever be mentioned in a court of law, the courts focused on the function of the privilege and determined that such statements could be introduced so long as they did not amount to an inquiry into a Member's conduct. Together, they thus represent a Millian advance in the law of privilege. Second, *Prebble* recognized that, although the courts still could not entertain challenges to things said or done in proceedings in Parliament, they could prevent lex parliamenti from adversely affecting the operations of lex terrae by staying any cases that would be unfairly influenced by assertions of privilege. Rather than allowing lex parliamenti to take primacy over lex terrae, the argument here was one of separate spheres: it was necessary to preserve lex parliamenti for the effective functioning of the Houses of Parliament, but the courts would also do their best to ensure that it did not adversely affect their own procedural fairness.

This, however, created a new procedural imbalance, as an MP who had been defamed might be left without remedy. The Defamation Act and the *Hamilton* decision thus added another layer of subtlety by allowing MPs to waive privilege insofar as it applied to them in a particular case. Note that there is nothing inconsistent about holding both that (a) parliamentary privilege is the privilege *of Parliament*, not of individual Members, and (b) that individual Members can waive privilege as it applies to them in particular cases.[111] Recall that at the heart of privilege is the need for a defense against improper outside interference in the affairs of the House. Both of the justifications for privilege that Lord Browne-Wilkinson gave in *Prebble* — that MPs and witnesses must be free to speak their minds and that conflict between the Houses and the courts must be avoided — fall under the general heading of preventing undue outside influence. This is necessary in order to ensure that the House can perform its legislative functions, which is why it is a privilege of the House and not of individual MPs. However, allowing MPs to waive it in no way harms these functions. MPs and witnesses may still speak altogether freely before the House without fear of ever being questioned in any other place unless they choose to be. Moreover, there is no possibility of institutional clash, as the MP or witness has voluntarily chosen to put himself or herself under the jurisdiction of the ordinary courts. It is true that a committee of the House could come to a conclusion different from that of an ordinary court on the same factual matter, but it is hard to see why this would be any more problematic than a criminal court and a civil court reaching different conclusions on the same factual matter. It may prove epistemically unsettling, but it hardly constitutes a political crisis. In any event, if the witness or MP likes the decision he or she has received from the committee, he or she is always free not to pursue the matter in court. These cases thus seem to have taken a significant step toward rendering peaceful coexistence between lex parliamenti and lex terrae possible, although they did not subsume either to the other.

Thus, the case law moved somewhat closer still to the Millian ideal in the late twentieth and early twenty-first centuries. Although *Graham-Campbell* and *Strauss* may have been something of a step backward, *Johnson-Smith*, *Pepper*, *Prebble*, the Defamation Act, and *Hamilton* all moved closer to the Millian paradigm. *Johnson-Smith* and *Pepper* allowed for better statutory interpretation (by allowing courts to refer to parliamentary debates), while retaining the functional protections of the speech privilege. The *Prebble* decision lowered the legal wall of privilege sufficiently that an MP could not attack and then retire safely behind its protection—that is, he or she could not sue and then use privilege to prevent the mounting of an effective defense. Such a suit would simply be stayed. The Defamation Act and *Hamilton* decisions further enmeshed the relationship between lex parliamenti and lex terrae by allowing the waiving of privilege. This effectively allows the procedural rules of lex terrae to predominate in defamation cases: a judge can simply tell an MP that he or she either must waive privilege or see his or her action stayed indefinitely.

THE *DEMICOLI* CASE

The issue has been further complicated by a recent ruling of the European Court of Human Rights which is reminiscent of the complete victory for lex terrae over lex parliamenti in the *Knollys* case. The editor of a political satire magazine was held in contempt of the Maltese House of Representatives, fined, and ordered to print in his magazine the resolution of the House concerning the contempt.[112] He argued that the contempt finding violated Article 6 of the European Convention on Human Rights, which guarantees a "fair and public hearing within a reasonable time by an independent and impartial tribunal established by law" to anyone against whom criminal charges are levied. The court concluded that the punitive nature of the proceedings and the potential severity of the punishment made the contempt proceedings criminal proceedings.[113] It also noted, "The two Members of the House whose behaviour in Parliament was criticised in the impugned article and who raised the breach of privilege in the House participated throughout in the proceedings against the accused, including the finding of guilt and . . . the sentencing."[114] This, it concluded, constituted a violation of the Article 6 impartiality requirement. It is unclear just how broadly the holding in *Demicoli* should be read: if one takes seriously the idea that all contempts are against the House as a whole, and not against individual Members, then no punitive (as opposed to regulatory or disciplinary) contempt of Parliament proceeding could ever survive Article 6 scrutiny (but, of course, neither could any such contempt of court proceeding). But even if one reads it narrowly to say simply that those directly criticized should not take part in contempt proceedings, it still suggests that rights granted by generally applicable law trump the special procedures of lex parliamenti.

Although decisions of the European Court of Human Rights may not be legally binding on the House of Commons,[115] they may be taken to have strong advisory force. In this role, *Demicoli* potentially has the most extreme Millian effects of any of the cases discussed above, as it holds out the possibility that even proceedings which take place within Parliament are subject to the procedural fairness restraints of lex terrae (or, in this case, *lex europa*), insofar as they involve punitive action and not merely internal regulation. Within Britain, however, both sides have generally sought to avoid conflict in recent years. Since the House no longer imprisons, there are fewer potential cases of clash between the courts and the House. Where courts have been called upon to hear cases dealing with lex parliamenti, they have largely followed the *Burdett/ Bradlaugh* settlement of proclaiming the primacy of lex terrae while simultaneously giving extremely wide deference to parliamentary claims of their own privileges. Thus, although the Millian settlement has never emerged clearly in British law, something approaching it has emerged in practice.

THE CURRENT STATE OF AFFAIRS

Wittke's assertion that "[c]ourts and Parliament are today in practical agreement that the law of Parliament is part of the law of the land"[116] thus seems a bit premature. In fact, it is not at all clear that the two bodies of law have been merged into one. It is an equally plausible interpretation of the nineteenth-, twentieth-, and twenty-first-century case law to say that the ordinary courts have simply been given the job of patrolling the boundaries between the two bodies of law, much as they were given the analogous job of patrolling the boundary between common law and canon law in the twelfth century.[117] As D. L. Keir and F. H. Lawson have noted, what we are left with are "two doctrines of privilege, the one held by the courts, the other by either House . . . and no way of resolving the real point at issue should conflict arise."[118] But we are also left with strong desires by both the courts and the Houses of Parliament to avoid such conflicts.

In 1999, a joint parliamentary committee on privilege made a number of recommendations — for example, criminalizing the acceptance of a bribe by a Member[119] — which would have moved the relationship between lex parliamenti and lex terrae significantly closer to interpretation 3. The committee also recommended that Parliament fully codify the law of parliamentary privilege.[120] These recommendations, had they been enacted, would have involved the courts in matters of parliamentary privilege to an extent heretofore seen only in *Knollys* and *Demicoli*. (It should be noted, however, that the committee recommended that certain matters, such as the Houses' punishment of their own Members,[121] should remain within the exclusive cognizance of the Houses.) The committee's recommendations have thus far not been enacted.

Conclusions

The question of how lex parliamenti should relate to lex terrae is fundamentally a question of institutional power and trust. Under the Blackstonian view of privilege, the Houses view other powerful institutions primarily as threats. The Blackstonian view sees the greatest threat to democratic rule as anything that might interfere with the functioning of the democratic part of the Constitution—that is, the House of Commons. On this view, lex parliamenti must be quarantined from any interference by outside forces. The courts—the royally controlled courts whose highest body is the House of Lords—cannot be allowed to meddle with affairs internal to Parliament. As *Rolle* makes abundantly clear, if these courts could interfere in Parliament, then Parliament could be threatened with impunity by other powerful actors (in the case of *Rolle*, by the King).

However, the rise of the Millian paradigm—a paradigm that focuses on the promotion of a tighter nexus between popular will and government action and therefore on applying the same law throughout the land—coincided with the increasing independence of the judiciary from the monarchy and with the increasing specialization of the judicial function within the House of Lords. (Of course, this coincidence was not coincidental—the same spirit driving the Millian conception of privilege was also driving the increasing liberalization of other aspects of the Constitution.) In this new political climate, allowing the judges to check potentially reckless or self-dealing actions by a House of Parliament was more conducive to furthering the democratic parts of the Constitution. The Millian conception of privilege thus focuses increasingly on giving the judges that check. Because the Millian paradigm has never been fully incorporated into the law, there are still obvious perversities in the relationship between lex parliamenti and lex terrae. For instance, Chief Justice Ellenborough's dicta in *Burdett* that the courts would not question a finding of contempt by a House of Parliament, but would question an imprisonment were it for something other than contempt, provides an incentive for the House simply to make a vague claim of contempt, without providing details, any time it wishes to imprison someone. Any judicial doctrine that actively encourages vagueness in commitment orders cannot be said fully to comport with the rule of law. However, as noted above, this problem has almost entirely been rendered moot by the fact that the Houses no longer imprison. The broader idea that certain actions of a House of the legislature are immune to judicial oversight, however, is very much alive, both in Britain and, as we shall see, in America as well.

2

Political Questions and Nonjusticiability

Article III of the American Constitution — as modified by the Eleventh Amendment — defines the jurisdiction of the federal judiciary. Yet it has long been accepted that there exists a category of cases that fall within these jurisdictional boundaries but nonetheless ought not to be heard in federal court.[1] Such cases are said to be *nonjusticiable* because they present *political questions* — that is, questions the final resolution of which is left to the political branches of government (the legislature and executive). In Erwin Chemerinsky's words, the political questions doctrine holds that "certain allegations of unconstitutional government conduct should not be ruled on by the federal courts even though all of the jurisdictional . . . requirements are met. . . . In other words, the 'political questions doctrine' refers to *subject matter* that the Court deems to be inappropriate for judicial review."[2] Louis Henkin more tartly characterized a political question as one "in which the courts forego their unique and paramount function of judicial review of constitutionality."[3]

Recent studies of the doctrine have largely been presented as arbitrating the debate between Herbert Wechsler and Alexander Bickel.[4] Wechsler argued that the judiciary had an absolute constitutional obligation to exercise judicial review and that therefore the political-questions doctrine came into play only when "the Constitution has committed to another agency of government the autonomous determination of the issue raised."[5] This requirement of (to use the later formulation of the U.S. Supreme Court) "a textually demonstrable constitutional commitment of the issue to a coordinate political department"[6] is, according to Wechsler, "*toto caelo* different from a broad discretion to abstain or intervene," as the courts see fit.[7] Bickel, however, argued that it was precisely this kind of broad discretion that allowed the courts to avoid potentially disastrous conflicts. "No good society can be unprincipled; and no viable society can be principle-ridden,"[8] he wrote. The role of the judiciary is to mediate this "tension between principle and expediency," which it can do "because at least in modern times it nearly always has three courses of action open to it: it may strike down legislation as inconsistent with principle; it may legitimate it; or it may do neither."[9] The political questions doctrine — one of the devices by which it does neither — is, therefore, one of prudence. It is an exercise of those "passive virtues" that allow the system to work without either the sclerotic and dogmatic application of principle regardless of consequences or the legitimation by the courts of actions which run contrary to basic principles.[10] That is, the courts' discretion to refrain from deciding a case allows society to be both good and viable.

While the Wechsler-Bickel debate is without doubt an interesting and fruitful one, I propose to approach the question from a somewhat different angle. Specifically, I would like to continue with the sort of structural/institutional analysis employed in the previous chapter to examine the conflict between lex parliamenti and lex terrae in Britain. While no one has ever seriously claimed that there exists a law of Congress — a *lex congressi*, as it were — separate from the law of the land, the courts have, to different degrees at different times, held that certain "political" controversies should not be subject to judicial oversight. Thus, although disputes over political questions are not as far ranging as those between lex parliamenti and lex terrae, they can be viewed along the same institutional lines. We can therefore return to the three possibilities discussed in chapter 1: (1) the courts can say nothing at all about political questions and must simply accept a House of Congress's assertions on the matter; (2) the courts can adjudicate on the extent, but not the interpretation or application, of political questions; and (3) the courts can review both the extent and (at least to some degree) the interpretation and application of political questions. The question with which we are faced, then, is which of these positions best comports with the popular sovereignty interpretation of the Constitution sketched in the Introduction. No student of the American Constitution has seriously suggested position 1 — unfettered congressional discretion over any area in which Congress merely claims such discretion would be flatly incompatible with both constitutional text and the popular sovereignty underlying that text. Position 3 quickly shades away from an issue of justiciability and toward an issue of simple deference.[11] The question, then, is whether this position of deference or the stronger justiciability principle in position 2 best fits the American constitutional order.

The political-questions doctrine has been held to apply to a number of areas, including foreign policy and controversies over whether a state has a republican form of government (as guaranteed by Article IV, section 4, of the Constitution).[12] Two areas, however, are of specific interest for our study of legislative privilege: (1) matters dealing with the internal organization of each House of Congress, and (2) matters surrounding impeachment proceedings. This chapter argues that simple deference is insufficient in both cases, and that, although the courts can define the outer limits of congressional power with respect to internal affairs and impeachment proceedings, they cannot interfere in those matters properly set aside as political.

Internal Organization of the Houses of Congress

TEXT AND HISTORY

The text of the Constitution explicitly gives the Houses of Congress wide powers in determining their internal organizations. Each House is granted the power to choose its own officers, to "[j]udge of the Elections, Returns and Qualifications of its own Members . . . [and] to compel the Attendance of absent Members, in such Manner, and under such Penalties as each House may provide," to "determine the Rules of its Proceedings, punish its Members for disorderly Behaviour, and, with the Concurrence of two thirds, expel a Member," and to keep those proceedings which "in their Judgment require Secrecy" out of their journals (which the Houses are required to publish "from time to time").[13] The provisions giving the Houses the power to choose their own officers, to judge the elections, returns, and qualifications of Members, and to compel the attendance of Members were almost entirely uncontroversial at the Founding, and there was ample precedent for them in existing state constitutions.[14] A few interesting questions were raised at Philadelphia regarding each House's power to expel Members (an issue we shall examine in more detail in chapter 10). In the working notes of the Committee of Detail, we find: "[Q]uaere. how far the right of expulsion may be proper."[15] The committee's initial answer was to include a caveat: "Each House may expel a Member, but not a second Time for the same Offence."[16] However, by the time the committee reported to the whole Convention, the caveat had been dropped.[17] Later, after a cursory debate in which Madison warned that "the right of expulsion . . . was too important to be exercised by a bare majority of a quorum: and in emergencies of faction might be dangerously abused," the Convention overwhelmingly adopted an amendment requiring a two-thirds vote for expulsion. The amended provision, along with the undebated provisions allowing each House to determine its own rules of procedure and to punish Members for disorderly behavior, was then agreed to unanimously.[18]

Of the provisions mentioned above, only the one dealing with the publishing of the journals was at all controversial, as it raised fears of congressional proceedings being hidden from public view. The Articles of Confederation had required that Congress

> publish the journal of their proceedings monthly, except such parts thereof relating to treaties, alliances or military operations, as in their judgement require secrecy; and the yeas and nays of the delegates of each State on any question shall be entered on the journal, when it is desired by any delegates of a State, or any of them, at his or their request shall be furnished with a transcript of the said journal, except such parts as are above excepted, to lay before the legislatures of the several States.[19]

At the Philadelphia Convention, the original wording from the Committee of Detail was, "The House of Representatives, and the Senate, when it shall be acting in a legislative capacity, shall keep a Journal of their proceedings, and shall, from time to time, publish them: and the yeas and nays of the members of each House, on any question, shall, at the desire of one-fifth part of the members present, be entered on the journal."[20] The Convention voted to strike out "when it shall be acting in a legislative capacity" and to add "except such parts thereof as in their judgment require secrecy."[21] James Wilson told the Convention, "The people have a right to know what their Agents are doing or have done, and it should not be in the option of the Legislature to conceal their proceedings."[22] George Mason concurred, arguing that "it would give a just alarm to the people, to make a conclave of their Legislature."[23] The requirement of maintaining and publishing a journal passed unanimously, as did the one-fifth requirement for recording votes. The secrecy exception, however, barely squeaked by, with six states voting for it, four states voting against, and New Hampshire divided.[24] The issue was returned to later in the Convention, when Mason and Elbridge Gerry tried to limit the secrecy rule to the Senate, so that the House of Representatives would have to publish all of its debates. (Their proposal lost on a three-to-seven vote, with South Carolina divided.)[25] Gerry listed "[t]he Power given to the Legislature over their Journals" as one of the reasons he refused to sign on to the completed document.[26] Patrick Henry, in the Virginia Ratifying Convention, demanded

> at least a plausible apology why Congress should keep their proceedings in secret. They have the power of keeping them secret as long as they please, for

the provision for a periodical publication is too inexplicit and ambiguous to avail any thing. The expression *from time to time*, as I have more than once observed, admits of any extension. They may carry on the most wicked and pernicious of schemes under the dark veil of secrecy. The liberties of a people never were, nor ever will be, secure when the transactions of their rulers may be concealed from them. The most iniquitous plots may be carried on against their liberty and happiness.[27]

Mason, also in the Virginia Ratifying Convention, thought the wording of the similar clause in the Articles of Confederation more felicitous. The proposed wording in the new Constitution, he said, "enables them to keep the negotiations about treaties secret. Under this veil they may conceal any thing and every thing. . . . The proceedings by [the Articles of Confederation] are to be published monthly, with certain exceptions. These are proper guards. It is not so here. On the contrary, they may conceal what they please."[28] Madison replied,

> All the state legislatures can keep secret what they think ought to be concealed. The British House of Commons can do it. They are in this respect under much less restraint than Congress. There never was any legislative assembly without a discretionary power of concealing important transactions, the publication of which might be detrimental to the community. There can be no real danger as long as the government is constructed on such principles.[29]

A similar discussion arose in the North Carolina Ratifying Convention, over both the question of secrecy and the ambiguity of "from time to time."[30] In ratifying the document, four states — New York, Rhode Island, Virginia, and North Carolina — explicitly called for an amendment to require the publication of the journals at least once per year and to limit the Houses' discretion over what could be kept secret.[31] No such amendment was ever passed.

INTERPRETATION AND CASE LAW

Given, then, what we know about these clauses, how ought they to be interpreted? Or, to be more precise, *who* ought to be tasked with interpreting them? Let us examine the clauses one by one. It should be remembered that in this chapter we are considering only the issue of justiciability; in future chapters, we shall return to the substantive interpretation of many of these clauses.

First, the provisions allowing each House to choose its own officers. There has been very little judicial interpretation of these provisions, but what interpretation there has been unambiguously supports the proposition that the courts may define the boundaries of political questions but may not venture inside. In *Murray v. Buchanan*,[32] the D.C. Circuit Court of Appeals was faced with the question of whether the practice of each House's hiring a chaplain violated the First Amendment prohibition against establishing a religion. Judge MacKinnon, noting that the chaplain has always been considered an officer of the House, wrote (in a special concurrence to a very brief *per curiam* opinion):

> Payment of the chaplains, in short, is clearly concomitant to Congress' constitutionally prescribed right to choose those officers in the first instance. It is therefore an act that is itself *textually committed to Congress by the Constitution*. Appellants' claim thus comes within the political question doctrine and for that reason it is beyond the scope of our review.[33]

However, there is a check on the Houses' running rampant with this power: the courts may inquire into whether a person truly is an officer of the House. Thus, in 1858, the federal Court of Claims decided (in a case with faint echoes of *Stockdale*) that the public printer of the House of Representatives was not, in fact, an officer of the House.[34]

Combined, these principles seem a sensible way of interpreting the clause, in light of textual and popular-sovereignty considerations. The scheme of separation of powers, with attendant checks and balances, so clearly established in the Constitution, requires that each branch be able to serve as a check on overreaching by the other branches.[35] When the branches check one another — when ambition is made to counteract ambition[36] — then no governmental actors can get away with promoting their own good at the expense of the common good. The Constitution — the people's document — sets up a system of checks on the people's public servants to ensure that they remain just that — servants to their sovereign masters. The judiciary may check the legislature by declaring laws incompatible with the people's higher law, the Constitution. But to allow the courts a voice in choosing the officers — including the agenda setters — of the Houses of Congress would be to allow them to strangle legislation in its infancy. Madison thought it essential that the separation of powers imply that "each department should have a will of its own; and consequently should be so constituted that the members of each should have as little agency as possible in the appointment of the members of the others."[37] He admitted — and attempted to justify — that the means of appointing judges was a departure from this principle, but, he argued, it must hold for the other branches. And if this is true for determining the *membership* of the branches of government, it must be even more so for determining their *leadership*. If the Houses are to perform their duties on behalf of the people, they must be free to order their affairs — including selecting their leadership — however they choose.[38] If they overstep their boundaries in making legislation, the courts can check the legislation itself.

Second, the provisions empowering each House to judge the elections, returns, and qualifications of Members and to compel the attendance of Members. Similar concerns are at work here. In a 1929 case concerning the Senate's authority to hold in contempt a witness called by a committee investigating alleged electoral irregularities in Pennsylvania, the Supreme Court held that judgments of a House of Congress under this provision are "beyond the authority of any other tribunal to review."[39] But the Court was called to inquire into the matter in significantly more detail in the 1969 case of *Powell v. Mc-Cormack*.[40] Adam Clayton Powell Jr. was a longtime Representative from New York. During the Eighty-ninth Congress (1965–66), a special subcommittee of the House found that he had committed several improprieties, including deceiving House authorities as to travel expenses and funneling illegal salary payments to his wife. No formal action was taken by the House, and Powell was reelected in 1966. When the Ninetieth Congress met in 1967, the House voted not to seat Powell and to establish a Select Committee to determine his eligibility to be seated. After a number of hearings, the committee recommended that he be censured, fined, and deprived of his seniority, but be seated in the House. However, on the floor, an amendment to the resolution was offered excluding Powell from taking his seat. The amendment was adopted by a vote of 248 to 176; the amended resolution was passed by a vote of 307 to 116; Powell was excluded, and the Speaker notified the governor of New York that the seat was vacant.[41] Powell and several of his constituents filed suit, and the case eventually made its way to the Supreme Court. The case raises myriad issues, and it will be returned to in several subsequent chapters. For now, it suffices to say that the issue here was one of exclusion (which falls under the House's power to judge the elections, qualifications, and returns of its Members) and not expulsion (which requires a two-thirds vote, and will be discussed below).[42] Given that the Constitution lays out age, citizenship, and residency requirements for Members of both Houses, the Court held that the only qualifications of which the House was allowed to judge were these.[43] Because Powell's exclusion was not based on these criteria, the Court ruled in his favor. As Chief Justice Warren wrote for the majority,

> A fundamental principle of our representative democracy is, in Hamilton's words, "that the people should choose whom they please to govern them." As Madison pointed out at the Convention, this principle is undermined as much by limiting whom the people can select as by limiting the franchise itself. In apparent agreement with this basic philosophy, the Convention adopted his

> suggestion limiting the power to expel. To allow essentially that same power to be exercised under the guise of judging qualifications, would be to ignore Madison's warning, borne out in the Wilkes case and some of Congress' own post–Civil War exclusion cases, against "vesting an improper & dangerous power in the Legislature." Moreover, it would effectively nullify the Convention's decision to require a two-thirds vote for expulsion. Unquestionably, Congress has an interest in preserving its institutional integrity, but in most cases that interest can be sufficiently safeguarded by the exercise of its power to punish its members for disorderly behavior and, in extreme cases, to expel a member with the concurrence of two-thirds. In short, both the intention of the Framers, to the extent it can be determined, and an examination of the basic principles of our democratic system persuade us that the Constitution does not vest in the Congress a discretionary power to deny membership by a majority vote.[44]

In other words, each House of Congress has the power to expel (as will be discussed below) and the power to exclude. But the House cannot do one in the guise of doing the other. The Court nowhere suggests that it could review the *content* of an exclusion decision—if, for instance, the House excluded a Member-elect after determining that he or she did not meet the constitutional age requirement, there is nothing here to suggest that a challenge to the House's determination would be justiciable.[45] The courts are simply policing the boundaries of congressional power; they are not straying inside those boundaries.

Subsequent decisions addressing these provisions can be read in the same light. In the 1972 case *Roudebush v. Hartke*, the Supreme Court held that a state's recount procedures do not violate this clause by usurping the role of the legislative House, because, as Justice Stewart wrote,

> a recount can be said to 'usurp' the Senate's function only if it frustrates the Senate's ability to make an independent final judgment. A recount does not prevent the Senate from independently evaluating the election any more than the initial count does. The Senate is free to accept or reject the apparent winner in either count, and, if it chooses, to conduct its own recount.[46]

In other words, the state's recount procedures were acceptable because they *preceded* any inquiry into the matter by the Senate. It seems clear from Justice Stewart's language, however, that the House's decision "to accept or reject the apparent winner" would not be open to review. Indeed, Stewart wrote that the Court "is without power to alter the Senate's judgment" and that "[w]hich candidate is entitled to be seated in the Senate is, to be sure, a nonjusticiable political question."[47] This point was amply made in a 1986 case from the D.C. Circuit Court of Appeals. Initial returns from a 1984 House of Representatives election in Indiana showed Democrat Frank McCloskey winning by a mere seventy-two votes (out of more than 230,000 cast). Corrections to the returns left his opponent, Republican Richard McIntyre, in the lead by thirty-four votes. Indiana's secretary of state certified McIntyre as the winner, and a subsequent recount showed him winning by 418 votes. Before the recount was completed, however, the House of Representatives refused to seat McIntyre and appointed a task force to investigate. The task force conducted its own recount under its own rules and found McCloskey the winner by four votes. The House voted to seat McCloskey. A group of citizens filed suit, demanding that McIntyre be seated.[48] Then-Judge Scalia, writing for the court, emphatically denied the justiciability of their claim: "Because the Constitution so unambiguously proscribes judicial review of the proceedings in the House of Representatives that led to the seating of McCloskey, we believe that further briefing and oral argument in this case would be pointless, and that the decision of the District Court should be summarily affirmed."[49] In discussing the relevance of *Powell* to the case at hand, Judge Scalia wrote that "the holding of the case [*Powell*] was simply that Article I, section 5 had no application, since the House action in question did *not* consist of judging 'qualifications' within the meaning of the provision," whereas "[i]n the present case, there is no doubt that a judgment of 'elections' is at issue."[50] In a previous case arising out of the same election dispute, Judge Easterbrook had written that "[t]he House is not only 'Judge' but also final arbiter. Its decisions about which ballots count, and who won, are not reviewable in any court."[51]

The gist of the decisions on these provisions seems, again, to be that the courts may define their boundaries, but only the Houses of Congress may rule on their content. The text of the Constitution seems clearly to leave these matters in the hands of the Houses — indeed, even Wechsler understands the "seating or expulsion of a Senator or Representative" to be a political question[52] — but precisely *what* is being left in the Houses' hands is a matter on which the courts may rule. This seems to comport well with the separation-of-powers concerns that, as we have seen, undergird popular sovereignty. The courts are unable to determine the membership of the legislature (as they could if they were the final word on election results), but they are able to prevent a self-dealing majority from excluding a duly elected Member on extraconstitutional grounds. Expulsion, as we shall see presently, requires a two-thirds vote, and it is unlikely that a single party will ever control two-thirds of either House, making it likely that Members will only be expelled for true transgressions. Separation of powers involves a delicate balance, and this conception of nonjusticiability seems to strike just that balance.

Third, the provisions allowing each House to determine its own rules of proceeding, punish Members, and, with a two-thirds vote, expel Members. Once again, we shall begin by considering the case law. In 1932, a case arose over the Senate's procedural rules. The rules of that House stated that, after the Senate had consented to an executive appointment (under Article II, section 2, clause 2), any Member voting with the majority could move for a reconsideration on either of the next two days of executive session of that House. If notification of the Senate's consent had already been sent to the president, the rules required that the president be requested to return the notification to the Senate while it was reconsidered. The Senate confirmed President Hoover's nomination of George Otis Smith to the Federal Power Commission on December 20, 1930, and the confirmation was sent to the president, who then delivered to Smith his commission on December 22. The Senate adjourned on the same day that it voted to confirm Smith, and did not reconvene until January 5, 1931. When it reconvened, a senator who had voted in the majority moved to reconsider the nomination, and the motion passed. The president was asked to return the resolution of confirmation, but he refused to do so on the grounds that Smith was already in office. The Senate later voted again on Smith's nomination, and this time voted it down. The Senate then petitioned for a writ of *quo warranto* to determine whether or not Smith lawfully held the position.[53] The Senate argued that, under its rules of proceeding, which it alone has the right to determine, it had not confirmed Smith. Justice Brandeis, for the Court, held for Smith, arguing that the normal meaning of a confirmation notification to the president was that the Senate had indeed confirmed the nominee. But most important for our considerations here was his assertion of the matter's justiciability: "As the construction to be given to the rules affects persons other than members of the Senate, the question presented is of necessity a judicial one."[54] This is best read as a limitation on the *scope* of the Senate's rulemaking power, rather than as a warrant to inquire substantively into it. That is, the issue was justiciable because the Senate claimed that its authority to determine the rules of *its own* proceedings extended to a power requiring the president to act in certain ways — that is, to return the confirmation resolution. The issue was justiciable because it was a case of circumscribing the Senate's rulemaking powers — declaring that they cannot extend to matters outside the Senate — rather than one of determining the Senate's rules.

Two lower-court cases support the proposition that, when the rules truly are internal to the House, they are nonjusticiable. In a 1975 case, the D.C. Circuit Court of Appeals found that a magazine's challenge to its being denied accreditation in the congressional press galleries was nonjusticiable.[55] In a subsequent case, the same Circuit dismissed a suit by Republican Members of the House of Representatives claiming that the Democratic majority in the House had denied them a proportionate share of the seats on committees and subcommittees.[56]

Although the court explicitly declined to base its ruling on the House's power to determine its own internal rules,[57] the instinct appears to be the same.

In another case from the same Circuit, a Congressman who had been indicted for misappropriating congressional funds argued that, in order for the court to determine whether the funds had been *mis*appropriated, it would have to inquire into the congressional rules governing appropriation of funds and that this question was nonjusticiable. Judge Ginsburg, writing for the court, dismissed this claim, arguing that, if taken seriously, it would "effectively insulate every Member of Congress from liability under certain criminal laws."[58] But Judge Ginsburg also noted that "a sufficiently ambiguous House Rule is non-justiciable" because "judicial interpretation of an ambiguous House Rule runs the risk of the court intruding into the sphere of influence reserved to the legislative branch under the Constitution."[59] It would seem, however, that Judge Ginsburg misunderstood the harm arising from judicial inquiry into the official conduct of Members of Congress. As we shall see in more detail in chapter 4, the harm is not simply the possibility that a judge might get the internal rules of the House *wrong*; rather, the concern is that judges simply should not be inquiring into how Members of Congress conduct congressional business. The concept of separation of powers necessitates that Members be given wide latitude to conduct their internal business free from oversight by the other branches; as we shall see in chapter 10, the Houses themselves are fully competent to punish Members who violate House rules.

Cases dealing with the punishment and expulsion of Members are not dissimilar. As noted above, the Court in *Powell* held that the House could not *exclude* Powell from taking his seat for any reason other than failure to meet those qualifications spelled out in the Constitution, but it pointedly declined to address the question of whether the House could have seated and then *expelled* him.[60] Indeed, federal courts do not seem ever to have been confronted with the question of expulsion, nor do they seem squarely to have dealt with the question of lesser punishments. In several decisions, however, the courts have made clear that the Houses' power to punish is not exclusive — that is, the fact that a House may punish its own Members does not grant those Members immunity from prosecution in ordinary courts for the same conduct (assuming, of course, that the conduct is not otherwise privileged).[61] Again, this seems to fit well with the idea that the courts cannot interfere with the House's internal procedures, but those procedures should not be allowed to extend their sphere and preempt the entertaining of legitimate cases by the courts.

Fourth, the provision requiring the publishing of a journal but allowing the House to keep parts of it secret. Here, too, the case law is slim, but interesting.

In 1892, the Supreme Court was asked to declare a law void in its entirety because

> such is the allegation — it is shown by the Congressional record of proceedings, reports of committees of each house, reports of committees of conference, and other papers printed by authority of Congress . . . that a section of the bill, as it finally passed, was not in the bill authenticated by the signatures of the presiding officers of the respective houses of Congress, and approved by the President.[62]

The argument was that the law had not, in fact, been passed by Congress, and therefore failed the constitutional requirements of a law.[63] Justice Harlan, for the Court, wrote:

> In view of the express requirements of the Constitution the correctness of this general principle cannot be doubted. There is no authority in the presiding officers of the House of Representatives and the Senate to attest by their signatures, nor in the President to approve, nor in the Secretary of State to receive and cause to be published, as a legislative act, any bill not passed by Congress.[64]

But, asked Justice Harlan, how was the Court to know whether a bill had, in fact, passed both Houses of Congress or not?[65] The appellants argued that the journals of the Houses provided conclusive evidence, but Justice Harlan replied both that what, precisely, was entered in the journals was "left to the discretion of the respective houses of Congress," and that the Constitution never specifies how the passage of a bill through both Houses should be authenticated.[66] The appellants, in contending that the journals must be the source of authentication, argued that "under any other view, it becomes possible for the Speaker of the House of Representatives and the President of the Senate [to] impose upon the people as a law a bill that was never passed by Congress," but Justice Harlan dismissed this view as "too remote to be seriously considered in the present inquiry."[67] Respect for the coordinate branches of government forbade him from considering that they might engage in such iniquity. In other words, the Court would not look behind the enrolled law.[68] Curiously, however, in another case decided on the same day, the Court *did* refer to the journals to determine that a quorum had in fact been present when the bill in question in that case was voted upon.[69]

It would seem that the Court was on more solid ground when it refused to look into the journals at all. If the provision was omitted accidentally, then the House could remedy this defect by passing the provision again. If it was omitted intentionally, then the House could discipline its presiding officer, even, if necessary, replace him. Judicial oversight of every quorum count and voting procedure in the House is surely a greater threat to popular sovereignty than the implausible possibility that the House will allow its presiding officer to run roughshod over its will. There seems to be no case law whatsoever on keeping certain parts of the journals secret or on how often the journals must be published. The text of the clause seems clearly to leave these determinations, too, in the hands of the Houses.

Impeachment

TEXT AND HISTORY

Four passages in the Constitution address the question of impeachment. The House of Representatives is given "sole Power of Impeachment," and the Senate has "sole Power to try all Impeachments," which it must do while sitting under "Oath or Affirmation." The chief justice is to preside over any presidential impeachment trials, and a two-thirds vote is needed to convict any impeached officer. A conviction "shall not extend further than to removal from Office, and disqualification to hold and enjoy any Office, Trust or Profit under the United States," but a convicted officer is still liable to be tried in the regular courts for the same offense for which he was impeached. Who may be impeached and for what are spelled out more clearly in Article II: "The President, Vice President and all civil Officers of the United States, shall be removed from Office on Impeachment for, and Conviction of, Treason, Bribery, or other high Crimes and Misdemeanors." Finally, Article III mandates that "[t]he Trial of all Crimes, except in Cases of Impeachment, shall be by Jury."[70]

The history of these clauses sheds significant light on the question of justiciability. The Virginia Plan, proposed in the Philadelphia Convention by Edmund Randolph, placed the "impeachment of any National officers" squarely within the jurisdiction of the "National Judiciary."[71] As originally laid before the Convention, this proposal passed unanimously.[72] William Patterson's New Jersey Plan also left impeachments in the hands of the judiciary.[73] Alexander Hamilton's alternative had impeachments being tried "by a Court to consist of the Chief or Judge of the Superior Court of Law of each State."[74] Later, in discussing who should appoint federal judges, George Mason remarked, "The mode of appointing the Judges may depend in some degree on the mode of trying impeachments, of the Executive. If the Judges were to form a tribunal for that purpose, they surely ought not to be appointed by the Executive."[75] Gouverneur Morris replied that "it would be improper for an impeachmt. of the Executive to be tried before the Judges."[76] Without further debate, the provision giving the judiciary jurisdiction over impeachment trials was struck out.[77]

The longest debate on impeachment occurred over the question of whether the president should be subject to it. Morris argued that he should not be—recourse to the voters at regular intervals was, he thought, sufficient.[78] After Mason pointed out that someone could fraudulently obtain the office by bribing the electors, and then retain the office because impeachment would not apply to him, Morris softened his position, admitting "corruption & some few other offenses to be such as ought to be impeachable; but thought the cases ought to be enumerated & defined."[79] Benjamin Franklin offered perhaps the most interesting defense of the impeachability of the president:

> What was the practice before this in cases where the chief Magistrate rendered himself obnoxious? Why recourse was had to assassination in wch. he was not only deprived of his life but of the opportunity of vindicating his character. It wd. be the best way therefore to provide in the Constitution for the regular punishment of the Executive when his misconduct should deserve it, and for his honorable acquittal when he should be unjustly accused.[80]

After Morris announced that he had come around—but that he hoped that the method of impeachment would not make the president "dependent on the Legislature"—the provision to make the president subject to impeachment passed handily.[81]

Early drafts from the Committee of Detail contain a number of variants. Some say that "Impeachments shall be by the H[ouse of] D[elegates] before the Senate and the judges of the federeal [*sic*] judicial Court."[82] Others say that impeachments are to be made in the House of Representatives and tried before the Supreme Court.[83] In the version that the committee reported to the whole Convention, the House of Representatives had sole power of impeachment, and the Supreme Court had original jurisdiction over impeachment trials.[84] The impeachment power in the House of Representatives was unanimously agreed to by the Convention.[85] Gouverneur Morris—who seemed to have trouble making up his mind on the issue—complained that the Supreme Court should not be the judge of presidential impeachment trials.[86] A committee appointed to address remaining contentious issues recommended that the trial of impeachments be conducted by the Senate, with a two-thirds vote necessary to convict.[87] Madison and others thought this made the president "improperly dependent" on the Senate, but Morris—who seems finally to have hit upon a formulation that met with his approval—"thought no other tribunal than the Senate could be trusted."[88] Madison's proposal to take the trial of impeachments away from the Senate was overwhelmingly defeated, and the matter seems finally to have been settled.[89]

Post-Philadelphia debates ran along much the same lines. George Mason complained in the Virginia Ratifying Convention that the proposed Constitution "has *married* the President and Senate — has made them man and wife. . . . They will be continually supporting and abiding each other: they will always consider their interest as united," and therefore allowing the Senate to try impeachments of the president is no check at all.[90] Patrick Henry called the impeachment power "a mere sham — a mere farce," asking, "Can there be any security where offenders mutually try one another?"[91] Madison replied that it was unlikely that a president could corrupt so many senators, and, even if he did, the biennial turnover in the Senate would furnish another check.[92] Still, Virginia, along with North Carolina and New York, called for an amendment moving impeachment trials out of the Senate.[93]

The debate in the press was similar. Luther Martin thought it unlikely that the House of Representatives would ever vote to impeach a president, as many Members would wish to be appointed to offices "of which he has the sole nomination." And even if the House impeached the president, the Senate would not convict, both because senators, too, would seek to be appointed to federal offices and because the Senate, "being constituted a privy council to the president, it is probable many of its leading and influential members may have advised or concurred in the very measures for which he may be impeached."[94] Antifederalist pamphleteer "The Federal Farmer" concurred, noting that the unlikelihood of an impeachment and conviction made the whole procedure "of but little importance."[95] And "Brutus" complained that while federal judges were impeachable, they were impeachable only for acts stemming from "wicked and corrupt motives," not for incompetence.[96] Hamilton was tasked with responding to these arguments on behalf of Publius. The subjects of impeachment, he wrote,

> are those offenses which proceed from the misconduct of public men, or, in other words, from the abuse or violation of some public trust. They are of a nature which may with particular propriety be denominated POLITICAL, as they relate chiefly to injuries done immediately to the society itself.[97]

Given the political nature of the offenses, "who can so properly be the inquisitors for the nation as the representatives of the nation themselves?"[98] Moreover, the division of labor between the House of Representatives as impeaching body and the Senate as trying body along with the requirement of two-thirds for a conviction serve to guard against political persecution.[99] Finally, it is not clear what the alternative would be — Hamilton notes that an officer who is impeached and convicted is still liable to be tried in the ordinary courts. "Would it be proper that the persons who had disposed of his fame, and his most valuable rights as a citizen, in one trial, should, in another trial, for the same offense, be also the disposers of his life and his fortune?"[100]

INTERPRETATION

Clearly, impeachment raises a number of interesting questions, most of which are beyond the purview of this study.[101] I have gone into some detail about the history of the impeachment provisions, however, to make this point: it was strongly debated — at Philadelphia, at the states' ratifying conventions, and in the press — whether the judiciary should have any role in impeachment proceedings. Indeed, as we have seen, the Supreme Court was at first tasked with original jurisdiction over impeachment trials. This jurisdiction was con-sciously — and controversially — taken away and given to the Senate. The only remaining role for the judiciary was the chief justice's job of presiding over the Senate during presidential impeachments. In other words, it was decided that the courts were not to be given a say in impeachments. Given how virulently this issue was debated at the time of the Founding, it would take an unusually compelling argument for making impeachment trials justiciable to overcome the weight of the historical evidence to the contrary.

In fact, however, there are at least two strong structural arguments for keeping impeachments away from the courts. The first is that judges them-selves are subject to impeachment proceedings. More specifically, Supreme Court justices are impeachable, and it would be dangerous to give a justice's eight colleagues final review power over his or her impeachment. Note that this would be a situation very different from the fact that each House of Congress has the last word on expelling one of its Members: Members of Congress must face the voters at regular intervals, and the voters would un-doubtedly not look favorably on a Member who shielded a guilty colleague. The justices, on the other hand, "hold their Offices during good Behaviour,"[102] with impeachment and conviction as the only way of removing them. Allow-ing a small, unelected body with life tenure to have the final word over the expulsion of its own members is, to say the least, dangerous to popular sov-ereignty.[103] Second, significant practical problems would arise from judicial review of impeachment convictions. Suppose the president were impeached and convicted. The vice president would become president. If the judiciary were then to declare that the impeachment conviction was illegal, what would happen? The vice president would have been illegally acting as president — would the laws he signed have effect? What if the vice president — now presi-dent — disagreed and refused to give up the office? How could the court en-force its order, given that the executive (the entirety of which is vested in the person of the president)[104] controls the enforcement mechanism? Whom would federal authorities — including, of course, the military — obey?[105] Or consider the impeachment and conviction of a federal judge. Federal law specifies the number and distribution of active federal judges.[106] But if a new judge had been nominated and confirmed to replace the impeached one, the reinstatement of the impeached judge would, in essence, constitute an order by the court to violate federal law. Would the new judge be allowed to keep his or her place? Would rulings he or she had issued be valid law? Could both judges continue to serve, in violation of the statutorily prescribed organization scheme of the federal judiciary? The combination of these structural and practical concerns with the obvious implication of the constitutional text and history has led even Wechsler to conclude that impeachments can never be justiciable.[107]

CASE LAW

Happily, the only significant judicial decision on the matter reached precisely the same conclusion. Walter L. Nixon Jr. was the chief judge of the United States District Court for the Southern District of Mississippi. In 1986, he was indicted and convicted on two counts of making false statements before a federal grand jury (the grand jury was investigating whether Nixon had accepted money in return for asking a local district attorney to halt a prosecution).[108] *Chutzpah* has often been said to be defined as when a man kills both his parents and begs the court for mercy because he's an orphan,[109] but the case of a federal judge who refuses to resign his position after being convicted of lying to a federal grand jury surely gives the traditional definition a run for its money. Judge Nixon continued to collect his federal judicial salary while residing in federal prison. In 1989, the House of Representatives adopted three articles of impeachment, and the Senate convicted Nixon on two of them, thus stripping him of his judgeship.[110] Nixon filed suit, claiming that the Senate's use of a committee to hold hearings and take evidence violated the constitutional duty of the Senate to "try" the impeachment.[111] This claim seems rather tenuous, but our concern here is with the justiciability issue. Chief Justice Rehnquist, for the Court, focused his textual argument on the fact that the Constitution gives the Senate "sole" power to try impeachments:

> The commonsense meaning of the word "sole" is that the Senate alone shall have authority to determine whether an individual should be acquitted or convicted. . . . If the courts may review the actions of the Senate in order to determine whether that body "tried" an impeached official, it is difficult to see how the Senate would be "functioning . . . independently and without assistance or interference" [the dictionary definition of "sole"].[112]

Rehnquist also noted that "[t]he parties do not offer evidence of a single word in the history of the Constitutional Convention or in contemporary commentary that even alludes to the possibility of judicial review in the context of the impeachment powers."[113] In addition, he made two structural/practical arguments. First, he argued that

> judicial review would be inconsistent with the Framers' insistence that our system be one of checks and balances. In our constitutional system, impeachment was designed to be the *only* check on the Judicial Branch by the Legislature. . . . Judicial involvement in impeachment proceedings, even if only for purposes of judicial review, is counterintuitive because it would eviscerate the "important constitutional check" placed on the Judiciary by the Framers.[114]

Second, in a nod to prudential concerns, Rehnquist added that "the lack of finality and the difficulty of fashioning relief counsel against justiciability."[115] In other words, Chief Justice Rehnquist, for the Court, hit on almost all of the themes discussed above: the textual and historical commitment of final say in impeachment trials to the Senate, the separation-of-powers argument, and the argument from the practical problems that would arise were impeachments justiciable.

Conclusions

When, at the Philadelphia Convention, Charles Pinckney and Gouverneur Morris proposed a clause declaring "that each House should be judge of the privilege of its own members," James Madison

> distinguished between the power of Judging of privileges previously & duly established, and the effect of the motion which would give a discretion to each House as to the extent of its own privileges. He suggested that it would be better to make provision for ascertaining by *law*, the privileges of each House, than to allow each House to decide for itself.[116]

Madison, then, recognized the essential difference discussed in this chapter — the difference between determining the scope of a privilege and determining its content. (It should be noted that Pinckney, in an 1800 speech on the Senate floor, argued along roughly the same lines as Madison, that the Constitution "never was intended to give Congress, or either branch, any but specified, and those very limited, privileges indeed.")[117] As we have seen, this distinction is essential to understanding how those political questions that deal with congressional matters ought to be interpreted. In these fields, as Madison suggested, the courts may define the scope of political questions, but they may not meddle in the content.

As we saw in chapter 1, this distinction is also essential to the conflict between lex parliamenti and lex terrae in Britain. Indeed, although the political-questions doctrine is not normally considered a part of congressional privilege in the United States, the striking similarity between it and this historical British conflict has impelled its inclusion in this book. They both play the same role — that is, both mandate that the final word on certain controversies be left with the Houses of the legislature. We have also seen that they are best viewed through a similar interpretive schema, where the three possibilities are: (1) the legislative House defines both the scope and the content of the question; (2) the courts define the extent of the House's power, but do not stray into it; and (3) the courts can review both the extent and the content of the question. As we have seen, Britain has slowly moved from a Blackstonian position — possibility 1 or a weak version of possibility 2 above — toward (but not all the way to) a Millian one — a stronger version of 2 or, in a few isolated cases, some version of 3. The popular sovereignty interpretation of the United States Constitution suggests a version of 2, and, as we have seen, the courts have by and large interpreted the political questions doctrine in precisely that way.

The balance both countries have reached seems well adapted to serve modern, liberal democracies. As we have seen, the paradigmatically Blackstonian decision in *Rolle* was necessary to protect the democratic element of the British Constitution from a powerful monarch. But today, the paradigm cases of jurisdictional clashes over privilege must include *Prebble* and *Hamilton* in Britain and *Powell* in America. That is, they must take into account that strong claims in favor of lex parliamenti or nonjusticiability can often work against modern, liberal conceptions of democracy. Of course, this should not be taken too far in the other direction, either — there clearly remains a sphere within which the Houses of the legislature ought to have the final say. Otherwise, we risk ceding too much power to unelected, life-tenured judges — a result that also does not comport well with liberal, democratic ideals. It seems appropriate, then, that both Millian Britain and popular-sovereignty-based America have reached the solution of retaining a separate sphere in which the Houses of the legislature have the final say, while allowing the courts to police the boundaries of that separate sphere.

3

Free Speech in Parliament

Freedom of speech is almost certainly the most important and best known privilege of Parliament.[1] It is, without a doubt, essential to the performance of their duties that Members of Parliament not face inappropriate consequences for what they say on the floor. But what constitutes an "inappropriate" consequence? That question is at the heart of the evolving meaning of the privilege of free speech. The Blackstonian model, as might be expected, took a much more expansive view of the threats to parliamentary independence and therefore protected MPs from a wider range of consequences. In this view, for example, the monarch, the courts, and the House of Lords were absolutely precluded from recognizing in any way what took place on the floor of the House of Commons — this extended even to a denial that assaults carried out on the floor of the House were punishable in the ordinary courts. This view, with its geographical focus on the floor of Parliament, did not extend privilege at all to the dealings of MPs with their constituents or with the press — indeed, it sometimes held the publication of parliamentary debates to be a breach of privilege (more on that topic in chapter 9). In contrast, the Millian view does place significant emphasis on contacts of MPs with their constituents and with the press. This view focuses on essential parliamentary functions — understood, by this time, to include making policy in line with the wishes of the people — and, to a degree, extends privilege to cover those essential functions, wherever they physically take place.

The Blackstonian Paradigm
EARLY CASES

The privilege of Members of Parliament to be free from questioning in any other place for their speeches in Parliament is undoubtedly an ancient one, stretching back at least to the reign of Richard II. In 1397, a bill was introduced in the House of Commons condemning the extravagant expenditures of the royal household. Richard demanded to know who had introduced the bill, and Thomas Haxey's name was given up. The Lords declared Haxey a traitor and condemned him to death, but the sentence was not carried out when the archbishop claimed Haxey as a clerk. In 1399, the new King Henry IV annulled the act condemning Haxey and granted Haxey's petition for a reversal of the judgment against him on the grounds that it was contrary to the liberties of the Commons. In the same year, the House of Commons itself also petitioned the King for an annulment of the judgment, an admission that the judgment had been erroneous and contrary to normal parliamentary procedure, and a restoration of Haxey's estate, which had been forfeited upon the Lords' judgment in 1397. Henry granted that petition as well.[2] In 1401, the King promised never to pay attention to unauthorized accounts of proceedings in Parliament again.[3] The acknowledgment that Richard's actions had been contrary to the traditional liberties and procedures of Parliament suggests that the privilege was not a new one in the late fourteenth century.

Thus, beginning in 1397, it is clear that the House of Commons saw its primary struggle as one against the monarch (and, to a lesser extent, the Lords and other powerful individuals), and its desire to assert itself and set a strong precedent for the defense of its privileges explains why it kept pursuing the matter, even after Henry had annulled the act condemning Haxey in 1399. Perhaps what is most interesting about the case is that the Commons exacted a promise from Henry that he would not pay attention to unauthorized accounts of its proceedings in the future. Because Parliament must struggle to remain outside the monarch's influence, freedom of debate is best guaranteed by secrecy.[4] (This point was amply made by another case from 1399, in which the bishop of Carlisle was arrested by a royal official and imprisoned in the Abbey of St. Alban's for declaring in Parliament that "the duke of Lancaster whom ye call king [that is, Henry], hath more trespassed to k. Richard & his realme, than king Richard hath done either to him, or us."[5] Clearly, speeches that could be conceived of as treasonous were not covered by privilege in the late fourteenth century—and since monarchs were likely to regard any strong criticism as treasonous, the parliamentary desire for secrecy was quite sensible.)

For the next several hundred years, cases of parliamentary free speech would involve, as the Haxey case did, instances of Parliament's defending its privileges against monarchs attempting to exert influence over its proceedings. For example, in 1451, Thomas Young, a Member for Bristol, proposed in Parliament that Richard, Duke of York should be declared heir to the Crown. For this, he was imprisoned in the Tower by the King. When, some time later, the duke had become Protector, Young petitioned for compensation for his sufferings, arguing that his imprisonment had violated the

> olde liberte and fredom of the Comyns of this Lande had, enjoyed and pre-scribed, fro the tyme that no mynde is, alle suche psones as for the tyme been assembled in eny Parlement for the same Comyn,' ought to have theire fredom to speke and sey in the Hous of their assemble, as to theym is thought conve-nyent or resonable, withoute eny maner chalange, charge, or punycion there-fore to be leyde to theym in eny wyse.[6]

The famous controversy over Richard Strode in 1512 was similar. Strode was the author of a bill in Commons to regulate certain abuses connected with the Cornwall tin industry, for which he was prosecuted in the Stannary Courts (equity courts with their origins in Celtic law, open to claims brought by the tinners of Cornwall), fined, and imprisoned.[7] He was released on a claim of privilege, whereupon he introduced what became known as Strode's Act. After annulling the judgment against Strode, the Act went on to state a claim of privilege in sweeping terms:

> All suits, accusements, condemnations, executions, fines, amerciaments, punishments, corrections, grants, charges, and impositions, put or had, or hereafter to be put or had unto or upon the said *Richard*, and to every other of the person or persons afore specified, that now be of this present parliament, or that of any parliament hereafter shall be, for any bill, speaking, reasoning, or declaring of any matter or matters, concerning the parliament to be com-muned and treated of, be utterly void and of none effect.[8]

The act further provided for a cause of action against anyone who "vexed, troubled, or otherwise charged" a Member of Parliament in one of the man-ners prohibited above.[9] In 1541, for the first time, the Speaker of the House of Commons included freedom of speech as one of the ancient rights of the House in his formal petition to the King at the beginning of the session.[10] Thereafter, it was claimed at the beginning of every session.[11] Thus, we see a number of pre-Elizabethan appeals to the ancient privilege of free speech in Parliament.[12]

ELIZABETH AND THE STUARTS VERSUS PARLIAMENT

Queen Elizabeth, too, frequently found herself in conflict with a group of parliamentarians, led by Peter Wentworth, over privilege. In 1566 (five years before Peter Wentworth became a Member of Parliament),[13] a number of Members criticized Elizabeth's refusal to address Parliament's petition on the issue of royal succession. Elizabeth summoned the Members who spoke out, delivered "a smart reproof,"[14] and forbade them to discuss such matters in the future. Afterward, Paul Wentworth — Peter's brother[15] — asked in the House of Commons whether the Queen's actions violated privilege. During the lengthy debate that ensued, Elizabeth summoned the Speaker and ordered him to end the debate, but to no effect. Eventually, Elizabeth backed down, although she made it known that she "desired the house to proceed no further in the matter at that time."[16] At the next session of Parliament, in 1571, the House of Commons learned that Walter Strickland had been called before the Queen's Council and prevented from attending Parliament because he had moved for the reformation of the Book of Common Prayer.[17] The Treasurer defended the Queen's actions by saying that Strickland was detained not for a speech made in the House but rather for drafting a bill that violated royal prerogative.[18] The House was not satisfied with this explanation; the Queen again yielded, and Strickland was allowed to return.[19] Up to this point, the controversies were all fairly straightforward instances of the Queen's attempting to interfere in the proceedings of Parliament, and, in each case, the Queen was forced to retreat to some degree. However, issues became somewhat more complicated in the 1575 session, when the Commons took up a bill on the rites and ceremonies of the Church, and the Queen again ordered them to stay out of religious affairs.[20] At that point, Peter Wentworth gave a lengthy floor speech on the Crown's infringements of the Commons' privileges. The House cut him off in the middle of his speech and ordered the Sergeant to take him into custody. After being examined by a committee of the Commons, Wentworth was committed to the Tower of London, where he remained for more than a month, until the Queen indicated that she was willing to have the House release him.[21] In 1587 and 1592, Wentworth again raised the issue, and he was sent back to the Tower by order of royal officials both times.[22] It is worth noting that Wentworth's three incarcerations raise two separate issues: whereas the first raises no issue of privilege — indeed, as the power to commit for contempt or breach of privilege is one of the privileges of Parliament (see chapter 9), Wentworth's incarceration by order of the House was in fact an *exercise* of parliamentary privilege — his imprisonments by royal officials certainly do raise the issue of outside interference in parliamentary debates. All three instances, however, provide us with what Carl Wittke called "a forceful comment on Tudor control of Parliaments,"[23] and what F. W. Maitland referred to as the Commons' "very submissive" role during Elizabeth's reign.[24] Indeed, when Coke, as the Commons' Speaker, presented the customary petition for freedom of speech at the beginning of the parliamentary session in 1593, he was met with a sharp reply by the Lord Keeper, on behalf of the Queen:

> Liberty of Speech is granted you; but how far this is to be thought on, there be two things of most necessity, and those two do most harm, which are wit and speech: the one exercised in invention, and the other in uttering things invented. Privilege of speech is granted, but you must know what privilege you have; not to speak every one what he listeth, or what cometh in his brain to utter that; but your privilege is *aye* or *no*. Wherefore, mr. Speaker, her maj.'s pleasure is, That if you perceive any idle heads, which will not stick to hazard their own estates, which will meddle with reforming the Church, and transforming the Common-wealth; and do exhibit any bills to such purpose, that you receive them not, until they be viewed and considered by those, who it is fitter should consider of such things, and can better judge of them.[25]

The Crown was thus advocating an extremely narrow interpretation of the scope of the speech privilege, in sharp contrast to the expansive liberty claimed by parliamentarians like Strickland and the Wentworth brothers. The clash between these rival interpretations illustrates the dangers of the monarch's having significant influence over Parliament. Elizabeth's control over Parliament meant that she was ultimately successful in keeping Parliament out of both religious affairs and issues of succession, and this degree of control doubtless served as a warning to future generations of parliamentarians to guard their privileges closely.

James I's relations with Parliament were even more fraught. In 1621, fiscal necessity compelled him to convene Parliament. While willing to grant James the subsidy he sought, the House first wanted to discuss the proposed marriage of the Prince of Wales to the Spanish Infanta. James saw the match as a means to collect a sizable dowry; the Commons saw it as a plot to spread the influence of Catholicism. Much as Elizabeth had done before him, the King ordered the House to stay out of the "mysteries of state."[26] The Commons replied with an appeal to "the ancient liberty of parl. for freedom of speech, jurisdiction, and just censure of the house, and other proceedings there," which, they noted, was their "ancient and undoubted right."[27] James retorted that, far from being an ancient right, parliamentary free speech was "derived from the grace and permission of our ancestors and us." But, he continued, he would be "as careful to maintain and preserve your lawful liberties and privileges, as ever any of our predecessors were," so long as the House stayed "within the limits of your duty" — that is, so long as it did not encroach upon royal prerogative.[28] The House disagreed, reasserting its claim that its privileges were its "ancient and undoubted birthright" and that in the handling and proceeding of those businesses every member of the house hath, and of right ought to have, Freedom of Speech, to propound, treat, reason and bring to conclusion, the same. . . . [A]nd that every such member of the said house hath like freedom from all impeachment, imprisonment and molestation (other than by the censure of the house itself) for, or concerning any bill, speaking, reasoning or declaring of any matter or matters, touching the parliament, or parliament business.[29]

James replied by sending for the Commons' journal, tearing out their protestation, declaring it "invalid, annulled, void, and of no effect," imprisoning some of the parliamentary ringleaders (including Coke), sending others off to Ireland as royal commissioners, and dissolving Parliament.[30]

The House of Commons' combativeness continued during the next major controversy over its privileges, during the reign of James's son, Charles I. On the final day of the session in 1629, in the course of a debate over the seizure of John Rolle's goods (see chapter 1), John Elliot delivered a speech "in which were divers malicious and seditious words, of dangerous consequence" (including a claim "That the Council and Judges had all conspired to trample under foot the Liberties of the Subjects").[31] While he was speaking, Denzil Hollis and Benjamin Valentine physically restrained the Speaker in his chair to prevent his interfering with Elliot's speech. A few days later, the three were arrested and brought before the King's Bench on criminal charges. They argued that the court had no jurisdiction over incidents that took place on the floor of Parliament, relying on Strode's Act, among other precedents. The justices unanimously disagreed, holding that criminal offenses occurring on the floor of Parliament were punishable in ordinary courts. They (rather implausibly, given the language quoted above) held that Strode's Act applied only to Strode's case, and that privilege prevented the actions of Parliament from being questioned, but not the actions of *Members* of Parliament.[32] A session of Parliament was not called again until 1640, and that Parliament — the "Short Parliament" — was dissolved three weeks after it assembled because it refused to grant the King money to put down a Scottish revolt until he made redress for the breaches of privilege in the *Rolle* and *Elliot* cases.[33] The "Long Parliament," assembled later in 1640, undertook an ambitious program of reform in 1641, designed to prevent royal abuses of power. These acts included a resolution declaring that the proceedings and judgment against Elliot, Hollis, and Valentine were breaches of privilege.[34] The outbreak of the Civil War prevented further parliamentary action on the case, but Parliament returned to the issue in the years after the Restoration. In 1667, Parliament declared that Strode's Act is a general law, extending to indemnify all and every the members of both houses of parliament, in all parliaments, for and touching any bills, speaking, reasoning, or declaring of any matter or matters, in and concerning the parliament to be communed and treated of, and is a declaratory law of the ancient and necessary rights and privileges of parliament.[35]

The next year, the House of Lords reversed the King's Bench judgment against Elliot et al., almost forty years after it had been handed down.[36]

Thus, in the *Elliot* case, we see the degree to which post-Elizabethan MPs were jealous of their privileges. Recall that Elliot's accomplices, Hollis and Valentine, had committed an assault on the floor of Parliament: they "laid violent hands upon the Speaker, to the great affrightment and disturbance of the house. And the Speaker being got out of the Chair, they by violence set him in the Chair again."[37] And yet Parliament was insistent that its privilege had been violated when they were tried and convicted. That is, in order to ensure a sufficient "safety zone" of independence, Parliament was willing to protest for more than forty years when a court punished several of its Members for assaulting its Speaker.

In 1680, William Williams, the Speaker of the House of Commons, acting in his official capacity, ordered the printing of a pamphlet (Dangerfield's *Narrative of the Late Popish Designs*) that was libelous of the Duke of York. Williams was hauled before the King's Bench on a charge of seditious libel. He claimed privilege on the grounds that his act was "done in time of parliament, and ordered to be done by the House of Commons."[38] The judges disagreed, with the chief justice asking: "Can the order of the House of Commons justify the scandalous, infamous, flagitious libel?"[39] Williams was fined £10,000, later reduced to £8,000. By the time of the verdict in 1686, Williams had lost his seat in Parliament and the Duke of York had become King James II, meaning that the House was not inclined to rise to Williams's defense.[40]

THE BILL OF RIGHTS

After James's abdication in 1689, and with the memory of the *Elliot* and *Williams* cases still fresh,[41] Parliament set about drafting the Bill of Rights. In the list of grievances at the beginning of that document, Parliament complained that James had instituted "prosecutions in the court of Kings bench, for matters and causes cognizable only in parliament." Article 9 thus guaranteed "[t]hat the freedom of speech, and debates or proceedings in parliament, ought not to be impeached or questioned in any court or place out of parliament."[42] Indeed, Sir George Treby, a Member of the Commons committee that drafted the Bill of Rights, told the House that the complaint about prosecutions in the King's Bench "was put in for the sake of one, once in your place [that is, the Speaker], Sir *William Williams*, who was punished out of Parliament for what he had done in Parliament."[43] The passage of Article 9 marks a significant turning point in the interpretation of the privilege of free speech. Indeed, several months after the Bill of Rights was promulgated, the House of Commons finally passed a resolution stating that the judgment against Williams was "an illegal Judgment, and against the Freedom of Parliament."[44]

PRIVILEGE AND THE PRESS

There were, however, post-1689 Blackstonian cases dealing with a separate but closely related line of case law: privilege and the press. It should first be noted that these cases dealt with qualified privilege (that is, privilege for actions done in good faith), which is legally an issue distinct from parliamentary privilege (qualified privilege is part of lex terrae, not lex parliamenti). However, discussions of qualified privileges that relate to the functioning of Parliament are clearly relevant to the topic here, and such discussions help to bring into focus the understandings of democratic government underlying interpretations of privilege. Because of their clear relevance to the larger issues under analysis here, such discussions are therefore included, but the reader is reminded that, legally, they fall under a separate head.

The first significant case dealing with privilege and the press in relation to Parliament is *R. v. Abingdon*, decided in 1794.[45] Lord Abingdon, in the course of a speech in the House of Lords accompanying the introduction of a bill to regulate the practice of attorneys, had accused his former attorney of improper conduct. Abingdon then, at his own expense, had his speech printed in several newspapers. The attorney sued for libel, and Abingdon claimed privilege. But Chief Justice Kenyon of the King's Bench held that privilege did not apply:

> [A]s to the words in question, had they been spoken in the House of Lords, and confined to its walls, that Court would have no jurisdiction to call his Lordship before them, to answer for them as an offence; but that in the present case, the offence was the publication under his authority and sanction, and at his expense: That a member of Parliament had certainly a right to publish his speech, but that speech should not be made the vehicle of slander against any individual; if it was, it was a libel.[46]

A similar case arose in 1813, when Thomas Creevey delivered a speech about the East India Company on the floor of the House of Commons. The speech contained an accusation of corruption against the Liverpool inspector-general of taxes. An erroneous report of the speech appeared in several newspapers and, to set the record straight, Creevey sent a copy of his speech to one of the newspapers with a request that the correct version be published. The newspaper complied, and the inspector-general sued for libel and won.[47] Relying largely on *Abingdon*, the King's Bench refused to order a new trial, holding that the publication was not privileged and that an MP did not have a right to correct misrepresentations of his speeches in the press. Chief Justice Ellenborough wrote that an MP has no right "to address [his speeches] as an oratio ad populum in order to explain his conduct to his constituents."[48] Justice Bayley noted,

> If any misrepresentation respecting [an MP's speeches] should go forth, there is a course perfectly familiar to all members, by which such misrepresentation may be set right, viz. by complaining to the House of the misrepresentation, and having the author of it at the Bar to answer such complaint: therefore it is not necessary for the purpose of correcting the misrepresentation that a member should be the publisher of his own speech.[49]

We can thus see the Blackstonian attitude in the *Abingdon* and *Creevey* cases. In essence, these cases stand for the principle that communicating with constituents is not one of the essential tasks of an MP. Indeed, *Creevey* even stood for the proposition that an MP should let a false account of one of his speeches circulate rather than publish a true accounting of a potentially libelous speech. The misrepresentation could be rectified, as Justice Bayley argued, by calling the author or publisher to the bar. Of course, that solution would in no way correct the misapprehension under which the MP's constituents would then be laboring. *Abingdon* and *Creevey* almost perfectly encapsulate the role of the voter in the Blackstonian conception of privilege: out of sight and out of mind.

An examination of the cases above, then, allows us to say a few things about the Blackstonian conception of the privilege of free speech. It is very much an inward-looking conception, focusing on interaction among MPs and between the Houses of Parliament and the monarch. Because the primary imperative for Parliament was to ensure its independence from the monarch and other powerful actors, it was a very jealous guard of its boundaries. Reports of what transpired on the floor were not to be made known to outsiders without consent of the House, and even criminal offenses committed on the floor were to be dealt with internally, so as not to allow royal officials and judges to interfere in any way. The flip side of this inward directedness was a lack of concern for the interaction between MPs and their constituents. When MPs spoke to one another, it was absolutely privileged; when they spoke to their constituents, not even a qualified privilege applied. Moreover, the very act of publicizing parliamentary debates could itself be considered a breach of privilege.[50] This inward directedness was the essence of the Blackstonian view of privilege.

The Millian Paradigm

One useful way to consider the difference between the Blackstonian and Millian paradigms is to consider how differently they understand the idea of a "proceeding in Parliament." Under the Blackstonian paradigm, in which Parliament seeks to build an impregnable wall around its powers, "in Parliament" can be defined almost entirely geographically. Speech — even speech that seems intimately related to parliamentary functions — taking place beyond the floor receives no protection, while even assaults are privileged, so long as they happen on the floor. In contrast, the Millian paradigm expands the purview of parliamentary privilege (and related qualified privileges) to take in tasks (such as communicating with constituents) that are functionally integral to, but sometimes geographically distant from, the workings of the Palace of Westminster.

STOCKDALE, WASON, AND BEACH

After the passage of the Bill of Rights and the corresponding shift of power from the monarch to Parliament, the focus of the protection of parliamentary speech shifted as well. Parliament was no longer as concerned with protecting itself from the monarch; rather, it now sought increased protections against suits by private individuals. The first major case after this shift was *Stockdale v. Hansard*[51] (which was mentioned briefly in chapter 1). In 1836, the printer Hansard published, by order of the House of Commons, a report by the inspector of prisons that called a book published by Stockdale "of a most disgusting nature" and "indecent and obscene in the extreme."[52] (It was an anatomy book.) Stockdale sued for libel, and the House of Commons produced a resolution stating its view that it alone had the right to pronounce upon the extent of its privileges, that this publication was privileged, and that "the institution or prosecution of any action, suit or other proceeding, for the purpose of bringing them into discussion or decision before any court or tribunal elsewhere than in Parliament, is a high breach of such Privilege, and renders all parties concerned therein amenable to its just displeasure, and to the punishment consequent thereon."[53] The Court of Queen's Bench disagreed and found for Stockdale, holding that parliamentary privilege did not extend to non-Members publishing libels for distribution to the general public, even if the publication was undertaken at the order of a House of Parliament. (It is

interesting to note that all three of the justices condemned the *Williams* decision, then distinguished it by noting that it was not the Speaker but rather the
private publisher who was the defendant here.[54]) When the sheriff of Middlesex sought to enforce the court's judgment, the House of Commons imprisoned the two men who shared the office of sheriff. The warrant stated
merely that the men were guilty of contempt and breach of the privileges of the
House of Commons. When they filed a petition for habeas corpus, the court
denied it on the well-established grounds that those imprisoned by a House of
Parliament could not be freed by the courts, because to do so would be to
encroach upon the House's power to determine for itself when someone has
committed contempt against it or breached its privilege[55] (see chapter 1).
Indeed, by some accounts, the Queen's Bench judges themselves were almost
arrested by the Commons.[56] However, they were not, and the sheriffs were
eventually released on a promise not to attempt again to enforce the judgment
against Hansard, whereupon "in an almost farcical turn of events, [the two
sheriffs] were then imprisoned for contempt of court."[57]

The *Stockdale* decision thus presents a strong clash between the two paradigms. While the Commons sought to publish one of its reports for the information of the public, the court refused to acknowledge that communication with
constituents was an essential part of parliamentary activity and thus refused to
extend privilege to cover the publication. (The jurisdictional conflict was discussed in chapter 1; here, my focus is on the clashing conceptions of the
parliamentary free-speech privilege.) It is instructive to consider the manner in
which the judges in *Stockdale* treated the *Williams* precedent. As noted above,
all of the justices agreed that the *Williams* case was wrongly decided and,
indeed, that one of the functions of Article 9 of the Bill of Rights was to prevent
a recurrence of *Williams*. But they distinguished *Stockdale* on the grounds that
it was not a Member of Parliament but rather a private publisher who was the
defendant. This is true, but the logic of privilege under the modern, Millian
view suggests that the publication should nonetheless have been privileged. If it
is essential to the functioning of Parliament that its proceedings be open to the
citizenry, then it is no less essential that citizens have access to its reports.[58] If
privilege precludes a judgment against the Speaker for ordering a publication —
which it does, and should, do — then how can privilege not also cover the
printer who carries out the Speaker's order? How can Hansard, who would
have been guilty of contempt of Parliament for refusing to publish the document, be guilty of libel for publishing it? Unhappy with the outcome in the
Queen's Bench, Parliament remedied the situation with the 1840 Parliamentary
Papers Act, which gave an absolute privilege to complete reports ordered

published by Parliament and a qualified privilege to extracts from reports ordered published by Parliament.[59]

Of course, there was no doubt that privilege still held for words spoken on the floor. In 1869, Rigby Wason accused Earl Russell, Lord Chelmsford, and the Lord Chief Baron of conspiracy to make untrue statements on the floor of the House of Lords. When the magistrate decided that Wason had not presented an indictable offense, he moved in the Court of Queen's Bench for a ruling calling on the magistrate to show cause. The justices of the Queen's Bench unanimously declined to grant the ruling.[60] Chief Justice Cockburn held, "It is clear that statements made by members of either House of Parliament in their places in the House, though they might be untrue to their knowledge, could not be made the foundation of civil or criminal proceedings, however injurious they might be to the interest of a third person. And a conspiracy to make such statements would not make the persons guilty of it amenable to the criminal law."[61]

The next case that must be touched upon was the 1972 decision in *Beach v. Freeson*[62] (another case dealing with qualified privilege). Reginald Freeson was a Member of the House of Commons who wrote a letter to the Law Society and the Lord Chancellor saying that a constituent had asked him to refer the law firm of Beach & Beach for investigation. Noting that he had received complaints from other constituents about the same firm, Freeson laid out the constituents' complaints in his letter. When the Beaches sued for libel, Freeson claimed qualified privilege as a defense, arguing that, as an MP, he "had an interest and a duty to communicate the information to the Law Society and the Lord Chancellor" and that "both the Law Society and the Lord Chancellor had a corresponding interest and duty to receive it."[63] The Queen's Bench agreed, with Justice Geoffrey Lane writing:

> It will be a sad day when a Member of Parliament has to look over his shoulder before ventilating, to the proper authority, criticisms about the work of a public servant or a professional man who is holding himself out in practice for the benefit of the public which he honestly believes to merit investigation.[64]

Qualified privilege was thus held to obtain.

By the time *Beach v. Freeson* was decided, the courts had clearly come around to the belief that privilege protected an MP's dealings with constituents as well as with other institutions of government. Freeson's letter was privileged because the court recognized that it was part of his job to be an advocate for the concerns of his constituents and that this involved both receiving letters from and sending letters to non-MPs. In other words, privilege was extended to cover proceedings intimately related to an essential parliamentary function, but not carried out on the floor of Parliament. This inclusion of constituents in the sphere of privilege is essentially Millian, and is very much opposed to the privilege of parliamentary secrecy that predominated under the Blackstonian paradigm.

PRIVILEGE AND OFFICIAL SECRETS

In 1938, Duncan Sandys, an MP and a junior officer in the Territorial Army, sent the secretary for war a draft of a question that he proposed to ask on the floor concerning London's air defenses. The secretary's advisers immediately realized that the question was based on highly classified information that should not have been available to a junior officer. As it turned out, Sandys had received the information from a more senior officer, who was under the impression that Sandys would only use it in communication with the secretary. The War Office's reaction was swift and severe, and after Sandys was given the impression that a violation of the Official Secrets Act may have occurred, he burned his notes and raised a question of privilege in the House of Commons. A military court of inquiry was convened, which Sandys was ordered to attend, and the House of Commons appointed a Select Committee to investigate. The Committee concluded that " 'the immunity of members from the criminal law in respect of acts done by them in the exercise of the functions of their office could not be confined to acts done within the four walls of the House' and would extend to a disclosure made by a Member to a Minister or by one Member to another even though it did not take place within the House. This implied a functional rather than a territorial conception of privilege."[65] That is, the committee's conclusion was appropriately Millian. However, the officer who provided the information to Sandys could be prosecuted under the act, and the committee was unclear as to whether Sandys could have been forced to testify about his source.[66] While it seems proper that someone who breaks the law in order to provide information to an MP be held accountable, it would also seem to impinge too closely on an MP's information-gathering function to require the Member to testify against those who provide him or her with information. Members of Parliament must be able to oversee the functioning of the government, and allowing them to receive information without being forced to testify as to its source is clearly important to this oversight function. A Millian interpretation of privilege would thus be solicitous of this role.

In 1986, journalist Duncan Campbell was working on a documentary in the BBC's "Secret Society" series. Campbell's film revealed British plans to put a spy satellite, code-named "Zircon," over the Indian Ocean. The BBC, concerned about the documentary, approached the government for advice. The government demanded that the program be shelved on national-security grounds. The BBC complied, but Campbell published his findings in an article in the *New Statesman*. The Special Branch of the Metropolitan Police carried out searches (authorized under the Official Secrets Act) of Campbell's home, the *New Statesman*'s offices, and the BBC's studio in Glasgow. Robin Cook, MP, acquired a copy of the BBC documentary and arranged a showing of it to Members of Parliament. The day that the screening was to take place, the attorney-general applied to the High Court for an injunction to prevent it. The application was unceremoniously denied. As A. W. Bradley put it, "It seems to have taken no more than one minute for Kennedy J. to reject this application, on the ground that it was for the House of Commons to regulate its own proceedings. What is notable in the matter is not the judge's decision — a refusal of the application was the only conceivable outcome, if a massive clash of jurisdictions between the High Court and the Commons was to be avoided — but that the Attorney-General, Sir Michael Havers, Q.C., should have thought it worthwhile or legitimate to make the application."[67] However, the attorney-general then asked the Speaker of the House to order that the film not be shown in the House of Commons. Because he could not immediately obtain the opinion of the House, the Speaker was allowed to make this decision on his own, and he assented. The government later asked the whole House to "confirm" the Speaker's "unprecedented" order, but the House refused.[68] A subsequent report by the House of Commons Committee of Privileges found that the Speaker acted within his proper authority.[69] It also concluded that the showing of the film was not a proceeding of the House, and therefore was not privileged — a conclusion that leaves the court's denial of the attorney-general's request for an injunction on rather tenuous grounds.[70] The Speaker's decision to bar the showing of the film clearly does not raise a question of privilege, as it involves an instance of the House regulating its own internal affairs. However, on the question of whether the showing of the film was entitled to privilege (that is, whether forces *outside* the House of Commons could have properly interfered with the screening), it would seem that the High Court was on firmer ground than the committee. After all, communication between Members is a paradigmatically parliamentary function, and a proper Millian interpretation of privilege would protect that function.

PRIVILEGE AND THE PRESS

We can also see an essentially Millian relationship in examining how Millian courts have dealt with cases of privilege and the press. Courts' attitudes toward such cases shifted significantly during the nineteenth century. In 1868 — fifty-five years after *Creevey* — the Queen's Bench considered in *Wason v. Walter* whether an accurate newspaper recounting of debates in Parliament was privileged.[71] The court held that it was due qualified privilege. Chief Justice Cockburn's reasoning is worth quoting at length:

> It seems to us impossible to doubt that it is of paramount public and national importance that the proceedings of the houses of parliament shall be communicated to the public, who have the deepest interest in knowing what passes within their walls, seeing that on what is there said and done, the welfare of the community depends. Where would be our confidence in the government of the country or in the legislature by which our laws are framed, and to whose charge the great interests of the country are committed, — where would be our attachment to the constitution under which we live, — if the proceedings of the great council of the realm were shrouded in secrecy and concealed from the knowledge of the nation? How could the communications between the representatives of the people and their constituents, which are so essential to the working of the representative system, be usefully carried on, if the constituencies were kept in ignorance of what their representatives are doing? What would become of the right of petitioning on all measures pending in parliament, the undoubted right of the subject, if the people are to be kept in ignorance of what is passing in either house? Can any man bring himself to doubt that the publicity given in modern times to what passes in parliament is essential to the maintenance of the relations subsisting between the government, the legislature, and the country at large?[72]

Although Cockburn claimed that this judgment was in no way inconsistent with *Abingdon* or *Creevey*,[73] it should be clear that there is at least a tension between the two former cases and *Wason v. Walter*. Whereas the two previous cases downplayed the importance of communication between constituents and MPs, the later case considers it of grave importance, especially "in modern times." This shift was a crucial one.

The holding in *Wason v. Walter* was reaffirmed in 1887, when the Exchequer Division held in *Dillon v. Balfour* that a Member was due absolute privilege for words spoken on the floor and qualified privilege for the publication of his speech in *Hansard's Parliamentary Debates*.[74] Chief Baron Palles asserted that qualified privilege was "conditional upon the words being published without malice, that is, for the purpose of informing the public of what took place in Parliament."[75] Note that, on facts very similar to *Abingdon* and *Creevey*, the court here reached the opposite conclusion and specifically held that the function of informing the public what happened in Parliament, so casually dismissed in *Creevey*, was in fact the very definition of good-faith publication.

Almost a century later, the holding in *Wason v. Walter* was expanded when the Queen's Bench ruled in *Cook v. Alexander* that qualified privilege extends to "parliamentary sketches" — that is, commentaries giving the reporter's impression of a debate in Parliament — as well.[76] Lord Denning wrote that "a parliamentary sketch is privileged if it is made fairly and honestly with the intention of giving an impression of the impact made on the hearers."[77] He clarified that "fairness in this regard means a fair presentation of what took place as it impressed the hearers";[78] in other words, a fair presentation of the impression left by a defamatory speech would still be privileged. The court's reasoning was explicitly based upon the public interest rationale of *Wason v. Walter*.[79]

The *Wason, Dillon,* and *Cook* press cases thus illustrate the shift to the Millian conception of privilege (here, qualified privilege). There is a stark difference between Chief Justice Cockburn's eloquent defense of the necessity of communication between MPs and their constituents in *Wason* (and its reaffirmation in *Dillon*) and earlier denials in *Abingdon* and *Creevey* that the functioning of Parliament requires anything of the sort. Moreover, the decisions in *Wason, Dillon,* and *Cook* illustrate again why the House of Commons, and not the judges of the Queen's Bench, had the better of the free-speech arguments in *Stockdale*. Consider that *Stockdale, Wason,* and *Cook* combined stand for the proposition that a newspaper's accounts of parliamentary debates are privileged, but when those debates are published *by order of the House*, then they are not privileged. Clearly, this is perverse; equally clearly, it is *Stockdale* that runs against the modern, Millian paradigm of privilege, as *Dillon* made clear.

However, in the 2004 case *Buchanan v. Jennings*,[80] the Privy Council unfortunately seems to have backtracked from the Millian focus on the importance of communication with constituents. The Privy Council held that a defamation action could lie against an MP who, in a news interview, affirmed without repeating a statement he had made on the floor of the House. This decision meant not only that the MP's communication with the public was unprivileged but also that the court would have to look into his statement on the floor — otherwise, it could not know what he was affirming to the news reporter. The Privy Council dismissed all concerns by noting that, in this case, "the propriety of the member's behaviour as a parliamentarian would not be in issue. Nor would his state of mind, motive or intention when saying what he did in Parliament."[81] This is true, but it ignores the fact that the effect of the ruling will be to chill a Member's ability to explain his actions and words on the floor to his constituents — and that relationship is supposed to be at the heart of the Millian paradigm of privilege.

A v. UNITED KINGDOM

Finally, the 2003 decision of the European Court of Human Rights in *A v. United Kingdom*[82] must be mentioned. During a debate on the floor of the House of Commons, Michael Stern, the MP for Bristol North-West, gave the name and address of one of his constituents and called her and her family "neighbours from hell."[83] More specifically, he reported that he had

> received reports of threats against other children; of fighting in the house, the garden and the street outside; of people coming and going 24 hours a day — in particular, a series of men late at night; of rubbish and stolen cars dumped nearby; of glass strewn in the road in the presence of [the applicant] and regular visitors; of alleged drug activity; and of all the other common regular annoyances to neighbours that are associated with a house of this type.[84]

Stern also noted that his purpose in giving this speech was "not just to draw attention to another example of neighbours from hell" but also to draw attention to what he saw as the baleful practices of local housing authorities.[85] The speech was covered in both the local and the national press, and the object of Stern's tirade — who denied the truth of most of the allegations — received hate mail and was subject to unpleasant encounters on the streets. In her suit before the European Court of Human Rights, she claimed, inter alia, that the British law of privilege violated Article 6(1) of the European Convention on Human Rights, which provides, "In the determination of his civil rights and obligations . . . , everyone is entitled to a fair and public hearing . . . by an independent and impartial tribunal established by law."[86] The court held that Article 6(1) did apply, but that competing interests more than balanced this right:

> [W]hile freedom of expression is important for everybody, it is especially so for an elected representative of the people. He or she represents the electorate, draws attention to their preoccupations and defends their interests. In a democracy, Parliament or such comparable bodies are the essential *fora* for political debate. Very weighty reasons must be advanced to justify interfering with the freedom of expression exercised therein. . . . [T]he Court believes that a rule of parliamentary immunity . . . cannot in principle be regarded as imposing a disproportionate restriction on the right of access to court as embodied in Art. 6(1).[87]

As N. W. Barber has noted, it is difficult to square Article 6(1)'s absolute language with the use of a balancing test, and the court might have been better advised to treat privilege as a substantive limit on individual rights — that is, to have said that privilege meant that the applicant had no right of action in this case, rather than saying that privilege meant that she could not vindicate her right.[88] Nevertheless, the court's focus on protecting freedom of expression in national parliaments suggests that the European Court of Human Rights, too, recognizes the essential role played by this ancient privilege.

Conclusions

It should be clear for at least two reasons that the performance of their duties requires that MPs have special protections of their speech, even in the modern era, when fear of offending the monarch is no longer a concern. First, the nature of their job requires MPs frequently to speak on controversial topics. Were they liable to be hauled into court at any time and made to defend themselves against anyone aggrieved by their statements, many MPs would soon find that they had no time for parliamentary business and that legal fees had sent them into debt. Because it is in the public interest that Members of Parliament conscientiously attend to their duties, it is likewise in the public interest that they not be vexed with a large number of (frequently baseless) lawsuits. Second, as S. A. de Smith colorfully put it, "It is often the public duty of an M.P. to make defamatory allegations about individuals and public and private bodies."[89] Colin Munro offers several examples of speeches on the floor of Parliament that, had they been delivered elsewhere, might have been found slanderous yet ultimately proved true and important to have in the public sphere.[90] One can imagine, too, situations in which legitimate speech by MPs might run afoul of the Official Secrets Act or laws against racial incitement[91] — or, at least, that fears of running afoul of such laws might chill legitimate speech on the floor.

However, it should also be clear that abuse of this privilege exists and is undesirable. As Geoffrey Marshall has noted, Parliament's free-speech privilege is "a breach in the general rule of law,"[92] and such a breach necessarily presents the possibility that an unchecked power will not be used responsibly. The most obvious example of abuse would be a speech in which an MP, for purely personal reasons, defames a non-MP. The only recourse open to the defamed citizen in this case is to attempt to persuade some other MP to bring the issue to the House's attention. In that case, the offending Member could be asked to withdraw the remarks, or the incident could be referred to the Committee of Privileges for a possible finding of contempt of Parliament. Unfortunately, in this, the injured citizen is completely dependent on the goodwill of other MPs: redress is a matter of grace, rather than one of right. While any solution will be imperfect, one way of addressing the issue would be for Parliament to create a more regularized enforcement mechanism, including a procedure by which citizens could bring instances that they believe to be abuses of privilege to the attention of a parliamentary committee.[93] (The Parliamentary Commissioner for Standards, who will be discussed in more detail in chapter 9, now has responsibility for receiving and investigating complaints about Members' conduct, but the process could undoubtedly be more regularized.) In the end, however, as Munro has noted, "on a robust view of the functions of members as tribunes of the people, we must simply be prepared to take the rough with the smooth."[94]

4

Free Speech in Congress

The United States Constitution guarantees that, "for any Speech or Debate in either House, [senators and representatives] shall not be questioned in any other Place."[1] This wording, of course, is immediately familiar as an adaptation — although not a straight importation — of Article 9 of the English Bill of Rights, discussed in the previous chapter. The ways in which this constitutional provision reacts to its English predecessor, and the ways in which it interacts with other American constitutional provisions — including the First Amendment — will prove instructive in developing a popular sovereignty-based account of its meaning.

Text and History

The Speech or Debate Clause seems to have been little discussed at the Philadelphia Convention. The Articles of Confederation had provided that "Freedom of speech and debate in Congress shall not be impeached or questioned in any Court, or place out of Congress."[2] Three state constitutions at the time of the Founding contained an explicit speech or debate privilege.[3] Early drafts from the Constitutional Convention's Committee of Detail said that Members of both Houses "shall be privileged from arrest (or assault) *personal restraint* during their attendance, for so long a time before and after, as may be necessary, for traveling to and from the legislature (and they shall have no other privilege whatsoever)."[4] That wording was removed, and a subsequent draft simply included the placeholder "Freedom of Speech."[5] In the final draft from the Committee of Detail, the wording was expanded and made nearly identical with the Speech or Debate Clause from the Articles of Confederation: "Freedom of Speech and Debate in the Legislature shall not be impeached or questioned in any Court or Place out of the Legislature."[6] That draft was approved by the entire Convention without dissent or even recorded debate.[7] The Committee of Style then gave the clause its final wording.[8] Likewise, the clause was completely uncontroversial at the states' ratification debates and in the debates in the press.[9]

Several of the Founders did later give their impressions of the clause. James Wilson, in his famous 1791 Lectures on Law, explained that,

> [i]n order to enable and encourage a representative of the publick to discharge his publick trust with firmness and success, it is indisputably necessary, that he should enjoy the fullest liberty of speech, and that he should be protected from the resentment of every one, however powerful, to whom the exercise of that liberty may occasion offence.[10]

James Madison commented only briefly on the issue, in an 1832 letter. "[T]he reason and necessity of the privilege must be the guide" to its interpretation, he wrote. He added that "[i]t is certain that the privilege has been abused in British precedents, and may have been in American also."[11] An interpretation focusing on the core functions of privilege, he suggested, may help to prevent such abuse.

Thomas Jefferson's most substantial comments on the privilege came during the Cabell affair. In 1797, Samuel J. Cabell, an Anti-Federalist Member of the national House of Representatives from Virginia, was charged with seditious libel for a letter he sent to constituents denouncing the Adams administration. Vice President Jefferson wrote an eloquent (if anonymous) petition to the Virginia House of Delegates asking it to take up the matter:

> [I]n order to give to the will of the people the influence it ought to have, and the information which may enable them to exercise it usefully, it was a part of the common law, adopted as the law of this land, that their representatives, in the discharge of their functions, should be free from the cognizance or coercion of the coordinate branches, Judiciary and Executive; and that their communications with their constituents should of right, as of duty also, be free, full, and unawed by any.[12]

Noting that these principles were the same for the national government as for the state,[13] Jefferson then launched into a passage that is worth quoting at length because it draws so explicitly the link between freedom of speech and debate on the floor of the legislature, freedom of communication with constituents, and popular sovereignty:

> [F]or the Judiciary to interpose in the legislative department between the constituent and his representative, to control them in the exercise of their functions or duties towards each other, to overawe the free correspondence which exists and ought to exist between them, to dictate what communications may pass between them, and to punish all others, to put the representative into jeopardy of criminal prosecution, of vexation, expense, and punishment before the Judiciary, if his communications, public or private, do not exactly square with their ideas of fact or right, or with their designs of wrong, is to put the legislative department under the feet of the Judiciary, is to leave us, indeed, the shadow, but to take away the substance of representation. . . . [It] is to do away the influence of the people over the proceedings of their representatives by excluding from their knowledge, by the terror of punishment, all but such information or misinformation as may suit their own [the judges'] views . . . and finally, [it] is to give to the Judiciary, and through them to the Executive, a complete preponderance over the legislature rendering ineffectual that wise and cautious distribution of powers made by the constitution between the three branches, and subordinating to the other two that branch which most immediately depends on the people themselves, and is responsible to them at short periods.[14]

Finally, Jefferson argued, the "right of free correspondence" between legislator and constituent is both a privilege of the House and "a natural right of every individual citizen."[15] Given that the privileges of the House flow from the right of citizens to govern themselves, how could it be otherwise?

However, Joseph Story, in his celebrated *Commentaries*, was decidedly less enthusiastic about the privilege:

> No man ought to have a right to defame others under color of a performance of the duties of his office. And if he does so in the actual discharge of his duties in Congress, that furnishes no reason why he should be enabled, through the medium of the press, to destroy the reputation and invade the repose of other citizens.[16]

But even Story had to acknowledge the force of the counterargument, when he agnostically noted that

> it has been recently insisted in Congress by very distinguished lawyers, that the privilege of speech and debate in Congress does extend to publication of the speech of the member. And they ground themselves upon an important distinction arising from the actual differences between English and American legislation. In the former the publication of the debates is not strictly lawful,

except by license of the House. In the latter it is a common right, exercised and supported by the direct encouragement of the body. This reasoning deserves a very attentive examination.[17]

He might have added that, as noted in chapter 2, the publication of the journals of each House of Congress is constitutionally mandated.

Interpretation

Congressional freedom of speech serves three distinct but related functions.[18] The first addresses separation-of-powers concerns: it is dangerous to give the executive and judiciary power over the legislature by allowing them to question legislators in court. This function should be given even more weight in the United States, where separation of powers is so prominent a feature of the constitutional structure, and Jefferson, as we saw above, was especially concerned with this role.[19] Second is Congress's informing function: the Houses have an obligation to communicate with their constituents — that is, their sovereign masters — for the purposes of both providing them with information about the workings of their government and receiving information from them so as to make the government work according to their wishes. The third function of legislative freedom of speech is to give legislators some "breathing room" — that is, to prevent a rash of suits that would interfere with their ability to do their jobs. By heeding Madison's advice and looking to "the reason and necessity" of congressional free speech, we shall greatly facilitate our interpretation of this important congressional privilege.

Failure fully to appreciate the function of free speech has led some otherwise thorough scholars to offer only partial interpretations of this congressional privilege. Having decided that the "ultimate focus [of the privilege] must be the functioning of the legislature according to the doctrine of the separation of powers," Robert Reinstein and Harvey Silverglate conclude that the privilege should be given broad scope against criminal suits brought by the executive, but narrow scope against civil suits in which private individuals assert that their rights have been violated.[20] Craig Bradley, in contrast, notes the Framers' disgust at infamous eighteenth-century English bribery cases and concludes that the privilege cannot have been intended "to provide corrupt congressmen with such a convenient haven from the consequences of their venality."[21] In other words, privilege is in fact *weakest* against executive-instigated criminal cases, according to Bradley. (It should be noted that the common-law courts in Britain have never had jurisdiction over bribery cases involving MPs,[22] although, as we shall see in chapter 9, the Houses of Parliament have dealt with bribery cases as contempts.) Still others have argued that the privilege must be absolute and broadly interpreted against all kinds of suits to protect the Houses of Congress from any outside interference.[23] Each of these approaches has suffered from an acute failure to ask the right questions.

Rather than considering how the privilege is best interpreted to further separation of powers or to prevent legislative self-dealing, we should ask how it is best interpreted to further popular sovereignty. It is, after all, in the name of preserving popular sovereignty that we declare separation of powers (and the attendant checks and balances) good, while declaring legislative self-dealing bad. David Lederkramer very sensibly writes that "the speech or debate clause ban on 'questioning' operates to prevent legislative deterrence and executive abuse. Where there is neither deterrence nor abuse there can be no 'questioning' within the meaning of the clause."[24] Put differently, "the clause was intended to bar any legal action involving legislative acts that would cause legislators to perform legislative tasks differently than they would have performed them but for the threatened legal action."[25] The privilege is, therefore, a "structural principle: it prevents, in general, the restructuring of governmental offices and powers in a way that would allow certain powers to subvert others."[26] The speech privilege, that is, operates to prevent the subversion of Congress's role in the American system of popular sovereignty.

What precisely this means will become clearer as we examine the Speech or Debate Clause case law, but before we come to that, we can clarify the issue somewhat by briefly considering the three most controversial questions surrounding the clause. First, there is the issue of information flowing *to* legislators. It seems clear that Members of Congress should be privileged in their information-gathering function. Their ability to legislate effectively is directly dependent on their ability to ascertain the relevant facts, and their ability to legislate in accordance with the will of the people is dependent on their ability to gauge that will. As James M. Landis noted, "Responsibility means judgment, and judgment, if the word implies its intelligent exercise, requires knowledge. . . . To deny Congress power to acquaint itself with facts is equivalent to requiring it to prescribe remedies in darkness."[27] In order to avoid this darkness, Members of Congress and their staffs must be able to meet with any sources and receive any information that is offered to them without fear of being brought into court. As Reinstein and Silverglate note, separation-of-powers concerns do come into play here: "If the executive can cut Congress off from relevant sources of information, it can expand its own powers into areas vested by the Constitution in the legislative branch. . . . [I]f key sources of confidential information are chilled, the very functioning of Congress itself is jeopardized."[28] It should be noted that nothing in my assertion that legislators should be free to meet with anyone and receive any information implies that legislators may *do* anything in pursuit of relevant information. Legislators would not, for example, be privileged if they were to break into a building and steal documents, but they should be able to make use of all information at their disposal without fear of being made to testify in court as to how they acquired that information.

Second, there is the issue of information flowing *from* legislators, either to executive agencies or to the public. Much as the Queen's Bench found in *Beach v. Freeson* (discussed in the previous chapter), legislators' communications with executive agencies ought to be privileged. These communications play three crucial roles: (1) they allow the Member of Congress to act as a sort of ombudsman over the executive agencies, ensuring that they do not abuse their authority;[29] (2) they serve to increase legislators' understanding of the implications of their policy decisions;[30] and (3) they serve as a conduit by which public concerns can be brought to the attention of the executive agencies.[31] As each of these roles tends to further popular sovereignty, and as threats of lawsuits or prosecution could easily convince legislators that this "intervening" role is not worth the risk, it seems clear that it ought to be privileged. Likewise, Members' communications with the public at large — both directly and via the media — ought to be privileged. As noted above, Jefferson considered the protection of the legislator's communication with the public to be one of the highest functions of privilege in a system of popular sovereignty. Reinstein and Silverglate note that the "heart of representative democracy is the communicative process between the people and their agents in government," and the representatives have an obligation to keep the people informed.[32] Indeed, in the context of its franking privileges, Congress itself has declared that "the conveying of information to the public, and the requesting of the views of the public, or the views and information of other authority of government" is part of "the official business, activities, and duties of the Congress of the United States."[33] As privilege conduces to fulfilling this obligation, communication with constituents ought to be privileged.

Third, there is the problem of bribery. Bribery presents a uniquely difficult set of challenges. On the one hand, it represents a strong threat to popular sovereignty. Bribed legislators have sold their public trust for private gain; the people can no longer be said to rule themselves through them. It may be thought unwise to trust a collegial, nonjudicial body with checking such egregious breaches of the public trust; this consideration counsels against extending privilege to bribery cases.[34] But this phrasing misconceptualizes the problem. No one favors privileging bribery per se. Rather, the question is whether allowing the courts to hear bribery cases will chill the exercise of legitimate privileged activity. Here, we see that popular-sovereignty concerns can also militate against allowing the courts to hear such cases. Reinstein and Silverglate explain the problem very succinctly: "[C]ongressmen often incur the favor of special-interest groups by proposing and voting for certain legislation; in return for this support, congressmen often receive generous campaign contributions. This may reflect a community of interest, or expectations on both sides, or it may be an outright bribe."[35] Moreover,

> [i]f a congressman decides to give a speech or cast a vote a certain way and he is indicted for having done so corruptly — as a result of a bribe — his motivation for the legislative activity is being called into question by the charge. . . . The decisionmaking process by which a congressman decides to speak or vote, or to remain silent or abstain, would seem to be as much a legislative act as a speech or vote itself. An indictment for exercising that decision improperly directly challenges this decisionmaking process.[36]

In other words, if, as asserted above, congressmen must be privileged in meeting with constituents and interest groups, and if, as seems apparent, motives for voting should receive privilege equal to the vote itself, and if, as Reinstein and Silverglate note, investigations into bribery allegations necessitate inquiring into both meetings with constituents and interest groups and how those meetings affected the Member's vote, then it seems to be an unavoidable conclusion that the courts must be prevented from hearing bribery cases against Members of Congress. As we have already seen, each House of Congress may "punish its Members for disorderly Behaviour,"[37] and it seems perfectly reasonable to think that this power extends to punishing former Members for disorderly acts done while Members. (The Houses' punishment powers will be the topic of chapter 10.) The House itself, then, has a role in punishing bribed Members, though not the "sole and exclusive" role, as Alexander Cella would have it.[38] The voters, too, may punish a Member, by making him a former Member. The courts, however, should have no role.

Each of these issues, and a number of ancillary ones, will become clearer as we examine the cases addressing them.

Cases

PROCEEDINGS ON THE FLOOR

The most important early American case on the free-speech privilege is not, in fact, a federal case at all. Rather, it was brought before the Supreme Judicial Court of Massachusetts in 1808, and it was brought under the provision of the Massachusetts Constitution that declared, "The freedom of deliberation, speech and debate, in either house of the legislature, is so essential to the rights of the people, that it cannot be the foundation of any accusation or prosecution, action or complaint, in any other court or place whatsoever."[39] The facts of the case were these: In the 1805 session of the Massachusetts House of Representatives, Benjamin Russell, at the request of William Coffin, moved a resolution authorizing the appointment of an additional notary public for Nantucket. Both Russell and Coffin were Members of the House. After Russell had moved the resolution, Micajah Coffin, another Member of the House, demanded to know where he had obtained the information that Nantucket needed an additional notary public. Russell replied that it was from a "respectable gentleman" from Nantucket. After the House had moved on to other business, Micajah Coffin crossed the floor to where Russell was involved in an informal conversation with other Members and again asked Russell who had provided the information. Upon finding out that it was William Coffin, Micajah Coffin exclaimed, "What, that convict?" When Russell asked him to explain, Micajah Coffin replied, "Don't thee know the business of the Nantucket Bank?" The Nantucket Bank had been robbed, and William Coffin had been tried and acquitted for the crime. When Russell told Micajah Coffin that William Coffin had been "honorably acquitted," Micajah Coffin replied, "That did not make him the less guilty, thee knows." William Coffin brought an action for slander against Micajah Coffin.[40] Micajah Coffin's defense rested upon a claim of privilege.

Chief Justice Parsons, for a unanimous court, began by interpreting the scope of the privilege broadly:

> These privileges are thus secured, not with the intention of protecting the members against prosecutions for their own benefit, but to support the rights of the people, by enabling their representatives to execute the functions of their office without fear of prosecutions, civil or criminal. I therefore think that the article ought not to be construed strictly, but liberally, that the full design of it may be answered. I will not confine it to delivering an opinion, uttering a speech, or haranguing in debate; but will extend it to the giving of a vote, to the making of a written report, and to every other act resulting from the nature, and in the execution, of the office; and I would define the article as securing to every member exemption from prosecution, for every thing said or done by him, as a representative, in the exercise of the functions of that office, without inquiring whether the exercise was regular according to the rules of the house, or irregular and against their rules. I do not confine the member to his place in the house; and I am satisfied that there are cases in which he is entitled to this privilege, when not within the walls of the representatives' chamber.[41]

However, wrote the chief justice, "When a representative is not acting as a member of the house, he is not entitled to any privileges above his fellow-citizens."[42] To determine whether Micajah Coffin's assertions were privileged or not, Parsons asked: "Was this inquiry, thus made, the act of a representative, discharging his duty, or of a private citizen, to gratify his curiosity?"[43] If the former, then it was privileged; if the latter, then it was not. The chief justice noted that the motion which gave rise to the conflict was no longer before the House when Micajah Coffin made the statements in question, and he therefore claimed that the statements could not have been made in an attempt to influence the outcome of the debate on the motion. Seeing no other possible justifications, he concluded that Micajah Coffin's motives for speaking as he did were

> to correct *Russell* for giving to the plaintiff the appellation of a respectable gentleman, and to justify the correction by asserting that an honorable acquittal, by the verdict of a jury, is not evidence of innocence. It is not, therefore, possible for me to presume that the defendant, in using thus publicly the defamatory words, even contemplated that he was in the discharge of any official duty.[44]

The assertions were therefore not privileged. In other words, after asserting that privilege had a broad, liberal scope, the court went on to apply it in a narrow, restrictive way.[45] It seems absurd to suppose that the fact that a matter is not *immediately* before the House makes any discussion of it nonlegislative in character. Moreover, even supposing that the matter had been settled for good, would it not be a legitimate legislative activity for Micajah Coffin to attempt to convince Russell that William Coffin should not be trusted as a source of information in the future? Finally, as Cella pointed out, the court's "restrictive application of the privilege doctrine forced it into an examination of the purposes, motives, and reasonableness of the legislative language and conduct involved, the very things which the privilege was historically developed to prevent."[46]

Interestingly, however, it is *Coffin*'s liberal dicta, rather than its restrictive holding, that has been enthusiastically taken up by the United States Supreme Court. In 1876, Hallett Kilbourn, who was not a Member of the House, refused to answer certain questions put to him by a special committee of the House of Representatives. Upon the House's order, he was imprisoned for forty-five days for contempt. He filed suit for false imprisonment against the Sergeant-at-Arms, the Speaker of the House, and the members of the committee.[47] The greater part of Justice Miller's opinion for the Court is taken up with holding that the order of the House imprisoning Kilbourn was void.[48] We shall return to this topic at some length in chapter 10. For our immediate purposes, we are more interested in the final part of the Court's opinion, where it asked whether those defendants who were Members of Congress were liable for this false imprisonment. After quoting from Chief Justice Denman's opinion in *Stockdale v. Hansard* to the effect that "whatever is done within the walls of either assembly must pass without question in any other place,"[49] Justice Miller moved on to *Coffin*. He noted that the case involved

> an action for slander, the offensive language being used in a conversation in the House of Representatives of the Massachusetts legislature. The words were not delivered in the course of a regular address or speech, though on the floor of the House while in session, but were used in a conversation between three of the members, when neither of them was addressing the chair.[50]

He then quoted precisely the liberal dicta quoted above, unmistakably giving the impression that the holding of the case had been to privilege the words. Noting that the decision was unanimous, Justice Miller called it, "perhaps, the most authoritative case in this country on the construction of the provision in regard to freedom of debate in legislative bodies."[51] He never got around to mentioning the holding in the case. And because Justice Miller got *Coffin* so wrong, he got the case before him right:

> It would be a narrow view of the constitutional provision to limit it to words spoken in debate. The reason of the rule is as forcible in its application to written reports presented in that body by its committees, to resolutions offered, which, though in writing, must be reproduced in speech, and to the act of voting, whether it is done vocally or by passing between the tellers. In short, to things generally done in a session of the House by one of its members in relation to the business before it.[52]

The Court thus held that the Members were privileged against a false-imprisonment suit based simply on the way they had voted on the contempt question. The Sergeant-at-Arms, however, was not privileged.

The next important case on legislative free speech did not arise for more than seventy years, but, when it did, it, too, abused *Coffin* while reaching the substantively correct result. This case, like *Coffin*, arose out of a state legislature, although the case was brought in federal court. William Brandhove filed suit against several members of the California Senate Fact-Finding Committee on Un-American Activities, claiming that a hearing of the committee was held not for any legislative purpose but rather for the purposes of intimidating him and preventing him from exercising his constitutional rights to free speech and to petition the legislature. He also claimed that the hearings denied him due process of law, equal protection of the laws, and the enjoyment of the privileges and immunities of United States citizenship.[53] Justice Frankfurter, for the Court, again quoted the entire passage of *Coffin* dicta quoted above, again without mentioning the holding of the case.[54] He then wrote,

The claim of an unworthy purpose does not destroy the privilege. Legislators are immune from deterrents to the uninhibited discharge of their legislative duty, not for their private indulgence but for the public good. One must not expect uncommon courage even in legislators. The privilege would be of little value if they could be subjected to the cost and inconvenience and distractions of a trial upon a conclusion of the pleader, or to the hazard of a judgment against them based upon a jury's speculation as to motives.[55]

This is indeed correct — and precisely the opposite of what the *Coffin* court held. On those grounds, the Court held that the common-law privileges of the legislature (because the case arose out of a state legislature, the Constitution's Speech or Debate Clause did not apply) made Brandhove's suit untenable. "Self-discipline and the voters" — not the courts — "must be the ultimate reliance for discouraging or correcting such abuses."[56] Courts should not be in the business of inquiring into the motives and propriety of legislative investigations.

In 1967, the Court held similarly in a case at the federal level. After Louisiana courts held that a series of raids carried out against the civil-rights group the Southern Conference Education Fund were illegal, those who had been targeted by the raids filed suit against, inter alia, the chairman and the counsel of the United States Senate Subcommittee on Internal Security. They claimed that the chairman and counsel had cooperated both before and after the raid with the Louisiana authorities who carried it out. Citing *Kilbourn* and *Tenney*, the Court, in a brief *per curiam* opinion, held that the chairman was privileged against any such suit. The counsel, however, was not — the Court held that the privilege was "less absolute, although applicable, when applied to officers or employees of a legislative body, rather than to legislators themselves."[57] The Court left unclear what the contours of a "less absolute, though applicable" privilege are.

Powell v. McCormack, which we encountered in chapter 2, also contains a brief section on the Speech or Debate Clause.[58] Chief Justice Warren, who cited *Kilbourn*, *Brandhove*, and *Dombrowski* — but who admirably refrained from citing *Coffin* — again noted that the clause has a broad reach: in addition to words spoken in debate, "Committee reports, resolutions, and the act of voting are equally covered, as are 'things generally done in a session of the House by one of its members in relation to the business before it.' "[59] Citing the James Wilson passage quoted above, the chief justice noted that the purpose of the clause is to ensure "that legislators are free to represent the interests of their constituents without fear that they will be later called to task in the courts for that representation."[60] However, the Court declined to extend the protection of the clause to employees of the House carrying out its orders.[61]

Finally, one lower-court case (reminiscent of the *Graham-Campbell* case, discussed in chapter 1, which determined that the House of Commons' bar could not be forced by the courts to abide by liquor-licensing laws) must be mentioned under this head. In 1982, Ed Jones, the chairman of the House of Representatives Subcommittee on Services, informed Anne Walker, the general manager of the House of Representatives Restaurant System, that she was being fired. Based on past statements Jones had made, Walker asserted that she had been fired because she was a woman. Jones, however, publicly accused her of mismanagement and skimming funds from the Restaurant System. Walker filed suit against Jones and subcommittee staff director Thomas Marshall, alleging physical and emotional distress and damage to reputation.[62] Jones and Marshall argued that the Speech or Debate Clause privileged them against her suit. The D.C. Circuit Court of Appeals, per then-Judge Ginsburg, held the Speech or Debate Clause inapplicable. After examining the cases described above, Judge Ginsburg concluded that "[t]he key consideration, Supreme Court decisions teach, is the act presented for examination, not the actor. Activities integral to the legislative process may not be examined . . . but peripheral activities not closely connected to the business of legislating do not enjoy Speech or Debate shelter."[63] Unlike congressional aides who help Members perform their legislative duties (a topic that will be discussed below), congressional employees who provide food for Members "cater to human needs that are not 'intimately cognate' . . . to the legislative process."[64] Decisions concerning them are not, therefore, covered by the Speech or Debate Clause.

INFORMATION FLOWING TO AND FROM LEGISLATORS

In 1971, Senator Mike Gravel convened a meeting of the Subcommittee on Buildings and Grounds, of which he was chairman, and, at the meeting, read extensively from a copy of a classified Department of Defense study titled *History of the United States Decision-Making Process on Viet Nam Policy*, more popularly known to history as the *Pentagon Papers*. The study bore a security classification of "Top Secret — Sensitive." After reading from it, Senator Gravel placed all forty-seven volumes in the public record. A few weeks later, there were press reports that members of Gravel's staff had spoken with an editor at M.I.T. Press and had arranged for the *Pentagon Papers* to be published by Beacon Press. The government, investigating crimes associated with the leaking of this classified report, subpoenaed Leonard Rodberg, one of Gravel's aides, and Howard Webber, the director of M.I.T. Press. Gravel intervened with a motion to quash the subpoenas, on the grounds that they violated his Speech or Debate Clause privilege (a claim similar to that made by Duncan Sandys in Britain in 1938).[65] The Court, per Justice White, began by asking whether Senator Gravel was privileged for his actions. The Court found it "incontrovertible" that he was privileged with respect to the subcommittee hearing because

> [t]he Speech or Debate Clause was designed to assure a co-equal branch of the government wide freedom of speech, debate, and deliberation without intimidation or threats from the Executive Branch. It thus protects Members against prosecutions that directly impinge upon or threaten the legislative process.[66]

This is not to suggest that the person who illegally provided the papers to Senator Gravel should be privileged, just as Gravel himself would not have been privileged for the act of breaking into the Pentagon and stealing them. However, the courts would impermissibly intrude on the legislative sphere if they sought to compel Gravel to testify as to how he received his information. Given that the senator was privileged, the question was then whether the privilege extended to his aide. The Court held that it did:

> [I]t is literally impossible, in view of the complexities of the modern legislative process, with Congress almost constantly in session and matters of legislative concern constantly proliferating, for Members of Congress to perform their legislative tasks without the help of aides and assistants; . . . the day-to-day work of such aides is so critical to the Members' performance that they must be treated as the latter's alter egos; and . . . if they are not so recognized, the central role of the Speech or Debate Clause — to prevent intimidation of legislators by the Executive and accountability before a possibly hostile judiciary . . . — will inevitably be diminished and frustrated.[67]

In essence, the Court made it clear that the Clause protects legislative *acts* (broadly understood), and that, insofar as the participation of aides is necessary for the proper performance of legislative acts, the privilege extends to those aides. By the same token, nonlegislative acts are not privileged, even if it is the Members of Congress themselves who perform them.

However, there was a second part to the Court's holding in *Gravel*: the senator's arrangement to publish the *Pentagon Papers* was not privileged, the Court held. Justice White noted that the privilege in Britain "was not viewed as protecting republication of an otherwise immune libel on the floor of the House,"[68] and in support of this statement, he cited *Stockdale*, *Williams*, *Abingdon*, and *Creevey*. He paused to note *Wason v. Walter* but dismissed it because "the immunity established in *Wason* was not founded on parliamentary privilege . . . but upon analogy to the privilege for reporting judicial proceedings."[69] Of course, this is true (as noted in the discussion of *Wason* in the previous chapter), but what it neglects is *Wason*'s eloquent discussion of the importance in a democratic system of communication between legislators and the public. Because the American Constitution is founded upon a much stronger basis of popular sovereignty than the British Constitution — even the British Constitution at its most Millian — that communication ought to be taken even more seriously in America. In glossing over *Wason* too quickly, the *Gravel* Court failed to understand this. Thus, Justice White wrote:

> The heart of the Clause is speech or debate in either House. Insofar as the Clause is construed to reach other matters, they must be an integral part of the deliberative and communicative processes by which Members participate in committee and House proceedings with respect to the consideration and passage or rejection of proposed legislation or with respect to other matters which the Constitution places within the jurisdiction of either House.[70]

But he failed to take into account that communication with the public — with the sovereign masters, of whom Senator Gravel and his colleagues were merely representatives — *is* an integral part of the job that the Constitution assigns to Members of Congress. And, indeed, the case of the *Pentagon Papers* makes it abundantly clear why: the *Papers* revealed a long-term pattern of arrogance, ineptitude, and deception on the part of U.S. policymakers concerning the war in Vietnam. When the executive has taken it upon itself to conceal evidence of its own misdeeds, surely legislators' oversight function permits — indeed, requires — them to reveal this information to the public.[71] The Court, unfortunately, missed this point entirely. Senator Sam Ervin, writing the year after the *Gravel* decision, excoriated the Court majority — no member of which, he tartly noted, "has spent any time in Congress" — on precisely this point.[72]

The next year, in *Doe v. McMillan*,[73] the Court again addressed the issue of the congressional informing function. In 1970, a special select subcommittee of the House of Representatives' Committee on the District of Columbia submitted to the Speaker of the House a 450-page report on the Washington, D.C., public school system. The report was subsequently printed and distributed by the Government Printing Office, pursuant to federal law. The report contained forty-five pages of attendance sheets, test papers, and documents related to disciplinary problems of specific students, whose names were not removed from the documents. A group of parents filed suit against the chairman, members, clerk, staff director, and counsel of the committee, a consultant and an investigator for the committee, the Superintendent of Documents and the Public Printer, the principal and one of the teachers at Jefferson Junior High School, and the United States of America, alleging invasion of privacy and reputational damage.[74] Justice White again wrote for the Court. After citing most of the cases mentioned thus far (and paying special attention to *Gravel*), he held that the Speech or Debate Clause barred the suit against the Members of

Congress, the committee staff, the consultant, and the investigator. Compiling the information, using it in a hearing, publishing it, and distributing it to other legislators, he held, were clearly legislative functions.[75] The fact that the inclusion of the children's names was gratuitous was irrelevant:

> Although we might disagree with the Committee as to whether it was neces-
> sary, or even remotely useful, to include the names of individual children in the
> evidence submitted to the Committee and in the Committee Report, we have
> no authority to oversee the judgment of the Committee in this respect or to
> impose liability on its Members if we disagree with their legislative judgment.[76]

However, the Court concluded that this protection did not extend to the Superintendent of Documents or the Public Printer, despite the fact that they were acting by order of the House.[77] Once again, the Court, under Justice White's guidance, failed to appreciate the importance of Congress's communications with the public. Justice White wrote:

> We cannot believe that the purpose of the Clause — "to prevent intimidation
> of legislators by the Executive and accountability before a possibly hostile
> judiciary" . . . — will suffer in the slightest if it is held that those who, at the
> direction of Congress or otherwise, distribute actionable material to the pub-
> lic at large have no automatic immunity under the Speech or Debate Clause
> but must respond to private suits to the extent that others must respond in
> light of the Constitution and applicable laws.[78]

It must be said that this shows a rather appalling lack of imagination. The power to bring such suits is the power to enjoin the distribution of the material. And that is the power to interfere with communications between Members of Congress and the public. It is, as Jefferson fretted, "to put the legislative department under the feet of the Judiciary." It is only by radically underestimating the importance of this communication to the American constitutional scheme of popular sovereignty that Justice White can suggest that a finding of privilege here would "be to invite gratuitous injury to citizens for little if any public purpose."[79] If it is not for the Court to disagree with Congress's legislative judgment, then how can it be for the Court to oversee Members' judgment about how and what to communicate to their constituents — that is, their sovereign?[80]

Just two years later, the Court again had the opportunity to address the scope of the Speech or Debate Clause. The Senate Subcommittee on Internal Security had, in 1970, held investigations into whether the United States Servicemen's Fund (USSF) was engaging in activities harmful to the morale of the Armed Forces. The subcommittee issued a subpoena to the USSF's bank for its bank records. The USSF and two of its members filed suit against the subcommittee, its chairman and members, its chief counsel, and the bank, seeking to enjoin implementation of the subpoena. The USSF claimed that the investigation was an abuse of the congressional investigating power and that its sole purpose was to harass the group's members and deter them from the constitutionally protected expression of their views.[81] Chief Justice Burger, for the Court (Justice White was in the Majority), held that the Speech or Debate Clause rendered the subcommittee's behavior immune from judicial review:

> Just as a criminal prosecution infringes upon the independence which the Clause is designed to preserve, a private civil action, whether for an injunction or damages, creates a distraction and forces Members to divert their time, energy, and attention from their legislative tasks to defend the litigation. Private civil actions also may be used to delay and disrupt the legislative function. Moreover, whether a criminal action is instituted by the Executive Branch, or a civil action is brought by private parties, judicial power is still brought to bear on Members of Congress and legislative independence is imperiled. We reaffirm that once it is determined that Members are acting within the "legitimate legislative sphere" the Speech or Debate Clause is an absolute bar to interference.[82]

Drawing from *Kilbourn*, *Gravel*, and *McMillan*, the Court understood the "legitimate legislative sphere" broadly, as encompassing anything done by Members in a session of the House, related to House business.[83] Thorough investigation plainly falls within this sphere. Moreover, no one plausibly could claim that Congress does not have the authority to inquire into threats to the morale of the Armed Forces.[84] In light of that, the Speech or Debate Clause provides immunity for the issuance of such a subpoena, because "[t]o hold that Members of Congress are protected for authorizing an investigation, but not for issuing a subpoena in exercise of that authorization, would be a contradiction denigrating the power granted to Congress in Art. I and would indirectly impair the deliberations of Congress."[85] Moreover, the Court, citing *Gravel*'s "alter ego" language, drew "no distinction between the Members and the Chief Counsel."[86] The Court also made it clear that it would not inquire into the subcommittee's motivations in holding the hearings—if the act is a legislative one, then the motive is irrelevant.[87] Within the area carved out as legitimate legislative activity, the privilege is absolute, even against actions that violate the rights of individuals.[88] The chief justice ended with a tart note directed at the appellate court, whose ruling he was overturning:

> This case illustrates vividly the harm that judicial interference may cause. A legislative inquiry has been frustrated for nearly five years, during which the Members and their aide have been obliged to devote time to consultation with

their counsel concerning the litigation, and have been distracted from the purpose of their inquiry. The Clause was written to prevent the need to be confronted by such "questioning" and to forbid invocation of judicial power to challenge the wisdom of Congress' use of its investigative authority.[89]

In other words, the lower courts' failure to apply the privilege led to precisely the kind of distraction from legislative duties that the privilege was meant to avoid.

But the chief justice sounded a more White-esque tone in his opinion (again, joined by Justice White) in the next Speech or Debate Clause case, *Hutchinson v. Proxmire*.[90] In 1975, Senator William Proxmire awarded his "Golden Fleece of the Month Award" (which he created to publicize what he considered to be especially egregious cases of wasteful government spending) to three federal agencies that had funded the work of behavioral scientist Ronald Hutchinson. Presenting the "award" consisted of giving a speech on the floor of the Senate and issuing a press release consisting of the text of the floor speech plus introductory and concluding sentences. A summary of the award was included in a newsletter the senator sent to more than a hundred thousand people, and he discussed the award on a television show. Morton Schwartz, the aide to Senator Proxmire who did the preparatory research for the award, contacted the federal agencies that had sponsored Hutchinson's research. Schwartz claimed the calls were merely to discuss the award; Hutchinson claimed that they were intended to persuade the agencies to withdraw their support for his work. Hutchinson filed suit against Proxmire and Schwartz, claiming reputational damage and interference with his contractual relationship with supporters of his research.[91] The chief justice wrote, "Whatever imprecision there may be in the term 'legislative activities,' it is clear that nothing in history or in the explicit language of the Clause suggests any intention to create an absolute privilege from liability or suit for defamatory statements made outside the Chamber."[92] He also noted approvingly Justice Story's assertion, quoted above, that "[n]o man ought to have a right to defame others under color of a performance of the duties of his office."[93] The chief justice, however, relegated to a footnote the other passage from Justice Story (also quoted above), in which he notes that the publication of floor speeches might well be privileged. In the footnote, Burger claims that Story "acknowledged the arguments to the contrary,"[94] although from the context it appears more that Story was agnostic between the two, rather than presenting the opposing position to his own. The chief justice also mentions *Abingdon* and *Creevey*,[95] although, curiously, there is nary a word about *Wason v. Walter*. Nor, of course, is Jefferson quoted on the importance of unfettered correspondence between representatives and their constituents. Instead, citing *Gravel* and *McMillan*, the Court held that a "speech by Proxmire in the Senate would be wholly immune and would be available to other Members of Congress and the public in the Congressional Record. But neither the newsletters nor the press release was 'essential to the deliberations of the Senate' and neither was part of the deliberative process."[96] This is, of course, explicitly predicated on the idea that communication with the public is insufficiently essential to a legislator's job to be privileged.[97] Indeed, it suggests that "the deliberative process" is something in which only legislators may engage—the sovereign public, in Chief Justice Burger's view, apparently does not participate in deliberations in a manner relevant to the legislative process. The case was distinguished from *McMillan* because the reports at issue there, while available to the public, were primarily intended for the use of other legislators. "Newsletters and press releases, by contrast, are primarily means of informing those outside the legislative forum," and are therefore not privileged.[98] This, of course, also explains why neither the Superintendent of Documents nor the Public Printer was privileged in *McMillan*. Their work, too, was directed toward the public.

Although the Supreme Court has not addressed the question of whether Speech or Debate Clause immunity protects communication between a legislator and an executive agency, a lower court has. In a case reminiscent of the *Strauss* case in Britain, the D.C. Circuit Court of Appeals was faced with *Chastain v. Sundquist*.[99] In 1985, Congressman Don Sundquist wrote a letter to the attorney-general expressing his concern that the Memphis Area Legal Services (MALS), and especially its staff attorney Wayne Chastain, were obstructing the enforcement of child support enforcement laws. Sundquist noted that MALS was federally funded and expressed displeasure that it should be attacking a federally funded child-support program. The letter asked the attorney-general to conduct whatever investigation he deemed warranted. The letter, along with a press release, was distributed to Memphis media outlets. Sundquist sent a similar letter to the Legal Services Corporation, accusing MALS of engaging in lobbying activities. This letter led to an investigation by the Legal Services Corporation, at the end of which Sundquist held a press conference claiming that the situation at MALS was even worse than he had thought. Chastain filed suit.[100] Judge Buckley, for the court, cited the cases discussed above for the proposition that "[t]he Clause thus does not protect acts that are not 'legislative in nature,' even if they are taken in a member's 'official capacity.' "[101] *Proxmire* made it plain that the statements to the press were not protected; moreover, since the letters to the attorney-general and the Legal Services Corporation "did not seek information or otherwise attempt to aid a congressional investigation . . . [but rather] attempted to influence the conduct of federal agencies,"[102] they were not privileged, either. Judge Buckley dramatically accused anyone who disagreed of attempting to re-write the Speech or Debate Clause to read, "[S]enators and representatives shall be privileged from questioning in any other place 'for any Speech or Debate in either House *or anywhere in respect of common law torts.*' "[103] This is patently false, even if we limit our consideration to common-law torts of defamation — the privilege shields legislators in the performance of their duties; it does not apply to their actions as private citizens. Thus, if Congressman Sundquist, as a result of a billing dispute with his own lawyer, had gone out and publicly slandered his lawyer, he would be liable like any other citizen. But both communication with constituents and communication with executive agencies are part of his job *as a legislator* and therefore ought to be privileged. Surely, it is much harder for congressmen to bring matters of public concern before executive agencies and oversee those agencies if they must worry about lawsuits every time they request an investigation.

BRIBERY

In 1963, Thomas Johnson, a former congressman, was indicted and convicted on seven counts of violating the federal conflict of interest statute and one count of conspiring to defraud the United States. Johnson and another congressman had allegedly agreed to exert influence on the Department of Justice to drop mail-fraud indictments against a Maryland savings and loan company and its directors. As part of the agreement, Johnson also delivered a favorable speech on the floor of the House, copies of which the company distributed to potential depositors. In return, Johnson received "campaign contributions" and "legal fees" from the company. These fees were not disclosed to the Department of Justice, and the jury presumably concluded that they were intended as bribes, rather than as bona fide campaign contributions or legal fees.[104] Justice Harlan, writing for the Court, held that some of the evidence taken at trial was clearly prohibited by the Speech or Debate Clause — questions about the details of and motives behind Johnson's floor speech were barred.[105] The Court also noted how central this evidence was to the government's case:

> The conspiracy theory depended upon a showing that the speech was made solely or primarily to serve private interests, and that Johnson in making it was not acting in good faith, that is, that he did not prepare or deliver the speech in the way an ordinary Congressman prepares or delivers an ordinary speech. Johnson's defense quite naturally was that his remarks were no different from the usual congressional speech, and to rebut the prosecution's case he introduced speeches of several other Congressmen speaking to the

same general subject, argued that his talk was occasioned by an unfair attack upon savings and loan associations in a Washington, D.C., newspaper, and asserted that the subject matter of the speech dealt with a topic of concern to his State and to his constituents. We see no escape from the conclusion that such an intensive judicial inquiry, made in the course of a prosecution by the Executive Branch under a general conspiracy statute, violates the express language of the Constitution and the policies which underlie it.[106]

This gets at the heart of the delicate balance underlying bribery cases. Accusations of bribery will often turn on the subjective motivations for legislative behavior, and they will often rely on evidence that consists of detailed examination of that legislative behavior. If the Speech or Debate Clause is to mean anything at all, as Jefferson noted, it must prohibit this sort of intensive scrutiny by the courts into the legislature. The Court agreed — looking at the history of the clause, it concluded that its primary purpose was "to prevent intimidation by the executive and accountability before a possibly hostile judiciary."[107] The Court thus held that no matters relating to the preparation or delivery of the speech on the floor could be introduced against Johnson at trial.

Bribery was again before the Court only six years later, in *United States v. Brewster*.[108] Senator Daniel Brewster was indicted for solicitation and acceptance of bribes in return for his vote on pending postage-rate legislation. Before trial, he moved to dismiss the indictment on the ground of Speech or Debate Clause immunity.[109] Chief Justice Burger, for the Court, began by noting that the English roots of the clause were not dispositive:

> Although the Speech or Debate Clause's historic roots are in English history, it must be interpreted in light of the American experience, and in the context of the American constitutional scheme of government rather than the English parliamentary system. We should bear in mind that the English system differs from ours in that their Parliament is the supreme authority, not a coordinate branch. Our speech or debate privilege was designed to preserve legislative independence, not supremacy. Our task, therefore, is to apply the Clause in such a way as to insure the independence of the legislature without altering the historic balance of the three co-equal branches of Government.[110]

The Court took notice of the fact that *Johnson* allowed a Member to be prosecuted for bribery "provided that the Government's case does not rely on legislative acts or the motivation for legislative acts."[111] To expand the privilege further than that, the Court held, would turn Members of Congress into "super-citizens, immune from criminal responsibility."[112] The Court also rejected the argument that Congress itself was well equipped to punish bribery, noting that the English analogy was inapt: whereas Parliament is "the High Court of Parliament," the American Congress has no such historical judicial role.[113] (Of course, as we shall see in chapter 10, the Houses of Congress in fact *have* punished for bribery in the past.) The question, then, was whether the facts at issue in *Brewster* allowed the government to make its case without reference to "legislative acts or the motivation for legislative acts." The Court held that they did: "The illegal conduct is taking or agreeing to take money for a promise to act in a certain way. There is no need for the Government to show that [Senator Brewster] fulfilled the alleged illegal bargain; acceptance of the bribe is the violation of the statute, not performance of the illegal promise."[114]

It is crucial to note that this rests on reasoning we have already rejected above — it relies on the assertion that Senator Brewster's meetings and discussions with constituents are not privileged. If, as the Court rightly held, matters related to the preparation and delivery of Congressman Johnson's floor speech were privileged, then why not Senator Brewster's meetings with those constituents who had an interest in postal-rate legislation? The chief justice wrote, "Taking a bribe is, obviously, no part of the legislative process or function; it is not a legislative act. It is not, by any conceivable interpretation, an act performed as a part of or even incidental to the role of a legislator."[115] But, as I have argued throughout, meeting and talking with constituents — including representatives of interest groups — *is* part of a legislator's official duties and thus ought to be privileged.[116] In his dissent, Justice White (joined by two colleagues) argued that the situation here was no different from *Johnson*: Members of Congress talk to constituents and representatives of interest groups all the time; Members receive campaign contributions, frequently from people whose causes the Members are likely to support; and this will generally be both legal and ethical.[117] Neither the executive nor the courts should have the power to interfere with, and thereby chill, this relationship between Member and constituent. It is this relationship — and not the act of receiving a bribe, as the Court blithely suggested — that ought to be privileged. Justice White concluded his dissent with a sharp nod to Congress: "The Speech or Debate Clause does not immunize corrupt Congressmen. It reserves the power to discipline in the Houses of Congress. I would insist that those Houses develop their own institutions and procedures for dealing with those in their midst who would prostitute the legislative process."[118]

The clause was again at issue in the 1979 case of *United States v. Helstoski*.[119] Between 1974 and 1976, while he was a Member of the House of Representatives, Henry Helstoski voluntarily appeared on ten occasions before grand juries investigating political corruption, including allegations that aliens had paid Members of Congress to introduce private immigration bills. Helstoski testified about his practices in introducing such bills, and he produced his files on them. Although he invoked his Fifth Amendment right against self-incrimination in some earlier appearances before the grand jury, it was not until his ninth appearance that he invoked Speech or Debate Clause immunity. In 1976, a grand jury indicted Helstoski for accepting money in return for promising to introduce and introducing private immigration bills. He moved to dismiss the indictment on Speech or Debate Clause grounds.[120] Chief Justice Burger, for the Court, began by noting that "[t]he Court's holdings in *United States v. Johnson* . . . and *United States v. Brewster* . . . leave no doubt that evidence of a legislative act of a Member may not be introduced by the Government in a prosecution."[121] The Court also rejected the government's two assertions that privilege had been waived. First, the Court, while explicitly declining to rule on the question of whether an individual Member could waive his Speech or Debate Clause privilege, held that no statement of Helstoski's was sufficient to constitute such a waiver, if one were possible.[122] The Court also rejected the idea that, in enacting a law[123] which made bribery of Members of Congress an offense prosecutable in ordinary federal courts, Congress itself had waived privilege in such cases. The Court again declined to decide whether such a waiver was possible, deciding only that it had not been effectuated here.[124] The evidence against Helstoski was therefore held inadmissible.

In order to square this holding with *Brewster*, the chief justice drew a curious temporal distinction: "[I]t is clear from the language of the Clause that protection extends only to an act that has already been performed. A promise to deliver a speech, to vote, or to solicit other votes at some future date is not 'speech or debate.' Likewise, a *promise* to introduce a bill is not a legislative act."[125] This temporal focus seems perverse: the evil of bribery is the fact that the legislator places his private good over the public good. But this is only the case if he *actually votes* a certain way because he was paid to. A legislator who takes money to vote one way and then votes another because she thinks it right may be defrauding the individual who attempted to bribe her, but she is not harming the common weal the way a bribed legislator does. The Court's temporal focus also cannot be taken entirely seriously — clearly, research that a Member of Congress (or one of his staffers) undertakes in order to prepare for a floor speech or vote is privileged (this is apparent from the *Gravel* holding). But if preparatory research is covered, then clearly the relevant consideration is not whether the act "has already been performed" or not. And if preparatory research is privileged, then why not preparatory meetings or correspondence with constituents?

A fleshing out of the concept of popular sovereignty, then, strongly suggests a wide scope for the free-speech privilege. Wide — but not unlimited. As the

Walker case about the House of Representatives Restaurant System made clear, certain functions — even functions geographically within the Capitol building — are sufficiently far removed from the duties of legislators as to remain unprivileged. Functions intimately related to their duties, however — speeches, debates, and votes, but also meetings and communications with constituents, special interest groups, and executive agencies — must be privileged in the service of popular sovereignty.

A Brief Note on the First Amendment

It is worth noting that all of these issues are affected by the First Amendment's Free Speech Clause. That Clause means not only that American law has a much higher burden of proof for libel or slander cases[126] but also that there are very few permissible types of criminal action for the spoken or written word.[127] Indeed, Akhil Reed Amar has argued that the Free Speech Clause of the First Amendment is best read as the popular-sovereignty analogue of the traditional free-speech privilege on the floor of Parliament:

> Don't We the Sovereign People of America necessarily have the same inherent rights of free political expression enjoyed by members of the Sovereign Parliament in England? . . . '[F]reedom of speech' had a rich tradition, in England and in the states, of guaranteeing absolute freedom of speech and debate within the sovereign legislature. And thus, the extension of this right to ordinary citizens in the First Amendment is indeed simply a textual recognition of the structural truth of American popular sovereignty.[128]

This argument does need to be qualified somewhat — the Article I Speech or Debate Clause offers somewhat more protection, albeit to many fewer people, than the Free Speech Clause. Whereas, for example, it is merely very difficult to prove a libel or slander case against a private individual, it is impossible to prove one against a Member for speech on the floor (and, as I have argued above, the same should hold true for communication with constituents). Still, the basic insight behind Amar's argument is a sound one, and it demonstrates quite nicely how a liberal, Millian conception of free speech in Parliament flowed into a popular-sovereignty conception of free speech in America.

Conclusions

We are thus in a position to look back over the development of the free-speech privilege in Anglo-American law. Beginning with (indeed, probably before) *Haxey* in 1397, Parliament and the courts in Britain developed the Blackstonian conception of privilege — speech and debate taking place on the floor of the House between Members was not to be questioned elsewhere. This privilege was understood to prohibit questioning, not only by the courts and the monarch but also by the public and the press (as we shall see when we examine breach of privilege and contempt of Parliament in chapter 9). At the same time, Blackstonian privilege did not extend at all to Members' communications with the public. As Lord Abingdon and Thomas Creevey discovered, privilege was not even extended to the republication of speeches delivered in Parliament.

Of course, the Tudor and Stuart monarchs were not enamored of even the limited speech privilege of the Blackstonian model, and conflicts — from Thomas Young to Peter Wentworth to William Williams — were frequent and intense. Still, the *Elliot* case, in which privilege was asserted (ultimately successfully) to shield an assault on the floor of the House of Commons (against the House's Speaker, no less!), demonstrates the absoluteness of the Blackstonian protection of behavior geographically internal to the House. But with the rise of the Millian paradigm of privilege (loosely centered around, but not sharply delineated by, the 1689 Bill of Rights), speech protection shifted to a functional view that, increasingly, encompassed Members' communications with the public at large. The ultimate victory by the Commons in *Stockdale* first suggested that publication was sufficiently integral to parliamentary duties to be privileged. *Beach v. Freeson*, *Wason v. Walter*, and *Cook v. Alexander* extended qualified privilege to communications with government agencies and to communications through the press, on the grounds that these functions were integral to Members' parliamentary duties, although the *Buchanan* decision was something of a retreat from this Millian position.

Grounded as it is in popular sovereignty, the American Constitution goes even further in protecting congressional speech. As we have seen, the Constitution, properly interpreted, absolutely privileges legislative activity, whether that activity is undertaken by the Member himself or by an aide, and whether it takes place on the floor of the House, in the press, in meetings with the public, or anywhere else. Nonlegislative activity, as we saw in *Walker v. Jones* (the House restaurant case), is not privileged. This has the consequence of precluding prosecution in the courts for most (if not all) bribery and corruption cases. However, this should not unduly trouble us: as we shall see in chapter 10, the Houses' own punishment powers extend to such cases. We should be more troubled by the fact that American courts have frequently failed to give appropriate consideration to the popular-sovereignty rationale underlying the speech privilege in America; as a consequence, they have tended to give short shrift to communication between Members and the public. The courts' failure here is all the sadder given that the First Amendment's extension of a similar free-speech right to all Americans provides a not-so-subtle hint about the proper role of popular sovereignty in interpreting the Article I Speech or Debate Clause.

5

Freedom from Civil Arrest and
Legal Process for Members of Parliament

The privilege against civil arrest and legal process during Parliament time is among the most ancient of Parliament's privileges. John Hatsell suggests that the privilege "must have been coeval with the existence of Parliaments, and . . . must, by some method or other, have been always adhered to and enforced."[1] However, the theory behind the privilege, and therefore the scope of the privilege, has changed significantly. In its origin, the privilege was intended to protect the King's right to have his Parliament meet without interference (and, indeed, it is related to the equally ancient privilege of freedom from private molestation, which will be discussed in chapter 9). In its earliest form, then, the privilege was a royal right and was enforced by officials of the Crown. However, as the Houses came into their own, the right took on a more distinctly Blackstonian hue. Here, the function of the privilege was to protect the Houses against all outsiders, and the Houses generally took enforcement into their own hands. Suits initiated by the Crown were treated the same as suits initiated by other citizens, and the House of Commons determined for itself how long before and after a session the privilege would last. The Blackstonian privilege extended to protection against being sued during Parliament time because responding to suits was so difficult that it would take a Member away from his parliamentary duties, almost as certainly as arresting him would.[2] Still, even in its Blackstonian phase, the privilege did not extend to freedom from criminal process and arrest, because it was not intended to place Members above the law, only to ensure that they could properly fulfill their constitutional role.[3] The Millian transition was primarily effected by a series of eighteenth-century statutes that eliminated the privilege against civil process and restricted the arrest privilege to Members and parliamentary officers, removing it from Members' menial servants. The Millian model also involved setting a more definite limit on the time of privilege for the Commons, extending it to forty days before and after a session of Parliament. (The Lords, as Members of a continuing body, always have privilege.) These changes created a more functional model of privilege — Members' menial servants were not necessary to the Members' constitutional role, and thus privilege was taken away from them. As civil process was increasingly handled by attorneys and travel became easier, it was less onerous for Members to defend themselves in court and attend to their duties; it was thus harder to justify a privilege against legal process. Finally, the privilege against civil arrest became markedly less important as the use of civil arrest diminished almost to the vanishing point.[4] This privilege is thus of interest today in relatively few cases but is worth studying for what it tells us about the history and development of privilege as a whole.

The Blackstonian Paradigm

RELIANCE ON THE KING

Early claims of this privilege make it clear that it was originally intended to serve the King's interests, not the institutional interests of an independent Parliament. The two earliest known assertions of the privilege arose in 1290, and both claimed privilege against legal process. That year, the Master of the Temple petitioned for leave to distrain for the rent of a house in London, the tenant of which was the bishop of St. David. The King replied that the action could not proceed during Parliament time, but would be permissible at other times.[5] That same year, Bogo de Clare, on behalf of the prior of the Holy Trinity in London, cited the Earl of Cornwall to appear before the archbishop of Canterbury. The King had also summoned the earl to Parliament. Bogo attempted to execute the prior's order during Parliament time and in Westminster Hall, whereupon both Bogo and the prior were summoned before the King and committed to the Tower of London for interfering in the workings of Parliament.[6] In the thirteenth century, Parliament was still principally the King's advisory council;[7] interference with a Parliament man was therefore treated as an offense against the King and punished by the King.

The earliest known case of the privilege of freedom from arrest dates from 1340. In 1330, John de Godessfeld had rented land and tenements in London from the King. He took such bad care of the property that he was prosecuted by Geoffrey de Aston on the King's behalf. After failing to show up for several court appearances in the Exchequer Court, he was caught and sent to the Fleet Prison in January 1340. That same month, he had been elected to Parliament from the borough of Bedford. His arrest came as he was preparing to take his seat in Parliament for the first time.[8] Three months later, the King ordered his release "on the grounds that the privilege of Commons' immunity from arrest had been flouted."[9] This suggests, of course, that the privilege was already well established at this point.

In 1404, the House of Commons sent a petition to Henry IV:

> [W]hereas, according to the custom of the realm, the lords, knights, citizens, and burgesses, coming to your Parliament at your command, staying there, and returning home to their countries, and their men and servants with them in the said Parliament, are under your special protection and defence, and ought not, for any debte, trespass, or other contract whatsoever, to be ar-rested, or any way imprisoned in the mean time; and now so it is, that many such men coming to your Parliament, and others their men and servants, during the said Parliament, have been arrested by them who had full knowl-edge that they so arrested were of the Parliament, or the men and servants of them of the Parliament as aforesaid, in contempt of you, great damage of the party, and delay of the business of your Parliament; may it please you to establish, that if any hereafter do arrest any such man coming to the Parlia-ment as aforesaid, or any of their men or servants remaining with them in the said Parliament, during the said Parliament, or any thing attempt contrary to the custom, he shall make fine and ransome unto you, and render treble damages to the party grieved.[10]

The King rejected this petition, not because he disagreed with its statements of rights but rather because he disapproved of the scope of the remedy.[11] The right itself — a privilege against arrest for Members and their servants during Parliament time and the time going to and coming from Parliament — was unquestioned, as was the arrested Member's right to be set at liberty.[12] Note, however, that the Commons had to appeal to the King to vindicate these rights and that, even under the House's own proposal, the King was to be compen-sated for the arrest of a Member of Parliament. Again, the implication is that this privilege exists to protect the King's council as it carries out his business.

In 1429,[13] William Larke, a servant to William Milrede, an MP from Lon-don, was arrested for trespass by suit of Margerie Janyns, brought before the King's Bench, and thrown into the Fleet Prison. The House of Commons petitioned for his release, while saving Janyns her remedy after the end of the present Parliament. The Commons also petitioned the King for a declaration that no Member of Parliament or servant of a Member could be arrested or detained in prison during Parliament time, "except for treason, felony, or surety of the peace."[14] The King, with the advice and consent of the Lords, granted the petition as to Larke but denied the request for a more general declaration.[15] (The Lords' participation was important because the consent of all three estates made the Commons' petition a special law, which allowed Janyns's remedy to be saved, in contravention of the then-prevailing rule that once a person had been arrested in execution, he could not be rearrested in the same case.)[16] The House of Lords later speculated that the King denied this request because the wording would have required the release of any justly imprisoned MPs as soon as Parliament was called into session. This was understood to be beyond the scope of the privilege.[17]

In 1453, the Duke of York accused Thomas Thorpe, the Speaker of the House of Commons, of trespass and theft. The duke filed suit in the Court of Exchequer, and, after a jury trial, Thorpe was found guilty. Damages were awarded to the duke, and Thorpe was sent to the Fleet until he could pay them. The Commons petitioned the King and the Lords for Thorpe's release, asserting a violation of their ancient liberties and privileges. The duke replied that

> the said Bille and Action were take and camed, and by processe of lawe juggement theruppon yeven again the said Thomas, in tyme of vacation of the same Parlement, and not in Parlement tyme; and also that if the said Thomas shuld be relessed by Privelegge of Parlement, or the type that the seid Duke be satisfied of his said dampmages and costes, the same Duke shuld be withoute remedie in that behalve.[18]

The Lords, declaring that they wanted neither to harm the privileges of the House of Commons nor to allow a failure of justice, asked the judges for their opinion of whether Thorpe "ought to be delivered from prison, by force and vertue of the Privelegge of Parlement or noo."[19] The judges replied that they should not answer the question, as it was not for judges of the lex terrae to "in eny wyse determine the Privelegge of this high Court of Parlement."[20] However, as to the question of how the common-law courts should react when faced with a writ of supersedeas (that is, a writ seeking to suspend execution of a judgment) asserting privilege of Parliament, the judges concluded that,

> if any persone that is a membre of this high Court of Parlement be arested in suche cases as be not for treason or felony, or suerte of the peas, or for a condempnation hadde before the Parlement, it is used that all such persones shuld be relessed of such arrestes and make an Attourney, so that they may have theire fredom and libertee, frely to entende upon the Parlement.[21]

The Lords decided that Thorpe should remain imprisoned and recommended to the lower house that it elect a new Speaker.[22] The Commons acquiesced.

Thus, although the judges supported an expansive privilege for the Commons, the outcome of the case was problematic for later advocates of a strong privilege for two reasons. First, and most obviously, the Lords won the battle of political will, and Thorpe remained in prison. Second, the Commons had attempted to vindicate their privileges by appealing to the Lords and the King. As we saw in the discussion of the *Shirley* case in chapter 1, the Commons would later become quite wary of arguments that their privileges required outside enforcement. Wittke suggests that these reasons explain why *Thorpe's Case* was "never much stressed by the later champions of privilege."[23]

However, in the immediate aftermath of *Thorpe's Case*, the House of Commons remained too weak to enforce its own privileges and was thus forced to rely on royal assistance. In 1460, when Walter Clerk, a Member of the House of Commons, was arrested for failure to pay a fine to the King, as well as for debts to others, the Commons had to petition the King (after receiving the advice and consent of the Lords) to release Clerk. The House reminded the King that the privilege "hath ever afore this tyme been and oweth to be, the same Commens to have fre commyng, goyng, and their abidyng" during Parliament time.[24] It also stipulated that the King's (and the other plaintiffs') rights would be saved, as Clerk could be legally pursued after Parliament was dissolved. The King assented, and Clerk was allowed to attend to his parliamentary duties.[25]

A similar case arose in 1474, when William Hyde, MP, was arrested at the suit of a private citizen for debts to several private citizens and to the King. The Commons again sought a royal writ ordering Hyde's release (again, after having received the Lords' consent), on the condition that he could be rearrested after the dissolution of Parliament. Again the King consented.[26] An interesting twist arose with the 1477 arrest of John Atwyll, MP.[27] In that case, the Commons stated the scope of their privilege thus: "[E]ny of theym shuld not be empleded in any action personell, nor be attached by their persone or goodes in their coming to any such Parlement, there abidyng, nor fro thens to their prope home resortyng."[28] Here, for the first time, we see the explicit assertion of a right not to be *impleaded* during Parliament time. Of course, such a claim was implicit in the *Master of the Temple* and *Bogo de Clare* cases, and altogether unnecessary in the *Atwyll* case, as Atwyll had actually been arrested. This may, perhaps, explain why the King gave his assent to the Commons' resolution, despite the fact that, only five years earlier, royal courts had held that privilege of Parliament does *not* extend to preventing Members from being impleaded during Parliament time.

In 1472, Bartholomew Donne brought suit for fourteen pounds, eighteen shillings against John Walsh, a servant of the Earl of Essex. Walsh produced a royal writ of supersedeas ordering that the action be stayed because, as

the servant of a Member of Parliament, he was privileged against being impleaded. The same year, John Ryver sued Robert Cosins to recover a debt, and
Cosins claimed privilege against legal process as a Member's servant.[29] In both
cases, the Barons of the Exchequer, after consulting with the other common
law judges, held that

> there was no such Custom, nor Priviledge then, nor in any former age or
> Parliaments, to exempt any Lords, Knights, Citizens, Burgesses, Barons of
> Ports or their necessary servants attending them, from any of these personal
> Actions and prosecutions of them during the Sessions of Parliament, but only
> from arrests and imprisonments of their persons in those Actions, and execu-
> tions grounded on them; whereupon they gave Judgment against both these
> Citizens and menial servants notwithstanding their Writs of *Supersedeas*.[30]

As a result, once the Houses started enforcing their own privileges, rather than
relying on royal writ, they would issue their orders to stay proceedings to the
plaintiff and his attorneys, rather than to the judges. "For [the judges] cannot
stay the trial, if the plaintiff will proceed, notwithstanding any such order; for it
is against the law [lex terrae]. But the plaintiff may be punished, if he contemn
the lords [or Commons'] order and break the privileges of Parliament."[31]

THE *FERRERS* CASE

The next major case marked a significant innovation in the enforcement
of the arrest privilege. In 1543, George Ferrers, an MP from Plymouth, was
arrested pursuant to an action for debt brought in the King's Bench while on
his way to Parliament in London. Upon being notified of Ferrers's arrest, the
Commons ordered its Sergeant to "forthwith repair to the Counter in Bread-
street, whither the said Ferrers was carried, and there to demand delivery of
the prisoner."[32] The jailers refused to release Ferrers and offered forcible re-
sistance to the Sergeant. The Sergeant "was driven to defend himself with his
mace of armes, and had the crown thereof broken by bearing off a stroke, and
his man stroken down."[33] The sheriffs of London arrived but sided with the
jailers. The Sergeant retreated and reported to the House. The House of Commons was so upset that it "rose up wholly, and retired to the Upper House,"
where the Speaker informed the Lords of their grievances.[34] The Lords declared the contempt "very great," and left its punishment in the hands of the
Commons. The Commons decided that the Sergeant should return to the
sheriffs, as before, and demand that Ferrers be delivered to him. Importantly,
the House refused the Lord Chancellor's offer to arm the Sergeant with a writ
for Ferrers's release, on the grounds that "all commandments and other acts
proceeding from the Neather House [the House of Commons], were to be

done and executed by their Serjeant without writ, only by shew of his mace, which was his warrant."[35] The sheriffs got wind of "how haynously the matter was taken"[36] and, deciding that discretion was the better part of valor, handed Ferrers over to the Sergeant. The House also demanded that the sheriffs and the jailers who had been involved in the fight with the Sergeant appear before it. On the House's orders, the Sergeant also arrested for contempt of Parliament the plaintiff in the suit against Ferrers.[37] The sheriffs and the plaintiff were sent to the Tower; the clerk most responsible for the fight was put in the Little Ease dungeon of the Tower; and five other jailers were sent to Newgate Prison.[38] After three days and the intervention of the Lord Mayor of London and other powerful friends, they were all released.[39]

Ferrers, in addition to being an MP, was also a servant of Henry VIII, and after Ferrers had been liberated, the King called in the Lord Chancellor, all of the judges, the Speaker of the House of Commons, and other prominent MPs, and delivered the following message:

> First, commending their wisdome in maintaining the Privileges of the House (which he would not have to be infringed in any point) alledged that he, being head of the Parliament, and attending in his own person upon the business thereof, ought in reason to have Privilege for him, and all his servants attending there upon him. So that if the said Ferrers had been no Burgess, but only his servant, that in respect thereof he was to have the Privilege, as well as any other. For I understand, quoth he, that you, not only for your own persons, but also for your necessary servants, even to your cooks and horsekeepers, enjoy the said Privilege. . . . And further, we be informed by our Judges, that we at no time stand so highly in our Estate Royal, as in the time of Parliament; wherein we as Head, and you as Members, are conjoin'd and knit together into one Body Politick, so as whatsoever offence or injury (during that time) is offered to the meanest Member of the House, is to be judg'd as done against our Person and the whole Court of Parliament; which prerogative of the Court is so great (as our learned Counsel informeth us) as all acts and processes coming out of any other inferior Courts, must for the time cease and give place to the highest.[40]

Beneath the superficial pleasantries of royal expressions of support for parliamentary actions, we can see a clash between the older, monarchical conception of privilege and the newer, Blackstonian model. After an initial moment of uncertainty in which it appealed to the House of Lords, the House of Commons insisted that it was the final word on the enforcement of its own privileges. It not only refrained from going to the King for help, it turned down proffered help from a royal official (the Lord Chancellor's offer of a writ of privilege), on the grounds that the Sergeant's mace was sufficient authority.

The House imprisoned the sheriffs, jailers, and plaintiff on its own authority and kept them in custody until it chose to release them. This was a strong assertion of the primacy of lex parliamenti, a Blackstonian claim that the House's privileges were paramount and that it alone would enforce them. In contrast, the King attempted to reassert the older view. His claim that his servants should be accorded parliamentary privilege is a claim that privilege is intended to help Members of Parliament serve the King. An offense against the House is to be treated as though it were "done against our Person." On Henry's view, the House of Commons is simply an instrument of royal governance; on the House's Blackstonian view, it is the democratic element in the state meant to balance the royal element. As we shall see, the Blackstonian view was ascendant, and it was the House's deeds, rather than Henry's words, that set the precedent for future assertions of the arrest privilege.

FREEDOM FROM CIVIL ARREST

In the 1545 *Chamond* case, discussed in chapter 1, we see the House of Commons continuing to take the initiative in enforcing its own privilege against arrest. There, the House of Commons directed the issuance of the writ of privilege, and, as Hatsell notes, within a few years, it became established "that no person should apply for a Writ of Privilege without a warrant for that purpose first obtained from the Speaker."[41]

In 1572, Lord Cromwell informed the House of Lords that he had been taken into custody by the sheriff of Norfolk for violating an injunction issued from the Court of Chancery.[42] After examining the precedents and finding no case in which a Lord of Parliament had been attached in a similar proceeding, the House declared the arrest "derogatory and prejudicial to the antient Privilege claimed to belong to the said Lords of this realm" and ordered Cromwell released.[43]

In 1586, the House of Commons was faced with a case in which a Mr. Martin,[44] a Member, was arrested while Parliament was prorogued. The arrest occurred more than twenty days before the House was set to reconvene. The House decided not to set a limit on the duration of privilege but rather declared that it extended for a "convenient time" before and after a sitting.[45] Twenty days was held to be within the "convenient time," but the House magnanimously decided not to punish the arrester for violating its freshly minted rule.[46] Similarly, in 1734, Colonel Pitt, a Member of the House of Commons, was arrested at the suit of several plaintiffs. The arrest came two days after Parliament had been dissolved. Pitt moved for his discharge on the grounds that his arrest came during the time of privilege. Although the motion was made in the Court of Common Pleas, the issue was seen to be sufficiently weighty for it to be argued at Sergeant's Inn before all of the justices of England.[47] The judges unanimously agreed that two days fell within the "convenient time" during which Members were privileged in going to and coming from Parliament.[48]

In 1592, Thomas Fitzherbert was arrested on a preexisting judgment of outlawry (for a debt to the Queen) two hours after his election to Parliament. He appealed to the House for a writ of privilege. The House had to consider, first, whether Fitzherbert, as an outlaw, was eligible to be elected; second, if he was, whether he was entitled to privilege; and third, if so, how he should be delivered from custody.[49] The House concluded that Fitzherbert was eligible and therefore was a Member of Parliament. However, the House decided that he was not entitled to privilege, for three reasons: (1) he was arrested before the election returns were official, (2) he was outlawed at the Queen's suit for not paying a debt to her, and (3) he was not arrested during the sitting of Parliament or while coming from or going to it.[50] As Hatsell notes, the third reason neglects the "convenient time" language of the *Martin* case, given that Fitzherbert's arrest came only sixteen days before the next meeting of Parliament.[51] In a case just over thirty years later, the House would extend privilege to a man imprisoned on mesne process and then elected to Parliament.[52]

The same year as the *Fitzherbert* case, Francis Neale, a Member of Parliament, informed the House that he had been arrested "by a Serjeant called *John Lightburn*, at the Suit of one *Wessellen Weblen* a Beer-Brewer."[53] Neale had secured his own release by paying the debt, but he brought the matter to the House's attention "in regard of the preservation of the Liberties and priviledges of this House."[54] The House ordered Weblen and Lightburn to attend upon it and, after some debate, threw them into the Tower, "there to remain during the pleasure of this House."[55] Three days later, the two were discharged, "paying their Fees."[56] This seems to be the first case in which the Commons extracted a fine for breaching the arrest privilege, although there is at least one other such case.[57] Similarly, in the 1604 *Shirley* case (discussed in detail in chapter 1), the House was quite willing to be aggressive in the vindication of its privilege against arrest.

Also in 1604, a new statute went into effect that obviated the need for special laws to save plaintiffs their remedies in cases filed against MPs during Parliament time.[58] The act provided that if a defendant had been released because of privilege, the plaintiff could receive a new writ of execution once Parliament time had ended, as if "no suche former Execution had bene taken forthe or served."[59] Thus, the remedies of well-meaning plaintiffs could be preserved without the need for constant recourse to the Lords and the King in order to pass special laws. Again, the Blackstonian logic is clear: Members are

not above the law, but, for the sake of the common weal, the ordinary operation of the lex terrae must be partially suspended during Parliament time.

In 1621, just before the House of Commons adjourned for the summer (a
period of more than five months), it adopted the following resolution, reportedly authored by Coke:

> That in case of any arrest or any distress of goods, serving any process,
> summoning the land of a Member, citation of summoning his person, arrest-
> ing his person, suing him in any court, or breaking any other Privilege of this
> House; a letter shall issue under Mr. Speaker's hand, for the party's relief
> therein, as if the Parliament was sitting; and the party refusing to obey it, to be
> censured at the next access.[60]

A Member proposed an amendment to protect creditors — "That in consideration of payment of debts, the land and goods of any Members, being debtors,
may not be privileged during this long recess"[61] — but the House voted it
down. As Wittke noted, this was "an unheard of extension of privilege,"[62] not
only because it extended the privilege for such a long time when Members
were not engaged in parliamentary business but also because it allowed the
Speaker alone to determine when a breach of privilege had occurred, and any
disobedience of his interpretation was to be treated as contempt.

In 1626, Charles I committed the Earl of Arundel to the Tower. The King did
not specify a reason, but it was thought that the cause was the marriage
(without royal blessing or approval) of Arundel's oldest son to Elizabeth Stuart,
the daughter of the late Duke of Lenox. Stuart was a royal ward, and Charles
reportedly had other plans for her.[63] The Lords were upset, but Charles sent
them a message asserting that Arundel "was restrained for a misdemeanor,
which was personal to his Majesty, and lay in the proper knowledge of his
Majesty, and had no relation to matters of Parliament."[64] The House of Lords
nonetheless resolved, "That the Privilege of this House is, that no Lord of
Parliament, sitting the Parliament, or within the usual times of Privilege of
Parliament, is to be imprisoned or restrained, without sentence or order of the
House, unless it be for Treason or Felony, or for refusing to give Surety for the
Peace."[65] The House then drew up a petition and remonstrance to the King,[66]
and the King promised a speedy reply. When more than a month had passed and
numerous petitions had gone unanswered, the Members of the House,

> seeing that, notwithstanding the most solemn promises so frequently re-
> peated, the King intended to delay giving them satisfaction till the end of the
> Session, and by that pitiful evasion to persist in the violation of their Priv-
> ileges, immediately resolve[d], "That all other business shall cease; and that
> consideration be had, how their Privileges may be preserved to posterity."[67]

The House then adjourned. The King, in dire need of funds and finding that all business would remain stopped until he satisfied the House, released Arundel fifteen days later.[68]

In 1628, Sir Henry Stanhope, an MP, was committed to prison by the Privy Council for challenging another gentleman to a duel. His arrest was declared to be "for the breach of the peace, and refusing to give security for the peace."[69] After examining the matter briefly, the House returned Stanhope to the Prison of the Marshalsea, where he was being held. This seems to constitute an acknowledgment that breach of the peace or refusal to give surety of the peace was an imprisonable offense for a Member. After Stanhope promised to keep the peace, he was released by order of the House.[70]

In January 1642,[71] as tensions between Parliament and Charles I mounted, the attorney-general brought accusations of treason before the House of Lords against Denzil Hollis, Arthur Haslerig, John Pym, John Hampden, and William Strowd, all Members of the House of Commons, and Lord Kimbolton, a Member of the Upper House. Royal officers sealed up those Members' houses and papers, and a royal sergeant was sent to arrest them.[72] Both Houses of Parliament declared that the sealing of the Members' homes and papers and the placing of a royal guard at Whitehall were breaches of privilege.[73] The Commons ordered their Sergeant to arrest the men who had sealed the doors of the Members.[74] The next day, the five accused Members of the Lower House were ordered to attend upon the House of Commons, but they were soon interrupted by a report that "his Majesty was coming with a guard of military men, commanders, and soldiers, to the House of Commons."[75] The House ordered the five to leave the premises in order to avoid forcible confrontation in Westminster Hall. Royal soldiers filled the Hall; the doors to the House of Commons were thrown open; and Charles ascended to the Speaker's chair.[76] Not seeing any of the five Members in attendance, he declared that, when he had sent his sergeant the day before, "I did expect obedience, and not a message."[77] He reminded the House that its privileges did not cover treason and demanded that the Members be yielded up to him when they returned to the House.[78] As he was leaving the House, a number of Members were heard to yell, "Privilege! Privilege!"[79] The next day, the Commons passed a resolution declaring the King's action

> a high breach of the Rights and Privileges of Parliament, and inconsistent with the liberty and freedom thereof; and therefore this House doth conceive they cannot, with the safety of their own persons, or indemnity of the Rights and Privileges of Parliament, sit here any longer without a full vindication of so high a breach, and sufficient guard wherein they may confide.[80]

The House then adjourned. When it later reconvened, it resolved that anyone who arrested any Member of Parliament

> by pretence of any warrant issuing out from the King . . . was guilty of the breach of the privilege of Parliament, and a public enemy of the common-wealth; and that the arresting any member of Parliament, by any warrant whatsoever, without consent of that House, whereof he is a member, is a breach of the privilege of Parliament: and the person that shall so arrest him is declared a public enemy of the commonwealth.[81]

The Blackstonian transformation of the arrest privilege had reached its zenith: whereas the privilege had once furthered Parliament's role as a royal hand-maiden, it was now asserted in the institutional interest of Parliament itself and in direct defiance of the King. Support for the Members was so great that the King was forced to remove his court from Whitehall to Hampton Court; the next day, the accused Members attended Parliament, "guarded by the Sheriffs, and Trained-bands of London and Westminster, and attended by a conflux of many thousands of people besides, making a great clamour against Bishops and Popish Lords, and for the privileges of Parliament."[82] At this point, the Civil War was all but inevitable, and the Members were never arrested.

FREEDOM FROM LEGAL PROCESS

We have already seen several assertions by Members that privilege pro-tected them from all legal process during Parliament time. That assertion arises as early as the 1290 *Master of the Temple* and *Bogo de Clare* cases. In the 1472 *Donne* and *Ryver* cases, the Barons of the Exchequer explicitly denied that privilege extended to all legal process, but five years later, in the *Atwyll* case, the Commons asserted, and the King agreed, that Members were privileged against being impleaded.[83]

In 1549, we find the House of Commons ordering four of its Members to excuse another Member from having to appear before the justices of the Com-mon Pleas.[84] In 1584, Richard Cook, MP, was served with a subpoena from the Court of Chancery. The House resolved that, "by the ancient liberties of this House, the Members of the same are privileged from being served with Subpœnas" and demanded that the subpoena to Cook be discharged and that no future subpoenas be issued to Members of the House.[85] When the House's emissaries presented this resolution in Chancery, the Lord Chancellor replied that "he thought this House had no such liberty of Privilege for Subpœnas, as they pretended; neither would he allow of any precedents of this House com-mitted unto them formerly used in that behalf, unless this House could also prove the same to have been likewise thereupon allowed and ratified also by the precedents in the said Court of Chancery."[86] The House could apparently find no such precedents. In a similar case the same year, Anthony Kirle served Alban Stepneth, a Member, with a subpoena out of Star Chamber. The subpoena was served during Parliament time, within Westminster Palace, and was accompanied by an attachment against Stepneth.[87] The Commons resolved that both the serving of the subpoena and the procuring of the attachment were contempts, and Kirle was taken into custody by the Sergeant and ordered to pay Stepneth's costs.[88] Six days later, Kirle was released, having apologized, paid the costs, and taken the Oath of Supremacy.[89] Thus, we see that, in the face of continuing judicial refusal to enforce the House's asserted right to freedom from legal process, the House simply took matters into its own hands and used its contempt power to punish those litigants who would serve Members with legal process.[90]

In 1588, before recessing, the Commons passed a resolution giving the Speaker the power during the vacation to issue warrants to the Lord Chancellor for the issuance of writs of supersedeas to suspend any civil suits against Members.[91] Sometimes, a letter from the Speaker alone was sufficient to stay proceedings. In 1605 and 1606, the Speaker wrote a number of letters to assize judges demanding the staying of trials in which Members were parties.[92] In 1606, the House granted the Speaker a general authority to write such letters whenever a Member required it.[93] In 1607, the Speaker wrote two such letters to the Barons of the Exchequer; this was the first time that such a letter had been written to one of the superior courts.[94] It appears that at least one of the letters was successful,[95] as were similar letters to lower courts.[96] However, in 1626, when the Speaker wrote a letter to the King's Bench demanding that it stay judgment against a Member of the House,

> [t]he Court was greatly offended at this, and would have returned a sharp answer to the Parliament, if it had not been dissolved; because it is against the oaths of the Judges to stay judgment, nec per Grand Seal, nec per Petit Seal, per le statute; but the way in such case is to procure a Supersedeas, which is a special Writ appointed in these cases: and this is to be allowed, being the legal course: But the letter is not to be regarded.[97]

However, as Hatsell noted, the fact that writs of supersedeas were almost never used at this point suggests that the House was increasingly taking matters into its own hands and holding plaintiffs themselves responsible for initiating legal action.[98]

On occasion, the judges, too, were cowed by the House's disciplinary powers. In 1697, Bourchier Wray petitioned the House of Commons in connection with his inheritance. A rival claimant to the estate, who was a Member of the House of Commons, had simply seized large portions of it, but the courts "will not meddle in the said Matters, though applied to, for fear of displeasing the House."[99] The House quickly resolved that "no Member of this House hath any Privilege in Cases of Breach of the Peace, or forcible Entries, or forcible Detainers."[100]

In 1606, the House made a sweeping claim of privilege for Members' goods. In a letter to the sheriff of Hampshire, the Speaker wrote that "the Privilege of Parliament, during the time of service there . . . reacheth as well to the goods, as person of every Member attendant for the time."[101] This privilege would shortly become instrumental in the House's dispute with Charles I, as we saw in the discussion of *Rolle's Case* in chapter 1.

ARREST PRIVILEGE FOR SERVANTS

As we have already seen in the *Larke*, *Walsh*, and *Cosins* cases, the arrest privilege extended not only to Members but to their servants as well. In 1575, Edward Smalley, a servant to Arthur Hall, an MP, was arrested for debt. The House granted Smalley privilege.[102] The House also appointed a committee to investigate the matter, and the committee reported that it found no precedent for

> setting at large by the Mace any person in Arrest but only by Writ, and that by divers precedents of Records perused by the said Committees it appeareth, that every Knight, Citizen and Burgess of this House which doth require priviledge [for a servant], hath used in that Case to take a corporal Oath before the Lord Chancellor, or Lord Keeper of the Great Seal for the time being, that the party for whom such Writ is prayed came up with him and was his Servant at the time of the Arrest made, and that Mr. *Hall* was thereupon moved by this House that he should repair to the Lord Keeper and make Oath in form aforesaid, and then to proceed to the taking of a Warrant for a Writ of priviledge for his said Servant according to the said Report of the said former precedents.[103]

The Committee's claim that it could find no precedent for setting Smalley free by use of the Mace alone is odd — as Hatsell notes, it "shews that they did not make a very diligent search; or proves that they did not consider Ferrers's Case merely in the light of an arrest for debt, but as an insult on the King and the House."[104] Indeed, the House itself soon came to the conclusion that the committee was mistaken. Perhaps because Hall refused to take an oath, Smalley was still in custody five days later when the House resolved that Smalley "shall be brought hither to Morrow by the Serjeant and set at liberty by Warrant of the Mace, and not by Writ."[105] The victory was a hollow one for Smalley, however — immediately after freeing him, the House itself arrested him.[106] The House adjudged Smalley guilty of contempt for intentionally getting himself arrested so that when he successfully asserted privilege he would be released and the underlying action would be dismissed.[107] (Note that this was prior to the passage of the 1604 act discussed above.)[108] Smalley was sent to the Tower for one month, ordered to repay the original debt, and assessed Sergeant's fees.[109]

In 1601, the House of Lords ordered the Keeper of Newgate Prison to release Vaughan, a servant to the Earl of Shrewsbury. The Keeper refused to comply, and the Lords committed him to the Fleet.[110] Upon examining the precedents, the House ordered the Lord Keeper to make out a writ of privilege to the sheriffs of London and Middlesex to bring Vaughan before it. The Lords then discharged both Vaughan and the Keeper of Newgate.[111] Hatsell concludes that an examination of the precedents must have convinced the Lords that "the regular and legal mode of bringing before them any prisoner in execution was not . . . by their Warrant sent by a Serjeant at Arms, but by an order to the Lord Keeper for a Writ of Privilege of Parliament."[112] Less than a month earlier, however, the House of Commons had used its Sergeant to free a Member's tailor, who had been arrested as the surety on a debt in default.[113] A few years later, the Commons sent their Sergeant to arrest a justice of the peace who had committed the coachman of an MP to Newgate. The House freed the coachman and released the justice of the peace when he acknowledged his fault.[114] And in 1610, privilege was extended to a Member's servant who had been arrested "for getting a woman with child."[115] The journals do not make it clear whether the Sergeant was sent to release him, but there is no record of any application to royal officials for aid.[116] In 1621, the House of Commons again made it quite clear that it could vindicate the privilege of Members' servants itself. The servant of Sir James Whitlock was arrested. The House brought the arresting parties to the bar, where they acknowledged their fault and begged forgiveness of the House and of the Member. Unsatisfied with this, the House ordered, "That they shall both ride upon one horse bare backed, back to back, from Westminster to the Exchange, with papers on their breasts with this inscription, 'For arresting a servant to a Member of the Commons House of Parliament.' "[117] In general, and in keeping with the Blackstonian framework, the Houses preferred to free arrested servants themselves, rather than to appeal to royal officials.

On occasion, the privileging of servants was stretched almost to the breaking point. In 1627, the House of Commons extended privilege to a farmer who had been a longtime lessee of a Member. As Prynne notes, this was an extension of privilege hitherto unknown.[118] Similarly, in 1645, the Speaker issued a warrant for the release of a Member's servant who had been impressed into military service. The impression was seen as a violation of the arrest privilege.[119]

A more serious problem with extending privilege to Members' servants, however, was that it allowed for serious abuses, most notably the sale and forgery of parliamentary protections. Protections were documents issued under the seal of a Member asserting that certain persons were their servants and demanding that they be free from arrest, imprisonment, and molestation during Parliament time.[120] In 1621, Lords Stafford and North complained to the House that "divers lewd Persons" were forging protections in their names.[121] One of the defendants confessed and was given the following sentence:

> That he the said *John Blunt* shall, To-morrow Morning (being *Wednesday*, the 28th of this *November*), stand on the Pillory here at *Westm.* with Papers on his Head, shewing his Offence, and further Punishment; and also that he shall stand on the Pillory in *Cheapesyde*, on *Saturday* following, with like Papers on his Head; and then shall be carried to *Bridewell*, and there remain during his Life, and be kept to Work for his Living.[122]

Blunt was by no means the only forger of protections to be so heavily punished.[123] Others got off comparatively lightly, with imprisonment "during the Pleasure of the House."[124] Still others were pilloried, but without the lifetime imprisonment.[125] And yet forging continued throughout the seventeenth century and well into the eighteenth.[126]

In 1641, the City of London complained in a petition to the House of Lords about "the great Multitudes and Inconveniency of Protections."[127] That same year, the House of Commons expelled a Member for selling twenty protections (for between seventeen and forty shillings apiece) to people who were not his servants.[128]

In 1691, John Pickering sued Thomas Powley in the Court of Common Pleas for a five hundred pound debt. George Wilson was sent to arrest Powley on Pickering's behalf. Lord Morley claimed that Powley was one of his servants and therefore privileged; as a result of this claim, Wilson was arrested by Black Rod.[129] Wilson petitioned the Lords, claiming that Powley had not been one of Morley's servants until after the arrest. After hearing several witnesses, the House came to the conclusion that Wilson was telling the truth. The House ordered Lord Morley to be sent to the Tower "for having given such a Protection as is contrary to the Orders of this House" and ordered Wilson freed.[130]

In 1745, Lady Mordington and Lady Cassillis tried to use privilege to prevent their illegal gambling houses from being shut down. The local officials trying to enforce the gaming laws provided the House of Lords with a letter from Lady Mordington in which she asserted that all of the employees of her Covent Garden gaming establishment were her "domestic Servants" and demanding "all those Privileges as belong to me, as a Peeress of *Great Brit-*

ain.[131] The House, however, was unimpressed and resolved that "no Person is entitled to Privilege of Peerage, against any Prosecution or Proceeding for keeping any Public or Common Gaming House, or any House, Room, or Place, for playing at any Game or Games prohibited by any Law now in Force."[132]

The Houses attempted to put a stop to these practices, but the sheer number of attempts attests to their relative futility. In 1660, the House of Commons, responding to a counterfeit protection, resolved:

> That the Privilege of this House, in point of Protection, from Arrests, doth belong to the Members of this House, and their menial Servants, only; and to the Officers attending the Service of this House: And that all Protections in Writing, granted by any Member of this House to any Person whatsoever, be forthwith called in; and are hereby declared to be null and void: And all Persons, whom this may concern, are required, upon all Occasions, to take notice of the Privilege belonging to the Members of this House, and their menial Servants, and of the Officers attending the Service of this House, at their Peril.[133]

The resolution must not have taken; ten years later, the House resolved:

> That no Member of this House do grant any Protection to any but such only as are their menial Servants: And that all Protections already granted to any other Persons besides menial Servants, be forthwith withdrawn, and called in.
> . . .
> [And:] That all Protections, and written Certificates, of the Members of this House, be declared void in Law; and be forthwith withdrawn, and called in; and that none be granted for the future; and that the Privilege of Members for their menial Servants be observed according to Law: And that, if any menial Servant shall be arrested and detained contrary to Privilege, he shall, upon Complaint thereof made, be discharged by Order from the Speaker.[134]

In 1677, another Commons resolution declared protections void and ordered that none be issued in the future. Any protection granted by a Member would render that Member "liable to the Censure of the House."[135] Privilege for Members' servants was again declared to "be observed, according to Law" — that is, "if any menial Servant shall be arrested, and detained, contrary to Privilege, he shall, upon Complaint thereof made, be discharged, by Order from Mr. Speaker."[136] This was declared a standing order of the House and ordered to be posted at Westminster, Chancery, the Inns of Court, and the Exchequer, and Members were ordered to send copies to their constituencies.[137] A mere two years later, the House again found itself passing a resolution that tracked the 1677 resolution almost verbatim.[138] This resolution, too, was ordered to be widely posted, suggesting that some did not get the message the first time.

In 1690, the House of Commons requested that municipal officials from Middlesex and London give them a list of protections claimed by Members of the House.[139] After the officials reported, and several Members denied that they had issued the protections listed under their name, the House resolved that

> all Protections, and written Certificates, of the Members of this House, be declared void in Law; and be forthwith withdrawn, and called in; and that none be granted for the future: And if any shall be granted by any Member, such Member shall be liable to the Censure of this House: And that the Privilege of Members for their menial Servants be observed according to Law; and that if any menial Servant shall be arrested, and detained, contrary to Privilege, he shall, upon Complaint thereof made unto the Speaker, be discharged by Order from him.[140]

This was again made a standing order of the House and ordered to be posted throughout Westminster Hall, the Inns of Court and Chancery, and the Exchequer, and to be sent throughout the country.[141] Moreover, those Members who had granted protections were made to give an account of them.[142] This order was repeated in 1695.[143]

In 1690, the House of Lords asked the sheriffs of London and Middlesex, the bailiff of Southwark, the Marshall of the Marshallsea, and the Steward of Westminster to bring in lists of all the protections granted by Members of the Upper House.[144] After reviewing the list, the House declared that

> all the Protections which are now given, by any Peer or Peers, or Members of this House, be, and are hereby declared to be, null and void to all Intents and Purposes whatsoever; and that for the future there shall be no Protection or Protections be allowed to be good, valid, or of any Effect, unless they be first entered in the parliament-office at *Westminster.*[145]

Moreover, the Clerk was to give the House regular accounts of who was issuing protections to whom, and for what purposes.[146] When a Lord's protections seemed excessive or otherwise suspicious, he was ordered to give an account to the House, as happened to the Earl of Huntingdon, the Earl of Aylesbury, and Lord Byron that very year.[147]

After reviewing the protections given, the House was obviously unsatisfied. Within a year, the Lords ordered that

> all Protections given by any Peer or Peers, or Members of this House, and entered in the Parliament Office at *Westm.* of the last Session of this Parlia-

ment, be, and are hereby, declared to be discontinued, null, and void to all Intents and Purposes whatsoever: And to the End that all Persons concerned may take Notice hereof, it is further ORDERED, That this Order be printed and published, and set upon the Doors of this House.[148]

Within a few months, the Duke of Northumberland, the Earls of Suffolk and Lincoln, and Lord Morley were called to task for granting protections in violation of this order. The protections they issued were nullified, but the House resolved that it was still proper to grant protections to menial servants of Members.[149]

In 1696, the House of Lords passed an order stating that "all written Protections given by any Lord of this House shall be, and are hereby, vacated and made void; and that, for the future, no Lord of this House shall give any written Protection to any Person whatsoever; and this Order to be fixed on the Doors of this House and *Westm'r Hall*."[150] The order clearly did not take, because the House ordered it to be read aloud in 1712.[151]

The Millian Paradigm

By the end of the seventeenth century, the arrest privilege had grown to such "huge dimensions" that "it became almost impossible to get any justice out of a member of parliament, and limits had to be set to what had become an intolerable nuisance."[152] The Millian turn in the arrest privilege began in the eighteenth century, as Parliament reacted with legislation to some of the abuses described above. The 1700 Parliamentary Privilege Act allowed suits to be brought against Members of either House or their servants "at any time from and immediately after the dissolution or prorogation of any parliament, until a new parliament shall meet, or the same be re-assembled and from and immediately after any adjournment of both houses of parliament for above the space of fourteen days, until both houses shall meet or re-assemble."[153] The act made clear that it did not in any way diminish the privilege against arrest, however. Three years later, another act allowed suits against any royal revenue official or other official of public trust for misconduct in the course of their duties and provided that parliamentary privilege would not stay or delay such suits if the official happened to be a Member of Parliament. Again, the act made it clear that the privilege against arrest was undiminished.[154]

The biggest change, however, was wrought by the 1770 Parliamentary Privilege Act. Under that act, suits could be brought against Members or their servants "at any time" — whether Parliament was sitting or not.[155] The act again reasserted the privilege against arrest, but only for Members of Parliament.

Servants were no longer privileged against arrest, which put an end to much of the corruption, including the selling of protections, described above.[156] This was clearly a Millian turn, in that it both extended the sphere of lex terrae and focused the privilege more clearly on the proper functioning of Parliament. Parliamentary staff would still be privileged,[157] which ensured that parliamentary functioning would not be affected, but the personal servants of Members, who may have had nothing to do with their parliamentary duties, no longer received privilege.

Not long before the 1770 act, the Court of Common Pleas had decided that John Wilkes was privileged against arrest for seditious libel because "a libel is not a breach of the peace. It tends to the breach of the peace, and that is the utmost. . . . But that which only tends to the breach of the peace cannot be a breach of it."[158] (The *Wilkes* case will be discussed in much greater detail in chapter 7.) This decision, however, was likely more a result of Lord Chief Justice Pratt's outrage at the politically motivated prosecution than a considered reflection upon the state of the law. After all, the 1628 arrest of Sir Henry Stanhope for challenging another gentleman to a duel was not a breach of privilege, despite the fact that the challenge was not an actual breach of the peace but only tended to the breach of the peace.[159] And when the House of Lords in 1745 resolved that privilege did not protect against arrests for operating a gambling house in violation of the law, it surely was not concluding that operating such an establishment was an actual breach of the peace.[160] Pratt's conclusion that not all indictable offenses subjected a Member to arrest was thus a historical novelty, and one that has not since been repeated.[161]

In 1814, Lord Cochrane, a hero of the Napoleonic Wars and a Member of the House of Commons, was indicted and convicted of conspiracy to commit stock-exchange fraud.[162] He was sentenced to one year in the King's Bench Prison and one hour in the pillory.[163] After his conviction, he was expelled from the House of Commons but was immediately reelected to his old seat.[164] After serving more than eight months of his sentence, Cochrane escaped from prison. He remained at large for a period of two weeks, at the end of which he entered the House of Commons chamber, which was empty at the time. There, he was arrested. The House Committee of Privileges had to consider whether this arrest was a breach of privilege.[165] The committee declared that it was unable to find any applicable precedents, but that, in its opinion, it did not think that the arresting officers had breached privilege.[166] Of course, were executive officials to have burst into the House chamber while the House was in session, it would have been a breach of privilege.[167] In keeping with the Millian spirit of the times, the committee here focused on functional considerations—that is, the fact that the House was not meeting—rather than geographical considerations—that is, the fact that the arrest took place on the House floor.

In 1831, the Court of Chancery held that a Member of the House of Commons could be arrested for criminal contempt, even if the contempt arose out of a civil case. In violation of a court order, Long Wellesley removed his infant daughter from the care of a court-appointed guardian. Wellesley, who was a Member of the House of Commons, was arrested, but asserted privilege. Lord Brougham held that privilege was not applicable:

> The line, then, which I draw is this,—that against all civil process privilege [against arrest] protects; but that against contempt for not obeying civil process, if that contempt is in its nature or by its incidents criminal, privilege protects not: that he who has privilege of Parliament in all civil matters, matters which whatever be the form are in substance of a civil nature, may plead it with success, but that he can in no criminal matter be heard to urge such privilege; . . . [Members] are no more protected than the rest of the king's subjects from commitment in execution of a sentence, where the sentence is that of a Court of competent jurisdiction, and has been duly and regularly pronounced.[168]

In other words, all criminal arrests fall outside of the scope of privilege. Indeed, Brougham explicitly noted that "a breach of the peace is not necessarily incident to the contempt,"[169] but he insisted that allowing Members to be arrested only for actual breaches of the peace would be placing Members too far outside the law. The decision here is again clearly a Millian one: private citizens cannot prevent a Member from performing his official functions by having him arrested, but neither can a Member use privilege as a means of acting wholly above the law. At the point at which their actions rise to violations of the criminal law, privilege ceases to shield them. If the court had ruled otherwise, Members would have returned to having a functional immunity against many civil actions—a Member could simply ignore a civil verdict, and that contempt would be unpunishable. That would be an unacceptable reversion to the Blackstonian interpretation of the arrest privilege.

In 1841, the Court of Common Pleas held that it was a violation of the 1770 act to issue a writ of *capias ad satisfaciendum*—that is, a writ to imprison a defendant with an outstanding judgment against him until the judgment is satisfied—against a Member of Parliament.[170] The plaintiff was aware that he could not enforce the writ; instead, he planned on the writ's being returned *non est inventus*—"he is not found"—which would then allow the plaintiff to seek a writ of *exigi facias*, which would eventually lead to the defendant's being outlawed.[171] The court held, however, that a writ could not issue when the enforcement of that writ would be illegal, even if the writ was never intended to be enforced.[172]

In 1847, the Court of Exchequer dispensed with the "convenient time" language of *Martin* and *Pitt* and declared, consistent with several centuries of actual parliamentary practice, that the Commons' privilege extended for forty days on either side of a meeting of Parliament.[173] Again, Peers, as members of a continuing body, enjoy privilege at all times.[174] This was a move away from the Blackstonian indefiniteness of *Martin* and *Pitt* and toward a Millian model in which the Commons' privilege is constrained by something other than its own sense of convenience.

In 1963, the Probate, Divorce, and Admiralty Division Court held that privilege prevented the imprisonment of a Peer who had violated a court order to turn over certain property to his wife.[175] In order to determine whether Lord Mowbray, the husband, could be arrested, the court had to determine whether contempt of court was a criminal act falling outside the privilege, or a civil wrong falling within it. The test the court chose to apply was "to see whether the arrest is to punish for a breach of the law or merely to compel performance of a civil obligation."[176] Finding that disobedience to a court order compelling the surrender of property fell into the latter category, the court refused to order Lord Mowbray arrested.[177]

The 1939 detention of Captain Ramsay, a Member of Parliament, under World War II Defense Regulations was held by the House of Commons not to involve a breach of privilege.[178] The committee apparently concluded that detention of a suspected disloyal subject during wartime was more akin to criminal imprisonment than civil arrest.

Conclusions

We have thus seen the rise and fall of the privilege against civil arrest and process. It arose as a means of protecting the King's access to his Parliament. It transformed into a Blackstonian instrument by which the Houses could protect themselves from interference from the monarch, as well as from vexatious suits that would keep them from their duties. The privilege was significantly weakened in the Millian transformation, as statutes decreased and then abolished the privilege against legal process and eliminated privilege for Members' servants. Although the privilege might still occasionally be relevant,[179] it is largely a historical artifact. It is, nonetheless, an important artifact. The privilege against civil arrest and process was one of the earliest of Parliament's privileges, and it was certainly one of the more important for much of parliamentary history. It thus adds an important piece to the larger puzzle we are examining and helps us see more clearly the development of British constitutionalism. We have seen how the movement from an ancient to a modern view of democracy necessitated and was facilitated by a change in the scope and nature of this privilege. What existed first in the service of the monarch was soon altered to serve an increasingly independent Parliament, sometimes even against the monarch (consider, especially, *Lord Arundel's Case* and the case of Hollis et al. in 1642). As democracy came increasingly to characterize the British Constitution as a whole, the privilege was altered again, this time to restrict its scope to that which was truly necessary to allow the Members of Parliament to perform their representative functions.

6

Freedom from Civil Arrest for
Members of Congress

The Constitution guarantees that Members of Congress "shall in all Cases, except Treason, Felony and Breach of the Peace, be privileged from Arrest during their Attendance at the Session of their respective Houses, and in going to and returning from the same."[1] Largely because there was comparatively little time between the adoption of the Constitution and the almost complete abolition of civil arrest in the United States,[2] this is the shortest chapter of our story. As we shall see, a popular sovereignty-based approach to the arrest privilege requires us to balance the need for the effective functioning of the ordinary justice system with the need for legislators to be able to perform their public duties.

Text and History

Like the Speech or Debate Clause, the Arrest Clause was not widely discussed at Philadelphia. The Articles of Confederation provided that "the members of Congress shall be protected in their persons from arrests and imprisonments, during the time of their going to and from, and attendance on congress, except for treason, felony, or breach of the peace."[3] Three state constitutions at the Founding contained arrest privileges. Maryland declared the "arresting on civil process" of any Member during the sitting of or on the way to or from the legislature to be a breach of privilege.[4] Massachusetts and New Hampshire both prohibited any Member of the legislature from being "arrested, or held to bail on mesne process, during his going unto, returning from, or his attending the general assembly."[5] As noted in chapter 4, a draft from the Constitutional Convention's Committee of Detail made Members of each House "privileged from arrest (or assault) *personal restraint* during their attendance, for so long a time before and after, as may be necessary, for traveling to and from the legislature (and they shall have no other privileges whatsoever)."[6] This was soon modified to: "The Members of each House shall, in all cases, except Treason, Felony & Breach of the Peace, be privileged from Arrest during their Attendance at Congress, and in going to and returning from it."[7] The "no other privileges whatsoever" language was dropped as the free-speech privilege was added.[8] Except for minor changes in punctuation and capitalization, this was the language that the committee reported to the whole Convention, and the Convention approved it unanimously. The Committee of Style gave it its final wording without altering the substance.[9] There was no recorded debate on the provision at any point. There was also no debate on the Arrest Clause at the states' ratifying conventions, and there was almost none in the press.[10]

In his 1791 Lectures on Law, James Wilson noted only, "This necessary privilege has continued substantially the same, since the time of the Saxons"[11] (a claim that chapter 5 should have belied). Thomas Jefferson had more to say about the privilege—oddly, he noted that the 1770 Parliamentary Privilege Act allowed the service of judicial process against Members of Parliament, but then asserted that Members of Congress retain the privilege against civil process.[12] Jefferson also quoted Blackstone on the necessity of keeping privileges indefinite, but then noted that the restrictive wording of the Arrest Clause was probably a reaction against "this view of the encroaching character of privilege," meant to "provide that the law shall bind equally on all."[13] In other words, he seems to have recognized that privileging Members against all civil process was a Blackstonian interpretation of the privilege, an interpretation that both Britain and the Founders had rejected. Yet he insisted that Members must be privileged against all civil process because civil summons would distract them too much from their duties.[14] He also considered the ways in which the arrest privilege might be enforced, including motion, habeas corpus, and writ, and he noted that the precise time during which the privilege applied would have to be judged on a case-by-case basis.[15]

Joseph Story, too, contemplated the arrest privilege in some detail. He gave the clause a wide construction, saying that it privileges Members of Congress "of course against all process, the disobedience to which is punishable by attachment of the person, such as a *subpœna ad respondendum, aut testifican-dum*, or a summons to serve on a jury, and (as has been justly observed) with reason, because a member has superior duties to perform in another place."[16] Story noted that the privilege extends only to Members and not to their servants or property, and he observed that this probably resulted from "a survey of the abuses of privilege which for a long time defeated in England the purposes of justice."[17] He argued that "breach of the peace" includes all indictable offenses, meaning that the clause applied to civil arrests only.[18] He noted that the time of privilege was left indefinite, rather than being limited to forty days on either side of a meeting of Congress.[19] Finally, he asserted that there were a number of ways in which the privilege could be enforced:

> The effect of this privilege is, that the arrest of the member is unlawful, and a trespass *ab initio*, for which he may maintain an action, or proceed against the aggressor by way of indictment. He may also be discharged by motion to a court of justice, or upon a writ of *habeas corpus*; and the arrest may also be punished as a contempt of the House.[20]

As we shall see, Jefferson and Story's understanding of the scope of the privilege — that is, that it prevents the service of any civil process — seems unduly inattentive to the lessons of those "abuses of privilege which for a long time defeated in England the purposes of justice."[21]

Interpretation

In light of the British history described in the previous chapter, as well as the fact that no state constitution privileged legislators against criminal arrest, Story was almost certainly correct that the clause was meant to apply to civil arrest only; "Treason, Felony, and Breach of the Peace" applies to all indictable offenses.[22] It is worth noting, however, that while the arrest privilege protects only against civil arrest, the speech and debate privilege rightly interpreted, as noted in chapter 4, may operate to prevent certain criminal prosecutions because those prosecutions require courts to delve into internal legislative business. The time of the arrest privilege is left indefinite, but it is well within judicial competence to determine whether a Member legitimately was going to or returning from a session of Congress (the substantial size difference between the United Kingdom and the United States may make a flexible standard more appropriate in the latter). Finally, contra Jefferson and Story, it seems evident that the privilege was not meant to apply to the service of civil process. The Framers would have been well aware of the 1770 Parliamentary Privilege Act and the abuses that gave rise to it, and the background assumption would thus have been that legislators were not privileged against the service of civil process. Had the Framers and Ratifiers intended to repudiate the background assumption of pre-Revolutionary British law, they would probably have found a clearer way to do so, and they probably would have discussed the alteration at length. Instead, as we have seen, nothing in the text or history of the Arrest Clause suggests that the Framers intended to alter this assumption.

Akhil Reed Amar and Neal Kumar Katyal, however, have taken a line closer to Jefferson and Story's and argued that

> "[a]rrest" may also be understood more functionally as extending to various civil cases that interfere with—that arrest—a person's performance of her duties in public office. This functional immunity avoids undemocratic results: functional civil arrests of members of Congress while it is in session might skew votes in Congress and penalize innocent third parties, namely, the American people.[23]

As noted above, this understanding is contrary to the Founding evidence, and Amar and Katyal nowhere discuss the 1770 Parliamentary Privilege Act.[24] Additionally, their structural point is not as strong as they make it sound — certainly, an *arrest* would prevent a Member from performing her public duties, and therefore a privilege against arrests is necessary to prevent Members from being taken away from their public duties, but the vast majority of the work in defending a lawsuit is done by attorneys, and their work can continue without unduly distracting the Member.[25] Certainly, judges should be flexible, especially in allowing Members to testify at times that would not require them to neglect their duties.[26] This, of course, is equally true when Members are subpoenaed as witnesses in cases to which they are not parties. But it is contrary to both the text and the history of the Arrest Clause to suggest that it privileges Members against all civil process. Moreover, Amar and Katyal's argument proves too much — on their reading, there is no principled reason why Members should not be privileged against *criminal* arrest as well. After all, a criminal arrest no less than a civil arrest "might skew votes in Congress and penalize innocent third parties, namely, the American people."[27] It seems a better interpretation to say that the Arrest Clause of the American Constitution, like its Millian British forebears, was intended to strike a balance between the competing demands of the ordinary justice system and the need for legislators to be able to perform their official duties. Criminal charges are sufficiently serious that, unless they run afoul of the speech or debate privilege, they may always be brought against a legislator.[28] A civil suit is not as serious — it generally alleges an offense against an individual or a discrete group, rather than one against the people as a whole — but the preparation of one's defense can largely be left to attorneys and is therefore unlikely to place a large burden on the legislator-defendant. The Constitution, thus, following the 1770 Parliamentary Privilege Act, allows civil suits against Members. However, the fact that arrest is permissible in the case of crimes does not mean that it is permissible in the relatively less serious case of civil suits. The seriousness of the action (an arrest that takes a Member away from his legislative duties), combined with the less serious nature of the justification (a civil suit), led to the constitutional judgment that civil arrests should not be allowed against legislators. In short, Amar and Katyal attempt to read the Arrest Clause as providing an absolute privilege for legislators to be (metaphorically) unfettered by the demands of the ordinary justice system during the time of privilege. But this reading not only conflicts with the history of the clause, it also conflicts with the clause's exception for criminal arrests. A more plausible reading would be to see the clause's deep structural logic as following the Millian British logic in balancing the need for an effective functioning of the ordinary law with the need for legislators able to perform their public duties. This reading leads to the conclusion that legislators must be (literally) unfettered in civil cases during the time of privilege, but they may be served with any civil process short of arrest, and they are subject to the criminal law (so long as its enforcement does not violate their speech or debate privilege).[29]

It does seem likely, however, that the Arrest Clause would apply in at least two situations other than arrest in a civil suit. First, it would be difficult to assert that a material witness[30] falls under the "Treason, Felony, and Breach of the Peace" exception. A person taken into custody as a material witness is not charged with any offense, and thus the arrest privilege would seem to prevent any Member of Congress from being arrested as a material witness. Second, civil confinement (for example, to a mental-health institution) should be unavailable against Members. As the Supreme Court has held, such confinement is not criminal,[31] and therefore does not fall under the Arrest Clause's exception for criminal offenses. However, the application of the privilege in the context of material witnesses or civil confinement never seems to have arisen in American courts.

Cases

The case law on the arrest privilege is sparse, but it comes to essentially the same conclusions as above. It did not start out that way, however. In 1787, James Martin, a delegate to the Pennsylvania Ratifying Convention, was served with process in a civil suit while in Philadelphia. Although this case obviously did not arise under the Constitution, it called for an interpretation of the common-law privilege that would greatly inform later interpretations of the constitutional privilege. Judge Shippen examined the history of British parliamentary privilege. After citing the 1700 Parliamentary Privilege Act, he concluded, "So, that before the rising of Parliament, and during the actual sitting of it, it appears, not only that, generally, a suit could not be commenced, but if it had been commenced before, it could not be prosecuted during that time."[32] He also took note of the 1703 Parliamentary Privilege Act, as well as an early edition of Blackstone's *Commentaries*.[33] He thus concluded that the British tradition favored privilege against civil suits during the sitting of the legislature and extended the same privilege to Martin.[34] Apparently, Judge Shippen was completely unaware of the 1770 Parliamentary Privilege Act, which eliminated the British privilege against being impleaded. Indeed, had Shippen consulted a more up-to-date edition of Blackstone, he would have noticed that the passage he cited in support of his view was no longer included in the work.[35] The *Martin* court was thus operating under a Blackstonian conception of privilege years after Blackstone himself had abandoned it.[36]

In an 1842 case almost identical to the 1628 *Stanhope* case discussed in the previous chapter, H. A. Wise, a Member of the House of Representatives, was arrested on a warrant charging probable cause to believe that he was about to breach the peace by fighting a duel with another member. Wise challenged the arrest on the grounds that it did not involve actual breach of the peace, and he was therefore privileged against it.[37] Although the court's reasoning is not recorded, the District of Columbia Criminal Court did not allow the privilege plea.[38] The government's argument for that result relied on the Queen's Bench's decision in *Stockdale v. Hansard* for the proposition that legislative privilege ought to be "rigidly scrutinized and kept within narrow limits."[39] The decision thus seems to be a recognition that "breach of the peace" should be read broadly, so as not to exempt Members from any criminal sanction. Indeed, as we saw in the previous chapter, breach of the peace was historically phrased as refusal to give surety for the peace, and certainly someone who intends to fight a duel can give no surety of the peace.

In 1869, Benjamin F. Butler, a Member of the House of Representatives, asserted privilege in response to an action of assumpsit. Chief Justice Chase, riding circuit, did not give the matter much thought:

> The primary intent of the clause of the constitution was exemption from civil arrest. The question before us, therefore, is the meaning of 'arrest.' If the privilege of exemption from arrest extends to exemption from summons, it extends equally to exemption from every other mode of commencing a suit. We think that the exemption is exemption from arrest with a view to imprisonment, and nothing else.[40]

In 1879, the Supreme Court for the District of Columbia faced the same question, but answered in a bit more detail. De Witt Giddings, a Member of the House of Representatives, claimed that he was privileged against service of process in an action for breach of contract.[41] The court briefly surveyed the British history discussed in the previous chapter, as well as some early American treatises.[42] Noting that the Founders would have been aware of the passage of the 1770 Parliamentary Privilege Act, the court argued: "It is impossible to believe that [the Founders] intended that the members of the Congress of the United States should have a greater extent of privilege in this matter, than belonged at that time to the Peers of Great Britain."[43] The court also noted that neither House of Congress had ever claimed that its Members were exempt from the service of civil process.[44] Finally, the court examined the *Bolton* precedent and noted that Judge Shippen had ignored the 1770 act and had worked from an outdated version of Blackstone's *Commentaries*.[45] Indeed, in a passage that, if written today, would elicit howls of outrage, the court declared that Shippen "relied upon a copy from one of the early editions of the Commentaries which he had probably studied in his youth and believed to be as unchanged and unchangeable as the Koran."[46] The court therefore held that no privilege against civil suits was appropriate.

In 1886, however, another federal circuit court held that the privilege did protect against the service of civil suits. Henry Markham, a Member of the House of Representatives from California, was on his way to a session of Congress in Washington when, to care for his sick children, he stopped at his brother's house in Milwaukee. While in Milwaukee, he was served with process in two civil suits. The court, referring to state court decisions and *Bolton*, held that

> it has been the law in this jurisdiction from territorial times that the privilege in such a case as that at bar extends to exemption from civil process, with or without actual arrest; and in the absence of more authoritative exposition of the constitutional provision from the supreme court of the United States, I shall hold that under that provision, the defendant, as a member of the congress of the United States, was entitled to exemption from service of process upon him, although it was not accompanied with an arrest of his person, provided the privilege was in force at the time of such service.[47]

The court was also faced with the question of whether Markham was "going to" Congress within the meaning of the Arrest Clause. The court's test was to inquire whether he was "in good faith on his way to the seat of government to enter upon the discharge of his public duties; that must have been the primary object of his journey."[48] Moreover, "[a] slight deviation from the usual route for rest, convenience, or because of family sickness, ought not to cause a loss of his privilege, if such deviation was but an incident to the principal journey."[49] The court thus held that Markham was privileged against the service of the civil suits.

However, the *Markham* line continued to be a minority point of view. In 1898, the Court of Appeals of the District of Columbia held that Milford Howard, a Member of the House of Representatives, was not privileged against the service of a civil suit. After a very brief survey of English and American cases,[50] the court quoted the language of the Arrest Clause itself and noted simply, "Language so plain does not leave room for interpretation. Save in certain cases mentioned [that is, treason, felony, and breach of the peace], Senators and Representatives are exempted from arrest, and nothing more."[51]

In 1908, the Supreme Court first addressed the clause. John Newton Williamson, a Member of the House of Representatives, was convicted of conspiring to suborn perjury. Williamson appealed his conviction, partly on the ground of privilege. After examining the British and American history of the phrase "treason, felony, and breach of the peace," Justice White for the Court concluded that the phrase applied to "all criminal offenses," and therefore that Williamson was not privileged against a conviction for conspiracy to suborn perjury.[52] Three decades earlier, a committee of the House of Representatives itself had come to the same conclusion.[53]

The Supreme Court returned to the Arrest Clause in 1934, this time to settle the question of whether it applied to the service of civil process. Samuel Ansell brought a libel suit against Senator Huey P. Long of Louisiana. Long moved to quash the summons on the grounds of privilege. The Court, per Justice Brandeis, cited the *Butler* case and noted, "Neither the Senate, nor the House of Representatives, has ever asserted such a claim in behalf of its members. Clause 1 defines the extent of the immunity. Its language is exact and leaves no room for a construction which would extend the privilege beyond the terms of the grant."[54] The Court concluded that, "[w]hen the Constitution was adopted, arrests in civil suits were still common in America. It is only to such arrests that the provision applies."[55] Referring to *Bolton* and similar cases, Justice Brandeis wrote that cases taking the contrary view "rest largely upon doubtful notions as to the historic privileges of members of Parliament before the enactment [of the 1770 Act]."[56] As we saw in the previous chapter, the view that, pre-1770, Members of Parliament largely enjoyed immunity from civil suits during Parliament time was not "doubtful"; however, the notion that the U.S. Constitution's Arrest Clause incorporated this immunity is not only doubtful, it is wrong.

One other case is worth noting for the manner in which the privilege was vindicated. In 1866, Charles V. Culver, a Member of the House of Representatives, was arrested on mesne process issuing from a Pennsylvania state court. A federal judge decided that Culver was not privileged. The House disagreed and passed a resolution ordering its Sergeant-at-Arms to "deliver forthwith the Hon. Charles V. Culver, a Member of this House . . . from the custody of the sheriff and jailer of [Venango County, Pennsylvania]."[57] The Sergeant did as he was ordered, and Culver was returned to his seat. Although they have rarely done so, the Houses of Congress are thus able, like the Houses of Parliament, to use their own officers to enforce their arrest privilege.

Conclusions

We have thus traced the arrest privilege from its rise in medieval England through its virtual obsolescence in both Britain and America. We have seen how it began as a right of the King not to have his council interrupted by the legal claims of mere subjects. Royal officials were the early enforcers of the privilege precisely because it was a royal privilege. It then evolved into a Blackstonian right meant to protect the House against all outsiders — the King as well as his subjects. The Houses themselves began to enforce the privilege, including enforcing it against the King in cases like *Arundel* and the Members accused of treason in 1642. However, as royal power declined and fear of an overbearing monarch was replaced with fear of a corrupt Parliament, the privilege began to take on a more Millian character. Throughout the eighteenth century, statutes gradually whittled down the privilege, until the 1770 act stripped all privilege from Members' servants and allowed the service of civil process against Members at any time. Only the civil arrest of Members remained impermissible.

It was this post-1770 Millian privilege that was written into the American Constitution in the form of the Arrest Clause. In America, as in Millian Britain, the privilege protects Members against civil arrest during legislative sessions and for a reasonable time on either side. In Britain, that time has long been set at forty days. In much larger America, it has been left undefined — in the early nineteenth century, a "reasonable" amount of time for a Maryland representative to return home might have been insufficient for a Louisiana representative.

In both Millian Britian and America, the interpretation of the arrest privilege seems to be based on a balancing between the need for the effective functioning of the judicial system and the need for effective representation of the people. When a legislator is accused of offending against the people as a whole — that is, when he is accused of committing a crime — it is sufficiently serious to justify the drastic step of arresting him and thereby rendering him unable to perform his legislative duties. Accusations of private wrongs — that is, civil suits — are important enough to merit the limited distractions of civil process but not important enough to warrant taking the legislator away from his duties entirely. Civil arrest is thus proscribed.

Of course, because civil arrest is now almost entirely a thing of the past in both Britain and America, this privilege is seldom a live issue anymore. However, its important role as one of the earliest and most strenuously contested privileges has allowed us to broaden considerably our understanding of the functions and development of privilege from its roots to the present day.

Disputed Parliamentary Elections

The history of parliamentary jurisdiction over electoral disputes follows a now familiar pattern of movement from the Blackstonian to the Millian. The House of Commons acquired the power from royal officials, then, after a while, became corrupt in its use of the power, and finally was forced to surrender much of that power. In brief, the Blackstonian model holds that the House of Commons must be the sole judge of disputed elections, on the grounds that allowing the intervention of any outside body would present a grave threat to the independence of the House and thus to the democratic element of the Constitution that it represents. The Millian model, on the other hand, sees as a greater threat the potential for corruption and self-dealing that arises when the House is allowed to be the sole judge of who has been duly elected to it. The Millian view thus seeks some outside institution that, as part of the democratic workings of the Constitution, can provide a check on the House.

The Blackstonian Paradigm

A Blackstonian view of parliamentary privilege would suggest that the House of Commons must have broad control over electoral disputes. Should royal officials, the House of Lords, or (royally appointed) judges be allowed to settle these disputes, the independence of the House of Commons would be gravely threatened. Since, as we have repeatedly seen, the Blackstonian view is highly protective of the independence of the House from any outside power, it follows that this view would not tolerate such interference.[1] And, indeed, an examination of the history of parliamentary jurisdiction over disputed elections shows that this view held for quite some time.

THE HOUSE'S EARLY ATTEMPTS TO ASSERT JURISDICTION

We first see the House of Commons taking a role in deciding disputed elections in the mid-sixteenth century. Prior to that, these controversies were decided by royal officials — a reminder that Parliament's origins are found in the King's Council, a group summoned by the King and serving as "court of law, advisory council, and exchequer all in one."[2] Because Parliament was originally summoned by the King for the purpose of helping to administer his realm, it was only reasonable that he would have final say as to its composition. Thus, for example, when Mathew de Cranthorn alleged a false return in an election in Devon in 1319, he did so in the form of a petition to the King's Council, which referred the dispute to the Court of Exchequer for resolution.[3] In 1384, Richard II and his Council themselves voided the election of Thomas Camoyes, who, as a baron, was ineligible for election to the House of Commons.[4] In 1409, the conduct of elections was placed under the jurisdiction of the justices of assize.[5] In 1413, after deciding that the election results from Rutland were "not sufficiently nor duly returned," the House of Commons "prayed the King and the Lords in Parliament, that this matter might be duly examined in Parliament." Henry IV turned the matter over to the House of Lords "to examine the said matter, and to do therein as to them should seem best in their discretions."[6]

But as the House of Commons gained in power and independence, it slowly came into its Blackstonian consciousness and began demanding jurisdiction over the election of its Members. In 1553, Alexander Nowell was returned as a Member for West Looe. Upon a challenge to his membership, the House appointed a committee to look into the matter. The committee reported back that Nowell was ineligible to sit in the House on the grounds of his "being a prebendary in Westminster and thereby having a voice in the convocation house." The House accepted the committee report, and the Speaker asked for a writ directing a new election for West Looe.[7] The West Looe election was significant, as it is the first in which the House took an active role in determining election results. And it was not long before this new role brought the House into conflict with other powers.

In the five years between the session of Parliament that met in 1575 and the session that was to meet in 1580, a number of Members had died, become seriously ill, or gone abroad in the Queen's service. The Lord Chancellor thus issued writs for the election of new Members to be chosen in time to attend the 1580 session. However, when the House met, it was moved that "divers Persons being newly returned in the Places of others, yet living, were not, or ought to be accounted, Members of this House."[8] Those who were newly returned were excused from the House while their membership was debated. Supporters of their right to sit argued that "it sufficeth to make suggestion in the Chancery, and to procure a Writ thereupon for a new Election. And to question this was to discredit the Lord Chancellor and to scandalize the Judicial Proceedings of that Court."[9] Here, then, we have what seems to be the first clash between the traditional role of royal authorities in determining disputed elections and the newly awakening Blackstonian consciousness of the House, which sought to control its own internal affairs and especially the election of its Members. After appointing a committee to look into the matter, the House readmitted those Members who were still living and voided the election of their replacements.[10] The House also issued a strong rebuke to the Lord Chancellor, in the form of a resolution stating

> [t]hat during the time of sitting of this Court, there do not at any time any Writ go out for the chusing or returning of any Knight, Citizen, Burgess, or Baron without the Warrant of this House first directed for the same to the Clerk of the Crown, according to the ancient Jurisdiction and Authority of this House in that behalf accustomed and used.[11]

Thus, the House asserted that it, and it alone, had the authority to determine whether a seat was open.

The first serious clash between the Commons' assertion of this right and the Crown's claim of jurisdiction in the same area came only six years later. In elections for a new Parliament to meet in 1586, two names were returned for Norfolk. Before the new Parliament met, the outcome of this election was protested in Chancery, and a writ for another election was issued. This second election returned one of the same names as the first election, but the second name was different.[12] When the House met, it took the Norfolk election under consideration, at which, "The Court took the alarm, and insisted that the Merits of the Election and Return were matters the House of Commons had no right or business to inquire into; and that it only belonged to the charge and office of the Lord Chancellor."[13] Indeed, Queen Elizabeth informed the House that it was "in truth impertinent" for it to consider the matter,[14] and she ordered the Lord Chancellor to look into the election returns with the aid of the judges. The House ignored the Queen's rebuke and appointed a committee to inquire into the matter. The committee declared that the first writ and return were "in matter and form perfect and duly executed," and that the second writ and return were therefore void.[15] Curiously, the committee also declared "that they understood that the Lord Chancellor and divers of the Judges, having examined the matter, were of the same opinion."[16] Nevertheless, the committee was adamant that it was "prejudicial to the privilege of the House to have the [matter] determined by others than such as were Members thereof. And though they thought very reverently of the said Lord Chancellor and Judges, and thought them competent Judges in their places; yet in this case they took them not for Judges in Parliament in this House."[17] The House accepted the committee's report, declared the first election good and the second void, and further declared,

> That it was a most perillous Precedent, that after two Knights of a County were duly Elected, any new Writ should issue out for a second Election without order of the House of Commons it self. . . .
>
> That the discussing and adjudging of this and such like differences, only belonged to the said House. . . .
>
> That though the Lord Chancellor and Judges were competent Judges in their proper Courts, yet they were not in Parliament.[18]

The Queen seems to have accepted the Commons' assertions, as the candidate returned in the first election but not the second (Thomas Farmer) took his seat in the House in 1586.[19]

GOODWYN-FORTESCUE AND ITS AFTERMATH

The precedent established by the House of Commons' victory in the 1586 Norfolk election dispute clearly played an important role in the next major election dispute, the *Goodwyn-Fortescue* controversy in 1604.[20] Sir Francis Goodwyn, who had been outlawed for personal debt, was returned as elected for the county of Buckinghamshire, but on the grounds of his outlawry, the Clerk of the Crown refused to receive the return. (King James, in his summons of Parliament, had forbidden the election of outlaws.)[21] On a second writ, Sir John Fortescue was returned. Fortescue was a Privy Councillor and held several royally appointed posts, and Wittke observes that James "seems to have had some personal interest in Fortescue's political fortunes."[22] The House of Commons thus presumably knew it was picking a fight with the Crown when it resolved that Goodwyn was the rightfully elected Member for Buckinghamshire.[23] The King referred the matter to the House of Lords, which sided with him and requested a conference with the House of Commons.[24] The Commons refused on the grounds that "it did not stand with the Honour and Order of the House, to give Account of any of their Proceedings or Doings."[25] The King then personally requested a conference, and the Commons accepted.[26] James insisted that "he had no Purpose to impeach [the House's] Privilege: But since they derived all Matters of Privilege from him, and by his Grant, he expected they should not be turned against him."[27] He claimed that disputed elections must be judged in Chancery and dismissed the 1586 Norfolk precedent on the grounds that it was decided in "the Time of a *Woman* [i.e., Queen Elizabeth], which *Sex* was not capable of *Mature Deliberation*."[28] The Commons refused to yield, and they sent to the King and House of Lords a formal petition, setting out their reasons for accepting Goodwyn as the rightfully returned Member, as well as asserting their jurisdiction over election returns.[29] Finally, the King proposed a compromise: neither Goodwyn nor Fortescue would have the Buckinghamshire seat, but instead yet another election would be held. The House assented, and a writ was issued for a new election.[30] The Commons also appointed a committee, which drew up *The Form of an Apology or Satisfaction of the House of Commons concerning their Privileges*, addressed to the King.[31] In the *Apology*, the House insisted that

> the House of Commons is the sole proper Judge of the Return of all such Writs, and of the Election of all such Members as belong unto it (without which the Freedom of Election were not entire) and that the *Chancery*, though as a standing Court under your Majesty, but to send out those Writs, and receive the Returns, and to preserve them; yet the same is done only for the Use of the Parliament, over which, neither the *Chancery*, nor any other Court ever had, or ought to have any manner of Jurisdiction.[32]

This is a striking statement — insisting that the function of a royal court was to act as a servant to a single House of Parliament. Certainly, the *Apology* is more intransigent than the compromise outcome of the *Goodwyn-Fortescue* case would seem to warrant. Indeed, commentators are divided on the question of precisely who emerged victorious from the controversy: Wittke insisted that "the struggle ended in a clear victory for the Commons,"[33] while John Glanville wrote that "the King in a manner compelled the House of Commons to yield up to him, the right of determining of the qualifications of the Members of that House."[34] Subsequent events favor Wittke's interpretation over Glanville's, but it was not immediately clear in 1604 exactly who had come out on top.

Fortunately, Glanville himself furnishes a wealth of information on electoral disputes soon after *Goodwyn-Fortescue*, in the form of his reports on cases decided by the House's Committee of Elections, of which he was the chair, in 1623 and 1624.[35] Several of these cases raise interesting issues. In one, the mayor of the borough of Winchelsey refused to allow Jonathan and Daniel

Tilden to vote, on the grounds that a local decree, passed fourteen years earlier, added a requirement that any voter must have been resident in the town for three months continuously before the election. When the Tildens attempted to vote anyway, the mayor threatened them with punishment and cast aspersions on the religious affiliation of their preferred candidate, Sir Alexander Temple. Temple and his opponent, John Finch, tied with eight votes apiece, and the mayor's vote for Finch was taken to break the tie in his favor.[36] The committee (whose report the House accepted) concluded that a local decree

> might make divers constitutions and bye-laws concerning their other affairs or government, [but] cannot alter the manner, or right, of election of barons, or burgesses, to the parliament, but is to that purpose utterly void; because, the commonwealth being interested in the freedom and consequence of such elections, the same cannot be restrained in any sort by any private ordinance whatsoever.[37]

It went on to note that the Tildens, "by the common-law of England," were entitled to vote.[38] This is important in the Blackstonian model: for the Commons to consolidate its power, it is essential that local officials not be able to interfere in the choice of its Members. The House voided the election and held the mayor in breach of privilege.[39] This decision was limited in a subsequent case, however, where the committee held that, even though a local ordinance could not disfranchise someone who came within the normal common law criteria for voting, "custom time out of mind used" could.[40] Custom, of course, would be less dangerous to the House, as it could not be immediately manipulated by local officials to control the House's membership.

The House's aim comes through even more clearly when we consider another case decided by the committee. In 1553, Queen Mary had granted a charter of incorporation to the town of Chippenham. The charter named a bailiff and twelve burgesses and said that the franchise for the town should rest with them and their descendants.[41] By 1623, this meant that a number of freemen of Chippenham who were eligible to vote under the common law were denied the franchise. They challenged the election returns before Glanville's committee, and the committee held that a royal charter could not set aside common-law rules:

> [T]he said charter of Queen Mary did not, nor could, alter the form and right of election for burgesses to the parliament, within the said borough, from the course there before, time out of mind, held. . . . [T]he charter, although it may incorporate this town, which was not incorporate before, or may alter the name, or form, of the corporation there, in matters concerning only them-

selves and their own government, rights and privileges; yet it cannot alter and abridge the general freedom and form of elections for burgesses to the parliament, wherein, as aforesaid, the commonwealth is interested.[42]

The committee went on to state that the common-law rule, which is most conducive to "the general liberty of the realm," is that "the greatest number of voices that reasonably may be had" should have the vote.[43] These three cases, combined, seem to stand for the proposition that only ancient custom (or, presumably, an act of Parliament) allows a locality to deviate from the common-law rules prescribing the franchise. The Blackstonian logic underlying that proposition seems to be that, whereas the courts, local officials, and royal officials may all present threats to the independence of the House, long-standing tradition cannot. And the committee's language about the liberty of the realm is consistent with the Blackstonian premise that the House, alone among the branches of government, speaks and acts for the people and protects their liberties. The committee also emphatically declared in the Chippenham case that it is "the antient and natural undoubted privilege and power of the said commons in parliament, *to examine the validity of elections and returns concerning their house and assembly, and to cause all undue returns, in that behalf, to be reformed; and to punish the offenders, concerning the same, according to justice.*"[44] By the early seventeenth century, then, the House was clearly unwilling to brook outside interference in its election disputes.

Half a century later, the courts, too, were recognizing the exclusive jurisdiction of the Commons over electoral disputes. In 1674, Sir Samuel Barnardiston brought suit against Sir William Soame, the sheriff of Suffolk, for having made a fraudulent double return. Barnardiston won and was awarded £800 in damages.[45] (Separately, the House of Commons came to the same conclusion and admitted Barnardiston to sit.)[46] Soame filed a motion before the King's Bench to arrest judgment, partially on the grounds that "the falsity or verity of the return is *only* examinable in the House of Commons, who are the sole judges, and will punish such falsities, and accordingly they have so done in this case, by committing the sheriff."[47] The King's Bench denied the motion, whereupon a writ of error was brought in the Exchequer Chamber.[48] The Exchequer Chamber reversed the judgment by a vote of six to two. Chief Justice North, in announcing the decision of the majority, wrote that "the parliament is the only proper judicature to determine the right of election, and to censure the behaviour of the sheriff. How then can the common law try a cause, that cannot determine of those things, without which the cause cannot be tried?"[49] Moreover, North claimed, even if the sheriff had maliciously made a fraudulent return, there was no injury done to Barnardiston, for "[t]o sit in parliament is a service in the member, for the benefit of the king and kingdom; and not for the particular profit of the member."[50] Barnardiston, then, could claim no damages. The dissenters argued that the wrongful denial of his place in the House was, indeed, an injury to Barnardiston, and that, while the House undoubtedly had jurisdiction over the outcome of elections, the awarding of damages for injuries was the business of the common-law courts.[51] On a writ of error, the House of Lords upheld the majority judgment from the Exchequer Chamber,[52] and thus upheld the principle that the House of Commons has sole jurisdiction over electoral disputes.

In two subsequent cases, the courts again declined to meddle in electoral disputes, deferring to the House of Commons. In the 1680 case of *Onslow v. Rapley*, another action for a fraudulent double return, the King's Bench held that "it would be great presumption in this Court to meddle with elections to Parliament."[53] In 1696, the Parliamentary Elections (Returns) Act gave a right of action against election officials in the Westminster courts to any parliamentary candidate aggrieved by a false or double return.[54] In *Prideaux v. Morris*,[55] however, the Queen's Bench gave a narrow interpretation to the statute. Chief Justice Holt held that no action for a false return lay "where there might be a determination in the House of Commons, because of the inconvenience of contrary resolutions."[56] However, where the House either has already determined the outcome of an election or cannot do so (for example, because of a dissolution), then an action will lie in the courts.[57] The courts, that is, must not decide an election contrary to the opinion of the House, but once there is no risk of that, they must be open to dispense justice to wronged parties. *Prideaux* thus foreshadowed Holt's opinions in the Aylesbury cases a few years later.

THE AYLESBURY CASES

The next major controversy over election jurisdiction came in the aftermath of the 1701 election in the borough of Aylesbury (the cases arising from this dispute were mentioned in the discussion of habeas corpus in chapter 1). Matthew Ashby was an inhabitant of Aylesbury and offered his vote in the election. The constables, however, refused to receive his vote, on the grounds that "in their opinions, [he was] no settled inhabitant there, nor did he ever contribute to the church or poor."[58] Ashby brought suit against the mayor and constables at the county assizes, which awarded him £5 in damages, having found that he was "duly qualified and intitled to give his vote," and that his vote "then and there of right ought to have been admitted."[59] On appeal, the Queen's Bench reversed, on the grounds that the action was not maintainable. Justice Gould stated, "This is a Parliamentary matter, and the Parliament is to judge whether the plaintiff had a right of electing or not."[60] Ashby only had injury done him if he had the right to vote, and only the House of Commons could determine whether he had the right to vote:

> [I]t may be this refusal of the plaintiff's vote may be no injury to him, according as the Parliament shall decide the matter; for they may adjudge, that he had no right to vote, whereby it will appear, the plaintiff was mistaken in his opinion as to his right of election, and consequently has sustained no injury by the defendant's denying to take his vote.[61]

Justice Powell concurred:

> The Parliament have a peculiar right to examine the due election of their members, which is to determine whether they are elected by proper electors, such as have a right to elect; for the right of voting is the great difficulty in the determination of the due election, and belongs to the Parliament to decide.[62]

Justice Powys did as well.[63] Chief Justice Holt, however, offered an eloquent dissent, in which he distinguished between the House's jurisdiction over cases questioning who may *sit* in Parliament and the courts' jurisdiction over cases questioning who may *vote* for Members of Parliament. The latter question, he insisted, was a matter of common law and thus within the purview of the common-law courts: "This right of voting is a right in the plaintiff by the common law, and consequently he shall maintain an action for the obstruction of it."[64] Indeed, the right to vote in parliamentary elections is not just any right; it is "a most transcendant thing, and of an high nature."[65] The violation of such an exalted right must be remedied,[66] yet the House can offer no remedy: the House cannot award monetary damages, and the counting of Ashby's vote would not change the outcome of the election. What, then, could the House do to make him whole?[67] Holt maintains that it is up to the courts to provide a remedy here: "This is a matter of property determinable before us. . . . [W]e do not deny [the House of Commons] their right of examining elections, but we must not be frighted when a matter of property comes before us, by saying it belongs to the Parliament; we must exert the Queen's jurisdiction."[68]

This disagreement over jurisdiction in the *Ashby* case almost perfectly illustrates the differences between the Blackstonian and Millian views of electoral disputes, with Justices Gould, Powell, and Powys representing the former and Chief Justice Holt representing the latter. For the justices in the majority, it was safeguarding the jurisdiction of the House that was most important. As Justice Powell noted, disputes over election results are often disputes over which votes count and which do not — to take the House's jurisdiction over the latter away is to diminish significantly its jurisdiction over the former. There was danger, then, in the courts' gaining too much power over the House of Commons — an especially acute danger when it is recalled that the House of Lords is the highest court of appeals. But Chief Justice Holt saw the matter altogether differently — for him, it was a matter of the fundamental right of Englishmen to vote for Members of the House of Commons. If the courts cannot protect this right, then self-dealing Members of the House can indefinitely expand their own powers at the expense of those whom they are supposed to represent. Both views envision threats to democracy, but whereas for the Blackstonians democracy is embodied by the House of Commons, which must be shielded from outside intervention, for the Millians democracy is threatened by the House of Commons, and only outside intervention can protect it.

The House of Lords, by a vote of fifty to sixteen, quickly reversed the decision of the Queen's Bench and adopted Holt's dissent.[69] The Lords echoed Holt on all of the important points. They, too, declared that Ashby had suffered damage, regardless of the fact that his vote would not have changed the outcome of the election — "his right and privilege is to give his suffrage, to be a party in the election; if he be excluded from it he is wronged, though the persons for whom he would have given his vote were elected."[70] They, too, noted that the House of Commons would be unable to provide a remedy for the wrong done to Ashby.[71] And they, too, distinguished between jurisdiction over who may sit in Parliament and jurisdiction over who may vote for Members:

> [W]ho has a right to sit in the House of Commons may be properly cognizable there; but who has a right to chuse, is a matter originally established, even before there is a parliament: a man has a right to his freehold by the common law, and the law having annexed his right of voting to his freehold, it is of the nature of his freehold, and must depend on it. The same law that gives him his right, must defend it for him.[72]

The House of Commons was furious. Numerous speeches were made arguing that the House had exclusive jurisdiction (and a few were made in defense of the Lords' decision).[73] It did not escape the attention of the House that, in Sir Humphry Mackworth's words, "If an action lies, and upon a judgment on that action a Writ of Error lies in the House of Peers, the Lords will be the sole judges at last, who have votes to chuse a House of Commons."[74] The House was presented with a five-part resolution.

> Resolved, 1. "That according to the known laws and usage of parliament, it is the sole right of the Commons of England in parliament assembled, except in cases otherwise provided for by act of parliament, to examine and determine all matters relating to the right of elections of their own members. . . .
> Resolved, 2. "That according to the known law and usage of parliament, neither the qualification of any elector, or the right of any person elected, is

cognizable or determinable elsewhere than before the Commons of England in parliament assembled, except in such cases as are specifically provided for by act of parliament.

The third resolution declared the unfairness to election officers of subjecting them to "vexatious" lawsuits and multiple jurisdictions; the fourth found Ashby in breach of privilege and contempt of Parliament; and the fifth declared that anyone who initiated such an action as Ashby's was guilty of breach and contempt.[75]

The first resolution passed unopposed. There then followed a brief but telling debate on the second resolution:

> Sir *William Strickland.* Mr. Speaker, I cannot agree to this Resolution; I think it deprives the people of England of their birthright. . . .
>
> Mr. *St. John.* I am for this, because I take it to be the greatest security for their liberty. The noble lord was pleased to take notice, that in the consequence [of allowing the common-law courts to rule in electoral disputes] the crown would have a great influence on those that are to return the members of the House of Commons; and when they were in, they might vote for one another.[76]

Here, again, we see concise encapsulations of the Blackstonian and Millian views. For Strickland — the Millian — the democratic right of the people to have their votes counted is at issue. The Blackstonian St. John also sees a threat to democracy — not the threat that the House will become too powerful at the expense of the people, but rather the threat that the House will become too weak at the hands of the royally controlled courts. Strickland sees the protection of democracy as requiring restraints on the House; St. John sees the protection of democracy as requiring restraints on other institutions' ability to interfere with the House. They are both talking about protecting democratic liberty, but they are talking past one another precisely because they are working in two very different paradigms. The House, of course, sided with the Blackstonian St. John — the remaining four resolutions passed without division.[77]

Now it was the Lords' turn to be furious. They passed a resolution insisting that the finding of breach of privilege against Ashby "is an unprecedented attempt upon the judicature of parliament, and is in effect to subject the law of England to the Votes of the House of Commons."[78] Meanwhile, soon after the House of Lords had ruled in Ashby's favor, John Paty and others filed suits similar to Ashby's, accusing the constables of Aylesbury of refusing to count their votes as well.[79] The House of Commons found Paty, his coplaintiffs, and their attorney in breach of privilege and contempt of Parliament, and ordered them imprisoned in Newgate.[80] (The Sergeant reported back to the House that his attempt to arrest Nicholas Lechmere, one of Paty's attorneys, was foiled when Lechmere "got out of his chamber in the Temple, two pair of stairs high, at the back window, by the help of his sheets and a rope.")[81] Their unsuccessful attempt to be freed on a writ of habeas corpus was discussed in chapter 1.

A series of conferences between the two Houses ensued, in which the level of acrimony continued to escalate. The Commons announced that the Lords' assertion of jurisdiction in the Ashby case threatened "the very being of an House of Commons," and they accused the Lords of attempting a power grab and plotting "to vent these new doctrines against the Commons of England, and with a design to overthrow their fundamental rights."[82] The Lords, in turn, accused the Commons of behaving like "that odious court called the Inquisition" and asserted that "[t]he most arbitrary governments cannot shew more direct instances of partiality and oppression" than the breach and contempt proceedings of the lower house.[83] The Commons, they charged, were assaulting the liberties of Englishmen.[84] This, again, seems a clear case of clashing paradigms. On the Blackstonian view, the Commons were right that giving the courts (and thereby the Lords) any power over elections was dangerous to the power of the House, and thereby to the liberties of the people. But on the Millian view, the Lords were right that the somewhat autocratic behavior by the House of Commons was a threat to the liberties of the people. The conflict ended, rather anticlimactically, with a deus ex machina: the Queen prorogued Parliament, thereby freeing those whom the Commons had imprisoned and leaving the principle unresolved.[85] The House, however, would continue to exercise jurisdiction over voting-rights cases throughout much of the eighteenth century.[86]

The Millian Paradigm

THE *WILKES* CASE

Maitland notes, "In the eighteenth century [the House of Commons' jurisdiction over disputed elections] was shamefully misused for party purposes. The question whether a member was duly returned or no became a question of confidence in the government."[87] Wittke concurs, noting the "many abuses of this privilege under George II and George III, when election disputes were time and again settled by mere party votes, regardless of the merits of the case or the expressed desires of the constituency which the candidate represented."[88] The famous *Wilkes* case of 1763–1770 is a good example of a parliamentary majority's use of its control over elections to thwart the will of the popular majority.[89] But the case's ultimate resolution also represents something of a tipping point in favor of privileging the voice of the people: the beginning of the ascent of the Millian model in determining electoral disputes can be seen in *Wilkes*.

In his newspaper the *North Briton*, no. 45, John Wilkes, an MP for Aylesbury, argued that certain statements made by the King before Parliament concerning the Peace of 1763 with Prussia were "most odious" and "most unjustifiable public declarations."[90] George III seems to have taken Wilkes's essay as a personal insult, and Lord Halifax, the King's secretary of state, issued a general warrant for the arrest and seizure of the papers of the "authors, printers and publishers of a seditious and treasonable paper, intitled, The North Briton, No 45."[91] Wilkes, among others, was arrested and had his house ransacked and his papers seized. He was committed to the Tower but applied to the King's Bench for a writ of habeas corpus. Before the court, he claimed freedom from arrest as a Member of Parliament and was freed on those grounds.[92] (The unique nature of this decision was discussed in chapter 5.) Wilkes also won trespass suits against Robert Wood (one of the men who carried out the search of his home) and Lord Halifax, on the grounds that the general warrant was illegal.[93] Both Houses of Parliament soon resolved, "That the Privilege of Parliament doth not extend to the case of writing and publishing Seditious Libels."[94] The House of Lords seized upon two of Wilkes's other publications — his *Essay on Woman* (an obscene parody of Pope's *Essay on Man*) and his *Veni Creator Paraphrased*. Wilkes had attached the name of Bishop Warburton, a Member of the House of Lords and an editor of Pope's *Works*, to the notes accompanying the *Essay on Woman*.[95] The bishop was not amused, and his colleagues were delighted to have presented to them a ready-made opportunity to go after Wilkes. The Lords declared Wilkes guilty of a breach of privilege and ordered him into Black Rod's custody.[96]

Wilkes was by now a cause célèbre among many members of the British public, for whom "Wilkes and Liberty!" became a rallying cry.[97] But the *North Briton*, no. 45, also brought him a different kind of fame: he was challenged to a duel by a fellow MP whom he had maligned in the work. After being injured, Wilkes fled to Paris.[98] While he was in France, the House of Commons ordered him to attend upon it. When he did not, he was voted guilty of contempt, declared guilty of libel over the *North Briton*, no. 45, and expelled from the House.[99] His expulsion, if anything, made him more popular. As Burke put it,

> I will not believe, what no other man living believes, that Mr. Wilkes was punished for the indecency of his publications, or the impiety of his ransacked closet. . . . I must conclude that Mr. Wilkes is the object of persecution. . . . That he is pursued for the spirited dispositions which are blended with his vices; for his unconquerable firmness, for his resolute, indefatigable, strenuous resistance against oppression.[100]

While he was abroad, Wilkes also lost two libel suits before the King's Bench.[101] When he failed to come to court five times, he was outlawed for his refusal to appear for judgment.[102] He returned to Britain in 1768 and surrendered to his outlawries, which were subsequently reversed on a technicality of wording.[103] The reversal of his outlawry revived the two outstanding libel judgments against him, and he was sentenced to twenty-two months in prison and fined £1,000.[104] The House of Lords affirmed the judgment.[105] In 1768, Wilkes also stood as a candidate for Parliament, despite his imprisonment. He lost in the election for London but won for Middlesex. The House of Commons declared him ineligible for membership and refused to allow him to take his seat.[106] A writ issued for a new election in Middlesex, and Wilkes was returned again, unanimously.[107] The procedure was repeated a third time, with the same (unanimous) result.[108] And again, although this fourth election was not unanimous. This time, the House simply declared his opponent the new Member for Middlesex, despite his having received only 296 votes to Wilkes's 1,143.[109] Here, as Wittke put it, was a case in which "the House of Commons, out of sheer vindictiveness, created a disability hitherto unknown to the law. Furthermore, by expelling Wilkes and barring him from membership, the Commons were interfering with the franchise rights and the rights of representation, guaranteed by law, to the voters of Middlesex."[110] Burke warned that

> [w]hen this submission is urged to us [although himself an MP, Burke used "us" to refer to his fellow subjects], in a contest between the representatives and ourselves, and where nothing can be put into their scale which is not taken from ours, they fancy us to be children when they tell us they are our representatives, our own flesh and blood, and that all the stripes they give us are for our own good. . . . They certainly will abuse it; because all men possessed of an uncontrolled power leading to the aggrandizement and profit of their own body have always abused it.[111]

It was a supremely Millian warning, and Burke did not shy away from explicitly stating this principle: "The House of Commons can never be a control on other parts of government, unless they are controlled themselves by their constituents; and unless these constituents possess some right in the choice of that House, which it is not in the power of that House to take away."[112] Wilkes himself understood the issue in the same way. As he later told the House,

> If you can reject those disagreeable to a majority, and expel whom you please, the House of Commons will be self-created and self-existing. You may expel till you approve, and thus in effect you nominate. The original idea of this House being the representative of the Commons of the realm will be lost. . . .

> By such manœuvres a minister may garble a House of Commons till not a single enemy of his own, or friend of his country, is left here, and the representation of the people in a great deal annihilated. . . . My expulsion was an easy victory over liberty and the constitution.[113]

Over "liberty and the constitution" understood in Millian terms, that is.

But Wilkes was nothing if not stubborn: he kept standing for election, and he kept winning. With the House having been co-opted by those sympathetic to the King, the people remained staunch in their support for Wilkes. In essence, having seen the corruption into which Blackstonian principles had allowed the House to fall, the people, with Wilkes as their champion, were demanding that their voice be respected. They were demanding movement toward Millian principles. Finally, in 1774, they won. Sixty thousand people had petitioned the Crown on Wilkes's behalf.[114] When he was again returned unopposed for Middlesex (and had been elected Lord Mayor of London), the House finally admitted him.[115] Eight years later, he succeeded in having all records of his case expunged from the House of Commons' journal "as being subversive of the rights of the whole body of electors of this kingdom."[116]

It should come as no surprise that Blackstone sided with the House and against Wilkes. He wrote,

> It is not only evident from precedents, that the house have a power of expulsion, but it is clear from the reason of the thing that they ought to have such a power. Otherwise the most unworthy and unfit representatives may sit in parliament, to the disgrace and detriment of the nation. Since it is not pretended that any such power is, or can be, lodged any where else. . . . [I]t would expose the judicature of the house of commons to the most flagrant insult and contempt; it would render the determination of the house of commons, totally nugatory, if the member whom they expelled to-day, should be forced upon them again to-morrow.[117]

Note that the voter is almost entirely absent from Blackstone's formulation, except as a sinister outside agent who might "force" an "unworthy and unfit" Member upon the House. There is no sense that the way to get rid of such unworthies is through the ballot. But by the end of the *Wilkes* controversy, those advocating a Blackstonian position were balanced by those advocating a Millian one, and the outcome of the controversy — Wilkes's eventual admission to the House and the expunging of his case from the journals — suggests that the Millian side was ascendant.

LEGISLATION AND THE COURTS

The subsequent history of the transition from Blackstonian to Millian came in the form of legislation, and it can be recounted briefly. The first statute addressing electoral jurisdiction was the 1770 Controverted Elections Act,[118] which turned jurisdiction over electoral disputes over to a fifteen-member committee of the House of Commons. The act specified a long and convoluted manner of choosing the fifteen members, which was supposed to ensure some level of impartiality. It was followed, almost a century later, by the Parliamentary Elections Act,[119] which gave jurisdiction over electoral disputes to the Court of Common Pleas (although the judges were to be drawn from all of the common-law courts). The Parliamentary Elections and Corrupt Practices Act of 1879 modified the procedure slightly, by requiring that cases of disputed elections be heard by two judges rather than one, but otherwise left it intact.[120]

It is worth examining a few of the cases that have arisen under this statutory regime in order to compare it with the old system of parliamentary jurisdiction. The Parliamentary Elections Act specified that,

> Until Rules of Court have been made in pursuance of this Act, and so far as such Rules do not extend, the Principles, Practice, and Rules on which Committees of the House of Commons have heretofore acted in dealing with Election Petitions shall be observed so far as may be by the Court and Judge in the Case of Election Petitions under this Act.[121]

This rule seems well suited to preserving the pragmatic political character of election-dispute resolution, but the question remains how well suited the courts are to exercising this role. The cases suggest that they have often, but not always, exercised it well. In an 1869 case arising out of the elections for the Borough of Tamworth, Justice Willes was called upon to determine whether the employment of a number of voters by an agent of one of the candidates constituted bribery and whether that agent had impermissibly sought to interfere with the election by causing "general drunkenness" amongst the voters.[122] After attempting to divine what he could of the agent's motives for hiring the voters, Justice Willes concluded that it did not constitute bribery; moreover, he held that the alcohol was provided to voters too far before the election effectively to cause general drunkenness for the election. He thus upheld the election result.

An 1874 case from the Borough of Bolton, however, suggested the primary pitfall of giving jurisdiction over electoral disputes to the courts: the legal rules constraining courts often leave them with too little freedom of action. The 1872 Ballot Act had required secret balloting, and Justice Mellor concluded that "a deliberate violation of the provision with regard to secrecy was attempted to be effected" in Bolton.[123] However, the act allowed only for the punishment of offenders; it did not allow for election results to be voided. Justice Mellor wrote that "[t]he punishment is specified by the Legislature; it must be found within the four corners of the Act of Parliament, and I have no power, neither has the common law any power, to supplement any additional penalty upon either the persons who transgressed the law or the persons for whose sake or in whose favour such an act may have been done."[124] This case suggests that the Millian granting of election jurisdiction to the courts was not an unqualified good — whereas a House of Parliament would have been able to exercise the discretion to void the election and order a new one in Bolton, the court was unable to do so. Still, in most cases, the courts had sufficient discretion effectively to adjudicate election disputes, voiding elections where improprieties or irregularities affected the outcome and upholding the election results where they did not.[125]

In 1964, the Queen's Bench Division was faced with an election dispute based on qualifications. Upon the death of his father in 1960, Tony Benn, an MP, became Viscount of Stansgate. In 1961, the House of Commons resolved that he had ceased to be a Member, by virtue of his peerage. Nevertheless, Benn stood in the by-election and received the highest number of votes. During the election campaign, his opponent sent notices to all voters in the district saying that Benn was ineligible to serve; these notices had also been published in the newspapers and posted at the entrance to the polling stations. After the election, Benn's opponent filed an election petition.[126] The court held that the fact that Benn had neither applied for nor received a summons to attend the House of Lords was immaterial — he was still ineligible to serve in the Commons. Moreover, the fact that the disqualification was made known to the voters meant that those who had voted for Benn had intentionally spoiled their vote. Hence, their votes were thrown out, and Benn's opponent was seated. This seems an unfortunate ruling — surely, there ought to be a strong presumption that more than 23,000 people did not intentionally spoil their votes. While a literal reading of the law may require that votes be considered spoiled if the ineligibility of the candidate was known to the voters, a pragmatic, Millian concern for the accurate representation of the people would militate strongly in favor of holding a new election.

In the 1997 election for Winchester, the returns showed Mark Oaten, the Liberal Democrat candidate, winning by just two votes over Gerry Malone, the Conservative candidate and incumbent. Malone filed an election petition on the grounds that fifty-five unstamped ballots had not been counted, and those would have given him a two-vote lead. The High Court agreed and ordered a new election, which Oaten won by 21,566 votes.[127] This seems the proper Millian outcome — after all, if effectuating the will of the voters is paramount, then an election in which there is legitimate and substantial uncertainty about the winner should be returned to the voters. Here, they decisively made their choice known the second time around.

In 1999, Fiona Jones, an MP, was convicted of knowingly making a false declaration about election expenditures, an offense that made her ineligible to sit in Parliament. Her seat was therefore declared vacant. However, before a by-election could be held, her conviction was quashed on appeal. The House then petitioned the Queen's Bench Division for a declaration that she was entitled to return to her seat.[128] The court granted the petition, which seems the appropriate decision—after all, if Jones was not guilty of an offense, then she was still her constituents' choice to represent them and should have been allowed to continue doing so.

It should also be noted that issues surrounding the qualifications of returned Members are still cognizable in the House itself. As we saw in chapter 1, the courts refused to intervene in the *Bradlaugh* controversy of the 1880s. As an atheist, Bradlaugh was not allowed to take the oath of office and therefore not allowed to take his seat. The courts held that the House alone could judge Bradlaugh's qualifications to sit.[129] In recent years, Sinn Fein Members have refused to take the oath of allegiance to the Queen and have thus been denied a seat in Parliament. In 2002, they were granted access to House facilities, office space, and office expenses, but not salaries.[130] The four Sinn Fein Members who have been elected to Parliament still have not taken the oath and therefore have not voted or participated from the floor. Disputes surrounding election returns themselves, however, are now wholly handled by the courts.

Conclusions

The ultimate outcome of the courts' assumption of jurisdiction over electoral disputes was the completion of the paradigm shift in jurisdiction over these cases from Blackstonian to Millian. With legislation putting the final determination of disputed elections in the hands of the courts, an outside check was imposed on possible self-dealing by the House of Commons. With the courts no longer perceived as a threat to democracy but rather as part of the functioning of a democratic system, giving them jurisdiction over disputed elections was seen as a way of tightening the nexus between the will of the people and the decisions of the House of Commons and thereby avoiding future *Wilkes*-type controversies. But, as we have seen, in some cases, courts are unable to exercise the sort of political pragmatic judgment that is often called for in determining election disputes.

As we shall see in the next chapter, giving the courts this power is a step that cannot be taken in America without an amendment to the Constitution. We shall also consider more fully the tradeoffs discussed above and offer some thoughts as to whether the Millian British position or the American one is preferable in a modern liberal democracy.

8

Disputed Congressional Elections

Judging election disputes and controversies over the qualifications of its Members is one of the privileges of each House of Congress, just as it was long one of the privileges of the House of Commons. By examining the shape and scope of this privilege, we shall better understand the role of the Houses of Congress within the American constitutional system of popular sovereignty. We shall also be able to see whether there are any reasons why the Constitution should not be amended to turn this role over to the courts, as the British have done.

Text and History

As noted in chapter 2, the provision of the Constitution making each House of Congress the "Judge of the Elections, Returns and Qualifications of its own Members" was almost entirely uncontroversial at the Founding.[1] But how were those elections to be judged, and what qualifications were necessary? A number of constitutional provisions speak to these questions. First, as to the question of who the electors are, the Constitution provides that "[t]he House of Representatives shall be composed of Members chosen every second Year by the People of the several States, and the Electors in each State shall have the Qualifications requisite for Electors of the most numerous Branch of the State Legislature."[2] Some of the Philadelphia Convention's leading lights were adamant about popular election of the lower house. Against arguments by Roger Sherman and Elbridge Gerry that Members of the House should be appointed by state legislatures, James Madison called popular election "essential to every plan of free Government."[3] James Wilson said that he was "for raising the federal pyramid to a considerable altitude, and for that reason wished to give it as broad a basis as possible."[4] Madison added that "the great fabric to be raised would be more stable and durable if it should rest on the solid foundation of the people themselves, than if it should stand merely on the pillars of the [state] Legislatures."[5] Against Gouverneur Morris and others who wanted to add a freehold requirement for House electors, Oliver Ellsworth replied that, "The people will not readily subscribe to the Natl. Constitution, if it should subject them to be disfranchised."[6] Pierce Butler concurred, noting that "[t]here is no right of which the people are more jealous than that of suffrage."[7] Perhaps decisive on the point was the venerated Benjamin Franklin's statement, "It is of great consequence that we shd. not depress the virtue & public spirit of our common people; of which they displayed a great deal during the war, and which contributed principally to the favorable issue of it."[8] Soon afterward, the Convention voted overwhelmingly against Morris's proposal to restrict the suffrage.[9] The next day, the clause making the House popularly elected and setting the qualifications for the electors the same as those for the most numerous branch of the state legislature was passed unanimously by the Convention.[10] A related clause, giving state executives the authority to issue writs of election to fill any House vacancies that might occur, passed unanimously and without debate.[11] Looking back with evident pride, Madison, writing as Publius, would ask, "Who are to be the electors of the federal representatives? Not the rich, more than the poor; not the learned, more than the ignorant; not the haughty heirs of distinguished names, more than the humble sons of obscure and unpropitious fortune. The electors are to be the great body of the people of the United States."[12] And a federalist pamphleteer, writing under the pseudonym "Plain Truth," made explicit the popular-sovereignty foundation of direct election of representatives: "It is more a government *of the people*, than the present [Confederation] Congress ever was, because, the members of Congress have been hitherto chosen by the legislatures of the several states. The proposed representatives are to be chosen 'BY THE PEOPLE.' If therefore it be not a confederation of *the states*, it is a popular compact, something more in favour of liberty."[13]

As for the Senate, the Constitution originally provided that "[t]he Senate of the United States shall be composed of two Senators from each State, chosen by the Legislature thereof, for six Years; and each Senator shall have one

Vote."[14] This clause was debated at great length. James Wilson wanted the Senate, too, to be chosen by direct election.[15] Edmund Randolph noted that the upper house "ought to be much smaller" than the lower one.[16] Rufus King pointed out that the upper house would either have to be "very numerous, or *the idea of proportion* among the States was to be disregarded."[17] Madison made it clear that he regarded any departure from the principle of proportionality to be "inadmissible, being evidently unjust."[18] The Convention reached agreement first on who was to elect the senators, voting overwhelmingly to give that job to state legislatures.[19] The Convention then agreed to a proposal by Hamilton and Wilson to make representation in the Senate "according to the same rule as in" the House[20] — that is, proportionality. But the taking of votes did not end debate on these issues. Wilson kept insisting that senators should be popularly elected, and Ellsworth, among others, continued to agitate for equal representation in the Senate.[21] Wilson, who strenuously opposed Ellsworth's proposal,[22] was to lose on both points. Realizing that the entire convention would never come to agreement on the issue of how senators were to be apportioned, the Convention decided to pass the buck to a committee.[23] The committee reported back in favor of equal representation for each state, and, after more debate, the Convention concurred.[24] Naturally, under this scheme, the legislature was empowered to fill any vacancy that arose, and if a vacancy occurred during a legislative recess, "the Executive [of the state] may make temporary Appointments until the next Meeting of the Legislature, which shall then fill such Vacancies."[25] (Wilson objected that giving the state executive this power "removes the appointment too far from the people" and is, in any case, unnecessary because "the Legislatures will meet so frequently," but he was substantially out-voted.)[26]

Equal representation for each state remains the rule in the Senate today, but the Seventeenth Amendment altered the other contentious decision: "The Senate of the United States shall be composed of two Senators from each State, elected by the people thereof, for six years; and each Senator shall have one vote. The electors in each State shall have the qualifications requisite for electors of the most numerous branch of the State legislatures."[27] The provision for filling vacancies, too, was amended: "When vacancies happen in the representation of any State in the Senate, the executive authority of such State shall issue writs of election to fill such vacancies: *Provided*, that the legislature of any State may empower the executive thereof to make temporary appointments until the people fill the vacancies by election as the legislature may direct."[28]

It is worth pausing briefly here to note what may seem a linguistic oddity in the clauses discussed above. In both Article I and the Seventeenth Amendment, it is explicitly stated that "each Senator shall have one Vote," yet it was seen as unnecessary to state that each representative would have one vote. To understand this, it must be recalled that the Constitution was being drafted against the background of the Articles of Confederation, which created a "confederacy," "a firm league of friendship," in which "sovereignty"—a word never used in the Constitution—was retained by each state.[29] Under the Articles, each state legislature could appoint anywhere between two and seven delegates to represent that state in the unicameral national Congress, but when it came time to vote, "each state shall have one vote."[30] Moreover, each state had the power, at any time, "to recal its delegates, or any of them, at any time within the year, and to send others in their stead, for the remainder of the Year."[31] Much like the General Assembly of the modern United Nations—which allows each member state to send up to five representatives but gives each state only one vote[32]—the Articles created something more akin to an international treaty regime than a nation. Because the proposed Senate was most reminiscent of the Confederation Congress—with equal representation for each state and election by state legislatures—the Framers felt the need to emphasize the difference. Indeed, a few of the Framers wanted the Senate to be more like the Confederation Congress. Luther Martin "was opposed to voting per Capita, as departing from the idea of the *States* being represented in the 2d. branch."[33] Martin was, however, significantly out-voted on the question.[34] He was right, though, that this was a departure from the Confederation idea that the states were to be represented—a departure with which Jefferson pronounced himself "much pleased."[35] Because senators were members of a *national* legislature, and not simply representatives of sovereign states at an international congress, they were to vote based on their own judgment. They could not be recalled,[36] nor did their state have control over their salary. And they were to vote as individuals, not as members of a delegation. Indeed, the Constitution went one step further to prevent states from exercising undue control over their Members of Congress, by providing that "[t]he Times, Places and Manner of holding Elections for Senators and Representatives, shall be prescribed in each State by the Legislature thereof; but the Congress may at any time by Law make or alter such Regulations, except as to the Places of chusing Senators."[37] South Carolinians Charles Pinckney and John Rutledge objected to the power given to Congress, but after responses from Nathaniel Gorham, James Madison, Rufus King, and Gouverneur Morris pointing out the abuses that state legislatures could perpetrate were Congress not given this power, the Convention agreed to it.[38] This power proved highly contentious in the ratification debates.[39]

The Constitution also has quite a bit to say about who is eligible to serve in

Congress. "No Person shall be a Representative who shall not have attained to the Age of twenty five Years, and been seven Years a Citizen of the United States, and who shall not, when elected, be an Inhabitant of that State in which he shall be chosen."[40] Similarly, "No Person shall be a Senator who shall not have attained to the Age of thirty Years, and been nine Years a Citizen of the United States, and who shall not, when elected, be an Inhabitant of that State for which he shall be chosen."[41] George Mason, who first proposed an age qualification for the House of Representatives, "thought it absurd that a man to day should not be permitted by the law to make a bargain for himself, and tomorrow should be authorized to manage the affairs of a great nation."[42] He wryly added, "It had been said that Congs. had proved a good school for our young men. It might be so for any thing he knew but if it were, he chose that they should bear the expence of their own education."[43] After that, the age qualification was agreed to without significant debate (as the similar qualification for the Senate had already been).[44] The original citizenship requirements reported to the Convention were for three years in the House and four in the Senate.[45] Mason, again, wanted a higher bar, arguing, "It might . . . happen that a rich foreign Nation, for example Great Britain, might send over her tools who might bribe their way into the Legislature for insidious purposes."[46] He therefore proposed a citizenship requirement of seven years for the House, which the Convention accepted.[47] Shortly thereafter, Morris proposed increasing the Senate citizenship requirement to fourteen years.[48] Pinckney supported him on the grounds that, "[a]s the Senate is to have the power of making treaties & managing our foreign affairs, there is peculiar danger and impropriety in opening its door to those who have foreign attachments."[49] Mason "highly approved," and toyed with the notion of limiting membership in the Senate to "natives."[50] But Morris and Pinckney were ably opposed on this question. Madison, saying that such a long citizenship requirement would "give a tincture of illiberality to the Constitution," added that it would "discourage the most desirable class of people from emigrating to the U.S."[51] Franklin, echoing his earlier arguments against restricting the franchise, noted, "We found in the Course of the Revolution, that many strangers served us faithfully — and that many natives took part agst. their Country."[52] The Scottish-born James Wilson injected a personal note, pointing out that "if the ideas of some gentlemen should be pursued," he would be unable to serve "under the very Constitution which he shared in the trust of making."[53] Still, the citizenship requirement for the Senate could not be left at four years when the requirement for the House had already been raised to seven. After voting down proposals for fourteen, thirteen, and ten years, the Convention settled on nine.[54] The Convention later returned to the citizenship requirement for the

House, with Elbridge Gerry echoing Mason's earlier concern: "Foreign powers will intermeddle in our affairs, and spare no expence to influence them. Persons having foreign attachments will be sent among us & insinuated into our councils, in order to be made instruments for their purposes."[55] But all of the proposed alternatives were voted down, and seven years stood.[56] Except for some debate as to whether "resident" or "inhabitant" was clearer, the inhabitance requirements for both houses were largely uncontroversial.[57] Mason was likely speaking for everyone present when he noted, "If residence be not required, Rich men of neighboring States, may employ with success the means of corruption in some particular district and thereby get into the public Councils after having failed in their own State. This is the practice in the boroughs of England."[58]

Most controversial, however, was a provision that did not make it into the Constitution: property requirements for membership in Congress. Following up on Mason's suggestion for a property requirement for senators, the draft reported by the Committee of Detail to the Convention contained a provision reading, "The Legislature of the United States shall have authority to establish such uniform qualifications of the members of each House, with regard to property, as to the said Legislature shall seem expedient."[59] Pinckney led off the debate on this proposal by noting that "he thought it essential that the members of the Legislature, the Executive, and the Judges — should be possessed of competent property to make them independent & respectable."[60] He proposed writing actual property requirements into the Constitution, but this proposal was resoundingly rejected.[61] Ellsworth pointed to the practical difficulty of establishing any sort of uniform property requirement: "The different circumstances of different parts of the U.S. and the probable difference between the present and future circumstances of the whole, render it improper to have either *uniform* or *fixed* qualifications."[62] Franklin, noting that "[s]ome of the greatest rogues he was ever acquainted with, were the richest rogues," added, "This Constitution will be much read and attended to in Europe, and if it should betray a great partiality to the rich — will not only hurt us in the esteem of the most liberal and enlightened men there, but discourage the common people from removing to this Country."[63] Madison spoke next:

> The qualifications of electors and elected were fundamental articles in a Republican Govt. and ought to be fixed by the Constitution. If the Legislature could regulate those of either, it can by degrees subvert the Constitution. A Republic may be converted into an aristocracy or oligarchy as well by limiting the number capable of being elected, as the number authorised to elect. In all cases where the representatives of the people will have a personal interest distinct from that of their Constituents, there was the same reason for being

jealous of them, as there was for relying on them with full confidence, when they had a common interest. This was one of the former cases. It was as improper as to allow them to fix their own wages, or their own privileges.[64]

A few minutes later, Madison added that "the British Parliamt. possessed the power of regulating the qualifications both of the electors, and the elected; and the abuse they had made of it was a lesson worthy of our attention."[65] He almost certainly had the *Wilkes* case in mind, and probably the *Ashby* case as well. The provision was voted down,[66] and no mention of property qualifications found their way into the Constitution. Mirroring his comments about the expansiveness of the American electorate, Madison wrote of the House of Representatives that, "[u]nder these reasonable limitations, the door of this part of the federal government is open to merit of every description, whether native or adoptive, whether young or old, and without regard to poverty or wealth, or to any particular profession of religious faith."[67]

In addition to the qualifications that did make it in, there are four specific *dis*qualifications listed in the document.[68] First, "No Senator or Representative shall, during the Time for which he was elected, be appointed to any civil Office under the Authority of the United States, which shall have been created, or the Emoluments whereof shall have been encreased during such time; and no Person holding any Office under the United States, shall be a Member of either House during his Continuance in Office."[69] Second, the federal government is tasked with guaranteeing "to every State in this Union a Republican Form of Government";[70] a state without a republican form of government would be ineligible to send Members to Congress. Third, Members of Congress "shall be bound by Oath or Affirmation, to support this Constitution"[71] — failure to take the oath would disqualify someone for membership. Finally, in the aftermath of the Civil War, the Constitution was amended to state that anyone "who, having previously taken an oath, as a member of Congress, or as an officer of the United States, or as a member of any State legislature, or as an executive or judicial officer of any State, to support the Constitution of the United States, shall have engaged in insurrection or rebellion against the same, or given aid or comfort to the enemies thereof" is ineligible, although "Congress may by a vote of two-thirds of each House, remove such disability."[72]

Interpretation

So what do all these constitutional provisions mean for the determination of cases of disputed elections and qualifications in the Houses of Congress? We shall see in some detail as we go through disputed election cases from both Houses, but first it will be useful to consider briefly three broad issues surrounding disputed congressional elections and qualifications. Those issues are: (1) the demands of a democratic system, (2) the question of whether the qualifications and disqualifications for Members of Congress listed in the Constitution are exhaustive, and (3) questions of procedure in deciding disputed elections or qualifications. As we examine these issues, it is important to remember that, as we saw in chapter 2, these questions are nonjusticiable: our conclusions here may be the best interpretation of legally binding restraints on Congress, but the courts cannot force Congress to follow the law in this area.

First, there is the broadest issue: democracy. The House and Senate were meant to be the components of a national democratic legislature. As we have seen, the Founders were particularly proud of (and adamant about) the popular election of the House of Representatives. In his famous 1791 Lectures on Law, Wilson argued that "free and equal elections" are the "original fountain, from which all the streams of administration flow. If this fountain is poisoned, the deleterious influence will extend to the remotest corners of the state: if this fountain continues pure and salubrious, the benign operation of its waters will diffuse universal health and soundness."[73] For the elections truly to be free and equal, suffrage had to be wide:

> The correct theory and the true principles of liberty require, that every citizen, whose circumstances do not render him necessarily dependent on the will of another, should possess a vote in electing those, by whose conduct his property, his reputation, his liberty, and his life, may be all most materially affected.[74]

By making anyone eligible to vote for the lower house of his state legislature eligible to vote for the House of Representatives, the Founders ensured that a high percentage of white males would have the vote. After the Founding, the internal logic of popular sovereignty in the federal Constitution led states to loosen their suffrage requirements until Tocqueville could observe that "all the states of the Union have adopted universal [white male] suffrage."[75]

What about the Senate? First, it is worth noting that, as we have seen, the Constitution requires each state to have a "Republican Form of Government." Senators were to be elected by republican state legislatures — at least one branch of which operated under the same suffrage rules that were in effect for the election of federal Representatives. Tocqueville observed that

> [t]he senators . . . do represent the result, albeit the indirect result, of universal suffrage, for the legislature which appoints the senators is no aristocratic or privileged body deriving its electoral right from itself; it essentially depends on the totality of citizens; it is generally annually elected by them, and they can always control its choice by giving it new members.[76]

Here, too, the post-Founding history is one of increasing populism, with a number of states adopting rules in the late nineteenth and early twentieth centuries whereby the people of the state voted for their senators in a referendum, the result of which was binding on the state legislature.[77] And, of course, in 1913, the Seventeenth Amendment changed the suffrage rules, making them the same as those for the House. The lesson to be drawn from the populist ideals of the Founding and the increasing populism in practice throughout American history is that "[i]nherent in this nation's fundamental commitment to a democratic and representative system of government is the right of the electors in each district to choose the individuals who are to represent them in the Congress."[78] Arrangements designed to flaunt or sidestep this right ought therefore to be viewed with deep suspicion.

Of course, there is a tension between this principle of democracy and the existence of *any* qualifications for representatives whatsoever. After all, if the voters have the right to be represented by whomever they choose, how can we justify excluding twenty year olds? But the three requirements — age, citizenship, and residency — spelled out in the Constitution make a great deal of sense once we recall the Founders' fear that their republic would become an aristocracy, that "the haughty heirs of distinguished names"[79] would entrench themselves in power. After all, who but the scion of a great family would have a districtwide reputation before his twenty-fifth birthday, or a statewide reputation before his thirtieth? What noninhabitant of a state or district would that state or district send to Congress, if not those "Rich men of neighboring States, . . . employ[ing] with success the means of corruption in some particular district,"[80] which Mason had feared and all of the Founders had seen in Britain? And were Mason and Gerry wholly wrong to suspect that immigrants secretly working for their native lands might bribe their way into Congress if a certain period of citizenship were not required for eligibility? The disqualifications serve similar purposes. The provision preventing Members of Congress from accepting during the time for which they were elected executive or judicial positions which were created or made more lucrative during that time, as well as the provision preventing anyone from simultaneously holding a position in the legislature and one of the other two branches, prevent legislators from corruptly enriching themselves by striking deals for appointment to offices. The disqualification of Members from states without republican governments ensures that a coup or revolt in one state cannot threaten the national councils. And the requirement of an oath — and the Fourteenth Amendment's subsequent disqualification of anyone who dishonors his oath — serves again to prevent the hijacking of the national legislature by traitors in a few states.

These requirements all make good republican sense, and, as we have seen, they were much debated. We have also seen that property qualifications were much debated — and rejected. And one of the rejected proposals was to give Congress the power to establish property qualifications. The implication is clear. In Hamilton's words (writing as Publius), the qualifications for membership "are defined and fixed in the Constitution, and are unalterable by the legislature."[81] Subsequent history suggests the same reading: "At least four constitutional amendments have been proposed which would add to the qualifications specified in the Constitution. Clearly if Congress already had the power to set its own qualifications, there would be little reason to attempt to amend the Constitution."[82] P. Allan Dionisopoulos argues to the contrary, but his arguments are unpersuasive. He claims that the clause forbidding any United States official from accepting "any present, Emolument, Office, or Title, of any kind whatever, from any King, Prince, or foreign State" without the "Consent of the Congress" and the clause giving Congress the "Power to declare the Punishment of Treason" serve as constitutional "sources of statutorily-defined disqualifications."[83] His argument is that both of these clauses give Congress a power of punishment (the former does so implicitly, the latter explicitly) and that disqualification to serve in Congress is a penalty; therefore, Congress may prescribe it.[84] This seems to rest on an obvious fallacy — the power to prescribe *a* punishment is not the power to prescribe *any* punishment. Clearly, Congress could not prescribe a "cruel and unusual" punishment,[85] for example. And Dionisopoulos gives us no independent reason to think that disqualification from Congress was one of the punishments meant to be available under these clauses.[86]

Structural considerations, however, strongly suggest that qualifications and disqualifications *should* be limited to those laid out in the Constitution. First, as noted above, these provisions were heavily debated and are consonant with republican thought. Other provisions, further limiting eligibility, would have to meet the same high bar of justification, in order to overcome the presumption in favor of letting the people choose whomever they like to represent them. The process of constitutional amendment, not ordinary lawmaking, is best situated to ensure that such a high bar is indeed overcome. Second, the Constitution provides that either House may expel Members by a two-thirds vote.[87] The expulsion power — which will be discussed in detail in chapter 10 — contains no specific criteria limiting its use, but it does require a supermajority, which makes it highly unlikely that it will ever be used in a partisan manner.[88] In the unlikely event, per Dionisopoulos, that an otherwise eligible person who had been convicted of treason was elected to Congress, he could be expelled immediately. But *excluding* a Member from Congress requires only a majority vote. If this could be done for reasons other than those specified in the Constitution, then the protection afforded by the supermajority requirement for expulsion would be easily evaded.[89] The Supreme Court agrees: the power of exclusion may be exercised only in judgment of those qualifications and disqualifications in the Constitution itself.[90]

Finally, there are a host of procedural questions surrounding congressional resolution of election or qualification disputes. The judging of elections or qualifications involves a mixture of law and politics, much as the judging of impeachments does. Legislative bodies considering these disputes should not be bound by all the rules of legal procedure — they should be able to take into account political practicalities that judges cannot. For example, even without evidence of specific cases of fraud or intimidation, a legislative body might find it suspicious that a certain district which, in the previous election, had ten thousand voters, eight thousand of whom voted for party A, suddenly now has only one thousand voters, nine hundred of whom voted for party B. The body might inquire into other possible explanations for this change, but if it does not find any other plausible explanations, it could conclude that significant fraud and/or intimidation has taken place, and it could invalidate the election on those grounds. It is unlikely that a judge could do the same absent specific evidence of illegal acts. While it is desirable that the Houses of Congress are not bound by technical legal procedures, it is also desirable that the procedures that the legislature does adopt are impartial and probative. It seems reasonable that these procedures ought to include the right for all parties to the dispute to be heard, to have assistance of counsel, to subpoena witnesses, to cross-examine witnesses, to be provided a written statement of any accusations against them, and to be furnished with written transcripts of all hearings.[91] Members of Congress sitting in judgment should make a bona fide effort to clear their minds both of partisan loyalty and of any personal relationship with the parties to the dispute.[92] Additionally, in close cases, the presumption should generally be in favor of vacating the election — that is, sending it back to the voters so that they can clarify their choice.

Indeed, Congress has made several attempts to codify in statute its procedures for judging disputed elections or qualifications. A 1798 law allowed parties to such a contest in the House of Representatives to subpoena witnesses to testify under oath, required the notification of the opposite party, and required transcripts to be taken of all testimony.[93] That law was set to expire automatically in 1800, but Congress extended it for an additional four years.[94] From 1804 to 1851, there was no statutory regime in place for either House. That year, another law was passed addressing disputed House of Representatives elections.[95] That law required notification of contest within thirty days of the official declaration of the result of the election in question and response by the returned Member to the notice of contest within a further thirty days. It also provided for the issuance of subpoenas, the production of relevant papers, and the taking of a transcript of testimony. A set of amendments passed in 1873 limited the taking of testimony to ninety days and allowed for the taking of depositions.[96] Minor alterations to the procedure were made by later amendments.[97] A 1969 law, still in effect, revised and elaborated upon the procedural details and, for the first time, applied to the Senate as well as the House.[98] But as Henry Dawes, who chaired the House Elections Committee from the Thirty-seventh through the Fortieth Congresses, noted, any statutory regime purporting to determine the procedure for adjudicating disputed elections or qualifications may be set aside by the House "at its pleasure, in whole or in part, as to one contest or as to all. This was understood by [the 1851 law's] framers; and all that they hoped to accomplish by it was to so demonstrate its utility that it would be adhered to as a wise rule, and in the strength of years and of usage it would gradually acquire the sanction and force of law."[99] Therefore, it is how the Houses have *actually* handled the cases that is most instructive, and it is to an examination of those cases that we now turn.

Cases

PROCEDURE WITHIN THE HOUSES OF CONGRESS

Electoral and qualifications disputes in the first several Congresses were primarily concerned with questions of how the inquiry was to be conducted. In the first such case to come before the House of Representatives, the Committee on Elections took testimony,[100] and then the House ordered it to issue a report with recommendations. After the committee did so, the House apparently changed its mind and examined all of the evidence itself.[101] In a subsequent case, testimony was allowed by deposition and counsel was heard for both sides in the trial, which took place before the Committee of the Whole House.[102] In the Third Congress, a trial took place before the Committee on Elections for the first time. The committee submitted its report to the House, which made a final judgment.[103]

For the most part, procedural modifications thereafter tended to be minor. In the Ninety-first Congress, the House was faced with the question of whether a losing candidate in a primary could challenge the election of a Member who was from another party, on the grounds that the returned Member faced an improperly chosen opponent in the general election. The Committee on House Administration recommended dismissing the complaint, on the grounds that the alleged irregularities in the primary involved neither the returned Member nor his general-election opponent. The House concurred and dismissed the contest.[104]

OVERSIGHT OF STATE ELECTION PROCEDURES

In *Spaulding v. Mead*, the House of Representatives in the Ninth Congress was faced with a situation in which Georgia law required election returns to be forwarded to the governor within twenty days of the election, and the governor had to certify the result five days after that. The governor did so, but the returns from three counties, which did not reach the governor until after the twenty-five-day deadline, would have thrown the election to the contestant. There was a dispute as to why those returns were late, but the committee held that the reason was immaterial, and that

> the returns of State officers are only *prima facie* evidence of the result of an election, and not conclusive on the House; that under the constitutional power of the House to judge of the elections, qualifications, and returns of members, it had the right to count these votes, though not returned in due time; and that as there was no fraud claimed, and no irregularity except the delay in transmission of the returns, the votes ought to be counted.[105]

This was the first time that the committee proposed to change the results of an election by counting votes that could not be counted under state law. The House sustained the committee report.[106] This seems an excellent example of a case in which the House's ability to judge according to the democratic spirit of the law rightfully took precedence over a narrow appeal to state law, and, indeed, a number of subsequent cases were to follow this lead. In later cases, for example, the House would determine that different spellings of the same name should be counted as votes for the same person and that electoral irregularities "related more to form than substance" would be disregarded.[107]

The most bitterly disputed antebellum election controversy arose over the representatives from New Jersey to the Twenty-sixth Congress. All New Jersey representatives were elected at large. In the 1838 election, the county clerks in Middlesex and Cumberland counties refused to count the votes from the townships of Millville and South Amboy. Without these votes, five Whig candidates would be elected; with them, five Democratic candidates would be elected. The House was so closely divided that these five seats would determine who controlled the chamber. The Whigs presented the House with a certificate of election from the governor; the Democrats presented the House with a certificate from the secretary of state asserting that they had the majority of all votes cast. While the issue was debated, the House remained unorganized for two weeks. At the end of those two weeks, the House decided not to admit either delegation, giving control of the House to the Democrats. Once the House was organized, a Committee of Elections was appointed, and the issue was referred to it. After hearing some, but not all, of the testimony offered, the committee reported that "the contesting (Democratic) delegation appeared *prima facie* to have 'received the greatest number of lawful votes.' "[108] As a result, the House voted to seat the Democrats, at least temporarily, while the investigation continued. When all the evidence was in, there were more than six hundred charges of illegal votes, "and the committee treated each of these individual votes as a distinct controversy. The testimony was examined, and separate arguments heard and separate votes taken on the question whether each voter voted, whether his vote was illegal, and whether it was shown for which candidates he voted."[109] The majority of the committee found for the Democrats, and, for the first time, the committee minority accused the majority of acting for partisan reasons: "We disclaim all design of charging the course adopted by the majority to corrupt intentions, but we are very reluctant to embrace the other branch of the alternative, and conclude, therefore, that some strange prejudice must have taken possession of the mind and led the judgment captive at will."[110] The report of the committee majority was adopted by a bare quorum of the House, with many Members refusing to vote.[111]

Soon thereafter — and probably with the New Jersey case in mind — Congress passed a law requiring all House elections to be by single-member districts.[112] Nevertheless, New Hampshire, Georgia, Mississippi, and Missouri elected their representatives to the Twenty-eighth Congress at large, and the elections were therefore challenged. The committee, determining for the first time that a federal law was unconstitutional, recommended that the Members from those states be seated. The committee reasoned that although Congress has the authority to regulate elections, it does not have the authority to "require the States to enact or enforce laws."[113] Because the states would have to draw district boundaries under the federal apportionment statute, that statute clearly required them to enact laws; therefore, it was unconstitutional. The committee minority argued in vain that "Congress has power to *alter* State regulations, and it is upon this power that the validity of the second section of the apportionment act rests. No State can prevent or circumscribe the action of Congress in this respect."[114] Moreover, argued the minority, "[a] law is constitutional if it is not contrary to the Constitution, and the constitutionality of a law of Congress can not depend on the forms of State laws."[115] The House did not formally agree to the majority report, but a decided majority voted to seat each Member elected on a general ticket.[116] On reflection, however, the committee minority would seem to have the better of this argument: if Congress has the authority to regulate the manner of elections, then surely it has the authority to require that state laws be in conformity with its regulations, even if that means that the state laws must be changed.

Relatedly, the Senate was faced with the question of what the Constitution meant when it required that "the Legislature" of a state choose its senators. In 1854, the Iowa legislature met in joint session to elect a senator. Although a majority of the total members of the state legislature was present, only a minority of the state senate was present. The convention elected James Harlan, but the state senate sent resolutions to the United States Senate protesting the election. The Judiciary Committee decided that the body electing Harlan was not the state legislature, as the Constitution used the term, and recommended that the seat be declared vacant. The full Senate concurred.[117] However, it appears that the objections were based primarily on the failure of the joint session to conform to Iowa law, rather than on the inherent impropriety of electing a senator with only a minority of one house of the state legislature present.[118] In a similar case from Indiana that arose during the same Congress, the Senate seated Members who were elected in a joint session attended by only a minority of the state senate.[119] Related was a question that arose in the Thirty-ninth Congress: could a state legislature decide that a candidate receiving a mere plurality of votes at a joint meeting of the houses of the legislature was duly elected? The Senate Judiciary Committee, noting that the state legislatures have the authority to prescribe the manner of electing senators, decided that a senator so elected should be seated. The Senate initially, by a one-vote majority, agreed with the committee but then, on a motion to reconsider, changed its mind and refused to seat the returned senator.[120]

In 1893, the Montana legislature adjourned, after a full session, without electing a senator. After the adjournment, the governor appointed Lee Mantle to fill the vacancy. The majority of the Committee on Privileges and Elections thought Mantle was entitled to a seat, but the minority held that this was not the sort of vacancy that the governor was empowered to fill. By a narrow margin, the Senate adopted the views of the minority, and Mantle was denied his seat.[121]

The arrival of the Seventeenth Amendment also brought unique challenges for the Senate. In 1913, after that amendment had been ratified, Senator Joseph Johnston of Alabama died. The Alabama legislature was in recess, and the governor appointed Frank Glass to fill the vacancy.[122] The Committee on Privileges and Elections then had to decide whether the governor had the authority to make this appointment, or whether the vacancy should have been filled by special election. The last clause of the Seventeenth Amendment reads, "This amendment shall not be so construed as to affect the election or term of any Senator chosen before it becomes valid as part of the Constitution." The majority of the committee, and the Senate as a whole, held that Glass was not entitled to the seat, because "[t]he length of the term may not be affected by the amendment, but the method of filling the vacancy became operative, upon its adoption."[123] The seat was subsequently filled by special election.

QUALIFICATIONS OF MEMBERS

The first case turning on challenged qualifications did not refer to the qualifications of a Member at all. The Third Congress's House Committee on Elections debated the constitutionality of the provision of the 1787 Northwest Ordinance[124] that allowed certain territories to send a nonvoting delegate to Congress. The committee concluded that it was constitutional, and the House concurred.[125]

In the Seventh Congress, the House Elections Committee decided that the acceptance of an officership in the militia of the District of Columbia constituted an "Office under the United States," which disqualified its holder from service in Congress. Holding a similar position in a state militia would not have been disqualifying, but because the District of Columbia militia was under federal command, the committee — and the House — determined that the seat in Congress was now vacant.[126] This seems to have been the right decision — the separation-of-powers purpose behind the disqualification would be seriously compromised if a Member of Congress were to be part of a chain of command at the head of which was the president.[127]

In the case of *Barney v. McCreery* in the Tenth Congress, the House Committee first faced the question of whether states could add qualifications for representatives. Under Maryland law, the town and county of Baltimore constituted one district, which was entitled to send two representatives to Congress. One had to be a resident of the city, and the other had to be a resident of the county. In the election for the city seat, the winner, William McCreery, was challenged on the grounds that he was not a resident of the city. The committee concluded that Maryland's law was unconstitutional, the first time that it was proposed for Congress to hold a state law unconstitutional. The House as a whole agreed with the committee's conclusions but was hesitant to vote explicitly that the state law was unconstitutional; the final vote was simply on the question of whether McCreery was entitled to his seat and did not address the grounds of that title. (The House overwhelmingly voted that he was entitled.)[128] Those who wanted — rightly — to make it clear that the Maryland law was unconstitutional appealed explicitly to popular-sovereignty-based reasoning:

> Congress was the creation of the people, not of the States, and the States can have no powers in regard to its election not expressly delegated by the Constitution. Any addition by the States to the constitutional qualifications would be an infringement on the reserved right of the people to elect any person to Congress not disqualified by the Constitution.[129]

Later cases would continue to hold that states had no authority to add qualifications to those listed in the Constitution.[130]

In the Fifteenth Congress, the question of ineligibility in the House due to executive service was raised again. When Samuel Herrick was elected to Congress, he was a federal district attorney. The Fourteenth Congress expired in March 1817; he resigned his position as district attorney in November; and he was seated in Congress in December. The question presented was whether he became a Member of Congress in March, thereby immediately vacating that office by continuing to serve as district attorney, or whether he did not become a Member until December. The committee concluded that he did not become a Member until December and was therefore allowed to retain his seat; the House concurred.[131] Given that the purpose of preventing the holding of simultaneous offices in the legislature and other branches is to preserve separation of powers, it seems correct that the disqualification would not come into operation until the new Member was actually exercising the powers of a Member of Congress.

One of the most controversial cases from the late nineteenth century also related to qualifications. Brigham H. Roberts, a polygamist, was elected to the House of Representatives from Utah. The committee, while noting that he was duly elected and met all of the qualifications listed in the Constitution, nonetheless was "unanimous in its belief that Mr. Roberts ought not to remain a member of the House of Representatives."[132] A majority of the committee favored excluding him; the rest thought expulsion the proper way to go. The majority examined the English precedents and concluded (correctly), "We have to say that after diligent search we find no cases where the House of Commons ever held or decided that it had not the right to exclude at the very threshold a member whose certificate or credentials were perfect and uncontested, although the ground of exclusion was not a want of legal qualifications."[133] The majority failed to note, however, that this was a case in which English parliamentary-sovereignty precedents should serve as a *contrast* to the popular-sovereignty-based rules underlying the American Constitution. Despite the minority's appeal to the structural reasoning discussed above, the majority concluded that Roberts's polygamy rendered him "ineligible, disqualified, unfit, and unworthy" of Membership in the House.[134] The House concurred with the majority and voted to exclude him, although the vote was well above the two-thirds that would have been necessary for expulsion.[135]

The citizenship qualification, too, was the subject of a House challenge. Henry Ellenbogen had been a citizen for only six years and five months when he was elected to the Seventy-third Congress. When the congressional term commenced, he was still not eligible. However, he did not present himself to the House until he had been a citizen for more than seven years. The committee held that the citizenship requirement, like the age requirement, could be met subsequent to election, and Ellenbogen was sworn in.[136]

The Senate's first challenge to a returned Member was also based on length of citizenship. The qualifications of Albert Gallatin, elected from Pennsylvania to the Third Congress, were challenged. He had come to Boston from his native Geneva in 1780 but had not taken an oath of allegiance to an American state (Virginia) until October 1785. Gallatin presented himself to be sworn in at the beginning of the Third Congress in December 1793. The Senate appointed a Select Committee to take testimony, and, after hearing these facts, it concluded that he had not been a citizen of the United States for the requisite nine years and was therefore ineligible to serve in the Senate.[137]

In the Eleventh Congress, the Senate was faced with the question of what it meant for someone to be an inhabitant of the state from which he was elected. Stanley Griswold moved to Ohio in September 1808 and was appointed by the governor to fill a Senate vacancy in May 1809. The Committee on Elections concluded that "the term of residence or other qualifications necessary to entitle a person to become an inhabitant of the State not being defined either by the constitution or laws of the State of Ohio, the certificate of the Governor that Griswold was a citizen thereof was sufficient."[138] The Senate concurred, and Griswold was seated.

Like the House in *Barney v. McCreery*, the Senate decided that the qualifications for office listed in the Constitution were exhaustive. The Illinois Constitution in effect in 1855 provided that the judges of the state supreme court were ineligible to serve in the federal government during the term for which they had been elected to the court, plus one year afterward. Lyman Trumbull had been elected to a nine-year term on the court in 1852. In 1853, he resigned his seat on the bench, and in 1855, he was elected to the United States Senate. Upon a challenge, the Senate decided both that the case did not fall within the disqualification of the state constitution, because Trumbull had resigned his seat more than a year before being elected to the Senate, and that the state had no authority to add qualifications to those listed in the Constitution.[139]

In a 1903 case reminiscent of Brigham Roberts's exclusion from the House for polygamy, Reed Smoot (also of Utah) was challenged simply on the grounds that he was a Mormon:

> The charges against Smoot grew out of his connection with the Mormon Church. A majority of the committee agreed that Smoot was not entitled to a seat but could not decide whether he should be excluded or expelled. The committee considered the following to be causes for removal: (1) Membership in a religious hierarchy that countenanced and encouraged polygamy and united church and state contrary to the spirit of the constitution; and (2) Smoot had taken an oath "of such a nature and character as that he is thereby disqualified from taking the oath of office required of a United States Sena-

tor." In the proceedings by the committee no evidence was presented tending to substantiate the charge that Reed Smoot was a polygamist and no such charge was made on the floor of the Senate; neither was his personal character assailed by Senators for or against the resolution.[140]

The Senate, however, declined to follow the committee's recommendation. Declaring, rightly, that Smoot could not be excluded if he met the constitutional qualifications and if he did not trigger any of the constitutional disqualifications, the Senate held that vacating Smoot's seat would require an expulsion. Less than half — and nowhere near the required two-thirds — of the Senate voted to expel Smoot, and he retained his seat. (Indeed, he was to remain in the Senate for thirty years.)

In 1935, Rush Holt, the winner of the West Virginia senatorial election, did not present himself to be sworn in until after his thirtieth birthday, which occurred several months after the beginning of the congressional session. His election was challenged on the grounds that he was ineligible for failing to meet the age qualification. The committee, noting that West Virginia voters had "full knowledge" that Holt would not turn thirty until several months into the session, held that he was entitled to his seat. The "date on which a Senator-elect presents himself to the Senate, is sworn, and takes his seat, should be determinative of the age qualifications under the Constitution," it decided.[141] The full Senate concurred. It is interesting that the committee noted that Holt's age was widely known. Had it not been, could the committee have decided differently, on the popular-sovereignty grounds that the people of West Virginia had not knowingly chosen to halve their Senate representation for the months before Holt could be sworn in? More likely, the proper response would have been that West Virginia voters (or Holt's opponent) should have done some more research into his background and made this fact widely known. But if Holt had actively lied about his age, then the committee might have had a strong case for excluding him.

ELECTORAL INTIMIDATION OR INTERFERENCE

In *Trigg v. Preston*, the Third Congress's House Committee on Elections determined that the brother of the returned Member from a district in Virginia had command of sixty to seventy federal troops and that those troops had intimidated and barred some voters who wanted to vote for the contestant. The committee therefore recommended vacating the election, but the House did not.[142] When the case came before the full House, Members argued "that Southern elections should not be judged by the standard of the Eastern States; that riots and intimidation were an established custom and quite a matter of course in all Southern elections; and that the election in question was much less disturbed than many others in regard to which there was no question."[143] Samuel Smith of Maryland educated his colleagues:

> In what way were elections for Southern members carried on? A man of influence came to the place of election with two or three hundred of his friends; and, to be sure, they would not, if they could help it, suffer any body on the other side to give a vote as long as they were there. It was certainly a very bad custom, and must very much surprise an Eastern member, but it was the custom, and perfectly known to be so.[144]

But the truly horrifying cases of electoral violence would come decades later, with the even more horrifying specter of civil war.

CIVIL WAR AND RECONSTRUCTION

The Thirty-fourth Congress (1855–57) saw the beginning of election controversies related to what would, in time, become the American Civil War. *Reeder v. Whitfield* dealt with an election for territorial delegate from Kansas to the House of Representatives. After the passage of the Kansas-Nebraska Act, the contestant of an election for delegate from Kansas claimed that the law under which the election was held was invalid, because the territorial legislature by which it was passed was not elected by the people of Kansas but was imposed upon them "by an armed invading force."[145] He alleged that a large number of illegal votes were cast by people who had "invaded" the Territory from Missouri (Missourians had an interest in doing so in order to ensure that the government in Kansas was friendly to slavery). The House empowered a three-Member committee to travel to Kansas and take evidence. Those Members found that

> each election held in the Territory had been carried by organized invasion from the State of Missouri; that the alleged Territorial legislature was an illegally constituted body, with no power to pass valid laws; that the election under which the sitting member held his seat was not held under any valid law, and could similarly only be regarded as an expression of the choice of those resident citizens who voted for him; that more resident citizens voted for the contestant than for the sitting member; and that in the present condition of the Territory a fair election could not be held.[146]

The committee majority recommended that the contestant be seated, but the House vacated the seat.[147]

The exact same territorial government then proceeded to hold a new election, at which John Whitfield, the winner of the previous invalidated election, "received *all* the votes cast."[148] The committee began by noting that the "election was held by officers and according to laws deriving their authority from the legislature of Kansas, which had already been decided by the House to be an illegal body and incapable of passing valid laws."[149] More remarkable, however, were the committee's conclusions as to the law under which the election was held:

> The law was an extraordinary one. It prescribed no period of residence as a qualification for voting, but only actual inhabitancy in the Territory at the moment of voting. . . . All the voters were required to take a test oath to support the fugitive-slave law and the Kansas-Nebraska act. The laws thus permitted any citizen of Missouri to vote who would swear that he was at the time of the election an inhabitant of Kansas, while disfranchising all of the citizens of Kansas who could not subscribe to a test oath committing themselves to the principles of the party in power. A large proportion of the citizens of Kansas did not vote at the election, both because they were disfranchised by the test oath and because they believed the election to be held without authority of law.[150]

If ever the Congress had been faced with a case in which concern for basic principles of democratic government called for the invalidation of an election, this was it. And, to its credit, that is precisely what the committee recommended. To its shame, however, the House tabled the committee's resolution, with the effect that Whitfield retained his seat.[151]

In the elections for the next Congress, Baltimore — in the border state of Maryland — was visited by "riots and violence, and . . . there was no such thing as a free expression of the will of the people."[152] The committee "called attention to the unprecedented character of the case, saying that it was not an ordinary question as to which of two candidates was legally elected, but 'the question involved is, Shall elections of members to the House of Representatives of the United States be free, fair, and open to the whole body of legal electors?' "[153] Noting that "there could be no such thing as an *election* unless all the voters were free to vote," the committee held that the election should be voided and the seat vacated.[154] Once again, however, the House tabled the matter, allowing the returned Member to retain his seat.[155]

As one might expect, the issues got even thornier once the war came. For example, Unionist voters in part of Tennessee elected a representative to Congress, even though Tennessee had already seceded. The Confederate governor refused to grant a certificate of election, and the sheriffs of all of the counties but one refused to return the votes cast. The claimant, however, had the returns of that single sheriff, as well as outside evidence that he had received more than two thousand votes. He also showed that "[o]n the day of the election there was not yet such an armed force in possession of the district as to prevent loyal voters from casting their votes."[156] He was seated. In the election from Virginia, however, a Unionist was denied a seat, having received only ten votes, none of which was canvassed or returned, and of which there was no evidence they were legally cast.[157]

In another Virginia case,

> the whole district, except the city of Alexandria, was in the armed occupation of the rebels, and that city was occupied by the troops of the United States, and was practically under martial law. No notice could be given to the people of the rest of the district, and they could not have held elections. They could not be held to have acquiesced in the result of the election, for "acquiescence presumes liberty to protest. In this instance that liberty did not exist."[158]

The returned Member was denied a seat. However, in a Louisiana case, where the districts were "in the complete control of the United States army"[159] and where the military governor had issued writs of election, the election results were upheld. The committee found that "[t]he election was participated in by a very large majority of the legal voters present in the parishes, and appeared to have been a very free and peaceable election."[160] To those questioning whether the military governor, General George Shepley, had the authority to issue writs of election, the committee replied,

> The Constitution required the United States to guarantee to each State a republican form of government. Representation was one of the essentials of such a government, and the right of the people to representation ought not to be dependent on the willingness of the rebel governor of Louisiana to order an election. Some one must assume the power to order the election. General Shepley assumed to act as governor of Louisiana, and his actions were acquiesced in by the people. The House ought at least to recognize him as *de facto* governor until his authority was contested by some one.[161]

The returned representatives were therefore seated. But in another case, again from Virginia, an election called by a military commander was invalidated. Major-General John Dix, commanding the Department of Virginia, had issued a proclamation fixing the time of the election and qualifications of the electors and "requiring all qualified voters to vote, under pain of being considered disloyal."[162] Moreover, because the rebels still controlled most of the district, writs of election were only issued to four of the eleven counties in the district. The committee found that "General Dix was not in any sense a military governor, and pretended to no civil functions."[163] Moreover, "The election could not be considered as a fair expression of the choice of the people, as it was only held in four of the eleven counties of the district and but a small fraction of the total vote was cast."[164] The election was therefore invalid, and the claimants were not seated.[165]

At first blush, these decisions from the Thirty-seventh Congress might seem ad hoc: one Unionist from a rebel state was seated; one was not; some representatives elected from districts under military control were seated; others were not. But the devil here is in the details, and with the details of the cases in view, we can see that the outcomes all make good democratic sense. A Unionist in Tennessee who receives two thousand votes, regularly cast but unreturned because of the treachery of state officials, has a legitimate claim to a seat; a Unionist in Virginia receiving only ten votes, which were not regularly cast, has no such legitimacy. Similarly, peaceful, regular elections in two Louisiana districts presided over by a military governor are legitimate in a way that irregular elections in a small part of one Virginia district, presided over by a military commander with no civilian authority, are not. In the chaos and flux of a civil war and military occupation, the committee seems to have done its best to seat those Members returned with a high degree of democratic legitimacy, while denying seats to those whose election could not reasonably be said to represent the expressed will of the people of their district.

During the war, Congress passed a law requiring that Congressmen-elect and other public officials swear an oath:

> I have never voluntarily borne arms against the United States since I have been a citizen thereof; that I have voluntarily given no aid, countenance, counsel, or encouragement to persons engaged in armed hostility thereto; that I have neither sought nor accepted nor attempted to exercise the functions of any office whatever, under any authority or pretend authority in hostility to the United States; that I have not yielded a voluntary support to any pretended government, authority, power or constitution within the United States, hostile or inimical thereto.[166]

In the war's aftermath, the test oath led to several controversies. In the Fortieth Congress, objections were made to the swearing in of the Members-elect from Kentucky on the grounds that they could not honestly take the oath. Five of the Members-elect were cleared of any charges of disloyalty and were sworn in; two others were found disloyal and were denied seats.[167] Somewhat different was the case of Roderick Butler, Member-elect from Tennessee. Butler had been elected to the postsecession Tennessee legislature and therefore had taken an oath of allegiance to the Confederacy, which made him ineligible to take the test oath.

> But it appeared that he had been elected to the legislature as the representative of the Union sentiment in his district, with the hope that he might be able to benefit those who were suffering for their loyalty. His district was so strongly Union that it had furnished more soldiers to the Federal Army than there were voters in it, and he was throughout the war known as one of the strongest and

most influential Union men in it. He had been singled out for especial persecution by the rebels, his property destroyed and plundered, lives of his family
put in danger, and himself arrested for treason.[168]

The committee recommended a joint resolution allowing Butler not to take the
oath. The joint resolution passed,[169] and Butler was sworn in. It should be
clear that, given Congress's inability to add qualifications for Members, the
test oath was unconstitutional. It went beyond Article VI's *prospective* oath
"to support this Constitution" and created a new disqualification for *former*
rebels. Certainly, former rebels could have been expelled from the House, but
the Constitution, as it stood in 1862, did not allow them to be excluded.
Congress implicitly acknowledged this by including the disqualification for
oath breakers in the Fourteenth Amendment, which was ratified in 1868.

Of course, the end of the war did not bring with it the end of racial antago-
nism, and, as the Black Codes and Jim Crow took hold, cases of violence and
intimidation at the polls returned, often in especially vicious form. In *Hunt v.
Sheldon*, the Forty-first Congress was faced with a case from Louisiana. Because this case was by no means unique, it is worth quoting the details at some
length:

> The main allegation . . . was that in certain parishes, constituting a large part
> of the State, the election was void by reason of violence and intimidation. At
> all the previous elections in these parishes since the beginning of the recon-
> struction period the Republican candidates had received a majority of the
> whole registered vote, but at this election the Republican vote suddenly fell to
> less than one-tenth the usual vote, and all but 20 of the votes that were cast
> were cast in eight country parishes. In the remaining parishes practically no
> Republican votes were cast, some parishes casting only 1 or 2 votes and others
> none at all. The cause of this remarkable result was found in the events which
> shortly preceded the election. A secret military organization, known as the
> "Knights of the White Camellia," was formed, which embraced practically all
> the Democratic voters in the State, and was able, in the city of New Orleans,
> to muster a force of over 15,000 armed men, all sworn to obey the commands
> of their authorized leaders. Out of this organization grew the KuKlux Klan in
> the country parishes and the Innocents in the city — bands of men operating in
> hideous disguises and devoted to the grosser sort of outrages. At first violence
> was generally avoided, and a system of social and business ostracism against
> Republican voters, contrasted with treatment of the opposite sort to such as
> would join Democratic organizations, was relied upon to break the Republi-
> can power. These methods proving ineffective, violence and murder were
> resorted to, and for some time the city of New Orleans and neighboring
> parishes were in a state of anarchy. Not less than 2,000 Republicans were
> killed or injured. There being no State militia, the civil authorities were en-

tirely without means of suppressing the disturbances, and the military force stationed at New Orleans was so small that the general in command declared that he had not enough force even to protect United States property if it should be attacked by the organization, which had taken practical control of the city. The result was that the riots and outrages continued until the civil authority was substantially surrendered to the riotous element by the appointment of a leading Democrat as chief of police. This produced a sort of peace, in the nature of a truce, and a comparatively peaceful condition was maintained up to and including the day of election, but only upon the express understanding that the Republicans would make no effort to poll their vote. Very many witnesses testified to the universal belief that if any attempt had been made to poll the Republican vote the scenes of violence and bloodshed would have been instantly renewed.

Under such a condition of affairs the committee held that the election was vitiated in the intimidated parishes. While there was no actual violence at the polls, the majority of Republicans refrained from voting under an actual and reasonable fear that any attempt on their part to vote would result in violence similar to that which had already taken place.[170]

The committee decided to throw out the returns from the parishes where intimidation had taken place and to count only the ones from the peaceable parishes. The winner of those parishes — Republican Lionel Sheldon — was awarded the seat.[171] It is worth noting that this is a case in which the presumption in favor of vacating a result was rightfully inoperative. That presumption is based upon the democratic idea that when the result is uncertain, the best course of action is to return to the voters and ask them to clarify their choice. Where, as here, there is every reason to think that a second election would be attended by the same violence and intimidation that attended the first, the committee was right simply to count the peaceable counties. However, this raises a further question. Suppose that the peaceable counties had voted for Sheldon's opponent. Suppose, that is, they were peaceable because they were Democratic strongholds, and therefore there was no need for intimidation in them. In that case, the committee would not have been justified in relying on the returns from the peaceable counties — doing so would have rewarded the instigators of violence and sent the highly undemocratic message that a candidate could win election by committing outrages in areas likely to vote against him, thereby invalidating the results from those areas. Here, again, we see how the political pragmatism of a legislative body can be better suited to the adjudication of electoral disputes than the legalism of a court. In subsequent cases, the House continued to hold that candidates could not benefit from intimidation and violence.[172] In one such case from Virginia, where blacks and whites were made to stand in separate lines to vote, and then election officials proceeded so slowly that all white votes were counted but many black votes were not by the time the polls closed, the committee held that "the rule was well established that the vote of a legal voter, tendered and illegally rejected, should be counted on a contest. They held, also, that the action of the voters in this case in standing in line and making every effort to reach the window amounted in law to a tender of their votes, and that the action of the judges in intentionally delaying the vote amounted in law to a rejection of the votes prevented from being cast."[173] Note again the — pragmatic, most likely correct, but almost certainly unjudicial — assumption that the blacks who did not get to vote would have voted Republican. How else could their votes be "counted" by the committee?

Of course, as the war receded further and further from memory, the House became less inclined to enforce the strong vision of Reconstruction that prevailed in the late 1860s and early 1870s. At the beginning of the twentieth century, the Fifty-eighth Congress faced a challenge to the South Carolina Constitution of 1895. Under the 1868 Reconstruction Act, which readmitted South Carolina into the Union, at no future time could the state constitution be changed so as to disfranchise those who had the right to vote under the state constitution recognized by Congress in 1868 (there were exceptions allowing for the disfranchising of convicted felons so long as they were convicted under "laws equally applicable to all the inhabitants of said State" and allowing the state to alter its residency requirement for voting).[174] South Carolina's 1868 Constitution did not contain any educational or property requirements for voters; the 1895 Constitution did.[175] The committee noted that

> if the House should unseat the contestee on the ground that no valid election was held or could be held in his district under the present constitution and election laws of South Carolina, a similar construction would require the House, in the case of contest, to unseat all of the Members from South Carolina and from most of the other Southern States, and that new elections could not be held to fill the vacancies until the respective constitutions of these States had been changed so as to comply with the reconstruction acts.[176]

The correct response, the committee determined, was to pass the buck: "If any citizen of South Carolina who was entitled to vote under the constitution of that State in 1868 is now deprived by the provisions of the present constitution, he has the right . . . to bring suit in a proper court for the purpose of enforcing his right or recovering damages for its denial."[177] This bowing to Jim Crow was an ignoble descent for the committee that had stood up for voting rights decades earlier.

As it had to the House, the coming of the Civil War presented a new set of challenges to the Senate. After the Senate had expelled its Members from the seceding states, an entity purporting to be the loyalist government of Virginia elected two replacement senators. When the question of admitting them came before the Senate,

> [s]ome Senators maintained that by admitting Messrs. Willey and Carlile to their seats the Senate would be undertaking to recognize a government of the State which was not the regular State government, even though that State government were in a state of rebellion; and that the Senate was bound to recognize the fact that the term of office of the Governor who was in rebellion had not expired, and that the credentials were not signed by him, but by another as Governor.[178]

Those arguments notwithstanding, the Senate seated the two Unionist Virginians. A seemingly similar case arose in Arkansas, where an entity purporting to be the free state government elected senators. The Senate Judiciary Committee noted both that relatively few Arkansas citizens took part in reorganizing the state government and that

> [a]t the time the claimants were elected, the State was occupied by hostile armies. While this state of things continued, and the right to exercise armed authority was claimed and exerted by the military power, it could not be said that a civil government, set up and continued only by the sufferance of the military, is that republican form of government which the Constitution requires the United States to guarantee to every State in the Union.[179]

The seat was thus denied. The question then naturally arose as to when a formerly rebellious state would be entitled to representation again. In a case from Louisiana, the Judiciary Committee answered that,

> the inhabitants of the State having been declared in a state of insurrection in pursuance of a law passed by the two Houses of Congress, the committee deemed it improper for the Senate to admit to seats Senators from Louisiana until by some joint action of both Houses there should be some recognition of an existing State government.[180]

The Senate also faced questions of loyalty. Much like his fellow Tennessean Roderick Butler, David Patterson held state office after secession in an attempt to represent and protect Unionist sentiment in the state. The Judiciary Committee recommended a joint resolution lifting Patterson's disability, and such a resolution passed the Senate but was tabled in the House. The Senate proceeded to seat Patterson, anyway, on the strength of a single-house resolution.[181] The loyalty of Philip Thomas, senator from Maryland, was also questioned, on two grounds: first, that, as secretary of the treasury in 1860, he had conspired to bankrupt the country and transfer much of the government's funds to the South, where they would be seized by rebels, and second, that he had given a disloyal speech.[182] The committee, examining these charges, reported that it found "nothing sufficient . . . to debar said Thomas from taking his seat, unless it be found in the fact of the son of said Thomas having entered the military service of the confederacy, and in circumstances connected with that fact or relating to it."[183] Although Thomas had, apparently, repeatedly attempted to dissuade his son from joining the Confederate army, when his son made it clear that he was going to do so, Thomas gave him $100 to take with him.[184] On those grounds—grounds that seem dangerously close to a corruption of blood—the Senate held that Thomas was not entitled to take the test oath and excluded him from taking his seat.[185]

In the Fortieth Congress, Joshua Hill and H. V. M. Miller, returned senators from Georgia, were challenged on the grounds that some Members of the state legislature that had elected them were ineligible to serve in the state legislature because they had served under the Confederacy and had not had the disqualification lifted, per the Fourteenth Amendment. The committee reported against admitting them to their seats, and no action was taken by the full Senate before the end of the Fortieth Congress, with the result that they were never seated in that Congress. However, in 1870, an act was passed declaring Georgia entitled to representation in Congress.[186] The committee then recommended that Hill and Miller be declared duly elected. However, Miller was still ineligible to serve, having been a surgeon in the Confederate army. By joint resolution, Miller was allowed to take a special oath, and both were seated.[187]

The Forty-first Congress also saw a challenge to the qualifications of Hiram R. Revels, senator from Mississippi and the first black senator in American history. It was contended that, in 1870, Revels had been a citizen for less than two years, rather than the nine requisite for Senate service. This argument turned on the infamous *Dred Scott* case, in which the Supreme Court had held that free blacks were not citizens under the Constitution.[188] Because *Dred Scott* was not overturned until the passage of the Fourteenth Amendment in 1868, the argument went, Revels had only then become a citizen of the United States. The Senate, to its credit, overwhelmingly rejected this argument, and Revels took his seat.[189]

VICTOR L. BERGER

It is, perhaps, fitting to conclude our case studies with a detailed look at the most famous exclusion case of the Progressive Era, a case that ties together a number of the threads discussed above. Victor L. Berger, who had served as a representative from Wisconsin in the Sixty-second Congress (1911–

13), was a member of the national executive committee of the Socialist Party (which he cofounded with Eugene V. Debs) and the editor in chief of the *Milwaukee Leader*. Through his post in the Party and his newspaper, Berger engaged in antiwar agitation, calling the United States' declaration of war in 1917 "a crime against the people of the United States and against the nations of the world." A Socialist Party publication recommended that women withhold their romantic affections from men who enlisted in the military.[190] In 1919, Berger was convicted under the Espionage Act of 1917[191] and sentenced to twenty years in prison. (His conviction was overturned by the Supreme Court in 1921 because the trial judge mishandled a motion to remove him from the case due to personal bias,[192] and the government chose not to reprosecute.) In 1918, just before his trial, Berger had been elected a representative from Wisconsin to the Sixty-sixth Congress; he was free on bail pending appeal when Congress assembled, and a special committee was appointed to consider his qualifications. All but one of the members of the committee recommended against seating him, and the holdout's objections were procedural, not substantive.[193]

The floor debate was especially vitriolic. Frederick Dallinger of Massachusetts led the attack. Appealing to the test-oath cases and the Brigham Roberts case, Dallinger argued that returned Members could be excluded on grounds not listed in the Constitution. Second, he argued that section 3 of the Fourteenth Amendment was applicable, since Berger had taken an oath as a Member of Congress in 1911. "[T]his man, Victor L. Berger, did give aid and comfort to the enemies of this country during this Great War," thundered Dallinger.[194] Dallinger was also careful to argue that this exclusion was for espionage, not for being a socialist:

> We do not care what his political or religious or economic beliefs are. Do not be misled. He came here before as a Socialist and was admitted. Myer London was admitted to this House as a Socialist. The American people do not care what a man's political, religious, or economic beliefs are, but they do care whether he is a loyal American.[195]

Berger probably did himself little good with his rambling ninety-minute defense,[196] most of which was dedicated to laying out in excruciating detail the socialist case against the war. He did, however, argue near the end that "[t]he qualifications of a Member of the House are clearly stated in the Constitution . . . the House has no right to add to these qualifications."[197] He also made the argument from popular sovereignty: "The fifth district of the State of Wisconsin is entitled to be represented by the man of its own choice. I say again, it is not the personal case of Victor Berger — representative government is on trial."[198] But Berger stood no chance, with other representatives being loudly applauded for increasingly over-the-top denunciations, culminating with Berger's fellow Wisconsinite James Monahan:

> Mr. Speaker, to-day the powers of evil, the emissaries of darkness, the foes of constitutional law and the civilization of the Nazarene, are knocking at the door of the House of Representatives, demanding admission for their representative, Victor L. Berger. Let us answer that challenge by hurling back the answer of heroic France at Verdun, and say to him, "You shall not pass."[199]

On the resolution to exclude Berger, 311 representatives voted yes; one voted no; and 119 did not vote.[200] The margin was, of course, well above what would have been necessary to expel him. In a sequence reminiscent of the *Wilkes* case, Berger was reelected to fill the vacancy created by his exclusion, and the House again refused to seat him. The seat remained vacant throughout the Sixty-sixth Congress. However, he was elected to and seated in the Sixty-eighth, Sixty-ninth, and Seventieth Congresses.[201]

The House was clearly wrong to think that it could legally exclude Berger for reasons not enumerated in the Constitution. But what about the Fourteenth Amendment argument? Berger *had* previously taken an oath to support the Constitution of the United States, and, if Dallinger et al. were right that he had then given "aid and comfort" to the enemies of the United States, he would be ineligible to serve under section 3 of the Fourteenth Amendment. Under a good reading of the First Amendment, Berger's speeches and writings could not have been seditious; however, under the interpretation prevailing at the time, they probably were.[202] Regardless, as we saw in chapter 2, the final judgment on the matter lay with the House.

Conclusions

C. H. Rammelkamp wryly noted that the Houses' exclusive right to judge the elections, returns, and qualifications of their Members "is an interesting survival of an idea which has been discarded by the parent who originated it."[203] Indeed, it does at first glance seem odd to have argued that the progression from a Blackstonian to a Millian paradigm in Britain meant taking election disputes away from the House and giving them to the courts, while also arguing that American popular sovereignty manifests itself in exclusive congressional jurisdiction over these disputes. But it is important to emphasize here the limits on each House's jurisdiction. Within the narrow confines of judging election returns and the enumerated qualifications and disqualifications, the House's judgment is final. As we have seen, the House is well suited to the mix of political and legal reasoning needed to judge such disputes. But, as we saw in chapter 2, courts may police the boundaries of congressional jurisdiction to ensure that neither House oversteps its bounds.

Moreover, in chapter 2, we examined the case of *Roudebush v. Hartke*,[204] in which the Supreme Court held that a state's recount procedures do not encroach upon the House's privilege of judging elections because the House is ultimately free to reject the state's conclusion and determine the winner for itself. There is no reason that what is true for state recounts could not also be true for federal judicial challenges. As we have seen, there are situations in which political reasoning is better suited to resolving electoral disputes than legal reasoning—for these cases, it makes sense for the Houses to retain the final say on election and qualification disputes. Indeed, we saw in the previous chapter two cases in which the courts in Britain were insufficiently flexible to arrive at the best outcome in an election dispute. In the 1874 *Bolton* case, the secrecy of the ballot was illegally compromised, but the law only allowed the judge to punish the offenders—he could not order a new election, even if he thought the offense affected the outcome of the election. Similarly, in the Tony Benn case in 1964, the court was constrained to rule that the overwhelming majority of voters had wasted their vote, and thus award the seat to a candidate who received far fewer votes than his opponent. A more appropriate result, as we have seen, would have been to order a new election. It is one of the great virtues of courts that they are constrained by the law, but some election disputes call for political pragmatism, rather than legal proceduralism.

Many other cases, however, are well suited to legal determination—as the bulk of post-1868 British election case law suggests. Perhaps, then, the ideal solution would be halfway between the British and the American solutions—allow the courts to hear election and qualification disputes, but with the understanding that their determinations can be overruled by the House. The public scrutiny that such a move would invite would ensure that the House used its overruling power sparingly and only in cases in which the courts' lack of institutional competence led to a miscarriage of justice. This would prevent the courts from being able to determine the composition of the legislature, while at the same time improving the quality of judging in election and qualification disputes. Additionally, the courts would retain their boundary-policing roles: they would still be charged with ensuring that the Houses were actually judging election or qualification disputes when they claimed that they were doing so. The Houses cannot exercise their disciplinary powers under the guise of exercising their election judging powers. And it is to an examination of the Houses' disciplinary powers in Britain and America that we now turn.

9

Breach of Privilege and Contempt of Parliament

Erskine May defines contempt of Parliament as "any act or omission which obstructs or impedes either House of Parliament in the performance of its functions, or which obstructs or impedes any Member or officer of such House in the discharge of his duty, or which has a tendency, directly or indirectly, to produce such results."[1] Breach of privilege comprises that subset of contempts in which a specific privilege of one of the Houses is attacked or infringed upon. Obviously, these categories are both broad and imprecise. How they are interpreted is of the utmost importance to the role that Parliament plays in the British Constitution. It should be apparent that the Blackstonian view will support a wider scope for breach and contempt than the Millian view—decisions justified under the Millian view will generally also be justified under the Blackstonian view, but not necessarily vice versa. For the Blackstonian view, it is appropriate to use breach and contempt proceedings to forestall anything that might damage the House's power or prestige. Under the Millian view, however, certain kinds of challenges are acceptable. The details will come into focus as we examine the history of breach and contempt proceedings.

The Blackstonian Paradigm

The Blackstonian view of breach and contempt is necessarily a wide one. As we have seen, the Blackstonian view of privilege perceives the House of

Commons to be the citadel of democracy in the government, besieged by other powerful forces. The House is thus justified in using even very blunt means to protect itself from outside manipulation.

THE *CHEDDRE* CASE

In 1404, Richard Cheddre, the servant to Thomas Brooke, a Member of Parliament from the county of Somerset, was "emblemished and maimed even to the peril of death" by one John Sallage.[2] The House was outraged and petitioned the King for a draconian system of punishments:

> [I]f any man shall kill or murther any that is come under your protection to Parliament, that it be adjudged treason; and if any do maim or disfigure any such so come under your protection, that he lose his hand; and if any do assault or beat any such so come, that he be imprisoned for a year, and make fine and ransome to the king: and that it would please you of your special grace hereafter to abstain from charters of pardon in such cases, unless that the parties be fully agreed.[3]

The King ordered Sallage to appear before the King's Bench and pay double damages, plus a fine and ransom to the King.[4] In 1433, a law was passed providing double damages, fine, and ransom as the punishment in any case in which a Member of Parliament was assaulted.[5] We thus see even very early parliaments being quite anxious to protect against contempts, although the assault on a Member (or his servant) was still seen as an offense against the King and was punished by royal justice.

SIXTEENTH-CENTURY CASES

In the sixteenth century, the House itself began punishing for contempt, rather than turning to royal officials for aid. A number of cases from that century show the various causes for which the House of Commons was willing to punish. In 1548, an MP named John Storie was sent to the Tower, probably for disrespectful remarks on the floor about Somerset the Protector.[6] In 1580, Arthur Hall, also an MP, was expelled, fined 500 marks, and sent to the Tower for a book he published that not only "reproach[ed] some particular good Members of the House, but [was] also very much slanderous and derogatory to the general authority, power and state of this House, and prejudicial to the validity of its proceedings, in making and establishing of laws."[7] In 1585, Dr. William Parry was the only Member of either House to oppose the "bill against Jesuits, Seminary Priests, and other such disobedient Persons."[8] Parry called it a "cruel, bloody and desperate law," which "would be of pernicious consequence to the English nation," but said that he would only explain his reasons to the Queen's Council, not to the House.[9] He was held in contempt and ordered into the Sergeant's custody.[10] After apologizing profusely, he was released from custody and readmitted to the House.[11] Soon after, however, he was found to be part of a plot to subvert the government and kill the Queen. He confessed before the Queen's Bench and was executed as a traitor.[12] In 1586, Mr. Bland—a private subject—was fined for insulting the House, and in 1588, Thomas Drurie was committed to the custody of the Sergeant for "having untruly reported and given out both to some of the Lords in the Upper House, and also to divers others Persons elsewhere, that he could have no justice in this House."[13]

The punishments of Storie and Parry are, perhaps, too blunt even for the Blackstonian view. In both instances, MPs were held in contempt merely for taking unpopular positions in floor speeches. Because the MPs' actions in these cases took place on the floor of Parliament, they did not threaten to bring the House into disrepute with either the public or another powerful institution, and there is no indication that the remarks were disruptive of the orderly functioning of the House. It did not increase the House's institutional power to hold these Members in contempt; rather, it was simply an expression by the House that it did not like what they had to say. Unlike in the cases of Storie and Parry, the punishments of Hall, Bland, and Drurie do fit within the Blackstonian model. They were all punished for casting aspersions on the House of Commons. Hall, by publishing his attack on the House, threatened to bring the House into disrepute among the public. This was dangerous enough for a body still attempting to assert its independence, but Drurie's case was even more severe. By complaining to the Lords about perceived injustices done him by the Commons, Drurie potentially gave the Lords justification for meddling in the affairs of the lower house. For a body concerned primarily with safeguarding and fortifying its role within the state, this was clearly intolerable, and insofar as the Blackstonian view suggests that the Commons needed to be concerned primarily with safeguarding and fortifying its role, these were appropriate Blackstonian uses of contempt proceedings.

IGNORING AN ORDER OF THE HOUSE AS CONTEMPT

The *Shirley*, *Shirley-Fagg*, and *Topham* cases, all discussed in chapter 1, demonstrate the use of contempt proceedings to punish ignoring an order of the House. In the 1604 *Shirley* case, the Warden of the Fleet was sent to the Tower for refusing to release Shirley when ordered to by the House. Probably more infuriating was the Warden's offer to release Shirley upon receipt of a writ from the Chancellor, which suggested that only royal officials, and not the House, had the power to secure an MP's release from prison. Similarly, in the

1675 *Shirley-Fagg* case, the Commons imprisoned both Shirley and his attorneys for continuing the suit against Fagg in contravention of the House's orders, and Fagg, for filing a response to Shirley's appeal in contravention of the orders of his own House. And in the 1689 *Topham* case, the House even went so far as to imprison judges of the King's Bench for allowing prosecutions against the Sergeant of the House. Indeed, it will be recalled that the House of Commons was having officers of the courts imprisoned for breaches of privilege arising from their attempts to enforce orders of the courts as late as the *Stockdale* controversy in the late 1830s.[14]

We can clearly see the Blackstonian dynamic at work in these cases. In the 1604 *Shirley* case, in order to protect its institutional power, the House needed to secure Shirley's release by itself, and, using its contempt power, that is precisely what it did. Similarly, in the 1675 *Shirley-Fagg* case, the House of Commons was so worried about an encroachment on its power by the upper house that it actually imprisoned its own Member simply for defending himself in front of the Lords. The implication was clear: if Members of the House of Commons were subject to the jurisdiction of the House of Lords, then the Lords had a strong institutional advantage over the lower house, and the Commons was prepared to use its contempt power to prevent the Lords from gaining the upper hand. *Jay v. Topham* stood for the same principle in the lower courts.

CONTEMPT TO PUNISH UNDESIRABLE SPEECH OR CONDUCT

One of the most obvious uses of the contempt power is the punishment of speech or behavior that is, literally, contemptuous of a Member or of the House. Thus, for example, in 1603, the House of Commons arrested, fined, and forced an apology from a yeoman of the King's Guard who prevented a Member of the House from accompanying his colleagues to the House of Lords.[15] Similarly, at various points, a number of people were called to the bar of the House and punished to varying degrees for insulting or slandering Members.[16]

The later stages of the *Burdett* case were discussed in chapter 1; however, its origins are pertinent to our discussion here. In 1810, the Commons had committed the publisher of a placard that advertised a debate on the conduct of two MPs. Sir Francis Burdett, an MP, wrote a letter to the *Cobbett's Weekly Political Register* denying that the House had the power to commit for such an offense. The House found that Burdett's letter was a "libellous and scandalous Paper, reflecting on the just Rights and Privileges of this House."[17] Burdett was found guilty of a breach of privilege and ordered to the Tower.[18] When the Sergeant went to arrest him, he had to force open his home—and he supposedly found Burdett busily teaching his infant son to read and translate the Magna Carta.[19] The court cases arising from the arrest are the subject of the discussion in chapter 1.

The *Burdett* case thus raises issues similar to those raised by the *Hall* and *Bland* cases in the late sixteenth century. Sir Francis Burdett's letter was a public denial that the House possessed powers that it claimed to possess. As such, it represented an institutional challenge of the sort that the Blackstonian conception of privilege was intended to combat. Holding Burdett in contempt was thus consonant with this conception of privilege.

PRESS CONTEMPTS

In 1641, the House of Commons passed a resolution prohibiting Members from distributing any account of the House's proceedings to non-Members.[20] The next year, it resolved that the printing or selling of accounts or proceedings of the House was a breach of privilege.[21] A similar resolution was again passed in 1694, ordering "News-Letter-Writers" not to "presume to intermeddle with the Debates, or any other Proceedings, of this House."[22] The order was repeated in 1722, and a similar one was passed in 1753 and another in 1762.[23] The House was not shy about punishing those who disobeyed its injunction against publishing. In 1695, Griffith Card and Jeremiah Stokes were reprimanded for publishing accounts of parliamentary proceedings, and the next year, John Dyer was ordered into the custody of the Sergeant for the same offense.[24] Dyer obviously failed to learn his lesson, as he was back before the House for the same offense within a year.[25] In 1703, we find the author, printer, and publisher of *The Observator* ordered into the Sergeant's custody for an article containing "Matters scandalous and malicious, reflecting upon the Proceedings of this House, and tending to the promoting Sedition in the Kingdom."[26] In 1721, the House of Lords resolved that "if, after the Death of any Lord of this House, any Person presume to publish in Print his Works, Life, or last Will, without Consent of his Heirs, Executors, Administrators, or Trustees, the same is a Breach of the Privilege of this House."[27] In 1728, the House of Commons hotly resolved, "That it is an Indignity to, and a Breach of the Privilege of, this House, for any Person to presume to give, in written or printed Newspapers, any Account, or Minutes, of the Debates, or other Proceedings of this House, or of any Committee thereof," and threatened to punish offending authors, printers, and publishers "with the utmost severity."[28] Indeed, as late as 1832, the proprietor of the *Dublin Evening Mail* was taken into custody for printing the report of a parliamentary committee before it was released for publication.[29]

Much like the *Abingdon* and *Creevey* cases discussed in chapter 3, the press cases discussed above also fall under the Blackstonian conception of privilege. The resolutions against publishing unauthorized reports of a House's proceedings and the punishments levied for flouting those resolutions demonstrate the Blackstonian conception's total lack of concern for communication between Members and their constituents. Again, the geographical focus of the Blackstonian conception is key: that which is said *inside* Parliament may only be released *outside* with the explicit permission of the House. In this way, information can be prevented from falling into the hands of those who might use it against the House. The control of information is, of course, a potent form of power.

This was clear again in 1956, when the editor of the *Sunday Express* was found guilty of contempt for an editorial criticizing the fact that petrol rationing in the wake of the Suez invasion would be less stringent for MPs than for their constituents.[30] The Committee of Privileges concluded that the editorial was meant to suggest that MPs were more interested in their own well-being than in that of the nation,[31] which it regarded as a grave attack on the dignity of the House and therefore a contempt. The editor was forced to apologize at the bar for showing such disrespect to the House.[32]

The *Sunday Express* case unfortunately demonstrates that the Blackstonian view persisted into the twentieth century in at least one instance. Here, a newspaper editor was, essentially, held in contempt for calling MPs hypocrites. The holding was justified on the grounds that the editorial soiled the good name of the House among the citizenry. The notion that the House must be protected from vigorous criticism in the press is surely a Blackstonian one — it rests on the fear that the House will lose power to some other institution, along with the sense that vigorous criticism is not really necessary to the proper functioning of the House. This was indeed a Blackstonian decision — even if it came at a time when such decisions were clearly no longer appropriate.

The Millian Paradigm

It should be noted that uses of the contempt power that are justified under the Millian paradigm would generally also be justified under the Blackstonian. The converse, however, is not true — the cases discussed above are largely justifiable on the Blackstonian view but not the Millian. The cases to which we come now are justifiable on both grounds, and by examining the Millian justifications for the use of the contempt power, we shall see how it is more restrictive than the Blackstonian and how that restriction serves to tighten the nexus between constituents and legislators.

FRAUD, BRIBERY, AND DISRUPTION

In 1701, Thomas Colepepper was committed to Newgate by the House. He had lost an election to the House by two votes, whereupon he protested, both publicly and in a petition to the House, that eight people who voted for his opponent — Thomas Blisse, by now an MP — received alms and were thus ineligible to vote. He also accused Blisse of buying a number of votes. Blisse denied that he had purchased votes, accused Colepepper of buying votes, and said that more people receiving alms had voted for Colepepper than had voted for him.[33] The House decided that Blisse was the duly elected Member, that Colepepper's petition was "scandalous, insolent, and seditious," and that Colepepper himself "hath been guilty of corrupt, scandalous, and indirect Practices, in endeavouring to procure himself to be elected a Burgess to serve in this present Parliament."[34]

After reviewing his complaint, the House determined that not only had Colepepper falsely accused his opponent of electoral fraud but Colepepper had, himself, committed electoral fraud. Of course, the possibility exists that Colepepper was right and the House was itself acting fraudulently by certifying the wrong winner. It was to prevent that possibility that Parliament turned over the judging of electoral disputes to the courts in 1868,[35] as we saw in chapter 7. But assuming that the House was correct — or at least acting in good faith — when it judged Colepepper to be guilty of electoral fraud, it was certainly within its purview to find him guilty of contempt, even on the more restrictive Millian view.

Bribery, too, has been treated as a contempt. Both Members receiving bribes and non-Members offering them have been punished by the House.[36] (As we have seen, the speech privilege has prevented the common-law courts from hearing bribery cases against MPs.) In 1695, the House of Commons resolved that "the Offer of any Money, or other Advantage, to any Member of Parliament, for the promoting of any Matter whatsoever, depending, or to be transacted, in Parliament, is a high Crime and Misdemeanor, and tends to the Subversion of the *English* Constitution."[37]

Moreover, the behavior of private citizens outside Parliament that has disrupted proceedings in Parliament has been considered a contempt. In 1780, the Commons held rioters in the streets outside the halls of Parliament in contempt. It announced generally, "That it is a gross Breach of the Privilege of this House, for any Person to obstruct and insult the Members, of this House in the coming to, or going from, the House, and to endeavour to compel the Members, by Force, to declare themselves in favour of or against any Proposition then depending, or expected to be brought, before the House."[38] In this, the House was simply following a much earlier suggestion of Edward Coke's:

> By the ancient law, and custome of the parliament a proclamation ought to be made in Westminster in the beginning of the parliament, that no man upon pain to lose all that he hath, should during the parliament in London, Westminster, or the suburbs, &c. wear any privy coat of plate, or goe armed, or that games or other playes of men, women, or children, or any other pastimes or strange shews should be there used during the parliament: and the reason hereof was, that the high court of parliament should not thereby be disturbed, nor the members thereof (which are to attend the arduous and urgent businesse of the church and commonwealth) should not be withdrawn.[39]

It remains the case today that disrupting a meeting of the House or one of its committees, or molesting or intimidating a Member, officer, or witness of either House, is a contempt.[40] Recall that the Millian view aims to tighten the fit between the wishes of the electorate and the actions of its representatives in Parliament. Attempted vote fraud is obviously a great affront to this view; the use of contempt to punish it is thus justified by Millian logic. Similarly, the Millian view justifies treating both bribery and the physical intimidation of MPs (by, for example, rioters) as contempt. Each of these is a case in which a minority is trying to exert disproportionate influence on the legislative process, and the Millian view of the role of privilege thus justifies treating them as contempts.

Likewise, telling lies on the floor of the House is a way of treating one's individual concerns as more significant than those of the nation and therefore constitutes Millian grounds for a contempt finding. Insofar as the free and open debate of policy is one of the functions of Parliament, lies hinder its effective functioning. The House of Commons was thus well within the Millian paradigm when it found John Profumo in contempt in 1963. Rumors had been circulating that Profumo, the secretary of state for war, had engaged in a relationship with a model who was also close with an attaché at the Soviet Embassy. In a statement before the House, Profumo denied having such an association, but he was later forced to admit that the rumors were true. His lie before the House was considered a serious contempt, although his subsequent resignation rendered the need for punishment moot.[41]

INTERFERENCE WITH THE COMPOSITION OF THE HOUSE OR THE EFFICACY OF ITS ORDERS

When the monarch was particularly irked by certain Members of Parliament, one way that he could deal with them was by appointing them to offices incompatible with their parliamentary status. We saw in chapter 3 that James I sent some Members off to Ireland as royal commissioners when they displeased him. Other nettlesome Members, however, could simply be appointed sheriffs. A sheriff was considered legally tied to his county, and service at Westminster was incompatible with this tie. Sheriffs were thus ineligible to serve in Parliament. The practice of appointing a Member a sheriff was known as "pricking for sheriff," and it was, not surprisingly, a source of irritation to the House.[42] In 1675, the House of Commons passed a resolution declaring it to be "a Breach of the Privilege of this House for any Member thereof to be made a Sheriff during the Continuance of the Parliament."[43] This bold move by the House was clearly justified on Millian grounds — after all, the power to remove vexatious Members of Parliament is the power to remove parliamentary opposition, and no theory of privilege aimed at facilitating the exercise of democratic governance could brook such a practice.

Just as the House could not tolerate interference with its composition, so too could it not tolerate interference with its orders. As noted in chapter 1, it was during one of its attempts to enforce the injunction against publishing reports of proceedings in Parliament that the House of Commons in 1771 ordered the arrest of a number of printers in London. The Lord Mayor, Brass Crosby, had the messenger of the Commons arrested as the messenger was trying to arrest a printer.[44] When he was called before the bar of the House, Crosby argued that his oath of office, which required him to protect the rights and liberties of the citizens, justified his action. The Commons, unsurprisingly, responded by sending him to the Tower for breach of privilege, where the Court of Common Pleas made him stay.[45] The Millian view of Parliament's contempt power clearly justifies the outcome of this case. Here, a local official imprisoned an officer of the House while that officer was acting under orders from the House. In other words, a local official (representing, therefore, a *national* minority) attempted to override the will of the national majority, as expressed by its representatives in Parliament, through force. Allowing the Lord Mayor to get away with it, then, would have been contrary to the purpose of the Millian conception of privilege; hence, the House's decision to hold the Lord Mayor in contempt was justified under the Millian paradigm.

PRESS CONTEMPTS

In *Wason v. Walter*, discussed in more detail in chapter 3, one of Wason's arguments was that the newspaper account was illegal because it violated the standing injunction against unauthorized accounts of debates on the floor. Chief Justice Cockburn concluded, in essence, that the injunction had become obsolete: "Practically, such publication is sanctioned by parliament; it is essential to the working of our parliamentary system, and to the welfare of the nation."[46] Although he acknowledged that "[s]hould either house of parliament ever be so ill-advised as to prevent its proceedings from being made known to the country — which certainly will never be the case — any publication of its debates made in contravention of its orders would be a matter between the house and the publisher," he also held that, until such time, the courts would treat the publication of debates as lawful.[47] The court's decision here that communication with constituents had come to be considered essential to the democratic functioning of the lower house was the first repudiation of the Blackstonian paradigm in press contempt cases. In 1971, the House of Commons would officially catch up to the *Wason* decision, when it resolved that "notwithstanding the Resolution of the House [in 1762] and other such Resolutions, this House will not entertain any complaint of contempt of the House or breach of privilege in respect of the publication of the Debates or Proceedings of the House or of its Committees, except when any such Debates or Proceedings shall have been conducted with closed doors or in private, or when such publication shall have been expressly prohibited by the House."[48] It should be noted, however, that the premature publication or leaking of parliamentary committee proceedings or reports remains a contempt.[49]

In 1956 — the same year as the (Blackstonian) *Sunday Express* case — the *Sunday Graphic* newspaper expressed disapproval over the position of Arthur Lewis, an MP, on the Suez invasion. The paper published his private phone number and encouraged its readers to call him if they felt similar disapproval. The result was that Lewis's "telephone was rendered useless by a flood of bitter and insulting calls."[50] The House of Commons, concluding that this inundation of phone calls hampered Lewis in his parliamentary duties, found the newspaper's editor in contempt, and he was forced to apologize at the bar.[51] The Millian conception justifies this finding. While the Millian conception seeks close communication between MPs and constituents, it must also provide limits to that communication. Harassment so extreme that it hinders MPs' ability to do their job is harmful, not beneficial, to democracy. It seems likely that the extreme invasion of privacy and personal harassment caused by publishing an MP's private phone number crosses this line and thus becomes a contempt.

THE NOLAN COMMITTEE REPORT

In 1994, the prime minister established the Committee on Standards in Public Life, under the chairmanship of Lord Nolan, in an effort to address public perceptions of declining ethical standards in public life. The committee's first report, issued in 1995, addressed standards for Members of Parliament (among others).[52] Several of the committee's recommendations with regard to Parliament addressed specific questions of the appropriateness of Members working as parliamentary consultants and of the disclosure of Members' financial interests. Most important for privilege purposes, however, was the committee's recommendation that the office of Parliamentary Commissioner for Standards be created. The commissioner would "take responsibility for advising Members on, and play[] an independent role in the enforcement of, the House's rules in respect of Members' conduct."[53] Specifically, when a complaint was raised about a Member's conduct, the commissioner would have the independent discretion to determine whether or not it merited investigation. Her investigations would be conducted privately, and she would have the power, via a Select Committee of the House, to summon witnesses, papers, and records. If she found the complaint unwarranted, she would dismiss the case, publicly stating her reasons. If she found the complaint warranted, she could either reach a settlement with the Member under investigation or refer the case to a special subcommittee of the Committee of Privileges for further, and public, investigation.[54] The Nolan Committee emphasized that this procedure would provide "the necessary detachment without recourse to the courts or indeed any surrender of privilege. The recommendations . . . should enable Members to secure a fair, thorough and expeditious hearing without removing jurisdiction from the House of Commons."[55] The recommendations thus allowed an increasingly effective and regularized mechanism for enforcing the rules governing Members' conduct without depriving the House of its exclusive jurisdiction over their behavior. Insofar as the House's internal rules operate to prevent corruption and self-dealing, this means that parliamentary behavior would be brought closer in line with the desires of the public, without giving a nonparliamentary body the final say over the content of lex parliamenti—in other words, a supremely Millian result. The House quickly adopted almost all of the Nolan Committee's recommendations with regard to the Parliamentary Commissioner for Standards, and the House has operated under the framework recommended by the Nolan Committee since.[56]

Abuses of the Contempt Power

We have already seen examples of the misuse of the breach and contempt power in the sixteenth-century *Storie* and *Parry* cases; sadly, those were not the last instances of such abuse. In 1621, the Commons attempted to use their contempt power to punish a non-Member for remarks made neither in nor about the House. Edward Floyd, a Catholic and a private subject, had made slanderous remarks about King James's Protestant son-in-law, the Elector Palatine, and had expressed satisfaction at the success of the Catholic cause in Germany. The House of Commons summoned Floyd to the bar, fined him £1,000, and sent him to the pillory. The Lords, believing this to fall outside the scope of contempt, considered the Commons' action an invasion of their judicial role. After several conferences between the Houses, the Commons gave in and turned the case over to the Lords, who claimed original jurisdiction. This proved cold comfort to Floyd: the Lords condemned him to life imprisonment, a fine of £5,000, and whipping and branding, and they, too, sent him to the pillory.[57] Here, the speaker was not an MP, was not speaking in Parliament, and was not speaking about Parliament. The finding that he was in contempt of Parliament was, then, nothing more than a ploy to silence him. Neither view of the role of privilege justifies this use of contempt. The House of Lords' subsequent punishment of Floyd for seditious libel may not be consonant with modern ideas of democratic justice, but it was consonant with the ideas of the time — and ultimately it was properly determined that the Lords, as a judicial body, could punish Floyd for a crime, but the Commons could not punish him for contempt.

The Houses also have a history of punishing as contempts or breaches of privilege actions that affect Members only in their capacity as private citizens. A mob that in 1640 destroyed a mill owned by the Countess of Exeter was held to be in breach of privilege, as were individuals who cut down trees, stole tin, trespassed into a mine, or killed rabbits or fish belonging to a Member.[58] Again, these seem to be clear abuses of the contempt power. While trespassing upon or destroying a Member's property, hunting his game, and so on, are undoubtedly illegal, it is hard to understand why they should be considered contempts of the House, assuming they were not done in order to intimidate or respond to the Member's official actions. They do not diminish the power of the House, nor do they prevent it from fulfilling its functions, nor do they prevent any individual Member from attending to his duties. They undoubtedly do present the allegedly injured Member with a forum more congenial to his claims, but this certainly does not justify taking the case out of the hands of the common-law courts.

Conclusions

Comparing these three categories of breach and contempt decisions — those justified only under the Blackstonian paradigm, those also justified under the Millian paradigm, and those not justified under either — helps to sharpen our understanding of how the Blackstonian and Millian paradigms treat contempt. The Blackstonian paradigm, as has been remarked before, treats privilege as a wall protecting the House's power from external forces that threaten it. Under this view, a contempt of Parliament is, quite literally, anything that might cause the House to be held in contempt — either by other powerful institutions or by the general public. For an institution struggling to assert its power in a hostile political landscape, anything that causes it to be held in contempt is a serious blow to its legitimacy. Because the Blackstonian view of privilege focuses on increasing the power of Parliament, as the most democratic institution in the state, it must erect strong barriers to prevent Parliament's legitimacy from being eroded. Hence, the Blackstonian view of privilege justifies contempt findings against those who publicly insult the House, refuse to carry out its orders, or publish its proceedings without its consent.

While the Blackstonian view thus uses breach and contempt findings to increase the power of Parliament, even at the expense of weak ties between Members of Parliament and their constituents, the Millian view holds that findings of contempt are only appropriate when used to punish an action that is detrimental to those ties. We thus find the Millian view justifying holdings of contempt in cases of electoral fraud, bribery, intimidation and harassment of Members, and attempts by local authorities to frustrate Parliament's intentions. (There is, of course, no bright line separating unacceptable intimidation or harassment from acceptable lobbying or presentation of views; marginal cases will always be contested, although the logic of the Millian position suggests that the benefit of the doubt ought to be given to the citizen expressing his or her views.) All of these are cases in which the actions of individuals or groups run counter to Parliament's ability to express the general will. Because the Millian view focuses on increasing the representativeness of an already powerful Parliament, it justifies the use of the contempt power only when something threatens the House's ability accurately to represent the people.

Finally, those contempt findings that cannot be said to serve democracy in any way (that is, on either the Blackstonian or Millian model) fall into the category of abuses of power. This includes the use of the contempt power to suppress unpopular speech. Note that this is different from suppressing speech that might harm the dignity of Parliament: the Blackstonian view (but not the Millian) allows for suppression of that kind of speech. And both views allow the punishment of speech that disrupts the functioning of the House. But orderly speeches made either on the floor (in which case no one outside the House would have access to them except by permission of the House) or in public but not about Parliament cannot touch upon the dignity of Parliament. Such speeches neither obstruct nor impede the House or its Members in the performance of their duties and thus are not punishable by contempt findings, even under the wide scope of the Blackstonian paradigm. Similarly, private offenses against Members that do not affect their ability to perform their jobs (for example, trespassing on their lands, hunting their game, and the like) are precisely that: *private* offenses, which ought to be punished in the common-law courts. They are certainly not issues that touch on Parliament's ability to carry out its function, and thus they are not fit subjects for contempt proceedings.

In the examination above, it is somewhat startling that cases which can only be justified under the Blackstonian paradigm arose as late as the 1950s. Indeed, Geoffrey Marshall has suggested that the *Sunday Express* case "did more to bring the House's privilege jurisdiction into disrepute than any other exercise of it in the twentieth century,"[59] and well it should have. The case was an anachronism: a Blackstonian decision in a Millian age. Contempt is undoubtedly a very tempting tool for Parliament — it enables the House to get its way through brute force. Perhaps because it is so tempting, it has proven susceptible to abuse. As we have seen, there are a number of cases in which the House has found breaches of privilege where no theory of privilege would find them. There have also been cases of Blackstonian findings of contempt within a solidly Millian political climate.

Although neither House has imprisoned anyone since 1880, contempt remains a powerful holding, one that the Select Committee on Parliamentary Privilege in 1967 concluded should be exercised "as sparingly as possible."[60] As can be seen from the paucity of recent cases, it has indeed been used sparingly since the 1950s. Ultimately, self-restraint on Parliament's part, the procedures put into place pursuant to the Nolan Committee Report, and the seeming end of imprisonment by Parliament (with an understanding that, should Parliament resume imprisonment, the courts might well have a role in reviewing it, as discussed in chapter 1) all combine to make abuses of this power increasingly unlikely and to ensure that Parliament's policy with respect to contempt findings is congruent with the Millian political climate in which it operates.

Punishment by Congress

As with the Houses of Parliament, if the Houses of Congress are to be able effectively to control their proceedings, they must be able to prevent both Members and non-Members from disrupting their orderly functioning. This is where their disciplinary powers come into play. A House can punish its Members, including expelling them, for conduct that is disruptive or that brings disrepute on the House, and it can punish non-Members for disrupting the House — either by impermissible interference or by refusing to cooperate with a legitimate request of the House. However, the Houses must strike a fine balance when exercising these powers — expulsion of Members threatens the right of their constituents to be represented by the person of their choice, and punishment of non-Members runs the risk of becoming something like a bill of attainder. By examining where those lines should be and have been drawn, we shall better understand the role this privilege plays in the American constitutional order.

Text and History

The power of the Houses of Congress to punish went almost entirely undiscussed at the Founding. As we saw in chapter 2, an early draft of the Constitution in the Committee of Detail contained the placeholder, "[Q]uaere.

how far the right of expulsion may be proper."[1] A subsequent draft gave each House the power "to punish its own Members for disorderly (and indecent) Behaviour" and allowed that "[e]ach House may expel a Member, but not a second Time for the same Offence."[2] Indeed, all three of the state constitutions at the Founding that gave the legislature a right of expulsion prohibited reexpulsion for the same offence.[3] However, by the time the committee had reported to the Convention, the provision had been changed to, "Each House may determine the rules of its proceedings; may punish its members for disorderly behaviour; and may expel a member."[4] In debate, Madison "observed that the right of expulsion . . . was too important to be exercised by a bare majority of a quorum: and in emergencies of faction might be dangerously abused. He moved that 'with the concurrence of ⅔' might be inserted between may & expel."[5] Edmund Randolph, George Mason, and Daniel Carroll voiced their approval; Gouverneur Morris thought that a majority was sufficient and that "[t]o require more may produce abuses on the side of the minority. A few men from factious motives may keep in a member who ought to be expelled."[6] Madison's proposal passed with ten states voting in favor, none against, and Morris's Pennsylvania delegation divided.[7] With no further debate, the clause assumed its final form: "Each House may determine the Rules of its Proceedings, punish its Members for disorderly Behaviour, and, with the Concurrence of two thirds, expel a Member."[8] There was no debate on the issue in the states' ratifying conventions or in the press.[9]

The Houses' power to punish non-Members has no explicit textual basis in the Constitution. At the Philadelphia Convention, Charles Pinckney did propose a provision reading,

> Each House shall be the Judge of its own privileges, and shall have authority to punish by imprisonment every person violating the same; or who, in the place where the Legislature may be sitting and during the time of its Session, shall threaten any of its members for any thing said or done in the House, or who shall assault any of them therefore — or who shall assault or arrest any witness or other person ordered to attend either of the Houses in his way going or returning; or who shall rescue any person arrested by their order.[10]

The proposal was referred to the Committee of Detail, where it died without recorded debate. Aside from Pinckney's short-lived proposal, the Houses' power to punish non-Members does not seem to have been considered in any of the other debates in the Philadelphia Convention, the states' ratifying conventions, or the press.

These issues were briefly touched upon by two of the great early interpreters of the Constitution. James Wilson, in his Lectures on Law, noted that Congress's disciplinary powers ensured that the congressional privilege of free speech did not give rise to verbal abuse: "Under the protection of privilege, to use indecency or licentiousness of language, in the course of debate, is disorderly behaviour, of a kind peculiarly base and ungentlemanly."[11] Wilson also noted that the Pennsylvania Constitution, unlike the final draft of the federal Constitution, explicitly prohibited a second expulsion for the same offense.

> The reason for the addition evidently is—that the member, who has offended, cannot be an object of a second expulsion, unless, since the offence given and punished by the first expulsion, he has been either reelected by his former constituents, or elected by others. In both cases, his election is a proof, that, in the opinion of his constituents, he either has not offended at all, or has been already sufficiently punished for his offence. The language of each opinion is, that he ought not to be expelled again: and the language of the constituents is a law to the house.[12]

Joseph Story, too, examined congressional disciplinary powers. "[T]he power to make rules would be nugatory," he noted, "unless it was coupled with a power to punish for disorderly behavior or disobedience to those rules."[13] This, of course, included even the power to expel.

> But such a power, so summary, and at the same time so subversive of the rights of the people, it was foreseen, might be exerted for mere purposes of faction or party, to remove a patriot or to aid a corrupt measure; and it has therefore been wisely guarded by the restriction, that there shall be a concurrence of two-thirds of the members to justify an expulsion.[14]

Story also noted that, although it was "remarkable" that the Constitution did not explicitly grant the Houses the power to punish non-Members for contempts, "yet it is obvious that unless such a power, to some extent, exists by implication, it is utterly impossible for either house to perform its constitutional functions."[15] He further noted that "the legislative body was the proper and exclusive forum to decide when the contempt existed, and when there was a breach of its privileges; and that the power to punish followed, as a necessary incident to the power to take cognizance of the offence."[16] However, as in Britain, the Houses' power to punish "is confined to punishment during the session of the legislative body, and cannot be extended beyond it."[17]

Interpretation
PUNISHING MEMBERS

The Houses' powers to punish Members and non-Members present two distinct issues, and they must be dealt with separately. First, we shall examine the power to punish Members. In addition to the power to expel, the punishments available to the Houses include imprisonment (which has never been used against a Member), censure or reprimand, fine, and loss of seniority, as well as the adverse publicity that comes with any finding of wrongdoing.[18] Gerald McLaughlin suggests that Members can also be suspended (although this has never been done), but he notes the problem that, "[d]uring the period of suspension, a member's constituents are deprived of the services of their representative without the power to send someone else in his place."[19] This is a fatal flaw for any claimed power to suspend—the Constitution guarantees each state two senators and a number of representatives proportionate to the state's population. Indeed, it even explicitly declares that "no State, without its Consent, shall be deprived of it's [*sic*] equal Suffrage in the Senate."[20] When a Member is expelled, dies, or retires, he may be replaced, and therefore his constituents are not deprived of representation; were a Member to be suspended, then his constituents would remain unrepresented for the duration of his punishment, and their constitutional right to representation would be denied. Punishment of a Member may not extend to his constituents.

Now that we have seen what punishments are available, it remains to consider what behavior Members may be punished *for*. First, it is important to note that the Constitution does not place any substantive restraints on what offenses are punishable by the Houses. The Houses can punish "for violations of statutory law, including crimes; for violations of internal congressional rules; or for any conduct which the House . . . finds has reflected discredit upon the institution."[21] Indeed, even purely private conduct by a Member that, in the House's opinion, reflects badly on it as an institution is punishable. There is, of course, a *procedural* restraint on expulsion—the requirement of a two-thirds supermajority—and collegiality and a sense that "there but for the grace of God go I" will generally operate to prevent unduly strict punishments. Although punishment decisions by the Houses are nonjusticiable (see chapter 2), the constitutional rights of free speech, freedom of religion, due process, and equal protection are relevant to Members deciding how to vote on a punishment resolution. Although the House can punish Members for words spoken in debate (or in any other context), it ought not to do so simply because those words express an unpopular or even abhorrent opinion. Similarly, no Member ought to be expelled for his religious beliefs or his race, gender, ethnicity, national origin, sexual orientation, and so forth. Moreover, although congressional proceedings do not and ought not follow judicial rules of procedure, they ought not be so summary as to violate due process.

Finally, there is the question of whether a Member can be expelled for behavior that both occurred and was known to his constituents before his election. Related is the question of whether a Member who has been expelled, then reelected, can be reexpelled for the same offense. It will be recalled that an early draft of the Constitution in the Committee of Detail prohibited a second expulsion for the same offense, but this provision was dropped. Nevertheless, it has traditionally been thought that Congress cannot expel for prior conduct or reexpel for the same conduct. Drawing on American outrage over the *Wilkes* case,[22] the argument has maintained that once the voters have indicated either their approval or their forgiveness of the Member's action by reelecting him, then it would be impermissibly antidemocratic for the House again to expel him for the same offense.[23] In the case of a second expulsion for the same offense, "the representatives of other states [would] have overridden the expressed will of the voters of the state or district thus deprived of its chosen representative."[24] While this traditional line of thought is admirable in the weight it places on democracy and popular sovereignty, and while it is undeniable that the House ought to be reticent to expel a Member twice for the same offense, a blanket prohibition on reexpulsion seems wrong. Recall that American popular sovereignty is a *national* popular sovereignty, and while locally elected representatives are clearly an important part of that system, representatives can act in ways that are approved of by their constituents while being antithetical to national popular sovereignty. Consider an example: Suppose that there is a bill under consideration that would open a new military base. The base would mean a significant boost to the economy of its locale, and the district in which it would be located is therefore strongly in favor of it. Now suppose that the Member representing that district offers a bribe to several of his fellow legislators to vote for the bill. This is certainly an expellable offense, and it is certainly antithetical to popular sovereignty. As we discussed in chapter 4, bribery is a means by which the interests of a well-funded minority are made to win out over a majority. But if the expelled Member's district is desperate or cynical enough, it may well approve of his "doing whatever it takes" to win the base for the area; it may, in fact, rally to his cause and reelect him. It would be odd indeed to suggest that, in the name of popular sovereignty, a briber cannot be kept out of Congress. Thus, while the Houses ought to be hesitant to reexpel a Member for the same offense, that option ought to be available for cases in which a Member acts antithetically to national popular sovereignty but in the interests of his constituents. It should additionally be noted that, had the Founders wished to prohibit reexpulsion for the same offense, they could simply have used the wording already familiar to them from the Delaware, Maryland, and Pennsylvania state constitutions. The fact that they did not do so suggests that no such prohibition was intended. The ratifiers, too, would have been familiar with these state constitutional counterparts and would have raised objections in the ratifying conventions had they wished a similar blanket prohibition to be included in the federal Constitution. It seems, then, that, for textual, structural, and historical reasons, the clause is best read not to place a blanket prohibition on reexpulsion for the same offense, although history would counsel that the Houses be reticent to do so.

PUNISHING NON-MEMBERS

The Houses' power to punish non-Members for contempt rests upon shakier footing than their power to punish Members. Nowhere in the Constitution is this power explicitly granted. However, as Story noted, it is difficult to imagine a legislative body functioning effectively without some such power — or, as C. S. Potts put it, the power is justified "on the ground of necessity."[25] Put differently, the ability to punish non-Members is structurally inherent in the very concept of a legislature; spelling it out in the document would simply have been redundant. It is certainly hard to deny that some power to punish non-Members is necessary for the House to carry out its business. The punishment power is thus justified under the general power of the Houses to regulate their own internal affairs. This means that, unlike Members, non-Members cannot be punished by the House for purely private activity. The alleged contempt or breach of privilege must in some way obstruct the functioning of the House. Contempts by non-Members fall into two broad categories: (1) impermissible interference with or attacks upon a Member or the House, and (2) refusal to cooperate with the House.

The former of these categories includes attempting to bribe a Member, assaulting a Member, and preventing Members from getting to the House. It should be noted that insulting the House or a Member — even in a defamatory way — does not fall within the House's ability to punish, as it does not disrupt the orderly functioning of the House. Indeed, it seems likely that the courts could grant habeas relief to anyone imprisoned by the House for speeches or writings outside the House. (Here, as in previous discussions, courts should be understood as having the power to police the boundaries, but not the content, of House punishment decisions. Speeches and writings made outside the House by non-Members simply do not fall within the area of the House's contempt powers.)

The Houses of Congress also have the right to demand the cooperation of private citizens — in the form of testimony or the production of evidence — in performing official functions, whether those functions are related to Congress's legislating role, its informing role, its oversight role, or its quasi-judicial role (that is, in cases of impeachment or disputed elections).[26] It simply is not

possible for Congress effectively to carry out investigations without the ability
to call witnesses and compel them to testify. As Allen Moreland put it, "In
practical terms, the inquisitorial authority of the Congress ends at the point
where a witness will be excused by the courts for refusing to obey a congressional summons to appear or to produce papers, or for refusing to answer questions posed by a member or committee of Congress."[27] Since Congress must
have broad inquisitorial powers — there are few subjects that do not fall under
the heading of either potential topics of legislation, oversight, or informing the
public — it follows that it must also have broad powers to subpoena witnesses
and evidence and to compel unwilling witnesses to testify. Because of this
broad power, the Houses of Congress should take care to ensure that procedural safeguards are in place — witnesses should have counsel available and
should be allowed to make pertinent explanatory statements.[28] However, as
we saw in chapters 2 and 4, these proceedings ought to remain the exclusive
province of the House — the courts will not be able to get involved without
running afoul of the speech or debate privilege, the same way they cannot get
involved in bribery cases without running afoul of that privilege.

Nevertheless, Congress has in fact delegated the task of punishing contempts to the courts, and the courts have upheld this delegation. In 1857,
Congress passed a law providing that anyone who refused to obey a congressional subpoena or refused to answer questions would be liable to criminal conviction "in addition to the pains and penalties now existing."[29] When a
witness's failure to appear or testify was reported to the House, the Speaker of
the House or president of the Senate was required to certify the fact to the
district attorney of the District of Columbia for prosecution. This remains the
law today, with the omission of "in addition to the pains and penalties now
existing" as the only significant modification.[30] The 1857 act also provided
immunity from criminal charges "for any fact or act touching which [a person]
shall be required to testify before either House of Congress or any committee
of either House."[31] The immunity provision was intended to prevent witnesses
from refusing to testify by citing their Fifth Amendment right against self-
incrimination. After some egregious abuse, the immunity provision was
amended in 1862 to allow for prosecution but to forbid the introduction of
testimony before Congress into evidence in that prosecution.[32] This was intended to prevent witnesses before Congress from using the Fifth Amendment
to escape testifying, while not providing blanket immunity to any criminal
lucky enough to get called before Congress to testify about his crimes. However, the Supreme Court in 1892 struck down a similarly worded immunity
clause in the context of testimony before a grand jury. The Court held that a
more expansive grant of immunity was necessary before testimony could be

forced — specifically, the wording had to be broad enough to prevent the use of the testimony in order to find other incriminating evidence.[33] Congress did not attempt to draw another immunity statute until 1954, when it passed the Compulsory Testimony Act, which applied only to national defense and security and was upheld by the Supreme Court.[34] That act was repealed in 1970 and replaced with a procedure by which, upon the request of a House or a committee thereof, a district court would order an unwilling witness to testify on the condition that "no testimony or other information compelled under the order (or any information directly or indirectly derived from such testimony or other information) may be used against the witness in any criminal case, except a prosecution for perjury, giving a false statement, or otherwise failing to comply with the order."[35] These provisions are still in effect.[36] Thus, while a good reading of the speech or debate privilege would leave the punishment of contempts solely in the hands of the House (subject to judicial oversight to ensure that the House was actually punishing *for contempt*), the current reading has in fact delegated it to the courts (although the Houses may still punish as well).

Now that we have sketched out the key issues involved in Congress's disciplinary powers, it will be instructive to examine a number of the prominent cases in which those powers have been exercised. This examination should help to flesh out the interpretive outline above.

Cases

PUNISHING MEMBERS

Quite a number of eighteenth- and nineteenth-century contempt cases involved assaults by one Member on another, an obvious contempt but often punished lightly, if at all. In the Fifth Congress, Roger Griswold taunted Matthew Lyon about Lyon's army record; in response, Lyon spat in Griswold's face.[37] While a resolution to expel Lyon was being considered by the House of Representatives' Committee on Privileges, the House passed a resolution declaring, "[T]his House will consider it a high breach of privilege if either of the Members shall enter into any personal contest until a decision of the House shall be had thereon."[38] Two days later, while the House was in session, Griswold assaulted Lyon with a cane while Lyon was seated at his desk. Lyon picked up the tongs from the House fireplace and fought back. While resolutions to expel both men were pending in committee, they pledged themselves before the Speaker to keep the peace. The expulsion resolutions were then overwhelmingly voted down.[39] In the Twenty-fifth Congress, William J. Graves killed his fellow House Member, Jonathan Cilley, in a duel. Graves had challenged Cilley to the duel because of Cilley's comments in debate on the floor. The committee was divided, but a majority held that this was a breach of privilege — indeed, "the highest offense that could be committed against either of the Houses of Congress."[40] It recommended that Graves be expelled and that the seconds — also House Members — be censured. The House tabled the matter.[41] The Senate was hardly more eager to punish its Members for assault. In the Thirty-first Congress,

> while Senator Foote of Mississippi was making a speech, Senator Benton of Missouri used threatening language toward his colleague without gaining the floor, indulged in menacing gestures toward him, and finally advanced toward him. Seeing the advance toward him, the Mississippi Senator backed away and drew a pistol from his pocket and cocked it, the pistol being a 5-chambered revolver, fully loaded.[42]

A special committee appointed to look into the matter recommended censure; its report, too, was tabled.

Finally, in the Thirty-ninth Congress, a Member of the House was punished for an assault on a fellow Member. In debate, Josiah Grinnell had "imputed cowardice to Mr. [Lovell] Rousseau in the latter's career as a soldier."[43] In response, Rousseau attacked Grinnell with a cane in the portico of the Capitol. The select committee appointed to look into the matter found that the imputation of cowardice to Rousseau was unjustified and a violation of House rules, but it also recommended the expulsion of Rousseau for the assault, which it concluded was a breach of privilege. The resolution to expel failed to garner the necessary two-thirds vote on the floor, but a motion to reprimand Rousseau instead passed. Rousseau resigned, but he was censured at the bar anyway.[44]

Perhaps the most infamous assault came during the Thirty-fourth Congress. In the course of his famous "Crime against Kansas" speech[45] on the Senate floor, Massachusetts Senator Charles Sumner spoke thus of South Carolina Senator Andrew Butler:

> The Senator from South Carolina has read many books of chivalry, and believes himself a chivalrous knight, with sentiments of honor and courage. Of course he has chosen a mistress to whom he has made his vows, and who, though ugly to others, is always lovely to him; though polluted in the sight of the world, is chaste in his sight — I mean the harlot, Slavery. For her, his tongue is always profuse in words. Let her be impeached in character, or any proposition made to shut her out from the extension of her wantonness, and no extravagance of matter or hardihood of assertion is then too great for this Senator. The frenzy of Don Quixote, in behalf of his wench, Dulcinea del Toboso, is all surpassed.[46]

Sumner continued for some time more in this vein. Three days later, Preston Brooks, a Member of the House of Representatives from South Carolina and a relative of Butler's, walked onto the floor of the Senate, approached Sumner's desk, and savagely beat him with a cane.[47] Indeed, so severe were Sumner's injuries that he was unable to resume his duties in the Senate for more than three years.[48] The House Committee appointed to investigate declared that the assault was "a most flagrant violation, not only of the privileges of the Senate and of the House, as coördinate branches of the legislative department of the Government, and the personal rights and privileges of the Senator, but of the rights of his constituents and of our character as a nation."[49] Both the Senate and the House explicitly recognized, however, that because Brooks was a Member of the House, the Senate could not punish him for contempt.[50] The majority of the House Committee recommended that Brooks be expelled.[51] When the proposed resolution came up for a vote, 121 voted to expel and 95 voted against—well short of the required two-thirds.[52] The same day, Brooks resigned.[53] He then stood for reelection in the special election to fill his seat, won, and was reseated without debate less than a month later.[54]

A second, and related, set of congressional discipline cases has arisen when Members have insulted either other Members or the House. In the Twenty-fifth Congress, a resolution was introduced to determine whether Alexander Duncan, a Member, was the author of a certain publication insulting Edward Stanly, another Member, and, if so, whether he was not "guilty of a violation of the privileges of this House; of an offense against its peace, dignity, and good order; and of such grossly indecent, ungentlemanly, disgraceful, and dishonorable misconduct, as renders him unworthy of a seat in this House, and justly liable to expulsion from the same."[55] After Duncan admitted to being the author of the publication in question, a Member offered an expulsion resolution. After opposition from John Quincy Adams, among others, the expulsion motion was withdrawn. The next day, a censure motion was introduced instead. After debate, the matter was tabled.

In the Fifty-seventh Congress, Senator John McLaurin, referring to a statement by Senator Benjamin Tillman, said that it was "a willful, malicious, and deliberate lie."[56] A brawl ensued. Both were held in contempt, and the matter was reported to the Committee on Privileges and Elections to consider punishment. The committee recommended censure, and the Senate concurred.[57] There was a debate on, but no resolution of, the question of whether the senators could vote after they had been held in contempt but before they had been punished: both voluntarily refrained from voting during that period.[58]

The House was certainly not in a mood to be forgiving when it was insulted as a body. In the Thirty-ninth Congress, John Chanler introduced the resolution:

> *Resolved*, That the independent, patriotic, and constitutional course of the President of the United States in seeking to protect by the veto power the rights of the people of this Union against the wicked and revolutionary acts of a few malignant and mischievous men meets with the approval of this House and deserves the cordial support of all loyal citizens of the United States.[59]

Naturally, the House did not take kindly to having acts that were approved by a majority of its Members called "wicked and revolutionary" or to having those Members called "malignant and mischievous." Neither did it appreciate Chanler's lauding of President Johnson, whom the House would impeach within two years. Robert Schenck introduced a resolution censuring Chanler for presenting a resolution insulting to the House. The censure passed on a vote of 72 to 30.[60] Similarly, during a debate on a reconstruction bill in the Fortieth Congress, Fernando Wood had the bad manners to call the bill a "monstrosity, a measure the most infamous of the many infamous acts of this infamous Congress."[61] The Speaker declared the words out of order, and Wood was censured by a vote of 114 to 39.

In the Forty-third Congress, John Young Brown managed both to insult an individual Member and to show contempt for the House as a whole. He was speaking on the floor against a motion of Benjamin Butler to recommit a civil- and political-rights bill:

> Now again that accusation has come from one—I speak not of men but of language, and within the rules of the House—that accusation against that people has come from one who is outlawed in his own home from respectable society; whose name is synonomous [*sic*] with falsehood; who is the champion, and has been on all occasions, of fraud; who is the apologist of thieves; who is such a prodigy of vice and meanness that to describe him would sicken imagination and exhaust invective.
>
> In Scotland years ago there was a man whose trade was murder, and who earned a livelihood by selling the bodies of his victims for gold. He linked his name to his crime, and to-day throughout the world it is known as "Burking."
>
> The SPEAKER. Does the Chair understand the gentleman to be referring in this language to a Member of the House?
>
> Mr. BROWN. No, sir; I am describing an individual who is in my mind's eye.
>
> The SPEAKER. The Chair understood the gentleman to refer to a member of the House.
>
> Mr. BROWN. No, sir; I call no names.
>
> This man's name was linked to his crime, and to-day throughout the world it is known as "Burking." If I wished to describe all that was pusillanimous in war, inhuman in peace, forbidden in morals, and infamous in politics, I should call it "Butlerism."[62]

Robert Hale introduced a censure resolution, both for Brown's words and for "the prevarication to the Speaker, by which he was enabled to complete the utterance of the language." After an expulsion resolution was introduced and then withdrawn for lack of adequate support, the censure resolution passed 161 to 79.[63]

In the Eighty-second Congress, the Senate Subcommittee on Privileges and Elections considered a resolution to expel Joseph McCarthy for, among other things, electoral improprieties. McCarthy claimed that the resolution was "a Communist smear," designed to punish him for "having exposed Communists in Government."[64] The subcommittee's report criticized McCarthy but did not recommend any action, and no action was taken by the Senate.[65] However, in the next Congress, the Senate censured McCarthy for his "noncooperation with and abuse of" the subcommittee in the previous Congress and for his "abuse of" the select committee in the current Congress.[66]

The Houses have also used their disciplinary powers to punish what might be called offenses against the nation — cases in which a Member has acted contrary to the national interest. During the Fifth Congress, President Adams showed the Houses a letter written by Senator William Blount laying out a plan to work with the British and Indian tribes to seize Spanish Florida and Louisiana — a plan against American and Spanish interests.[67] A select committee held hearings, allowing Blount to be represented by counsel and to be furnished with copies of relevant documents.[68] The committee's report ultimately recommended expulsion, and the Senate adopted the report by a vote of 25 to 1, thereby expelling him.[69]

In the Tenth Congress, the Senate was faced with accusations of treason against John Smith, who was an associate of Aaron Burr. Samuel Maclay introduced a resolution calling for a select committee to "inquire whether it be compatible with the honor and privileges of this House" that Smith continue to sit.[70] The committee, in a report delivered by John Quincy Adams, concluded that despite Burr's acquittal in the courts on treason charges,

> the conspiracy of Aaron Burr and his associates against the peace, union, and liberties of these States is of such a character, and that its existence is established by such a mass of concurring and mutually corroborative testimony that it is incompatible not only with the honor and privileges of this House, but with the deepest interests of this nation, that any person engaged in it should be permitted to hold a seat in the Senate of the United States.[71]

On procedural matters, the committee concluded that it was not "bound in this inquiry by any other rules than those of natural justice and equity, due to a brother Senator on the one part and to their country on the other." The technical rules of courts would not be incorporated: "[T]he power of expelling a member must, in its nature, be discretionary, and in its exercise always more summary than the tardy process of judicial tribunals."[72] The committee also pondered the purpose of the expulsion power:

> The power of expelling a member for misconduct results, on the principles of common sense, from the interest of the nation, that the high trust of legislation should be invested in pure hands. When the trust is elective it is not to be presumed that the constituent body will commit the deposite [sic] to the keeping of worthless characters. But when a man, whom his fellow-citizens have honored with their confidence, on the pledge of a spotless reputation, has degraded himself by the commission of infamous crimes, which become suddenly and unexpectedly revealed to the world, defective indeed would be that institution which should be impotent to discard from its bosom the contagion of such a member; which should have no remedy of amputation to apply until the poison had reached the heart.
>
> The question upon the trial of a criminal cause, before the courts of common law, is not between guilt and innocence, but between guilt and the possibility of innocence. If a doubt can possibly be raised, either by the ingenuity of the party or of his counsel, or by the operation of general rules in their unforeseen application to particular cases, that doubt must be decisive for acquittal, and the verdict of not guilty, perhaps, in nine cases out of ten, means no more than that the guilt of the party has not been demonstrated in the precise, specific, and narrow forms prescribed by law. The humane spirit of the laws multiplies the barriers for the protection of innocence, and freely admits that these barriers may be abused for the shelter of guilt. It avows a strong partiality favorable to the person upon trial, and acknowledges the preference that ten guilty should escape rather than that one innocent should suffer. The interest of the public that a particular crime should be punished is but as one to ten compared with the interest of the party that innocence should be spared. . . .
>
> But when a member of a legislative body lies under the imputation of aggravated offenses, and the determination upon his cause can operate only to remove him from a station of extensive powers and important trust, this disproportion between the interest of the public and the interest of the individual disappears; if any disproportion exist, it is of an opposite kind. It is not better that ten traitors should be members of this Senate than that one innocent man should suffer expulsion. In either case, no doubt, the evil would be great. But, in the former it would strike at the vitals of the nation; in the latter it might, though deeply to be lamented, only be the calamity of an individual.
> . . .
> [The committee Members] believe that the very purpose for which this power was given was to preserve the Legislature from the first approaches of

infection. That it was made discretionary because it could not exist under the procrastination of general rules; that its processes must be summary, because it would be rendered nugatory by delay.[73]

The committee submitted to the Senate testimony to show that Smith was a part of Burr's conspiracy, as well as Smith's response, and it recommended a resolution of expulsion.[74] The full Senate allowed Smith to be heard by counsel before it but denied his requests to be informed specifically of the charges against him and to have process to compel the attendance of witnesses.[75] The issue was debated at length in the Senate, but the final vote (nineteen to ten) fell just short of the two-thirds needed for expulsion.[76] Smith thus remained in the Senate.

The tables turned somewhat in the Twenty-seventh Congress, when John Quincy Adams was the subject of a censure resolution for presenting to the House a petition of some of his constituents calling for the peaceful dissolution of the Union on the grounds that "a vast proportion of the resources of one section of the Union is annually drained to sustain the views and course of another section without any adequate return."[77] In response, one Member offered a resolution censuring Adams, while another offered a resolution accusing him of treason. The matter was ultimately tabled.[78]

In the next session of Congress, Senator Benjamin Tappan was censured for releasing to the press a copy of a treaty of annexation just signed between the president and the Republic of Texas. The treaty was supposed to be considered in secret. After Tappan apologized, no more than a mild censure was seen as necessary.[79]

There were also, of course, a number of punishment cases surrounding the Civil War. In the Thirty-seventh Congress, the names of eight senators who had "withdrawn from the Senate following the secession of the States they represented" were stricken from the roll.[80] Another eleven senators were expelled for adherence to the Confederacy, and three more were expelled for evincing Confederate sympathies.[81] The House expelled three Members for joining in the rebellion against the Union.[82] The House also censured Alexander Long for declaring himself in favor of recognizing the Confederacy and Benjamin Harris for declaring on the floor, "The South asked you to let them live in peace. But no; you said you would bring them into subjection. That is not done yet; and God Almighty grant that it never may be. I hope that you will never subjugate the South."[83]

Finally, we must examine the most banal set of congressional discipline cases—those dealing with misconduct, corruption, and criminal activity by Members. In the Fourth Congress, a Senate select committee was appointed to investigate accusations of fraud and perjury against Humphrey Marshall. The crimes were alleged to have been committed before his election to the Senate and were public knowledge. The committee held that the Senate had no jurisdiction over the matter — that it was properly cognizable only in a court of law. The Senate concurred in the committee report.[84] In the Fifth Congress, a resolution was introduced in the House to expel Matthew Lyon (the same Matthew Lyon who was almost expelled earlier in the same session for spitting in his colleague's face) because of his previous conviction under the Sedition Act. It was urged in Lyon's favor that his conviction had been public knowledge before his election; the vote on the resolution was 49 to 45 to expel, so Lyon retained his seat.[85] In this case, it was appropriate to let constituents' approval stand as a barrier to expulsion for a prior offense, as Lyon's conviction was not for an act that benefited his district at the expense of the nation.

In the Thirty-fourth Congress, Orsamus Matteson was investigated for corruption. To escape an expulsion resolution, he resigned.[86] He was then elected to the Thirty-fifth Congress, and a resolution was introduced to expel him.[87] Thomas Harris, who introduced the expulsion resolution, urged that it was "proper, not as a punishment but as a purification of the House."[88] The matter was referred to a special committee, which resolved that it was "inexpedient" for the House to take any further action in regard to the expulsion resolution. The outrage over the *Wilkes* case was cited in support of the proposition that Members could not be punished for actions before they took their seat. The matter was tabled.[89] In the Forty-second Congress, Oakes Ames and James Brooks were censured in connection with the Credit Mobilier scandal (in which shares of the company, which relied heavily on government subsidies, were sold to Members of Congress for less than market value). Although their actions had taken place before their election, they had remained unknown until after the election. A select committee investigating the matter had concluded that it could punish Members for acts prior to election even if their constituents had known of those acts, but the Judiciary Committee, which was also investigating the scandal, issued a contrary report. That issue was not decided by the House, but the two were censured.[90]

In the Thirty-seventh Congress, Senator James Simmons took money to use his influence over the heads of the departments in procuring an order authorizing a certain person to manufacture rifles for the army and navy. The Senate Judiciary Committee determined that such conduct was "entirely indefensible" and "highly improper" but that, because the conduct was not illegal at the time it took place, it would be unfair to punish it severely. No action was taken, and Simmons later resigned.[91] In the Forty-first Congress, Roderick Butler was censured by the House for taking money to appoint a cadet to West

Point.[92] In the next Congress, Alexander Caldwell resigned while facing an expulsion resolution because he had paid a potential opponent not to run against him for election to the Senate.[93] In 1967, Senator Thomas Dodd became the first senator to be investigated by the new Senate Select Committee on Standards and Conduct. The committee recommended that he be censured for financial impropriety, and the Senate voted 92 to 5 to censure him.[94] In 1970, he lost his party's nomination, ran for reelection as an independent, and finished third.[95] In 1978, the committee — which had been renamed the Select Committee on Ethics — began investigating Senator Herman Talmadge, who admitted that he "received most of his pocket money in small amounts of cash from constituents."[96] The committee determined that he either "knew, or should have known" about substantial improprieties and recommended that he be "denounced" (despite confusion on the part of the Senate parliamentarian as to what, precisely, a denouncement was).[97] On the Senate floor, Talmadge did not contest the committee's proposed resolution, which passed 81 to 15. The next year, he was defeated in his quest for reelection.[98] More recent instances of congressional discipline have dealt with everything from sexual misconduct (Senator Robert Packwood resigned while facing an expulsion resolution over sexual harassment; Representatives Gerry Studds and Daniel Crane were censured for having sexual relations with teenage House pages) to bribery (three Members resigned, one was expelled, and three lost their seats before the House could take any action against them in the early 1980s "Abscam" scandal) to improperly using influence (Representative Barney Frank was reprimanded for using his influence to fix parking tickets and shorten the probation period of a male prostitute with whom he had a relationship).[99] Perhaps most infamously, Representative James Traficant — a man with long ties to the Mafia — was expelled from the House after being convicted on charges of bribery, racketeering, and improper use of congressional staffers.[100]

Taken together, these cases suggest many of the issues discussed in the previous section. The Houses can punish and have punished Members for any action they deem disruptive or objectionable, including, but not limited to, assaults, insults, behavior antithetical to the national interest, and corruption. The punishment has primarily taken the form of censure, although on very rare occasions the Houses have expelled Members. In recent years, the Houses have also fined Members in several cases.[101]

PUNISHING NON-MEMBERS

In the Fourth Congress, three Members informed the House of Representatives that Robert Randall attempted to bribe them to support his memorial for the grant of a tract of land. The House passed a resolution directing the Speaker to issue a warrant, directed to the Sergeant-at-Arms, to arrest Randall. Another Member informed the House that Charles Whitney, thought to be an associate of Randall's, had attempted to bribe him. A warrant was also issued for Whitney's arrest. Randall and Whitney were both taken into custody and "held subject to the further direction of the House."[102] They were brought before the bar of the House and questioned and were permitted representation by counsel. The House determined that accusations against Randall and Whitney were to be put in writing and entered into the journal. Members and other witnesses were to testify under oath, and the trial was to take place at the bar of the House, rather than by committee. Randall was found guilty of contempt of the House and breach of the privileges of the House. He was reprimanded at the bar and committed to the Sergeant's custody "until further order of this House." A week later, he was discharged. Whitney was discharged immediately.[103]

Another bribery case arose in the Fifteenth Congress, when Lewis Williams laid before the House a letter from Colonel John Anderson in which Anderson requested Williams to accept $500 as "part pay for extra trouble" in furthering claims from the River Raisin.[104] Anderson was arrested by order of the House, but a debate arose over whether the House could punish him:

> It was objected that neither the Constitution nor the law gave any authority to the House to punish, and that the great and oppressive powers assumed in this respect by the British Parliament were no precedent here. The House might protect itself from indecorum and insult, but might not punish individuals for acts done elsewhere. It was better to suffer a hundred insults than to trample on the rights of the individual.[105]

The matter was referred to the Committee on Privileges, which recommended that Anderson be questioned at the bar of the House. He was allowed counsel, given process to summon witnesses, and furnished with a copy of the letter of accusation against him. After questioning, Anderson was found guilty of contempt and breach of privilege, reprimanded at the bar, and released.[106] Anderson then brought suit against the Sergeant for assault and battery and false imprisonment, and the case made its way to the Supreme Court. Justice Johnson, for the Court, wrote that the question presented was simply whether the Houses of Congress could punish for contempts committed by outsiders.[107] Were the Court to answer in the negative, the result would be the "total annihilation of the power of the House of Representatives to guard itself from contempts, [leaving] it exposed to every indignity and interruption that rudeness, caprice, or even conspiracy, may meditate against it."[108] The Houses, therefore, must have the power to punish for contempt, subject to the restraints that the punishment could only take the form of imprisonment, and the imprisonment could not extend beyond the adjournment or dissolution of the House.[109]

As with contempts by Members, a number of contempts by non-Members involved assaults upon Members. In the Twenty-second Congress, Samuel Houston (who had until recently been a representative from Tennessee) attacked William Stanbery as Stanbery was walking home in reprisal for Stanbery's comments in a floor debate. Houston was taken into custody by order of the House.[110] Against the arrest, James Polk "took the ground that the law of the District of Columbia was the proper remedy for the Member, and indorsed the sentiment that precedents from the House of Commons were repugnant to the spirit and genius of republican institutions."[111] Edward Everett argued in response, "If the time should ever come when the House would not assume the injuries inflicted on its Members as done to itself, the Constitution would no longer be worth living under."[112] Houston was brought to the bar of the House, where he was allowed counsel and process for summoning witnesses.[113] He "admitted the assault and beating because of words reported to have been uttered in debate by Mr. Stanberry; but denied any intention to commit any contempt or breach of privilege, or that such had really been committed."[114] Nevertheless, he was found guilty of contempt and breach of privilege by a vote of 106 to 88. He was reprimanded at the bar and discharged.[115] A similar case arose with a similar result in the Thirty-eighth Congress.[116]

During the Forty-first Congress, Patrick Woods assaulted Representative Charles Porter in the city of Richmond, Virginia. A resolution was submitted calling for Woods's arrest; to this was objected that it had not been shown that Woods assaulted Porter because of Porter's official duties. The Speaker "decided that any assault on a Member, which that Member, in his capacity as such, brings to the attention of the House, must be ruled as a question of privilege." Woods was therefore arrested and brought to the bar.[117] The Judiciary Committee reported that "[i]t appears, from an uninterrupted series of cases, both in this country and in England, from which we derived our parliamentary law, that all assaults made upon the reputation, character, and persons of Members have ever been held as breaches of the privileges of the legislative body of which the Member was a part, and as high crimes and misdemeanors." The committee also noted that Woods could not be imprisoned by the House for any longer than the duration of the current Congress.[118] The House held Woods in breach of privilege and sentenced him to three months in jail, which was longer than the current session of the House, but not longer than the current Congress.[119]

Verbal "assaults" were also punished by the Houses, although, as we have seen, the Houses' power to do so is questionable at best. In the Sixth Congress, the Senate Committee on Privileges determined that certain articles in a Philadelphia newspaper called the *General Advertiser* or *Aurora* contained

> assertions and pretended information respecting the Senate and the committee of the Senate, and their proceedings, which are false, defamatory, scandalous, and malicious, tending to defame the Senate of the United States, and to bring them into contempt and disrepute, and to excite against them the hatred of the good people of the United States; and . . . the said publication is a high breach of the privileges of this House.[120]

The resolution, which passed the Senate, also ordered William Duane, the editor of the newspaper, to attend the bar of the Senate. Having attended once and requested the assistance of counsel, which was granted, Duane refused to attend upon the Senate again. He was declared guilty of contempt, and the Sergeant was ordered to take him into custody.[121] (Technically, the contempt for which Duane was arrested was refusing to attend on the Senate when ordered to do so;[122] clearly, however, he was being punished for his writing.) The Senate also voted to request that the president instruct law enforcement officers to prosecute Duane for the contents of his article. Upon conviction, he was sentenced to thirty days' imprisonment.[123] In the Twenty-ninth Congress, after the *New York Tribune* published a letter that was "personally abusive" toward a Member of the House, the House expelled all reporters and letter writers for the paper from its chamber.[124] In the Thirtieth Congress, John Nugent was committed for contempt by the Senate for publishing in the *New York Herald* a treaty that was pending before the Senate in executive session.[125] His petition for a writ of habeas corpus was denied, with the District of Columbia Circuit Court holding that each House "has power to punish for contempts of its authority in cases of which it has jurisdiction," and that each House "is the sole judge of its own contempts," its determinations unreviewable by the courts.[126] Again, note that the courts *can* police the boundaries of the Houses' contempt power — the power extends only to cases *of which the House has jurisdiction*. But within those cases, its jurisdiction is exclusive. The court here was simply wrong to think that punishments for newspaper articles fell within that jurisdiction. In a speech case from the Thirty-ninth Congress, James Blaine offered in the House a letter from Provost-Marshal-General James Fry impugning the official conduct of Roscoe Conkling, a Member. The House agreed to resolutions proposed by a select committee calling the allegations in the letter "wholly without foundation in truth" and "a gross violation of the privileges of such Member [Conkling] and of this House."[127]

In 1915, a federal grand jury, convened by United States District Attorney H. Snowden Marshall, investigated a Member of the House of Representatives for violation of the Sherman Anti-Trust Act. The Member accused Marshall of official misfeasance and nonfeasance, accusations that were taken up by a subcommittee of the Judiciary Committee. An article appeared in a newspaper accusing the committee of attempting to frustrate the proceedings of the grand jury. Marshall admitted in a letter to the subcommittee that he was the source of the charges in the article; the letter went on to restate the charges "in amplified form in language which was certainly unparliamentary and manifestly ill-tempered and which was well calculated to arouse the indignation not only of the members of the subcommittee but of those of the House generally."[128] This letter was also provided to the press. The House declared this a contempt and breach of privilege and ordered Marshall's arrest. He petitioned for a writ of habeas corpus. The district court refused to grant it, but the Supreme Court reversed. Chief Justice White, for the Court, held that each House has the power "to deal with contempt in so far as that authority was necessary to preserve and carry out the legislative authority given."[129] This power "rests simply upon the implication that the right has been given to do that which is essential to the execution of some other and substantive authority expressly conferred."[130] But, the Court held, that condition was not met here:

> [T]he contempt was deemed to result from the writing of the letter not because of any obstruction to the performance of legislative duty resulting from the letter or because the preservation of the power of the House to carry out its legislative authority was endangered by its writing, but because of the effect and operation which the irritating and ill-tempered statements made in the letter would produce upon the public mind or because of the sense of indignation which it may be assumed was produced by the letter upon the members of the committee and of the House generally. But to state this situation is to demonstrate that the contempt relied upon was not intrinsic to the right of the House to preserve the means of discharging its legislative duties, but was extrinsic to the discharge of such duties and related only to the presumed operation which the letter might have upon the public mind and the indignation naturally felt by members of the committee on the subject. But these considerations plainly serve to mark the broad boundary line which separates the limited implied power to deal with classes of acts as contempts for self-preservation and the comprehensive legislative power to provide by law for punishment for wrongful acts.[131]

Again, note the scope/content distinction here: the House can punish within that class of acts which truly constitute contempts against it; however, it cannot punish for general "wrongful acts" in the guise of its contempt power.

Probably the most significant type of contempt is contempt by witnesses called to testify before a House (or a committee thereof). In the Twelfth Congress, Nathaniel Rounsavell refused to answer the questions of a select committee, and the House directed the Sergeant to bring him to the bar.[132] At the bar, Rounsavell refused to answer again, and he was committed to the custody of the Sergeant. After a time, he apologized and professed himself ready to testify, but "then a resolution was adopted purging him of contempt and declaring that, by reason of the explanation of a Member, it was not necessary to inquire further." He was discharged.[133]

In the Thirty-fifth Congress, John Wolcott refused fully to answer a question propounded to him by a select committee of the House. The partial answer he had given, he claimed,

> is a full answer to everything which such a question may involve, falling under the jurisdiction of the House of Representatives, touching the inquiry which the committee are constituted, and could only be constituted, to investigate. . . . I most respectfully submit that the question in its present form is not of itself "pertinent" to the only inquiry which the House, in this instance, has a legal right to institute.[134]

The committee concluded that this was a contempt and asked that Wolcott be arrested; after debate, the House agreed. Wolcott continued to argue at the bar that the question put to him was not pertinent and therefore not within the committee's (or the House's) power to ask.[135] The House then voted to imprison Wolcott until he indicated his willingness to answer the question. Several weeks later, the House voted to release Wolcott into the custody of the marshal of the District of Columbia for prosecution in the courts on charges of contempt of Congress, under the 1857 act.[136]

In the next Congress, the Senate appointed a committee to inquire into the invasion and seizure of the armory and arsenal at Harper's Ferry. Thaddeus Hyatt, summoned as a witness, did not appear, and the Senate ordered his arrest.[137] At the bar, Hyatt questioned the authority of the committee and refused to answer the questions, on the grounds, inter alia, that:

> The inquisition delegated to the committee, being an inquiry as to who committed crimes, was a judicial one, and a usurpation of the functions of the judiciary.
> The object of the inquisition being unconstitutional, the Senate could have no power to compel the attendance of witnesses before the committee.
> The investigations being made with a view to legislation can not give the Senate authority to make a judicial inquisition as to the authors of specific crimes, if it would not otherwise have possessed such authority.[138]

Hyatt's answer was deemed unacceptable, and he was imprisoned. Against the imprisonment resolution, Charles Sumner argued that the Senate could not compel testimony for legislative purposes only. Nonetheless, the vote went against him.[139]

In the Forty-second Congress, during a House investigation of the Credit Mobilier scandal, Joseph Stewart was asked for the names of the persons to whom he had given certain bonds he had received. He refused to answer, on the grounds that in the transactions in question he was an attorney acting on behalf of clients.[140] The committee denied that attorney-client privilege protected Stewart from having to disclose the name of his clients, and he was ordered to the bar of the House.[141] He presented his argument at the bar, but it was deemed insufficient and he was held in contempt. He continued to refuse to answer the questions and was held for nearly a month, until he was released near the end of the session.[142] In the next Congress, when called in front of a House committee investigating allegations against the Pacific Mail Steamship Company, Richard Irwin refused to reveal to whom he had paid $750,000. He acknowledged that it was paid out "for the purposes of procuring the subsidy" for the company, but he claimed that none of it had been paid to any Members or Officers of Congress.[143] When the committee asked to whom it had been paid, he replied that

> the jurisdiction of the committee did not give it authority to demand an answer to the question; that the jurisdiction of the committee and the House was exhausted when it appeared that none of the money was paid by him to any person under the jurisdiction of the House; that the matter arose in a prior Congress, over which the present committee and House were without jurisdiction; that as an honorable man he had no right to disclose relations existing between himself and others on a matter not within the jurisdiction of the House; and finally that the committee was not empowered by any order or resolution of the House to ask the question.[144]

The committee disagreed and proposed a resolution for Irwin's arrest. The House concurred, and Irwin was brought to the bar; when he continued to refuse to answer the questions, he was held in contempt and imprisoned. He later agreed to answer the questions and was released.[145]

The Forty-fourth Congress saw clashes over the Houses' contempt power take a federalist turn. For refusing to obey a subpoena requiring the production of papers relating to the presidential election, the House ordered the arrest of four members of a Louisiana state canvassing board.[146] The subpoena had required them to produce

> all returns of elections, all consolidated statements of supervisors of elections, all statements of votes, and tally sheets for each polling place at the late election for electors for President and Vice-President of the United States,

together with all affidavits, depositions, protests, and other written proofs in their possession or under their control, touching the said election in certain parishes.[147]

The board members claimed that, as members of a state body, their actions were not reviewable by any federal body. Noting that "[c]harges of fraud had been made against this returning board, and the witnesses were subpoenaed to appear and testify in regard to the charges," the committee proposed a resolution ordering them arrested, and the resolution passed. At the bar, they were held in contempt and ordered imprisoned until they produced the required papers. They were held for more than a month, until the committee investigation was at an end, and they were released (apparently without ever having surrendered the papers).[148]

In the Forty-fourth Congress, the House of Representatives Select Committee on the Real Estate Pool and Jay Cooke Indebtedness was impaneled to inquire into the loss of a significant sum of federal money deposited by the secretary of the navy in Jay Cooke & Co. bank when the bank went bankrupt. The committee subpoenaed Hallet Kilbourn to testify before it and produce papers. He appeared before the committee but refused to produce certain books and papers and to answer certain questions, "on the ground that the subject involved was a purely private matter and had no relation, in the remotest degree, to any public interest whatsoever."[149] The House adopted a resolution for Kilbourn's arrest. Kilbourn denied that the House had the power to punish him, as it had "transferred the whole power of trial and punishment to the criminal courts of the District" by statute. He continued to refuse to answer the House's questions, at which point he was held in contempt and kept in the jail of the District of Columbia.[150] He was also indicted in federal court, but the House refused to release him from its custody to stand trial.[151] Kilbourn filed for a writ of habeas corpus; the House Judiciary Committee recommended that the House refuse to produce Kilbourn, but the House ultimately adopted a substitute resolution directing the Sergeant to bring Kilbourn before the court but to argue that he was duly held by authority of the House.[152] When the Sergeant did so, the judge ordered Kilbourn released by the House into the custody of the marshal of the District of Columbia.[153] Kilbourn then filed a false imprisonment suit against the Sergeant and several Members of the House, which wound its way to the Supreme Court. Justice Miller, for the Court, wrote that

> we are sure that no person can be punished for contumacy as a witness before either House, unless his testimony is required in a matter into which that House has jurisdiction to inquire, and we feel equally sure that neither of

these bodies possesses the general power of making inquiry into the private affairs of the citizen.[154]

Examining the preamble and resolution under which the House committee was empowered to conduct its investigation, the Court held that the hearings were clearly judicial in character, and therefore outside the authority of the House.[155] And if the House could not lawfully hold the hearings, then it could not compel Kilbourn to testify at them.[156] The Court therefore rejected *Anderson*'s contention that the Houses have a broad power of contempt, unreviewable by the courts.[157] As noted in chapter 4, the Court went on to hold that the Members were privileged against Kilbourn's suit, but the Sergeant was not. The Court here was far too restrictive as to what constituted a legitimate purpose of the House. The scandal that the committee was investigating involved the loss of a significant sum of federal money by the secretary of the navy — surely the investigation could have resulted in impeachment proceedings. Even if impeachment was not considered, Congress's oversight function gives it the authority to bring government failures to the public attention. Moreover, "may it not be possible that such an investigation would show the need of legislation to prevent future secretaries from making 'improvident deposits,' or to limit the power of trustees in bankruptcy to prefer some creditors over others? How does it come about that the court can know beforehand whether a situation may not be developed by inquiry calling for legislation?"[158] All of these are legitimate legislative purposes, and the committee had reason to believe that the papers in Kilbourn's possession were pertinent to the inquiry. The Court's inability to see these legitimate purposes in the committee's inquiry was the Court's failure, not the committee's.

The Forty-fifth Congress had to address the issue of whether forcing a government official to provide evidence that might be used against him in impeachment proceedings was forcing him to incriminate himself. The House Committee on Expenditures in the State Department was investigating allegations of official misconduct against George Seward, minister to China. The committee subpoenaed papers from Seward. Seward refused to produce them, and "his counsel presented an argument that the said George F. Seward was protected by the constitutional guaranty that 'no person shall be compelled in any criminal case to be a witness against himself.' "[159] The committee denied that these were criminal proceedings and recommended that Seward be arrested and brought to the bar, which he was. At the bar, Seward contended that the committee was investigating with a view to impeaching him and that therefore the constitutional protection was operative.[160] The issue was referred to the Judiciary Committee, and Seward was released on his own recognizance. Subsequently, the Expenditures Committee did report articles of impeachment against Seward.[161] The Judiciary Committee then reported that he could not be compelled to produce the evidence against himself in an impeachment proceeding.[162]

In the Fifty-third Congress, Elverton Chapman had refused to answer pertinent questions before a Senate select committee investigating charges that there had been corruption in connection with the passage of a tariff bill.[163] Along with a number of other similarly uncooperative witnesses, Chapman's case was certified to the district attorney for the District of Columbia for proceedings in the courts. No further action was taken by the Senate. After he was convicted, Chapman challenged the contempt law, and his challenge reached the Supreme Court. In his decision for the Court, Chief Justice Fuller noted that each House of Congress "necessarily possesses the inherent power of self-protection."[164] The case was distinguished from *Kilbourn* because "[s]pecific charges publicly made against Senators had been brought to the attention of the Senate, and the Senate had determined that investigation was necessary. The subject-matter as affecting the Senate was within the jurisdiction of the Senate."[165] Although the preamble and resolutions did not specifically say that the hearings were for the purpose of considering censure or expulsion, that was not fatal to the constitutionality of the hearings because the Court "cannot assume on this record that the action of the Senate was without a legitimate object, and so encroach upon the province of that body."[166] The Court also upheld the 1857 law making contempt of either House a crime punishable in the ordinary courts. It held both that Congress did have the constitutional power to make such a law and that the concurrent jurisdictions of the House and the courts over the same action did not constitute double jeopardy.[167] It thus upheld Chapman's conviction. While the Court in *Chapman* was careful not to overrule *Kilbourn*, it is hard to miss the very different tone of the two cases. The *Kilbourn* Court's insistence that the case did not present an issue into which Congress might legitimately inquire — including its refusal to consider that legislation might be promulgated on the topic as a result of what the committee learned — was replaced by the *Chapman* Court's refusal to assume that the Senate was acting without a legitimate purpose. Indeed, in the 1927 case *McGrain v. Daugherty*,[168] the Court explicitly held that a House could punish a witness for contempt for refusing to answer questions from a committee designed to obtain information for the purpose of legislating.

The Court also took a broader view of the contempt power in the 1935 case *Jurney v. MacCracken*.[169] After a Senate committee subpoenaed papers from William MacCracken, he permitted those papers to be destroyed. The Senate ordered him to the bar to explain why he should not be held in contempt; when he refused to attend, he was arrested. He petitioned for a writ of habeas corpus, on the grounds that the Senate could only punish for contempt "as a means of removing an existing obstruction to the performance of its duties; [and] the power to punish ceases as soon as the obstruction has been removed, or its removal has become impossible."[170] As the destruction of the papers made the production of them to the committee impossible, he argued, the contempt power no longer reached him. Justice Brandeis, for the Court, was unconvinced, noting that the use of the contempt power to vindicate "the established and essential privilege of requiring the production of evidence" was historically well established and fully appropriate.[171] The Court was also unconvinced by MacCracken's argument that the 1857 act had removed the Houses' power to punish for contempt on their own and given it wholly over to the courts, noting that *Chapman* had already settled the issue.[172]

However, with the advent of the McCarthy era in legislative hearings, the courts again began to narrow the scope of permissible legislative inquiries. Edward Rumely was the secretary of a group called the Committee for Constitutional Government, which, among other things, sold politically controversial books. In 1949, the House Select Committee on Lobbying Activities asked for the names of those who had made bulk purchases for further redistribution, and Rumely refused to answer. The House cited him for contempt, and he was convicted in the courts under the contempt statute. On appeal, the Supreme Court overturned the conviction.[173] Justice Frankfurter, for the Court, held that the committee had exceeded the scope of its authorizing resolution, as the distribution of books to the public was not a form of lobbying. In a series of subsequent cases, lower courts built upon this ruling, holding that the government in contempt prosecutions had an obligation to show the source of authority for the investigation, that the question was within that authority, and that the witness's refusal to answer was willful and deliberate, and holding that grants of investigative authority would be construed narrowly.[174]

However, in a series of challenges, the basic project of the most (in)famous of the Communist-hunting committees, the House Committee on Un-American Activities, was held to be constitutional. In *Barsky v. United States*,[175] the District of Columbia Circuit Court of Appeals held that

> Congress is charged with part of the responsibility imposed upon the federal government by that clause of the Constitution which provides that 'The United States shall guarantee to every State in this Union a Republican Form of Government. . . .' Art. 4, Sec. 4. This clause alone would supply the authority for Congressional inquiry into potential threats to the republican forms of the governments of the States.
>
> If Congress has power to inquire into the subjects of Communism and the Communist Party, it has power to identify the individuals who believe in

Communism and those who belong to the party. . . . In our view, it would be sheer folly as a matter of governmental policy for an existing governmental [*sic*] to refrain from inquiry into potential threats to its existence or security until danger was clear and present. And for the judicial branch of government to hold the legislative branch to be without power to make such inquiry until the danger is clear and present, would be absurd. How, except upon inquiry, would the Congress know whether the danger is clear and present? There is a vast difference between the necessities for inquiry and the necessities for action. The latter may be only when danger is clear and present, but the former is when danger is reasonably represented as potential.[176]

Other lower-court decisions have held similarly,[177] and, in 1959, the Supreme Court employed a balancing test between the individual's claimed First Amendment rights not to testify about his political and religious beliefs and associations, on the one hand, and the government's interest in determining the extent of Communist infiltration into the field of higher education, on the other. Justice Harlan, for the Court, held that "the balance between the individual and the governmental interests here at stake must be struck in favor of the latter, and that therefore the provisions of the First Amendment have not been offended."[178]

The courts have also provided sadly illustrative studies on the danger of judicial meddling in internal House rules related to contempt. To take just one example, in 1949, the Supreme Court overturned a conviction for perjury in front of a committee on the grounds that the statute criminalized perjury before a "competent tribunal," which the committee was not at the time, because a quorum was not present.[179] The next year, the Supreme Court upheld a conviction for perjury in front of a committee when a quorum of the committee was not present because the statute in that case did not require a "competent tribunal."[180] In dicta, however, the Court suggested that a witness might legally refuse to testify before a committee until a quorum was present, but that this reason for refusing to testify must be raised at the time, and not as a *post hoc* justification.[181] Two years later, an appellate court upheld a conviction for perjury where the committee's authorizing resolution specified that one Member constituted a quorum for the purposes of taking testimony.[182] Surely, this rather absurd back-and-forth points to the basic unwisdom of judicial inquiry into internal House rules. If enough Members of the House vote to hold a witness in contempt and vote either to punish her or to refer her to the courts for punishment, then what business do the courts have inquiring into whether the hearing was duly constituted? The House clearly thought it was, and its word on its own rules ought to be final. Likewise, if the House thinks that a committee's questioning of witnesses is within the scope of the authority that the House delegated to the committee, then what business do the courts have disagreeing?

Conclusions

We have seen, then, that the Houses have very broad discretion to punish their own Members, subject only to the requirement that the punishment of expulsion requires a two-thirds supermajority, and that they have a narrower discretion to punish non-Members. The punishment of non-Members must be for obstructing the functioning of the House in some way. This entails either impermissible interference with the House or a Member or refusal to cooperate with the legitimate requests of the House. Impermissible interference should not be interpreted as including verbal attacks on the House or on a Member, but the House's power to require testimony or evidence should be given broad latitude, as the Houses perform a number of different functions, each of which opens numerous avenues of potential inquiry. The House must have access to any information pertinent to a legitimate inquiry, and one goal of the contempt power is to give it a means of obtaining that access. As we have seen in cases like *Marshall v. Gordon*, the courts can police the boundaries to ensure that non-Members are not punished for actions that do not in any way obstruct the House. We have also seen that the Houses have almost entirely surrendered their punishment power over non-Members to the courts, although their constitutional authority for doing so is dubious, at best. Judicial inquiry into contempts of Congress requires the courts to probe into the internal procedures of the Houses; however, as we have seen throughout, preventing such probing is one of the functions of privilege.

We have also seen here, perhaps more clearly than in any of the previous chapters, the way in which British precedents affected the development of American law. Specifically, the *Wilkes* case looms, both for good and for ill, over all of the American case law. The *Wilkes* case has had a salutary influence in that it has served to focus attention on the ways in which the Houses' punishment powers can be used to thwart popular sovereignty; it has had a deleterious influence in that it has been successfully invoked in arguments for an absolute ban on reexpulsion for the same offense, a ban that, as we have seen, can itself have anti-popular-sovereignty consequences in certain situations.

British contempt case law has provided cautionary tales in other ways as well. As we have seen, the Houses of Congress—unlike the Houses of Parliament—have consistently taken care to ensure that they only punish non-Members for offenses against the Houses or Members qua Members. Whereas the Houses of Parliament have punished non-Members who poached on Members' land, the Houses of Congress have taken care only to punish for offenses related to the functioning of the House.

This is, of course, not to claim that Congress has not abused its contempt powers. To take just one example, it has, on occasion, been too quick to punish both Members and non-Members for speech. However, mistakes in interpreting congressional punishing powers have largely been mistakes in the other direction — that is, interpreting the power too narrowly and allowing the courts too broad a role. Included under this head are the various statutory regimes that give the courts the power to punish for contempt of Congress, a power that requires impermissible judicial meddling into the internal rules and procedures of the Houses. It is in the context of prosecutions under these statutes that many of the unfortunate court cases examined above arose.

Conclusion

Legislative privilege has historically been a powerful tool of the British Parliament and the American Congress. Like any tool, it can be used properly or it can be abused, and, indeed, history provides many examples of each. As Carl Wittke has (perhaps a bit hyperbolically) noted,

> Privilege has been both the bulwark of English liberty and the most ruthless oppressor of the rights of the subject. It has proved a means for the advancement of democracy and representative government and institutions in the hands of some, and again, it has been a tool of oppression in the hands of a corrupt, mercenary, time-serving oligarchy of politicians desirous of perpetuating their power.[1]

And yet it is clearly as "a means for the advancement of democracy and representative government and institutions" that privilege fulfills its true purpose. When privilege is functioning properly, it serves to strengthen democracy in the British and American constitutions.

I have throughout this book made extensive use of grand concepts like democracy, representation, and popular sovereignty. It may, perhaps, be objected that my account of these concepts is undertheorized. However, it has been one of the aims of this work to show how meaning can be given to these terms, not through abstract speculation, but rather through concrete analysis of texts, history, and institutional structures. So, where has this exercise brought us? It is time to back away from our portal and return to the big questions with which this book began.

As the British Constitution has evolved, so has the understanding of what constitutes the democratic part of it. Under a Constitution that was mixed in the ancient sense — containing monarchical, aristocratic, and democratic elements — the democratic part was easy to locate. It resided in the House of Commons. Because this democratic citadel of the Constitution was easy to localize, it was also easy to reinforce: strengthen the House of Commons and you strengthen democracy; weaken the House, and the democratic element of the Constitution will begin to fade, as the monarchical and aristocratic elements encroach on its powers. It was in such a political milieu that what I have throughout termed the Blackstonian approach to privilege was appropriate. That approach sought precisely to strengthen the walls of the citadel of democracy, the legal protections surrounding the House of Commons. It denied that the courts (whose judges were royally appointed and whose highest court of appeals was the entire body of the House of Lords) could have any say as to the content, or even the extent, of the House's privileges; it sought absolute protection from outside questioning for anything done on the floor of the House; it sought an expansive freedom from civil arrest and process; it gave the House exclusive jurisdiction over disputes concerning the election and qualifications of its Members; and it allowed the House to use its punitive powers to attack anyone who threatened its power or prestige (prestige being, of course, a significant source of power). It was almost completely unconcerned with the role of the constituent: the House was identified with democracy; the constituent was at best an afterthought (and at worst a potential nuisance to the MP).

As time passed, the democratic part of the Constitution grew stronger, while the monarchical and aristocratic parts withered. Executive powers effectively passed from the monarch to the ministers of the House of Commons; those same ministers effectively took over the appointing of judges; the appellate functions of the House of Lords were increasingly handled by a small group of professional judges within that body; and the power of the House of Lords vis-à-vis the Commons was in decline. Of course, these changes by no means came about all at once, but, over a period of several centuries, the British Constitution slowly transformed itself from a mixed constitution in the ancient sense into a modern liberal democratic constitution. To the degree that separation of powers can be said to characterize the British Constitution, it is now seen as separation between legislative, executive, and judicial functions — all of them elements of a liberal democracy — rather than separation between monarchical, aristocratic, and democratic elements.

And with this shift in the nature of the British Constitution came a corresponding shift in the role of parliamentary privilege within the Constitution. The Millian approach to privilege takes a fundamentally democratic constitution as its starting point. From there, it envisions the promotion of popular control over the government to be the function of privilege. Because it can no longer be said that one part of the Constitution is "the democratic part," the Millian approach to privilege no longer focuses on strengthening one part of the Constitution at the expense of others. Rather, it takes a functional approach, focusing on which particular functions of which institutions require protection (and from whom). The Millian approach allows different (democratic) elements of the Constitution to check one another, in an attempt to ensure that no part of the Constitution strays too far from its legitimizing force: popular consent. It thus gives an expanded (although not unlimited) role to the courts in determining the extent, and sometimes even the content, of privilege; it expands to protect certain speech that takes place far from the floor of the House, while contracting so as no longer to cover, for example, assaults that take place on the floor; it eliminates the privilege against the initiation of civil suits, at the same time that the privilege against civil arrest is losing relevance; it gives jurisdiction over election disputes to the common-law courts; and it envisions a much more limited role for breach and contempt proceedings.

It should be abundantly clear, then, that neither the Blackstonian nor the Millian conception is right or wrong. Each was simply appropriate at a different stage of British constitutional development. Blackstonian decisions have been inappropriate for some time, and are certainly inappropriate today, because the assumptions of the Millian model fit the modern political situation much better than do those of the Blackstonian model: in modern Britain, the entire Constitution is broadly democratic, not just part of it. It should also be clear that Blackstonian and Millian are not binary positions: they are opposite ends of a spectrum, and cases frequently fall somewhere in the middle. The cases are considered in terms of one of the two paradigms, but it should be remembered that these paradigms are simply heuristic models projected backward onto historical cases. The fit will never be perfect, and much can be learned from the cases in the middle.

The American Founders introduced the idea of popular sovereignty into the equation, in the process making the nexus between the will of the people and the actions of the legislators even more central to interpretations of privilege than it is under the Millian paradigm in Britain. As we have seen throughout, privilege under the American Constitution is best interpreted as facilitating the people's access to and communication with their elected representatives. But it is also important to keep in mind that popular sovereignty deals first and foremost with the people *in their collective capacity*. Of course, the protection of certain individual rights is central to popular sovereignty, but it should not be thought that popular sovereignty will always be solicitous of the rights of the individual over the mechanisms that allow popular self-government to function effectively. The private citizen who is egregiously slandered on the floor of the House has been wronged, and it is to be hoped that the House would see fit to punish the Member who so wronged him or her. But the wrong done to individual interests does not outweigh the systemic virtue of protecting speech on the floor from questioning in any other place.

As we have seen, the popular sovereignty interpretation of privilege means that, while the final determination of certain "political questions" is left with the Houses of Congress, the courts police the boundary line. While freedom of speech is absolute and expansive for Members of Congress, it is also very strong and very broad for ordinary citizens. While Members enjoy freedom from civil arrest, they are not free from other civil process or from criminal arrest. While disputes over elections and qualifications are judged by the House, they may only judge based on those qualifications and disqualifications enumerated in the Constitution itself. And while the Houses may punish both Members and non-Members, a two-thirds supermajority is necessary to expel a member, and the courts may ensure that non-Members are punished only for activities disruptive to the functioning of the House.

We have also seen that the evolution of privilege in both counties is ongoing. In Britain, the European Convention on Human Rights — whose impact has just started to become apparent in the *Demicoli* and *A v. United Kingdom* cases — may continue to reshape parliamentary privilege well into the future. In America, the pendulum has, in many cases, swung too far in the direction of giving the courts jurisdiction over matters properly cognizable only by the Houses of Congress; it is to be hoped that this trend will reverse itself and the proper balance will be restored. Although fights over the scope of legislative privilege may not have quite the same import today that they did under the first Queen Elizabeth, the fact that such fights continue to arise points to the continuing importance of the issue. Moreover, the historical significance of the doctrine is not to be dismissed. As I have argued throughout, the history of privilege is the history of democracy in the British and American constitutions. Just as the development of democracy sheds light on the changing role of privilege, so too the changing role of privilege sheds light on the development of democracy in two of the exemplars of modern democratic constitutionalism.

Notes

Introduction

1. Vernon Bogdanor, *Britain: The Political Constitution, in* Constitutions in Democratic Politics 54–55 (Vernon Bogdanor ed., 1988) (citing Dicey's unpublished lectures on the Comparative Study of Constitutions).

2. Adam Ferguson, An Essay on the History of Civil Society 119 (Fania Oz-Salzberger ed., Cambridge Univ. Press 1995) (1767).

3. *See* 1 Friedrich Hayek, Law, Legislation, and Liberty 37 (1973).

4. J. R. Pole, Political Representation in England and the Origins of the American Republic 408 (1971).

5. Sidney Low, The Governance of England 12 (1904).

6. *But see* Akhil Reed Amar, *The Supreme Court, 1999 Term — Foreword: The Document and the Doctrine,* 114 Harv. L. Rev. 26 (2000) (noting that, while not confusing the two, many judges and scholars suffer from an unfortunate tendency to privilege judicial doctrine over the Constitution itself).

7. *See* J. G. A. Pocock, The Machiavellian Moment: Florentine Political Thought and the Atlantic Republican Tradition 547 (1975) (noting that "there is no British Jefferson. Democratization, when it came, arrived by the medieval technique of expanding the king-in-parliament to include new categories of counselors and representatives").

8. Carl Wittke, The History of English Parliamentary Privilege (photo. reprint 1970) (1921).

9. Mary Patterson Clarke, Parliamentary Privilege in the American Colonies (1943).

10. 1 William Blackstone, Commentaries on the Laws of England 159 (1st ed. photo. reprint 1979) (1765).

11. James R. Stoner Jr., Common Law and Liberal Theory: Coke, Hobbes, and the Origins of American Constitutionalism 163 (1992). *See also* Herbert Storing, *William Blackstone, in* History of Political Philosophy 594– 606 (2d ed., Leo Strauss & Joseph Cropsey eds., 1972) (noting Blackstone's liberalism); Richard Posner, *Blackstone and Bentham*, 19 J. L. & Econ. 569 (noting same).

12. 1 Blackstone, *supra* note 10, at 157.

13. 1 *id.* at 156.

14. *See* William Blackstone, *The Case of the Late Election for the County of Middlesex, Considered on the Principles of the Constitution, and the Authorities of Law, in* An Interesting Appendix to Sir William Blackstone's Commentaries on the Laws of England 101 (Philadelphia, Bell 1773).

15. Wittke, *supra* note 8, at 203.

16. John Stuart Mill, *Considerations on Representative Government, in* Utilitarianism, On Liberty, Considerations on Representative Government, Remarks on Bentham's Philosophy 234 (Geraint Williams ed., Everyman 1993) (1861).

17. *Id.* at 349.

18. Walter Bagehot, The English Constitution 101 (1st ed., Miles Taylor ed., Oxford Univ. Press 2001) (1867).

19. A. V. Dicey, Introduction to the Study of the Law of the Constitution 302 (8th ed., Liberty Fund 1982) (1915).

20. *Id.* at 285. *See also* Jeffrey Goldsworthy, The Sovereignty of Parliament: History and Philosophy 219–20, 228 (1999).

21. Stockdale v. Hansard, 112 Eng. Rep. 1112, 1182; 9 Ad. & E. 1, 184–85 (Q.B. 1839).

22. 112 Eng. Rep. at 1182; 9 Ad. & E. at 185.

23. Patricia M. Leopold, *Freedom of Speech in Parliament — Its Misuse and Proposals for Reform*, 1981 Pub. L. 30, 32 (quoting *Report from the Select Committee on the Official Secrets Act*, H.C. 101, at xiv (1938– 39)). *See also* Simon Wigley, *Parliamentary Immunity: Protecting Democracy or Protecting Corruption?*, 11 J. Pol. Phil. 23, 27 (2003).

24. The great constitutional historian Charles Howard McIlwain argues that the most important difference between ancient and modern constitutionalism is that the moderns think of the constitution as fundamental law, conceptually (if not temporally) antecedent to all acts of government. The ancients, in contrast, understood the constitution of a state to be a description of the state as it actually is, including its social, economic, and political structure. McIlwain thus sees the ancient/modern divide as running between the *politeia* of Plato and Aristotle and the *res publica* of Cicero, Seneca, and Polybius. The Roman and English constitutions thus fall on the same side of McIlwain's great divide. Charles Howard McIlwain, Constitutionalism: Ancient and Modern (rev. ed. 1947).

But McIlwain's schema seems less than fully useful — and not simply because, on his criteria, the British Constitution would be best described as always having one foot in the ancient scheme and one in the modern. McIlwain argues that "those checks and balances so admired by Polybius and Machiavelli and so despised by Mommsen . . . while possibly the most original of Rome's permanent contributions to constitutionalism, are very far indeed from being the most important then, or the most significant now." *Id.* at 42–43.

However, I shall argue that it is precisely the ways in which those checks and balances have shifted over the years that allows us to mark the difference between ancient and modern republican constitutionalism.

25. *See, e.g.,* Polybius, The Rise of the Roman Empire 303–18 (Ian Scott-Kilvert trans., Penguin 1979) (c. 160 B.C.); Cicero, The Republic 17–33 (Niall Rudd trans., Oxford Univ. Press 1998) (c. 52 B.C.); Niccolò Machiavelli, The Discourses 109–11 (Leslie J. Walker trans., Bernard Crick ed., Penguin 1998) (1531). *See also* Goldsworthy, *supra* note 20, at 75; Pocock, *supra* note 7, at 365, 479.

26. *See, e.g.,* Pole, *supra* note 4, at 415 ("In the British Constitution, the House of Commons represented the democracy; but in rejecting the contention that Walpole's practices of corruption were necessary in order to preserve the Constitution, [Boling-broke] added that the combined Lords and Crown would prevent a democratic tyranny by the Commons."); McIlwain, *supra* note 24, at 115 ("This principle of the people's consent and of parliament as the channel of this consent, reasserted by Wentworth and Coke in 1621, is a very ancient one.").

27. *See* Clarke, *supra* note 9, at 1–2 ("There came a time in the nineteenth century when these two concepts had to be separated, because even a representative institution can become autocratic; but for a long period the privilege of parliament was defended as one of the chief means of upholding and preserving the liberty of the subject."). *See also id.* at 10, 131 (noting same).

28. *See* Montesquieu, The Spirit of the Laws 156–66 (Anne M. Cohler, Basia Carolyn Miller & Harold Samuel Stone trans. & eds., Cambridge Univ. Press 1989) (1748). *See also* Geoffrey Marshall, *Hansard and the Interpretation of Statutes, in* The Law and Parliament 139–40 (Dawn Oliver & Gavin Drewry eds., 1998) (noting the "conscious growth of a separation of powers" in British constitutional history).

29. Goldsworthy, *supra* note 20, at 68.

30. For significantly more detail on the popular-sovereignty foundations of the Constitution than it is possible to provide here, see Amar, *supra* note 6; Akhil Reed Amar, America's Constitution: A Biography 5–53 (2005).

31. U.S. Const. preamble.

32. *Id.* art. VII, cl. 1 (Ratification Clause); *id.* art VI, cl. 2 (Supremacy Clause).

33. *Id.* amdts. IX, X.

34. United States v. Darby, 312 U.S. 100, 124 (1941) (discussing only the Tenth Amendment, but the point applies equally to the Ninth).

35. U.S. Const. amdt. XXVII. The Twenty-seventh Amendment was originally submitted to the states as part of the proposed Bill of Rights in 1789. It was not ratified, however, until 1992.

36. 2 The Records of the Federal Convention of 1787, at 120 (Max Farrand ed., rev. ed. 1966) [hereinafter Farrand's Records].

37. 2 *id.* at 150.

38. Articles of Confederation preamble.

39. The Federalist No. 39, at 243 (James Madison) (Clinton Rossiter ed., Mentor 1961) [hereinafter all citations are to this edition].

40. Akhil Reed Amar, *Of Sovereignty and Federalism,* 96 Yale L. J. 1425, 1452–53 n.113 (1987). *See also* Bernard Bailyn, The Ideological Origins of the American Revolu-

tion 206–07 & n.47 (enlarged ed. 1992) (noting that the sentence *"imperium in imperio*
is the greatest of all political solecisms"* was "one of the most commonplace phrases of
eighteenth-century political theory" and tracing some of its uses); Gordon S. Wood, The
Creation of the American Republic, 1776–1787, at 351–53, 527–29 (reprint 1998)
(1969) (citing more examples of same); John V. Orth, *History and the Eleventh Amendment,* 75 Notre Dame L. Rev. 1147, 1157 (2000) ("At the time of the drafting of the
United States Constitution, it was axiomatic that sovereignty was indivisible: there could
be no imperium in imperio.").

    41. Wood, *supra* note 40, at 345 (quoting Alexander Hamilton). *See also* 2 The De-
bates in the Several State Conventions, On the Adoption of the Federal Constitution, as
Recommended by the General Convention at Philadelphia, in 1787, at 455 (Jonathan
Elliot ed., 2d ed. reprinted Philadelphia, J. B. Lippincott 1907) (1836) (James Wilson: "It
has not been, nor, I presume, will it be denied, that somewhere there is, and of necessity
must be, a supreme, absolute, and uncontrollable authority. This, I believe, may justly be
termed the *sovereign* power; for, from that gentleman's (Mr. Findley) account of the
matter, it cannot be sovereign unless it is supreme; for, says he, a subordinate sovereignty
is no sovereignty at all." Wilson then goes on to say that, in the American system that
sovereignty resides in the people) [hereinafter Elliot's Debates]; Akhil Reed Amar, *The
Consent of the Governed: Constitutional Amendment Outside Article V,* 94 Colum. L.
Rev. 457, 507 (1994) ("[James] Wilson built his argument axiomatically on the idea that
sovereignty was absolute and indivisible. This view was almost universally held in the
1780s. Divided sovereignty was seen as a logical contradiction, a 'solecism.' Indeed, so
far as I can tell, Madison was the only major figure who believed in it. Why did virtually
no one follow Madison's lead on this point? Perhaps because they understood—as did
Wilson and [Jefferson] Davis, for example—that 'divided' or 'mixed' popular sovereignty was no popular sovereignty. A fundamental principle for republican government
was that the majority should rule, and divided sovereignty betrayed that fundamental
principle. The formal principle of popular sovereignty, in other words, cannot tell us
whether we should be a state people, or a national people, but it does insist that we be one
or the other. (And since Davis was wrong, Wilson must be right.) For if sovereignty can
indeed be divided—as only Madison believed—then We the People today cannot control
our fate." Internal citations omitted); Helen K. Michael, *The Role of Natural Law in
Early American Constitutionalism: Did the Founders Contemplate Judicial Enforcement
of 'Unwritten' Individual Rights?,* 69 N.C. L. Rev. 421, 458 n.214 (1991) ("Perhaps
more importantly, the theory of popular ratification enabled proponents of the new
Constitution to rebut the Antifederalist charge that the national government would con-
sume the state governments because the indivisible nature of sovereignty conflicted with
the maintenance of concurrent sovereignties. The Antifederalists insisted that this charac-
teristic of sovereignty dictated that either the national or state governments must be
supreme, arguing that 'two co-ordinate sovereignties would be a solecism in politics[ ]'
and that 'it would be contrary to the nature of things that both should exist together—
one or the other would necessarily triumph in the fullness of dominion.' The Federalists'
argument that the people, not their servants in the state legislature, possessed this indivisible sovereignty deprived the Antifederalists' objection of any real force." Internal citations omitted.).

42. 1 Farrand's Records, *supra* note 36, at 477.

43. The Federalist No. 46, at 294 (James Madison) (emphasis added).

44. The Federalist No. 49, at 313–14 (James Madison).

45. The Federalist No. 22, at 152 (Alexander Hamilton).

46. The Federalist No. 78, at 467 (Alexander Hamilton).

47. 1 The Debate on the Constitution 299 (Bernard Bailyn ed., 1993) (Letter from Timothy Pickering to Charles Tillinghast (Dec. 24, 1787)) [hereinafter Bailyn's Debate]. *See also* 1 *id.* at 301 (Letter from Timothy Pickering to Charles Tillinghast (Dec. 24, 1787)).

48. 1 *id.* at 155 ("An Examination into the Leading Principles of the Federal Constitution," by "A Citizen of America" [Noah Webster] (Oct. 17, 1787)).

49. For other similar statements from federalists in the popular press, *see, e.g.*, 1 *id.* at 748 (Letter from Samuel Holden Parsons to William Cushing (Jan. 11, 1788)); 2 *id.* at 287 ("Observations on the Constitution," by "A Columbian Patriot" [Mercy Otis Warren] (Feb. 1788)); 2 *id.* at 417 (Letter from Benjamin Rush to David Ramsay (April 19, 1788)); 2 *id.* at 507 (David Ramsay's Oration at Charleston, South Carolina (May 27, 1788)).

50. 3 Elliot's Debates, *supra* note 41, at 22.

51. 3 *id.* at 37.

52. 3 *id.* at 28.

53. *See, e.g.*, 2 *id.* at 432–33, 434–35, 437, 443–44, 456, 497–99 (James Wilson in the Pennsylvania convention); 4 *id.* at 161 (Archibald Maclaine in the North Carolina convention).

54. U.S. Const. art. VII, cl. 1.

55. James Wilson, *Oration to Celebrate the Adoption of the Constitution of the United States, in* 2 The Works of James Wilson 774 (Robert Green McCloskey ed., 1967). *See also* Jed Rubenfeld, *Reading the Constitution as Spoken*, 104 Yale L. J. 1119, 1143 (1995) (noting that, before the American Constitution, constitution formation was wholly omitted from political typologies: "If, before America, political liberty could have been thought to require a democratic constitution, democracy was never thought to require democratic constitution formation."); Gordon S. Wood, The Radicalism of the American Revolution 243 (1991) (America "became the first society in the modern world to bring ordinary people into the affairs of government—not just as voters but as actual rulers. This participation of common people in government became the essence of American democracy, and the Revolution made it so.").

56. 1 Farrand's Records, *supra* note 36, at 122.

57. 2 *id.* at 88.

58. 2 *id.* at 88–89.

59. 2 *id.* at 94. It might be asked what made the ratifying conventions so different from ordinary state legislatures. First, eighteenth-century political theory understood conventions to be special assemblies of the people themselves, in their sovereign capacity. *See* Amar, *supra* note 40, at 1459. Second, several of the states followed up on this understood meaning of conventions by allowing broader suffrage in the election for delegates to the states' ratifying conventions than they did in normal legislative elections. *See* Amar, *supra* note 30, at 5–53, 308–12.

60. 17 U.S. (4 Wheat.) 316 (1819).

61. *Id.* at 363.

62. *Id.* at 403.

63. *Id.* at 403–05.

64. Amar, *supra* note 6, at 35.

65. For one version of this critique, see Thurgood Marshall, *Reflections on the Bicentennial of the United States Constitution,* 101 Harv. L. Rev. 1 (1987).

66. Plutarch, *Solon, in* The Rise and Fall of Athens: Nine Greek Lives 47, 67 (Ian Scott-Kilvert trans., Penguin 1960) (emphasis added).

67. John V.A. Fine, The Ancient Greeks: A Critical History 103 (1983).

68. 1 Bruce Ackerman, We the People: Foundations 88 (1991).

69. 1 *id.* at 88–89.

70. 1 *id.* at 141.

71. John Hart Ely, Democracy and Distrust: A Theory of Judicial Review 125 (1980).

72. U.S. Const. amdts. XVII (direct election of senators), XV (enfranchisement of blacks), XIX (enfranchisement of women), XXIII (giving District residents the right to vote for presidential electors but not giving them representation in Congress), XXIV (elimination of poll taxes), XXVI (enfranchisement of eighteen-year-olds).

73. Ely, *supra* note 71, at 99. *See also id.* at 120 ("We cannot trust the ins to decide who stays out.").

74. The Federalist No. 47, at 301 (James Madison).

75. The Federalist No. 48, at 308 (James Madison).

76. *See* Anita Bernstein, Note, *Executive Targeting of Congressmen as a Violation of the Arrest Clause,* 94 Yale L. J. 647, 662–63 (1985) ("Legislative privilege is a force for equality between branches, not superiority of congressmen over their fellow citizens.").

77. This picture will be further complicated in a moment by the addition of nonprincipled motives for the actors involved.

78. This seemingly intuitive suggestion is at the heart of Quentin Skinner's insistence that an interpreter must take note of text, context, *and* authorial intent — no one or two of these in isolation is sufficient. *See* Quentin Skinner, *Meaning and Understanding in the History of Ideas, in* Meaning and Context: Quentin Skinner and His Critics 29–67 (James Tully ed., 1988).

79. This is not dissimilar from Dworkin's understanding of "law as integrity," by which "propositions of law are true if they figure in or follow from the principles of justice, fairness, and procedural due process that provide the best constructive interpretation of the community's legal practice." Ronald Dworkin, Law's Empire 225 (1986).

80. *See, e.g.,* Friedrich Schleiermacher, *Hermeneutics, in* Hermeneutics and Criticism 24 (Andrew Bowie trans. & ed., Cambridge Univ. Press 1998) (c. 1828).

81. Hans-Georg Gadamer, Truth and Method 293 (2nd rev. ed., Joel Weinsheimer & Donald G. Marshall eds., 1989).

82. *See* chapters 3 and 4 for more on freedom of speech in the Houses of Parliament and Congress.

83. The paradigm case would be the 1734 arrest by royal authorities of John Peter Zenger, the publisher of the New York *Weekly Journal,* for seditious libel, stemming from his newspaper's criticism of the royal governor. Zenger's case became a cause célèbre

among rebellious colonists. *See generally* Harold L. Nelson, *Seditious Libel in Colonial America*, 3 Am. J. Legal Hist. 160 (1959); sources cited in *id.* at 160 n.1. *See also* chapter 4's concluding section on the First Amendment.

84. *See* Cohen v. California, 403 U.S. 15, 25 (1971) ("one man's vulgarity is another's lyric").

85. For a profound and subtle unpacking of this idea, see Jed Rubenfeld, Freedom and Time: A Theory of Constitutional Self-Government (2001).

Chapter One. Lex Parliamenti vs. Lex Terrae

1. William Blackstone, *The Case of the Late Election for the County of Middlesex, Considered on the Principles of the Constitution, and the Authorities of Law, in* An Interesting Appendix to Sir William Blackstone's Commentaries on the Laws of England 64–65 (Philadelphia, Bell 1773). *See* Edward Coke, The Fourth Part of the Institutes of the Laws of England, Concerning the Jurisdiction of Courts 15 (reprint London, Brooke 1797) (1644).

2. Blackstone, *supra* note 1, at 66.

3. Executors of Skewys v. Chamond, 73 Eng. Rep. 131; 1 Dyer 59b (K.B. 1545).

4. 1 John Hatsell, Precedents of Proceedings in the House of Commons 233 (rev. ed., London, Hansard 1818).

5. 1 *id.* at 239.

6. G. W. Prothero, *The Parliamentary Privilege of Freedom from Arrest, and Sir Thomas Shirley's Case, 1604,* 8 Eng. Hist. Rev. 733, 734 (1893). *See also* 1 William Cobbett, Parliamentary History of England 1028–30 (London, Hansard 1806).

7. Prothero, *supra* note 6, at 735. The bill is printed in *id.* at 738.

8. *Id.* at 735.

9. *Id.* at 736.

10. *Id.* The bill is printed in *id.* at 739.

11. *Id.* at 736. For a chilling description of the Little Ease, see Albert Camus, The Fall 80–81 (Justin O'Brien trans., 2000) (1956).

12. Prothero, *supra* note 6, at 737.

13. *Id.* at 735.

14. Shirley v. Fagg, 6 State Tr. 1121, 1127–28 (H.L. 1675).

15. *Id.* at 1131–33.

16. *Id.* at 1134, 1143, 1146–47.

17. Carl Wittke, The History of English Parliamentary Privilege 84 (photo. reprint 1970) (1921).

18. *Fagg,* 6 State Tr. at 1148–54.

19. *Id.* at 1158–68.

20. 9 *Journals of the House of Commons* 381.

21. *Fagg,* 6 State Tr. at 1187–88; Wittke, *supra* note 17, at 88–89.

22. Jay v. Topham, 12 State Tr. 821, 822 (H.C. 1689).

23. *Id.* at 834.

24. Tonnage and poundage were taxes on imports and exports traditionally granted by Parliament to English monarchs, and they represented the largest single item of revenue

for the Crown. In 1625, Charles I's first Parliament refused to grant him tonnage and poundage, whereupon Charles prorogued Parliament and attempted to collect the duties anyway. Merchants revolted, refusing to pay, which forced Charles to recall Parliament and ask it to grant him tonnage and poundage, thus setting up the fight with Rolle, among others. For an excellent description of the entire controversy, see Linda S. Popofsky, *The Crisis over Tonnage and Poundage in Parliament in 1629*, 126 Past & Present 44 (1990).

25. 2 Cobbett, *supra* note 6, at 437.

26. 2 *id.* at 442–43.

27. 2 *id.* at 477–83, 488–91.

28. 2 *id.* at 491–504.

29. 2 *Journals of the House of Commons* 960.

30. 5 *Journals of the House of Commons* 221.

31. Streater's Case, 5 State Tr. 365, 376–86 (U.B. 1653).

32. *Id.* at 380–81.

33. *Id.* at 381.

34. *Id.* at 386.

35. *Id.* at 386–87.

36. *Id.* at 392.

37. *Id.* at 392, 401–02.

38. Shaftesbury's Case, 86 Eng. Rep. 792, 793; 1 Mod. 144, 144 (K.B. 1676). *See also* 6 State Tr. 1269 (K.B. 1677).

39. 86 Eng. Rep. at 795; 1 Mod. at 147–48.

40. 6 State Tr. at 1294–96.

41. 86 Eng. Rep. at 797–99; 1 Mod. at 153–57.

42. 86 Eng. Rep. at 798; 1 Mod. at 154.

43. 86 Eng. Rep. at 799–800; 1 Mod. at 157–58.

44. 92 Eng. Rep. 232; 2 Ld. Raym. 1105 (Q.B. 1705); 90 Eng. Rep. 1189; Holt K.B. 526 (Q.B. 1705).

45. The Queen's Bench agreed with the House, with Chief Justice Holt dissenting, but the House of Lords reversed, holding that the ordinary courts could indeed determine voter qualifications. *See* Ashby v. White, 92 Eng. Rep. 126; 2 Ld. Raym. 938 (Q.B. 1703). *See also* 92 Eng. Rep. 710; 3 Ld. Raym. 320 (K.B. 1702) (translation of the Latin pleading before the King's Bench); 14 State Tr. 695 (H.C., H.L. & Q.B. 1704–05).

46. *Paty*, 92 Eng. Rep. at 233; 2 Ld. Raym. at 1106–07.

47. 92 Eng. Rep. at 233; 2 Ld. Raym. at 1107.

48. 92 Eng. Rep. at 237; 2 Ld. Raym. at 1113.

49. 92 Eng. Rep. at 236; 2 Ld. Raym. at 1112.

50. *See* Murray's Case, 95 Eng. Rep. 629; 1 Wils. K.B. 299 (K.B. 1751); R. v. Hobhouse, 2 Chitty 207 (K.B. 1820). The issue would, however, become moot after the Houses ceased imprisoning people for breach or contempt. *See* Report of the Joint Committee on Parliamentary Privilege, H.L. Paper 43-I & H.C. 214-I, at 13 (1999) (noting that the House of Lords has not imprisoned anyone since the early nineteenth century and the House of Commons has not imprisoned anyone since 1880) [hereinafter Joint Committee Report].

51. Brass Crosby's Case, 95 Eng. Rep. 1005, 1006–07; 3 Wils. K.B. 188, 191–92 (C.P. 1771).

52. 95 Eng. Rep. at 1007–08; 3 Wils. K.B. at 193–94.

53. 95 Eng. Rep. at 1013; 3 Wils. K.B. at 202.

54. 95 Eng. Rep. at 1014; 3 Wils. K.B. at 204–05.

55. R. v. Knollys, 91 Eng. Rep. 904; 1 Ld. Raym. 10 (K.B. 1695).

56. 91 Eng. Rep. at 905; 1 Ld. Raym. at 11.

57. 91 Eng. Rep. at 907; 1 Ld. Raym. at 16.

58. 91 Eng. Rep. at 906; 1 Ld. Raym. at 14.

59. 91 Eng. Rep. at 907; 1 Ld. Raym. at 16.

60. 91 Eng. Rep. at 909; 1 Ld. Raym. at 18.

61. *See* 1 Hatsell, *supra* note 4, at 281–322; Wittke, *supra* note 17, at 128; chapter 9 of this book.

62. 65 *Journals of the House of Commons* 260–70, 285.

63. 65 *id.* at 355.

64. Burdett v. Abbott, 104 Eng. Rep. 501, 502–05; 14 East 1, 3–10 (K.B. 1811).

65. 104 Eng. Rep. at 530–31; 14 East at 78.

66. 104 Eng. Rep. at 532–33; 14 East at 83–84.

67. 104 Eng. Rep. at 559; 14 East at 152.

68. 104 Eng. Rep. at 558–59; 14 East at 150–51.

69. *See* 2 Frederick Pollock & Frederic William Maitland, The History of English Law Before the Time of Edward I, at 198 (2d ed. reprint Cambridge Univ. Press 1968) (1898).

70. Burdett v. Abbott, 3 Eng. Rep. 1289, 1301–02; 5 Dow 165, 200–01 (H.L. 1817).

71. 112 Eng. Rep. 1112; 9 Ad. & E. 1 (Q.B. 1839).

72. 112 Eng. Rep. at 1168; 9 Ad. & E. at 147–48.

73. Wittke, *supra* note 17, at 150.

74. *See* Case of the Sheriff of Middlesex, 113 Eng. Rep. 419; 11 Ad. & E. 273 (Q.B. 1840).

75. Colin R. Munro, Studies in Constitutional Law 236–37 (2d ed. 1999).

76. 3 & 4 Vict., c. 9 (1840). For an interesting historical analysis of the Act, see Patricia M. Leopold, *The Parliamentary Papers Act 1840 and Its Application Today*, 1990 Pub. L. 183.

77. Bradlaugh v. Erskine, 31 Wkly. Rept'r 365 (Q.B. 1883).

78. 29 Vict., c. 19 (1866).

79. Bradlaugh v. Gossett, 12 Q.B.D. 271, 276–77, 278, 280–82, 285 (Q.B. 1884).

80. *Id.* at 278.

81. *Id.* at 286–87.

82. R. v. Graham-Campbell, [1935] 1 K.B. 594.

83. *Id.* at 598–99.

84. *Id.* at 602.

85. *See* Geoffrey Lock, *Statute Law and Case Law Applicable to Parliament, in* The Law and Parliament 53, 55–57 (Dawn Oliver & Gavin Drewry eds., 1998) (noting the anachronistic nature of *Graham-Campbell*).

86. *In re* Parliamentary Privilege Act 1770, [1958] A.C. 331 (P.C.).

87. It should be noted that the committee's decision was rejected by a narrow vote in the House of Commons, which resolved that the letter did not constitute a proceeding in Parliament and was therefore not privileged. *See* Joint Committee Report, *supra* note 50, at 32. As we shall see in chapter 3, this seems an unnecessarily narrow (and un-Millian) interpretation of the scope of protected parliamentary duties.

88. 10 Geo. 3, c. 50 (1770).

89. *Strauss,* [1958] A.C. at 350.

90. It was finally published as an appendix to G. F. Lock, *Parliamentary Privilege and the Courts: The Avoidance of Conflict,* 1985 Pub. L. 64, 80–92.

91. *Id.* at 89.

92. *See also* Joint Committee Report, *supra* note 50, at 83 (recommending a statutory reversal of *Strauss*).

93. [1972] 1 Q.B. 522.

94. *Id.* at 529–30.

95. *Id.* at 530.

96. [1993] A.C. 593 (H.L.).

97. *Id.* at 638.

98. *Id.* at 639.

99. *Id.*

100. The reasoning in *Pepper* would thus seem to overrule Rost v. Edwards, [1990] 2 W.L.R. 1280 (Q.B.). In that case, the Queen's Bench Division held that the fact of a Member's appointment to and subsequent deselection from a parliamentary committee was inadmissible in court. Justice Popplewell acknowledged that "neither freedom of speech nor the dignity of the House will have been affected," *id.* at 1291, but considered himself bound by precedent. *See id.* at 1290. In *Rost,* as in *Pepper,* the evidence would not have constituted a questioning of parliamentary behavior, and thus allowing it into evidence would not have chilled parliamentary debate.

101. *Pepper,* [1993] A.C. at 645.

102. Prebble v. Television New Zealand Ltd., [1995] 1 A.C. 321 (P.C.).

103. *Id.* at 334.

104. *Id.* at 335.

105. *Id.* at 338.

106. *Id.*

107. Allason v. Haines, 145 N.L.J. 1576 (Q.B. 1995).

108. Defamation Act, 1996, c. 31, § 13.

109. [2001] 1 A.C. 395 (H.L.).

110. *Id.* at 408.

111. Thus, the criticisms voiced in the Joint Committee Report, *supra* note 50, at 24 & n.84, and the sources cited therein, are inapt. If a privilege can be a privilege of the House, though it is asserted and relied upon by an individual Member (as the committee acknowledged), then why can it not equally be a privilege of the House, though it is *waived* by an individual Member?

112. Demicoli v. Malta, 14 Eur. H.R. Rep. 47 (1992).

113. *Id.* at 61–63.

114. *Id.* at 64.

115. *See* Human Rights Act, 1998, c. 42, § 6.

116. Wittke, *supra* note 17, at 171.

117. Indeed, this seems to be Lord Brown-Wilkinson's interpretation in *Pepper. See supra* text accompanying note 101.

118. D. L. Keir & F. H. Lawson, Cases in Constitutional Law 255 (6th ed. 1979). *See also* Thomas Erskine May, Erskine May's Treatise on the Law, Privileges, Proceedings and Usage of Parliament 176 (William McKay ed., 23d ed. 2004) ("[T]he boundary between the competence of the law courts and the jurisdiction of either House in matters of privilege is still not entirely determined.").

119. Joint Committee Report, *supra* note 50, at 47.

120. *Id.* at 97.

121. *Id.* at 78.

Chapter Two. Political Questions and Nonjusticiability

1. As early as 1803, Chief Justice Marshall wrote that it is not the role of the courts "to enquire how the executive, or executive officers, perform duties in which they have a discretion. Questions, in their nature political, or which are, by the constitution and laws, submitted to the executive, can never be made in this court." Marbury v. Madison, 5 U.S. (1 Cranch) 137, 170 (1803).

2. Erwin Chemerinsky, Federal Jurisdiction 142 (2d ed. 1994).

3. Louis Henkin, *Is There a 'Political Question' Doctrine?*, 85 Yale L. J. 597, 599 (1976).

4. *See* Alexander M. Bickel, The Least Dangerous Branch 111–98 (2d ed. 1986); Alexander M. Bickel, *The Supreme Court, 1960 Term — Foreword: The Passive Virtues*, 75 Harv. L. Rev. 40 (1961) [hereinafter Bickel, *Passive Virtues*]; Herbert Wechsler, *Toward Neutral Principles of Constitutional Law*, 73 Harv. L. Rev. 1 (1959). Other participants in the debate include Henkin, *supra* note 3; Martin H. Redish, *Judicial Review and the "Political Question,"* 79 Nw. U. L. Rev. 1031 (1985); Fritz W. Scharpf, *Judicial Review and the Political Question: A Functional Analysis*, 75 Yale L. J. 517 (1966).

5. Wechsler, *supra* note 4, at 7–8.

6. Baker v. Carr, 369 U.S. 186, 217 (1962) (finding this among several characteristics which may mark a case as falling under the political-questions doctrine).

7. Wechsler, *supra* note 4, at 9.

8. Bickel, *Passive Virtues, supra* note 4, at 49.

9. *Id.* at 50.

10. *See id.* at 46–51.

11. *See* Henkin, *supra* note 3, at 605; Redish, *supra* note 4, at 1048–49.

12. For good summaries of the doctrine as a whole, see Chemerinsky, *supra* note 2, at 142–66; Paul M. Bator et al., Hart and Wechsler's The Federal Courts and the Federal System 270–94 (3d ed. 1988).

13. U.S. Const. art. I, § 2, cl. 5 (selection of officers in the House of Representatives); *id.* art. I, § 3, cl. 5 (selection of officers in the Senate); *id.* art. I, § 5, cl. 1 (Elections, Returns, and Qualifications Clause and Compelled Attendance Clause); *id.* art. I, § 5, cl. 2 (Rules, Punishment, and Expulsion Clause); *id.* art. I, § 5, cl. 3 (Journals Clause).

14. On the Founding debates, see 2 The Records of the Federal Convention of 1787, at 231 (Max Farrand ed., rev. ed. 1966) (Philadelphia Convention unanimously agreeing to the provision giving the House of Representatives power to choose its own officers) [hereinafter Farrand's Records]; 2 *id.* at 239 (Philadelphia Convention unanimously agreeing to the provision giving the Senate power to choose its own officers); 2 *id.* at 254 (Philadelphia Convention unanimously agreeing to the provision making each House the judge of the elections, returns, and qualifications of its Members); 2 *id.* at 253–54 (Philadelphia Convention overwhelmingly agreeing to the provision giving each House the power to compel the attendance of its Members). None of these provisions caused controversy in the state ratifying conventions, either. *See* 1–5 The Debates in the Several State Conventions, On the Adoption of the Federal Constitution, as Recommended by the General Convention at Philadelphia, in 1787 (Jonathan Elliot ed., 2d ed. reprinted Philadelphia, J. B. Lippincott 1907) (1836) [hereinafter Elliot's Debates]. *But see* 4 The Complete Anti-Federalist 142 (Herbert J. Storing ed., 1981) ("Cornelius" complaining that the power to judge the qualifications of Members is "equal to that of a negative on elections in general").

Of the original thirteen states, twelve had constitutional provisions allowing legislative houses to choose their own officers. *See* Conn. Charter of 1662, *continued in force by* Conn. Const. of 1776, para. 1; Del. Const. of 1776, art. V; Ga. Const. of 1777, art. VII; Md. Const. of 1776, art. XXIV; Mass. Const. of 1780, pt. II, ch. 1, § 2, art. VII (Senate); *id.* pt. II, ch. 1, § 3, art. X (House of Representatives); N.H. Const. of 1784, pt. II, Senate, para. 12; *id.* pt. II, House of Representatives, para. 12; N.J. Const. of 1776, art. V; N.Y. Const. of 1777, art. IX; N.C. Const. of 1776, art. X; Pa. Const. of 1776, § 9; S.C. Const. of 1778, art. XVIII; Va. Const. of 1776, para. 5. The single exception was Rhode Island, which was still using its 1663 colonial charter.

Eight Founding states had constitutional provisions giving legislative houses the power to judge the elections, returns, and qualifications of their Members. *See* Del. Const. of 1776, art. V; Md. Const. of 1776, arts. IX, XXI; Mass. Const. of 1780, pt. II, ch. 1, § 2, art. IV; *id.* pt. II, ch. 1, § 3, art. X; N.H. Const. of 1784, pt. II, Senate, para. 9; N.J. Const. of 1776, art. V; N.Y. Const. of 1777, art. IX; N.C. Const. of 1776, art. X; Pa. Const. of 1776, § 9.

15. 2 Farrand's Records, *supra* note 14, at 140.

16. 2 *id.* at 156.

17. 2 *id.* at 180.

18. 2 *id.* at 254. Once again, Elliot's Debates, *supra* note 14, shows no contention over these provisions in the state ratifying conventions.

19. Articles of Confederation art. IX, cl. 7.

20. 2 Farrand's Records, *supra* note 14, at 180.

21. 2 *id.* at 247.

22. 2 *id.* at 260.

23. *Id.*

24. *Id.*

25. 2 *id.* at 613.

26. 2 *id.* at 635.

27. 3 Elliot's Debates, *supra* note 14, at 169–70.

28. 3 *id.* at 404.

29. 3 *id.* at 409.

30. 4 *id.* at 72–73.

31. 1 *id.* at 330 (New York); 1 *id.* at 336 (Rhode Island); 3 *id.* at 659–60 (Virginia); 4 *id.* at 245 (North Carolina).

32. 720 F.2d 689 (D.C. Cir. 1983) (en banc).

33. *Id.* at 692 (MacKinnon, J., concurring specially) (internal footnotes omitted).

34. Nicholson v. United States, 1858 U.S. Ct. Cl. LEXIS 68.

35. *See* The Federalist No. 48, at 308 (James Madison) (Clinton Rossiter ed., 1961) ("[U]nless these departments be so far connected and blended as to give to each a constitutional control over the others, the degree of separation which the maxim requires, as essential to a free government, can never in practice be duly maintained.") [hereinafter all citations are to this edition].

36. *See* The Federalist No. 51, at 322 (James Madison).

37. *Id.* at 321.

38. *See* 1 Joseph Story, Commentaries on the Constitution of the United States § 741, at 544–45 (Melville M. Bigelow ed., Boston, Little, Brown & Co. rev. ed. 1891).

39. Barry v. United States *ex rel.* Cunningham, 279 U.S. 597, 613 (1929).

40. 395 U.S. 486 (1969).

41. *Id.* at 489–93.

42. *Id.* at 506–12.

43. *Id.* at 521–22. *See* U.S. Const. art. I, § 2, cl. 2 (qualifications for representatives); *id.* art. I, § 3, cl. 3 (qualifications for senators). For a detailed defense of the principle that the qualifications listed in the Constitution are exhaustive, see chapter 8.

44. *Powell,* 395 U.S. at 547–48 (internal citations omitted). For more on the *Wilkes* case mentioned by the chief justice, see chapter 7.

45. *See Powell,* 395 U.S. at 521 n.42 ("Consistent with this interpretation, federal courts might still be barred by the political question doctrine from reviewing the House's factual determination that a member did not meet one of the standing qualifications. This is an issue not presented in this case and we express no view as to its resolution.").

46. Roudebush v. Hartke, 405 U.S. 15, 25–26 (1972) (internal footnotes omitted).

47. *Id.* at 18–19.

48. Morgan v. United States, 801 F.2d 445, 445–46 (D.C. Cir. 1986), *cert. denied,* 480 U.S. 911 (1987).

49. *Id.* at 446–47.

50. *Id.* at 448.

51. McIntyre v. Fallahay, 766 F.2d 1078, 1081 (7th Cir. 1985).

52. Wechsler, *supra* note 4, at 8.

53. United States v. Smith, 286 U.S. 6, 26–31 (1932).

54. *Id.* at 33.

55. Consumers Union v. Periodical Correspondents' Association, 515 F.2d 1341 (D.C. Cir. 1975), *cert. denied,* 423 U.S. 1051 (1976).

56. Vander Jagt v. O'Neill, 699 F.2d 1166 (D.C. Cir. 1983), *cert. denied,* 464 U.S. 823 (1983).

57. *Id.* at 1168. It chose instead to base its ruling on the somewhat fuzzier grounds that

"prudential and separation-of-powers concerns counsel us not to exercise our judicial power." *Id.*

58. United States v. Rostenkowski, 59 F.3d 1291, 1305 (D.C. Cir. 1995).

59. *Id.* at 1306.

60. Powell v. McCormack, 395 U.S. 486, 507 n.27 (1969) ("Since we conclude that Powell was excluded from the 90th Congress, we express no view on what limitations may exist on Congress' power to expel or otherwise punish a member once he has been seated.").

61. United States v. Brewster, 408 U.S. 501, 520–24 (1972); Burton v. United States, 202 U.S. 344, 366–67 (1906); United States v. Myers, 635 F.2d 932, 937–38 (2d Cir. 1980), *cert. denied*, 449 U.S. 956 (1980).

62. Field v. Clark, 143 U.S. 649, 668–69 (1892).

63. *See* U.S. Const. art. I, § 7.

64. *Field*, 143 U.S. at 669.

65. *Id.* at 670.

66. *Id.* at 670–71.

67. *Id.* at 672–73.

68. *Id.* at 680.

69. United States v. Ballin, 144 U.S. 1 (1892).

70. U.S. Const. art. I, § 2, cl. 5; *id.* art. I, § 3, cl. 6–7; *id.* art. II, § 4; *id.* art. III, § 2, cl. 3.

71. 1 Farrand's Records, *supra* note 14, at 21–22.

72. 1 *id.* at 224, 231, 238.

73. 1 *id.* at 244.

74. 1 *id.* at 292–93.

75. 2 *id.* at 41–42.

76. 2 *id.* at 42.

77. 2 *id.* at 39, 46.

78. 2 *id.* at 64. *See also* 2 *id.* at 53.

79. 2 *id.* at 65.

80. 2 *id.* at 65.

81. 2 *id.* at 68–69.

82. 2 *id.* at 136. *See also* 2 *id.* at 159, 172–73. "House of Delegates" was the name in early drafts of what later became the House of Representatives.

83. 2 *id.* at 145, 147, 157.

84. 2 *id.* at 178–79 (impeachments); 2 *id.* at 186–87 (impeachment trials).

85. 2 *id.* at 231.

86. 2 *id.* at 427.

87. 2 *id.* at 493.

88. 2 *id.* at 551.

89. 2 *id.* at 551–52.

90. 3 Elliot's Debates, *supra* note 14, at 493–94.

91. 3 *id.* at 512.

92. 3 *id.* at 516.

93. 3 *id.* at 661 (Virginia); 4 *id.* at 246 (North Carolina); 1 *id.* at 331 (New York).

94. 1 The Debate on the Constitution 654–55 (Bernard Bailyn ed., 1993) (Luther Martin's "The Genuine Information, IX" (Jan. 29, 1788)) [hereinafter Bailyn's Debate].

95. 1 *id.* at 265 ("The Federal Farmer, III" (Oct. 10, 1787)).

96. 2 *id.* at 375 ("Brutus, XV" (March 20, 1788)).

97. The Federalist No. 65, at 396 (Alexander Hamilton).

98. *Id.* at 397.

99. The Federalist No. 66, at 402 (Alexander Hamilton).

100. The Federalist No. 65, at 399 (Alexander Hamilton).

101. For an excellent introduction to all of the issues involved, see Charles L. Black Jr., Impeachment: A Handbook (reissued 1998) (1974). Black limits his study to presidential impeachment, but many of the issues he addresses are relevant to any impeachment. *See also* 1 Story, *supra* note 38, §§ 742–813, at 545–92.

102. U.S. Const. art. III, § 1.

103. *See* 1 Story, *supra* note 38, § 762, at 558, § 768, at 562.

104. *See* U.S. Const. art. II, § 1, cl. 1.

105. For a discussion of the practical problems involved in judicial overturning of a presidential impeachment, see Black, *supra* note 101, at 53–55, 61–62.

106. *See* 28 U.S.C. § 1 (2000) (Supreme Court); 28 U.S.C. § 44 (2000) (Courts of Appeals); 28 U.S.C. § 133 (2000) (District Courts).

107. *See* Wechsler, *supra* note 4, at 8; *see also* Black, *supra* note 101, at 23, 62.

108. For details of the case against Nixon, see United States v. Nixon, 816 F.2d 1022 (5th Cir. 1987), *cert. denied*, 484 U.S. 1026 (1988).

109. *See* Alex Kozinski & Eugene Volokh, *Lawsuit, Shmawsuit*, 103 Yale L. J. 463, 467 (1993). It might be argued that this is, in fact, an exemplification, rather than a definition, but far be it from me so to *kibitz* in Kozinski and Volokh's writing. *See id.* at 463 n.4, 464 & n.6, 467.

110. Nixon v. United States, 506 U.S. 224, 226–28 (1993).

111. *Id.* at 228.

112. *Id.* at 231.

113. *Id.* at 233.

114. *Id.* at 234–35 (citing Hamilton in Federalist No. 81).

115. *Id.* at 236.

116. 2 Farrand's Records, *supra* note 14, at 502–03.

117. 10 Annals of Congress 72 (1800).

Chapter Three. Free Speech in Parliament

1. *See, e.g.*, Report of the Joint Committee on Parliamentary Privilege, H.L. Paper 43-I & H.C. 214-I, at 1 (1999) ("Freedom of speech. . . . is the single most important parliamentary privilege.") [hereinafter Joint Committee Report].

2. *See* Henry Elsynge, The Manner of Holding Parliaments in England 179–81 (London, Richardson & Clark rev. ed. 1768); F. W. Maitland, The Constitutional History of England 241 (H. A. L. Fisher ed., reprint Cambridge Univ. Press 1963) (1908); Carl Wittke, The History of English Parliamentary Privilege 23–24 (photo. reprint 1970) (1921).

3. Wittke, *supra* note 2, at 24. J. E. Neale argues that Haxey's case was not an example of the free-speech privilege because there was no evidence that Haxey was a Member and because privilege was not a plea against a charge of treason. *See* J. E. Neale, *The Com-*

mons' Privilege of Free Speech in Parliament, in 2 Historical Studies of the English Parliament 149 (E. B. Fryde & Edward Miller eds., 1970). But Neale ignores Henry's promise to respect the House's privacy in the future, a promise which suggests that, regardless of Haxey's status, the House regarded interference in its internal debates as a violation of its privileges.

4. *See* J. R. Pole, Political Representation in England and the Origins of the American Republic 402 (1966) ("The liberty of Parliament included its privacy. . . . But [this privacy] was never thought of as being a popular liberty.").

5. Raphaell Holinshed, The Third Volume of Chronicles, beginning at duke William the Norman, Commonlie Called the Conqueror; and Descending by Degrees of Yeeres to All the Kings and Queenes of England in their Orderlie Successions 512 (London, Denham 1587). *See also* Elsynge, *supra* note 2, at 218–19.

6. 5 *Rotuli Parliamentorum* 337.

7. *See* 1 John Hatsell, Precedents of Proceedings in the House of Commons 85–86 (rev. ed., London, Hansard 1818); Maitland, *supra* note 2, at 242; Wittke, *supra* note 2, at 25.

8. Strode's Act, 4 Hen. 8, c. 8 (1512).

9. *Id.*

10. Elsynge, *supra* note 2, at 176; Maitland, *supra* note 2, at 242; Wittke, *supra* note 2, at 23.

11. For a history of the speaker's petition, *see* Neale, *supra* note 3, at 157–59.

12. Neale's attempts to show that no such privilege existed before Elizabeth are unpersuasive. His dismissal of *Haxey* is, as I have argued above, inappropriate. *See supra* note 3. He claims that *Young* was a historical anomaly. *See* Neale, *supra* note 3, at 170. And then he ignores *Strode* entirely! Naturally, *Young* will appear anomalous to a historian who ignores or dismisses other similar cases.

13. J. E. Neale, *Peter Wentworth*, 39 Eng. Hist. Rev. 36, 38 (1924).

14. 1 William Cobbett, Parliamentary History of England 716 (London, Hansard 1806).

15. 8 J. B. Black, The Oxford History of England: The Reign of Elizabeth, 1558–1603, at 223 (George Clark ed., 2d ed. 1959).

16. 1 Cobbett, *supra* note 14, at 716.

17. 1 *id.* at 761, 765.

18. 1 *id.* at 761–62.

19. 1 *id.* at 765.

20. 1 *id.* at 781–82.

21. 1 *id.* at 784–98, 802.

22. 1 *id.* at 851–53, 870; Wittke, *supra* note 2, at 27; Neale, *supra* note 13, at 49; J. E. Neale, *Peter Wentworth (Continued)*, 39 Eng. Hist. Rev. 175, 190–92 (1924); 8 Black, *supra* note 15, at 224–26.

23. Wittke, *supra* note 2, at 28.

24. Maitland, *supra* note 2, at 242.

25. The Lord Keeper's Further Answer, *in* 3 The Selected Writings of Sir Edward Coke 1190 (Steve Sheppard ed., 2003). J. E. Neale discovered a slightly different version of the speech in a manuscript in the British Museum, but the general tenor is the same:

> For libertie of speech her maiestie commaundeth me to tell yow, that to saye yea or no to Bills, god forbid that any man should be restrained or afrayde to answear accor-

dinge to his best likinge, with some shorte declaracion of his reason therin, and therin to haue a free uoyce, which is the uerye trew libertie of the house, Not as some suppose to speake there of All causes as him listeth, and to frame a forme of Relligion, or a state of gouernment as to their idle braynes shall seeme meetest, She sayth no king fitt for his state will suffer such absurdities.

J. E. Neale, *The Lord Keeper's Speech to the Parliament of 1592/3,* 31 Eng. Hist. Rev. 128, 136–37 (1916).

26. 1 Cobbett, *supra* note 14, at 1326–27.

27. 1 *id.* at 1335.

28. 1 *id.* at 1344.

29. 1 *id.* at 1361.

30. 1 *id.* at 1362–71; 1 Hatsell, *supra* note 7, at 140– 41; 2 Hannis Taylor, The Origin and Growth of the English Constitution 249 (Boston, Houghton, Mifflin 1898).

31. R. v. Elliot, Hollis & Valentine, 3 State Tr. 293, 293–94 (K.B. 1629).

32. *See id.* at 306–07 (Jones, J., expressing this view); *id.* at 307 (Hyde, C.J., expressing this view); *id.* at 308 (Whitlocke, J., expressing this view).

33. Theodore F. T. Plucknett, Taswell-Langmead's English Constitutional History 389–92 (11th ed. 1960).

34. *Elliot,* 3 State Tr. at 310–312.

35. *Id.* at 314–15.

36. *Id.* at 332–33. *See also* 1 Hatsell, *supra* note 7, at 250–58.

37. *Elliot,* 3 State Tr. at 294.

38. R. v. Williams, 13 State Tr. 1369, 1382 (K.B. 1686).

39. *Id.* at 1437.

40. G.F. Lock, *Parliamentary Privilege and the Courts: The Avoidance of Conflict,* 1985 Pub. L. 64, 74. For a good brief account of Williams's life, see Lois G. Schwoerer, The Declaration of Rights, 1689, at 53– 55 (1981).

41. *See* Lock, *supra* note 40; Schwoerer, *supra* note 40, at 85; S. A. de Smith, *Parliamentary Privilege and the Bill of Rights,* 21 Mod. L. Rev. 465, 478 (1958).

42. 1 Wm. & M., sess. 2, c. 2 (1689).

43. 9 Anchitell Grey, Debates of the House of Commons, From the Year 1667 to the Year 1694, at 81 (London, Henry, Cave & Emonson 1763).

44. 10 *Journals of the House of Commons* 215.

45. 170 Eng. Rep. 337; 1 Esp. 226 (K.B. 1794).

46. 170 Eng. Rep. at 338; 1 Esp. at 228.

47. R. v. Creevey, 105 Eng. Rep. 102, 102; 1 M. & S. 273, 273– 74 (K.B. 1813).

48. 105 Eng. Rep. at 104; 1 M. & S. at 278.

49. 105 Eng. Rep. at 105; 1 M. & S. at 280–81.

50. *See* the "Press Contempts" section of chapter 9.

51. 112 Eng. Rep. 1112; 9 Ad. & E. 1 (Q.B. 1839).

52. 112 Eng. Rep. at 1112–13; 9 Ad. & E. at 1–2.

53. 92 *Journals of the House of Commons* 418.

54. *See Stockdale,* 112 Eng. Rep. at 1160; 9 Ad. & E. at 124– 26 (Denman, C.J.); 112 Eng. Rep. at 1177; 9 Ad. & E. at 171–72 (Littledale, J.); 112 Eng. Rep. at 1187–88; 9 Ad. & E. at 200– 01 (Patteson, J.).

55. Case of the Sheriff of Middlesex, 113 Eng. Rep. 419; 11 Ad. & E. 273 (Q.B. 1840).

56. Lock, *supra* note 40, at 65–66.

57. Colin R. Munro, Studies in Constitutional Law 236–37 (2d ed. 1999).

58. In oral arguments, the attorney-general noted that "[t]he theory of the constitution supposes a constant intercourse between the representative and the constituent. The constituent petitions the House and the House informs the constituent," and this informing role often involves the publication of parliamentary proceedings. *Stockdale*, 112 Eng. Rep. at 1146; 9 Ad. & E. at 87.

59. 3 & 4 Vict., c. 9 (1840). *See generally* Patricia M. Leopold, *The Parliamentary Papers Act 1840 and Its Application Today*, 1990 Pub. L. 183.

60. *Ex parte* Wason, 4 L.R.-Q.B. 573 (1869).

61. *Id.* at 576.

62. [1972] 1 Q.B. 14.

63. *Id.* at 16.

64. *Id.* at 24.

65. Clive Parry, *Legislatures and Secrecy*, 67 Harv. L. Rev. 737, 777 (1954) (quoting Report from the Select Committee on the Official Secrets Acts, H.C. 101 at ¶¶ 6, 7 (1939) [hereinafter Official Secrets Acts Report]).

66. *Id.* at 781 (citing Official Secrets Acts Report, *supra* note 65, ¶¶ 10–14).

67. A. W. Bradley, Comment, *Parliamentary Privilege and the Zircon Affair*, 1987 Pub. L. 1, 2.

68. *Id.*

69. A. W. Bradley, Comment, *Parliamentary Privilege, Zircon and National Security*, 1987 Pub. L. 488, 489–90 (citing Committee of Privileges, Speaker's Order of 22 January 1987 on a Matter of National Security, H.C. 365 (1987)).

70. *See id.* at 491–92.

71. Wason v. Walter, [1868] 4 Q.B. 73.

72. *Id.* at 89.

73. *Id.* at 94–95.

74. 20 L.R. Ir. 600, 611, 617–18 (Ex. D. 1887).

75. *Id.* at 617–18.

76. Cook v. Alexander, [1974] 1 Q.B. 279.

77. *Id.* at 288.

78. *Id.* at 289.

79. *Id.* at 287–88.

80. Times (London), July 19, 2004, at 53 (P.C.).

81. *Id.*

82. 36 Eur. H.R. Rep. 917 (2003).

83. *Id.* at 921.

84. *Id.* at 922.

85. *Id.* at 921.

86. *See id.* at 932–33.

87. *Id.* at 937.

88. N. W. Barber, *Parliamentary Immunity and Human Rights*, 119 Law Q. Rev. 557, 558–59 (2003).

89. De Smith, *supra* note 41, at 481. *See also* Geoffrey Marshall, *The House of Commons and Its Privileges, in* The House of Commons in the Twentieth Century 213 (S. A. Walkland ed., 1979) ("Undoubtedly there have been scandals and misdemeanours exposed that might not have been exposed had members not believed themselves to be protected by an absolute immunity.").

90. Munro, *supra* note 57, at 243. These include an espionage accusation, an exposé of the "methods of the infamous property racketeer Peter Rachman," and MPs' public airings of their "suspicions of the media magnate Robert Maxwell and the businessman Asil Nadir," all of which turned out to be well founded.

91. For a hypothetical example dealing with the latter, see Patricia M. Leopold, *Freedom of Speech in Parliament — Its Misuse and Proposals for Reform*, 1981 Pub. L. 30, 31. *See also* Joint Committee Report, *supra* note 1, at 57 ("We cannot rule out the possibility there may be occasions when the benefit, in the public interest, of disclosure of a secret matter by a member outweighs any harm caused thereby.").

92. Marshall, *supra* note 89, at 211.

93. *See* Leopold, *supra* note 91, at 39–40 (arguing for the need for such a procedure).

94. Munro, *supra* note 57, at 245.

Chapter Four. Free Speech in Congress

1. U.S. Const. art. I, § 6, cl. 1.

2. Articles of Confederation art. V, cl. 5.

3. Md. Const. of 1776, Declaration of Rights, art. VIII ("[F]reedom of speech and debates, or proceedings in the Legislature, ought not to be impeached in any other court or judicature."); Mass. Const. of 1780, pt. I, art. XXI ("The freedom of deliberation, speech, and debate, in either house of the legislature, is so essential to the rights of the people, that it cannot be the foundation of any accusation or prosecution, action or complaint, in any other court or place whatsoever."); N.H. Const. of 1784, pt. I, art. XXX ("The freedom of deliberation, speech, and debate, in either house of the legislature, is so essential to the rights of the people, that it cannot be the foundation of any action, complaint, or prosecution, in any other court or place whatsoever.").

4. 2 The Records of the Federal Convention of 1787, at 140 (Max Farrand ed., rev. ed. 1966) (House of Delegates); 2 *id.* at 141 (Senate).

5. 2 *id.* at 156.

6. 2 *id.* at 166. This draft was reported to the full Convention. 2 *id.* at 180.

7. 2 *id.* at 254.

8. 2 *id.* at 593.

9. On the states' ratification debates, see generally 1–5 The Debates in the Several State Conventions, On the Adoption of the Federal Constitution, as Recommended by the General Convention at Philadelphia, in 1787 (Jonathan Elliot ed., 2d ed. reprinted Philadelphia, J. B. Lippincott 1907) (1836). On the debates in the press, see generally The Federalist; 1–7 The Complete Anti-Federalist (Herbert J. Storing ed., 1981); 1–2 The Debate on the Constitution (Bernard Bailyn ed., 1993).

10. James Wilson, *Lectures on Law, Part Two: Of the Constitutions of the United States and of Pennsylvania — Of the Legislative Department, in* 1 The Works of James Wilson 421 (Robert Green McCloskey ed., 1967).

11. James Madison, Letter to Philip Doddridge (June 6, 1832), *in* 4 Letters and Other Writings of James Madison 221 (New York, R. Worthington 1884).

12. Thomas Jefferson, *Petition to the Virginia House of Delegates, in* 8 The Works of Thomas Jefferson 322 (Paul Leicester Ford ed., 1904).

13. 8 *id.* at 323.

14. 8 *id.* at 325–27.

15. 8 *id.* at 327.

16. 1 Joseph Story, Commentaries on the Constitution of the United States § 866, at 632 (Melville M. Bigelow ed., Boston, Little, Brown rev. ed. 1891).

17. *Id.*

18. *See, e.g.,* David M. Lederkramer, *A Statutory Proposal for Case-by-Case Congressional Waiver of the Speech or Debate Privilege in Bribery Cases,* 3 Cardozo L. Rev. 465 (1982); Leon R. Yankwich, *The Immunity of Congressional Speech—Its Origin, Meaning and Scope,* 99 U. Pa. L. Rev. 960 (1951); Michael R. Seghetti, Note, *Speech or Debate Immunity: Preserving Legislative Independence While Cutting Costs of Congressional Immunity,* 60 Notre Dame L. Rev. 589 (1985).

19. Related, of course, is a federalist concern: *state* governments cannot interfere with congressional speech or debate, either.

20. Robert J. Reinstein & Harvey A. Silverglate, *Legislative Privilege and the Separation of Powers,* 86 Harv. L. Rev. 1113, 1146 (1973). Reinstein and Silverglate are not alone in this view—*see also* Sharon A. Rudnick, *Speech or Debate Clause Immunity for Congressional Hiring Practices: Its Necessity and Its Implications,* 28 UCLA L. Rev. 217 (1980).

21. Craig M. Bradley, *The Speech or Debate Clause: Bastion of Congressional Independence or Haven for Corruption?,* 57 N.C. L. Rev. 197, 210, 214 (1979).

22. *See* O. Hood Phillips, Paul Jackson & Patricia Leopold, Constitutional and Administrative Law 275 (8th ed. 2001); Report of the Joint Committee on Parliamentary Privilege, H.L. Paper 43-I & H.C. 214-I, at 40 (1999).

23. *See* Alexander J. Cella, *The Doctrine of Legislative Privilege of Speech or Debate: The New Interpretation as a Threat to Legislative Coequality,* 8 Suffolk U. L. Rev. 1019 (1974) [hereinafter Cella, *New Interpretation*]; Alexander J. Cella, *The Doctrine of Legislative Privilege of Freedom of Speech and Debate: Its Past, Present and Future as a Bar to Criminal Prosecutions in the Courts,* 2 Suffolk U. L. Rev. 1 (1968) [hereinafter Cella, *Criminal Prosecutions*]; Yankwich, *supra* note 18.

24. Lederkramer, *supra* note 18, at 468.

25. *Id.* at 476.

26. *Id.* at 516.

27. James M. Landis, *Constitutional Limitations on the Congressional Power of Investigation,* 40 Harv. L. Rev. 153, 205, 209 (1926).

28. Reinstein & Silverglate, *supra* note 20, at 1154–55, 1157.

29. *See id.* at 1163.

30. *See* Cella, *New Interpretation, supra* note 23, at 1072.

31. *See* Reinstein & Silverglate, *supra* note 20, at 1163–64.

32. *Id.* at 1150. *See also* Cella, *New Interpretation, supra* note 23, at 1075.

33. 39 U.S.C. § 3210 (2000).

34. *See* Bradley, *supra* note 21; Rudnick, *supra* note 20; Note, *The Bribed Congress-man's Immunity from Prosecution*, 75 Yale L. J. 335 (1965).

35. Reinstein & Silverglate, *supra* note 20, at 1160.

36. *Id.* at 1162 (internal footnote omitted).

37. U.S. Const. art. I, § 5, cl. 2.

38. Cella, *New Interpretation, supra* note 23, at 1088.

39. Mass. Const. art. XXI.

40. Coffin v. Coffin, 4 Mass. 1, 24–25 (1808).

41. *Id.* at 27.

42. *Id.* at 28.

43. *Id.* at 29.

44. *Id.* at 30.

45. *See* Cella, *Criminal Prosecutions, supra* note 23, at 27–28.

46. *Id.* at 30.

47. Kilbourn v. Thompson, 103 U.S. 168, 170–78 (1880).

48. *See id.* at 181–201.

49. Stockdale v. Hansard, 112 Eng. Rep. 1112, 1156; 9 Ad. & E. 1, 114 (Q.B. 1839), *quoted in Kilbourn*, 103 U.S. at 202.

50. *Kilbourn*, 103 U.S. at 203.

51. *Id.* at 203–04.

52. *Id.* at 204.

53. Tenney v. Brandhove, 341 U.S. 367, 369–71 (1951).

54. *Id.* at 373–74.

55. *Id.* at 377.

56. *Id.* at 378.

57. Dombrowski v. Eastland, 387 U.S. 82, 85 (1967) (per curiam).

58. 395 U.S. 486, 501–06 (1969).

59. *Id.* at 502 (quoting *Kilbourn*, 103 U.S. at 204).

60. *Id.* at 503.

61. *Id.* at 504.

62. Walker v. Jones, 733 F.2d 923, 925–27 (D.C. Cir. 1984).

63. *Id.* at 929.

64. *Id.* at 931 (citing Davis v. Passman, 544 F.2d 865, 879 (5th Cir. 1977)).

65. Gravel v. United States, 408 U.S. 606, 608–10 (1972).

66. *Id.* at 615–16.

67. *Id.* at 616–17 (internal citation omitted).

68. *Id.* at 622.

69. *Id.* at 623 n.14 (internal citation omitted).

70. *Id.* at 625.

71. Justice Douglas eloquently made this point in his dissent, *see id.* at 634–37 (Douglas, J., dissenting), as did Justice Brennan, *see id.* at 649–64 (Brennan, J., dissenting).

72. Hon. Sam J. Ervin Jr., *The* Gravel *and* Brewster *Cases: An Assault on Congressional Independence*, 59 Va. L. Rev. 175, 184–85 (1973).

73. 412 U.S. 306 (1973).

74. *Id.* at 307–09.

75. *Id.* at 312.

76. *Id.* at 313.

77. *Id.* at 315–16.

78. *Id.* at 316 (internal citations omitted).

79. *Id.* at 317.

80. On this point, see especially Justice Blackmun's partial dissent, *id.* at 332–38 (Blackmun, J., concurring in part and dissenting in part). *See also id.* at 331–32 (Burger, C.J., concurring in part and dissenting in part); *id.* at 338–45 (Rehnquist, J., concurring in part and dissenting in part). Justice Rehnquist specifically expressed outrage at the possibility of injunctive relief, *id.* at 344–45 (Rehnquist, J., concurring in part and dissenting in part).

81. Eastland v. United States Servicemen's Fund, 421 U.S. 491, 493–95 (1975).

82. *Id.* at 503.

83. *Id.*

84. *Id.* at 504–07.

85. *Id.* at 505.

86. *Id.* at 507.

87. *Id.* at 508–09.

88. *Id.* at 509–11.

89. *Id.* at 511.

90. 443 U.S. 111 (1979).

91. *Id.* at 113–18.

92. *Id.* at 127.

93. 1 Story, *supra* note 16, § 866, at 632, *quoted in Hutchinson,* 443 U.S. at 128.

94. *Hutchinson,* 443 U.S. at 128 n.13.

95. *Id.* at 129.

96. *Id.* at 130.

97. *See id.* at 133.

98. *Id.*

99. 833 F.2d 311 (D.C. Cir. 1987).

100. *Id.* at 312–13.

101. *Id.* at 314.

102. *Id.* at 315.

103. *Id.* at 325.

104. United States v. Johnson, 383 U.S. 169, 170–72 (1966).

105. *Id.* at 173–74.

106. *Id.* at 177.

107. *Id.* at 181.

108. 408 U.S. 501 (1972).

109. *Id.* at 502–03.

110. *Id.* at 508 (internal footnote omitted).

111. *Id.* at 512.

112. *Id.* at 516.

113. *Id.* at 518.

114. *Id.* at 526.

115. *Id.*

116. *See* Ervin, *supra* note 72, at 186 (*Brewster* "regards constituent work as 'political' and therefore not entitled to protection. By labeling such activities 'errands' and assuming that they are performed for base political reasons, the Court demeans many legitimate acts performed by Congressmen in their representative capacities and in their roles as ombudsmen between the people and their government.").

117. *See Brewster*, 408 U.S. at 556–58 (White, J., dissenting).

118. *Id.* at 563 (White, J., dissenting).

119. 442 U.S. 477 (1979).

120. *Id.* at 479–84.

121. *Id.* at 487 (internal citations omitted).

122. *Id.* at 490–92.

123. 18 U.S.C. § 201 (2000).

124. *Helstoski*, 442 U.S. at 492–93.

125. *Id.* at 490.

126. *See* New York Times Co. v. Sullivan, 376 U.S. 254 (1964) (standard for defamation of public officials is "actual malice" — that the statement was made with knowledge of its falsity or reckless disregard for its truth or falsity); Gertz v. Robert Welch, Inc., 418 U.S. 323 (1974) (strict liability — i.e., liability without fault — may not be the standard for defamation even of nonpublic figures); Philadelphia Newspapers v. Hepps, 475 U.S. 767 (1986) (First Amendment prohibits states from applying the common-law rule putting the burden of proof on the defendant to establish truth as a defense to a defamation action brought by a nonpublic figure).

127. *See* Watts v. United States, 394 U.S. 705 (1969) (per curiam) (overturning a conviction under a statute criminalizing threats against the life of the president, on the grounds that the statute could not permissibly cover political hyperbole); Brandenburg v. Ohio, 395 U.S. 444 (1969) (per curiam) (advocacy of the use of force or the violation of the law may only be proscribed when it is directed toward inciting, and is likely to incite, imminent lawless action); Cohen v. California, 403 U.S. 15 (1971) (overturning a conviction for using offensive language in public); New York Times Co. v. United States, 403 U.S. 713 (1971) (per curiam) (prior restraint on publication is impermissible); Hess v. Indiana, 414 U.S. 105 (1973) (per curiam) (advocacy of illegal action at some indefinite future time is insufficient to meet the *Brandenburg* threshold, and therefore may not be proscribed); NAACP v. Claiborne Hardware Co., 458 U.S. 886 (1982) (advocates must be free to make strong emotional appeals without carefully weighing their words, so long as they do not incite lawless action).

Prosecutions for seditious libel early in the Republic — like the case of Samuel Cabell discussed above, or prosecutions under the Sedition Act of 1798, 1 Stat. 596 (1798) — were undoubtedly unconstitutional, as President Jefferson argued when he pardoned those convicted under the act and allowed it to expire in 1801. The Supreme Court never ruled on these cases because, under the Judiciary Act of 1789, 1 Stat. 73 (1789), it lacked the jurisdiction to hear criminal appeals from the circuit courts. The circuit-court cases surrounding the act, especially United States v. Callender, 25 F. Cas. 239 (C.C.D. Va. 1800), were highly controversial, and the impeachment of Justice Chase was largely a result of his high-handed management of the *Callender* case, which he heard as circuit justice. *See generally* Akhil Reed Amar, The Bill of Rights: Creation and Reconstruction 98–103 (1998).

    128. Amar, *supra* note 127, at 223–24.

Chapter Five. Freedom from Civil Arrest and Legal Process for Members of Parliament

    1. John Hatsell, Precedents of Proceedings in the House of Commons 9 (rev. ed., London, Hansard 1818).

    2. *See* 1 William Blackstone, Commentaries on the Laws of England 160 (1st ed. photo. reprint 1979) (1765). *See also* Cassidy v. Steuart, 133 Eng. Rep. 817, 834 n.(a)[1]; 2 Man. & G. 437, 470 n.(a)[1] (C.P. 1841).

    3. *See* 1 Hatsell, *supra* note 1, at 206 ("[T]here is not a single instance of a Member's claiming the Privilege of Parliament, to withdraw himself from the criminal law of the land: for offences against the public peace they always thought themselves amenable to the laws of their country: they were contented with being substantially secured from any violence from the Crown, or its Ministers; but readily submitted themselves to the judicature of the King's Bench, the legal Court of criminal jurisdiction; well knowing that 'Privilege which is allowed in case of public service for the Commonwealth, must not be used for the danger of the Commonwealth.'" (Internal footnotes omitted.)).

    4. *See* Act for Abolishing Arrest on Mesne Process in Civil Actions, 1 & 2 Vict., c. 110 (1838); Debtors Act, 32 & 33 Vict., c. 62 (1869). *See also* F. W. Maitland, The Constitutional History of England 377 (H. A. L. Fisher ed., reprint Cambridge Univ. Press 1963) (1908) ("Freedom from arrest is now no very important matter, because this immunity does not extend to imprisonment on the charge of an indictable offence, and in 1869 imprisonment for debt was abolished."); Thomas Erskine May, Erskine May's Treatise on the Law, Privileges, Proceedings and Usage of Parliament 88 (William McKay ed., 23d ed. 2004) ("[I]mprisonment in civil process has been practically abolished."); O. Hood Phillips, Paul Jackson & Patricia Leopold, Constitutional and Administrative Law 280 (8th ed. 2001) ("[T]his privilege has lost most of its importance and only applies to a few cases."); Luke Owen Pike, A Constitutional History of the House of Lords 259 (London, Macmillan 1894) ("[C]omparatively few opportunities now occur for the exercise of the ancient privilege [of freedom from civil arrest]."); Report of the Joint Committee on Parliamentary Privilege, H.L. Paper 43-I & H.C. 214-I, at 11 (1999) ("Freedom from arrest has little application today."); *id.* at 85 ("The immunity lost most of its importance in 1870 when, with a few exceptions, imprisonment for debt was abolished.").

    5. Henry Elsynge, The Manner of Holding Parliaments in England 185 (London, Richardson & Clark rev. ed. 1768); 1 Hatsell, *supra* note 1, at 3.

    6. Elsynge, *supra* note 5, at 184–85; 1 Hatsell, *supra* note 1, at 3–6; Carl Wittke, The History of English Parliamentary Privilege 47–48 (photo. reprint 1970) (1921).

    7. *See* 1 Frederick Pollock & Frederic William Maitland, The History of English Law Before the Time of Edward I, at 199–200 (2d ed. reprint Cambridge Univ. Press 1968) (1898). *See also* chapter 7.

    8. W. N. Bryant, *Commons' Immunity from Arrest: The Earliest Known Case (1340)*, 43 Bull. Inst. Hist. Res. 214, 214 (1970).

9. *Id.*

10. Elsynge, *supra* note 5, at 186–87.

11. *See id.* at 187–88; 1 Hatsell, *supra* note 1, at 14; William Prynne, The Fourth Part of a Brief Register, Kalender and Survey of the Several Kinds, Forms of Parliamentary Writs 725 (London, Ratcliffe 1664).

12. *See* Elsynge, *supra* note 5, at 187–88.

13. Wittke misstates the year of *Larke* as 1492. *See* Wittke, *supra* note 6, at 39. This is most likely due to a misreading of the regnal year in which the case occurred, 8 Hen. VI, as 8 Hen. VII.

14. 4 *Rotuli Parliamentorum* 357–58.

15. 4 *id.* at 358.

16. *See* 1 Hatsell, *supra* note 1, at 110–11; 1 William Cobbett, Parliamentary History of England 555 (London, Hansard 1806).

17. Elsynge, *supra* note 5, at 217–18. Hatsell is skeptical of this explanation, noting that the King could simply have altered the wording of the statement before issuing it. 1 Hatsell, *supra* note 1, at 21–22.

18. 5 *Rotuli Parliamentorum* 239.

19. *Id.*

20. *Id.*

21. 5 *id.* at 240.

22. *Id.*

23. Wittke, *supra* note 6, at 34. *See also* 1 Hatsell, *supra* note 1, at 33–34.

24. 5 *Rotuli Parliamentorum* 374–75.

25. 5 *id.* at 375.

26. 6 *id.* at 160–61.

27. *See* 6 *id.* at 191–92.

28. 6 *id.* at 191.

29. 1 Hatsell, *supra* note 1, at 41–43.

30. Prynne, *supra* note 11, at 764–65.

31. Elsynge, *supra* note 5, at 253–54. For more on the Houses' powers to punish, see chapter 9.

32. 1 Hatsell, *supra* note 1, at 53.

33. 1 *id.* at 53–54.

34. 1 *id.* at 54.

35. *Id.*

36. 1 *id.* at 54–55.

37. On the general topic of contempt, see chapter 9.

38. 1 Hatsell, *supra* note 1, at 55.

39. *Id.*

40. 1 *id.* at 56–57.

41. 1 *id.* at 64. *See* Executors of Skewys v. Chamond, 73 Eng. Rep. 131, 135; 1 Dyer 59b, 61a–b (K.B. 1545).

42. 1 Hatsell, *supra* note 1, at 87.

43. 1 *id.* at 88.

44. It is unclear whether the Member in question was Nicholas Martin of Bere Alston

or Henry Martyn of Wilton. *See* 3 P.W. Hasler, The History of Parliament: The House of Commons, 1558–1603, at 22, 26 (1981).

45. 1 Hatsell, *supra* note 1, at 100.

46. *Id.*

47. Colonel Pitt's Case, 27 Eng. Rep. 767, 769; Ridg. t. H. 91, 96 (Ch. 1734); Holiday v. Pitt, 93 Eng. Rep. 984, 985; 2 Str. 985, 985 (K.B. 1734).

48. 27 Eng. Rep. at 769; Ridg. t. H. at 96; 93 Eng. Rep. at 986; 2 Str. at 988.

49. 1 Hatsell, *supra* note 1, at 107.

50. 1 *id.* at 108.

51. *Id.*

52. *See* 1 *id.* at 165.

53. Simonds D'Ewes, The Journals of All the Parliaments During the Reign of Queen Elizabeth 518 (Paul Bowes ed., London, Starkey 1682).

54. *Id.*

55. *Id.* at 519.

56. *Id.* at 520.

57. *See* 4 *Journals of the House of Commons* 254.

58. *See supra* text accompanying note 16.

59. Parliamentary Privilege Act, 1 Jac. 1, c. 13 (1604).

60. 1 Hatsell, *supra* note 1, at 163.

61. *Id.*

62. Wittke, *supra* note 6, at 37.

63. 1 Hatsell, *supra* note 1, at 142. *But see* Vernon F. Snow, *The Arundel Case, 1626,* 26 The Historian 323 (1964) (suggesting that, while Charles was indeed displeased about the marriage, he was also upset because Arundel undermined the position of the Duke of Buckingham, a royal favorite, in the House of Lords).

64. 1 Hatsell, *supra* note 1, at 143.

65. 1 *id.* at 144.

66. *See* Elsynge, *supra* note 5, at 224–26.

67. 1 Hatsell, *supra* note 1, at 146.

68. 1 *id.* at 147; Snow, *supra* note 63, at 345–46.

69. 1 Hatsell, *supra* note 1, at 152.

70. *Id.*

71. Hatsell misstates the year as 1641 (or, perhaps, he was anachronistically using Old Style dating). *See* 1 *id.* at 265. However, 1642 (New Style) is clearly the correct date. *See, e.g.,* 1 Edward Earl of Clarendon, The History of the Rebellion and Civil Wars in England 555 (Oxford, Clarendon Press new ed. 1807); Lois G. Schwoerer, *"The Fittest Subject for a King's Quarrel": An Essay on the Militia Controversy 1641–1642,* 11 J. British Stud. 45, 46 (1971).

72. 1 Hatsell, *supra* note 1, at 265–67.

73. 1 *id.* at 266.

74. 1 *id.* at 268.

75. 1 *id.* at 271.

76. 1 *id.* at 271–72.

77. 1 *id.* at 272.

78. 1 *id.* at 272–73.

79. 1 *id.* at 273.

80. 1 *id.* at 274.

81. 1 Clarendon, *supra* note 71, at 584–85.

82. 1 *id.* at 590–91.

83. Auxiliary to the privilege against being impleaded is a traditional exemption of Members of Parliament from jury service. *See, e.g.,* D'Ewes, *supra* note 53, at 560; 1 Hatsell, *supra* note 1, at 171, 174; 81 *Journals of the House of Commons* 82, 87–88. *See also* Erskine May, *supra* note 4, at 125 n.6. This exemption was recently abolished. *See* Criminal Justice Act, 2003, c. 44, § 321, sched. 33; Erskine May, *supra* note 4, at 125.

84. 1 *Journals of the House of Commons* 11.

85. 1 Hatsell, *supra* note 1, at 96.

86. 1 *id.* at 97.

87. 1 *id.* at 97–98.

88. 1 *id.* at 98–99.

89. 1 *id.* at 99.

90. For other examples of the House punishing the issuing of subpoenas against its Members, see D'Ewes, *supra* note 53, at 647, 651, 655–56; 1 Hatsell, *supra* note 1, at 118–19; 1 *Journals of the House of Commons* 371, 655, 922, 928.

91. D'Ewes, *supra* note 53, at 436.

92. 1 Hatsell, *supra* note 1, at 176–77.

93. 1 *id.* at 177. A similar authority was granted in 1620. *See* 1 *Journals of the House of Commons* 525.

94. 1 Hatsell, *supra* note 1, at 178.

95. Hatsell reports that, almost a month after the letter was sent, the plaintiff in the suit against the Member, "finding he could get no redress by course of law, had employed force, and had entered upon the house and goods in question, and kept possession by force and violence." Only the fact that Parliament was prorogued shortly thereafter kept the plaintiff from being cited for contempt of Parliament. *Id.*

96. *See, e.g.,* 1 *Journals of the House of Commons* 342–43, 804; 8 *id.* at 601, 603.

97. 1 Hatsell, *supra* note 1, at 185.

98. *See* 1 *id.* at 186–87.

99. 11 *Journals of the House of Commons* 784.

100. *Id.*

101. 1 Hatsell, *supra* note 1, at 188.

102. D'Ewes, *supra* note 53, at 248–49.

103. *Id.* at 249.

104. 1 Hatsell, *supra* note 1, at 90–91.

105. D'Ewes, *supra* note 53, at 250.

106. *Id.* at 251.

107. *Id.* at 254.

108. *See supra* text accompanying notes 58–59. *See also supra* text accompanying note 16.

109. D'Ewes, *supra* note 53, at 258.

110. 1 Hatsell, *supra* note 1, at 117.

111. 1 *id.* at 118.

112. *Id.*

113. Heywood Townshend, Historical Collections: Or, An Exact Account of the Proceedings of the Four Last Parliaments of Q. Elizabeth of Famous Memory 196 (London, Basset, Crooke & Cademan 1680).

114. George Petyt, Lex Parliamentaria: Or, A Treatise of the Law and Custom of the Parliaments of England 282 (London, Goodwin 1690).

115. 1 Hatsell, *supra* note 1, at 133.

116. *See id.*; 1 *Journals of the House of Commons* 438, 440, 441.

117. 1 Hatsell, *supra* note 1, at 165.

118. Prynne, *supra* note 11, at 845.

119. 4 *Journals of the House of Commons* 316.

120. *See* Wittke, *supra* note 6, at 41.

121. 3 *Journals of the House of Lords* 170.

122. 3 *id.* at 172.

123. *See, e.g.,* 4 *id.* at 65 (forger of Lord Morley's seal on a protection ordered imprisoned, pilloried at Westminster and Cheapside, and heavily fined).

124. 3 *id.* at 525.

125. *See* 3 *id.* at 550–51, 558.

126. *See, e.g.,* 10 *Journals of the House of Commons* 296, 332; 14 *Journals of the House of Lords* 457, 461; 28 *id.* at 201.

127. 4 *Journals of the House of Lords* 258.

128. 2 *Journals of the House of Commons* 301.

129. 15 *Journals of the House of Lords* 15.

130. 15 *id.* at 16.

131. 26 *Journals of the House of Lords* 492.

132. *Id.*

133. 8 *Journals of the House of Commons* 184.

134. 9 *id.* at 157.

135. 9 *id.* at 435.

136. *Id.*

137. *Id.*

138. 9 *id.* at 607.

139. 10 *id.* at 332.

140. 10 *id.* at 340.

141. *Id.*

142. 10 *id.* at 340–41.

143. 11 *id.* at 219.

144. 14 *Journals of the House of Lords* 436.

145. 14 *id.* at 441.

146. *Id.*

147. 14 *id.* at 462.

148. 14 *id.* at 521.

149. 14 *id.* at 606.

150. 16 *id.* at 83.

151. 19 *id.* at 431.

152. Maitland, *supra* note 4, at 244.

153. Parliamentary Privilege Act, 12 & 13 W. & M., c. 3 (1700). The original act applied only to suits in a list of enumerated courts. Later, Parliamentary Privilege Act, 11 Geo. 2, c. 24 (1738), expanded the 1700 act to include all British (and Irish) courts of record.

154. Parliamentary Privilege Act, 2 & 3 Ann., c. 18 (1703).

155. Parliamentary Privilege Act, 10 Geo. 3, c. 50 (1770). In the 1773 edition of his *Commentaries*, Blackstone noted that Members were no longer privileged against the service of civil process. *See* 1 William Blackstone, Commentaries on the Laws of England 165 (5th ed. Oxford, Clarendon Press 1773).

156. *See* Wittke, *supra* note 6, at 43.

157. *See* Erskine May, *supra* note 4, at 126–27.

158. Wilkes' Case, 19 State Tr. 981, 989–90 (C.P. 1763).

159. *See supra* text accompanying notes 69–70.

160. *See supra* text accompanying notes 131–132.

161. *See* Erskine May, *supra* note 4, at 84 ("[I]t had always been recognized that privilege could not be pleaded against criminal offences, then adequately summed up as treason, felony, and breach of the peace."); *id.* at 119 ("The privilege of freedom from arrest has never been allowed to interfere with the administration of criminal justice." Internal footnote omitted.). *See also id.* at 84 (citing 1831 House of Commons Committee of Privileges report noting that privilege is not claimable for any indictable offense).

162. Specifically, he and a number of others were convicted of "conspiring by false news to induce the subjects of our Lord the King to believe that Napoleon Bonaparte was dead, and thereby to occasion a rise in funds and to injure such of the King's subjects as should on the 21st of February 1814 purchase any share in the said funds." Christopher Lloyd, Lord Cochrane: Seaman, Radical, Liberator 118–19 (1947). It is not at all clear that Cochrane was actually involved in the scheme, but he was careless in preparing his defense. *See id.* at 119–20.

163. *Id.* at 126.

164. *Id.* at 128–31.

165. 1 Hatsell, *supra* note 1, at 278–79.

166. 1 *id.* at 279–80.

167. *See* Erskine May, *supra* note 4, at 142.

168. Mr. Long Wellesley's Case, 39 Eng. Rep. 538, 548; 2 Russ. & M. 639, 665–66 (Ch. 1831).

169. 39 Eng. Rep. at 548; 2 Russ. & M. at 667.

170. Cassidy v. Steuart, 133 Eng. Rep. 817; 2 Man. & G. 437 (C.P. 1841).

171. 133 Eng. Rep. at 818, 834; 2 Man. & G. at 439–40, 470.

172. 133 Eng. Rep. at 834; 2 Man. & G. at 470–71.

173. Goudy v. Dumcombe, 154 Eng. Rep. 183, 1 Exch. 430 (1847). On the actual parliamentary practice of the time, see Erskine May, *supra* note 4, at 126; Wittke, *supra* note 6, at 52–54; Geoffrey Marshall, *The House of Commons and Its Privileges, in* The House of Commons in the Twentieth Century 210 (S. A. Walkland ed., 1979).

174. Erskine May, *supra* note 4, at 126; Wittke, *supra* note 6, at 52.

175. Stourton v. Stourton, [1963] 1 All E.R. 606 (P.).

176. *Id.* at 609.

177. *Id.* at 610.

178. *See* Richard Griffiths, Patriotism Perverted: Captain Ramsay, The Right Club and British Anti-Semitism, 1939–40, at 274, 285, 287–92 (1998); Marshall, *supra* note 173, at 209; Cornelius P. Cotter, *Emergency Detention in Wartime: The British Experience*, 6 Stan. L. Rev. 238, 278–80 (1954). *See also* Erskine May, *supra* note 4, at 121.

179. *See, e.g.,* Patricia M. Leopold, *The Compulsory Detention of Peers*, 1985 Pub. L. 9.

Chapter Six. Freedom from Civil Arrest for Members of Congress

1. U.S. Const. art. I, § 6, cl. 1.

2. *See* Wheeler Yule Fisher, *Congressional Exemption from Suit and Responsibility and the Long Case*, 3 Geo. Wash. L. Rev. 231, 234 (1935) ("The great democratic upheaval of the nineteenth century swept away much of this legislation [allowing for civil arrest]. Kentucky in 1821 was the first state to abolish imprisonment for debt as part of her debtor relief policy. New York followed in 1831 and by 1857 nearly all states had enacted this form of relief. At the present [1935] the remedy of arrest in aid of civil process has largely disappeared except in a few states for an absconding debtor. Some few other states provide for arrest in civil action for personal injuries. Others allow arrest of a fiduciary who appropriates to his own use. Outside of these few exceptions the present importance of this provision [the Arrest Clause] is small." (Internal footnotes omitted.)). *See also* 5 Am. Jur. 2d *Arrest* § 73 (2005) ("It has been said that the circumstances in which arrest and imprisonment on civil process are available are so narrowly restricted that, for all practical purposes, this mechanism is virtually extinct as an incident of the commencement and maintenance of civil actions.").

3. Articles of Confederation art. V, cl. 5.

4. Md. Const. of 1776, art. XII.

5. Mass. Const. of 1780, pt. II, ch. 1, § 3, art. X; *see also* N.H. Const. of 1784, pt. II, House of Representatives, para. 11 (almost identical language to the Massachusetts provision).

6. 2 The Records of the Federal Convention of 1787, at 140, 141 (Max Farrand ed., rev. ed. 1966) [hereinafter Farrand's Records].

7. 2 *id.* at 156–57.

8. *See* chapter 4.

9. 2 Farrand's Records, *supra* note 6, at 180, 254, 593.

10. On the state ratifying conventions, see 1–5 The Debates in the Several State Conventions, On the Adoption of the Federal Constitution, as Recommended by the General Convention at Philadelphia, in 1787 (Jonathan Elliot ed., 2d ed. reprinted Philadelphia, J. B. Lippincott 1907) (1836).

The only press comments I have encountered are Montezuma's crack that "we [Federalists] have framed a privilege clause, by which they may laugh at the fools who trusted them; but we have given out that this clause was provided, only that the members might be able without interruption, to deliberate on the important business of their country," 3

The Complete Anti-Federalist 54 (Herbert J. Storing ed., 1981) (Montezuma, Oct. 17, 1787), and Agrippa's proposal that "[n]o officer of Congress shall be free from arrest for debt by authority of the state in which the debt shall be due," 2 The Debate on the Constitution 159 (Bernard Bailyn ed., 1993) (Agrippa XVIII, Feb. 5, 1788). *The Federalist Papers* are silent on the clause.

11. James Wilson, *Lectures on Law, Part Two: Of the Constitutions of the United States and of Pennsylvania — Of the Legislative Department, in* 1 The Works of James Wilson 420 (Robert Green McCloskey ed., 1967).

12. Thomas Jefferson, *Manual of Parliamentary Practice* (1812), *in* Constitution of the United States of America with the Amendments Thereto: To Which Are Added Jefferson's Manual of Parliamentary Practice, the Standing Rules and Orders for Conducting Business in The House of Representatives and Senate of the United States, and Barclay's Digest 52–53 (Washington, Government Printing Office 1867).

13. *Id.* at 53.

14. *Id.* at 54–55.

15. *Id.* at 53–54.

16. 1 Joseph Story, Commentaries on the Constitution of the United States § 860, at 628 (Melville M. Bigelow ed., Boston, Little, Brown rev. ed. 1891).

17. 1 *id.* § 862, at 629.

18. 1 *id.* § 865, at 629–30.

19. 1 *id.* § 864, at 629.

20. 1 *id.* § 863, at 629.

21. 1 *id.* § 862, at 629.

22. Thomas Davies, relying on the *Wilkes* case, disagrees. *See* Thomas Y. Davies, *The Fictional Character of Law-and-Order Originalism: A Case Study of the Distortions and Evasions of Framing-Era Arrest Doctrine in* Atwater v. Lago Vista, 37 Wake Forest L. Rev. 239, 293–97 (2002). However, as we saw in the previous chapter, the *Wilkes* decision constituted a departure from the settled understanding of the scope of the privilege, and this aspect of the *Wilkes* decision has never been followed on either side of the Atlantic.

23. Akhil Reed Amar & Neal Kumar Katyal, *Executive Privileges and Immunities: The* Nixon *and* Clinton *Cases,* 108 Harv. L. Rev. 701, 711–12 (1995) (internal footnote omitted).

24. *See* William F. Allen, Note, *President Clinton's Claim of Temporary Immunity: Constitutionalism in the Air,* 11 J. L. & Pol. 555, 589 (1995); Bradford E. Biegon, Note, *Presidential Immunity in Civil Actions: An Analysis Based Upon Text, History and Blackstone's Commentaries,* 82 Va. L. Rev. 677 (1996). *See also* Amar & Katyal, *supra* note 23, at 710 (Amar and Katyal acknowledging that the English debates on parliamentary privilege were "well known to the Framers").

25. *See* Oliver P. Field, *The Constitutional Privileges of Legislators: Exemption from Arrest and Action for Defamation,* 9 Minn. L. Rev. 442, 455 (1925) (noting that "the work of preparing for a case, calling witnesses and the other work incidental to law suits is performed by an attorney, and does not usually demand the personal attention of the legislator").

26. *See id.* at 454–55 (noting that statutes, as well as judicial discretion, can operate to

minimize a Member's distraction from his legislative duties caused by defending against a civil suit).

27. Amar & Katyal, *supra* note 23, at 712.

28. Anita Bernstein has argued that executive "targeting" (defined as investigating a person, rather than a crime) of Members of Congress raises Arrest Clause issues. She proposed that a special "court of legislative integrity" be established to pre-clear all investigations of Members. *See* Anita Bernstein, Note, *Executive Targeting of Congressmen as a Violation of the Arrest Clause*, 94 Yale L. J. 647 (1985). While few would deny that targeting is an abuse of the executive's law-enforcement powers, a more appropriate remedy would seem to lie in the Houses' investigative powers. The Speech or Debate Clause allows targeted Members freely to accuse the executive of targeting them, and legislators are unlikely to be enthused about the targeting of one of their own. Congressional committees could investigate any such accusations, and, if the executive truly was engaged in targeting, the voters would likely be turned off by this abuse of power. Bernstein acknowledges the possibility of congressional investigation into allegations of targeting but concludes that, "[b]y the time a congressman has the opportunity to raise claims post hoc, the targeting has done most of its work." *Id.* at 657. This, however, ignores the fact that congressional investigation will have a deterrent effect: Presidents are less likely to order law-enforcement agencies to target a Member because they fear that the targeting will be discovered and the voters will disapprove. Bernstein's attempt to bring targeting under the ambit of the Arrest Clause, while creative, is thus unnecessary.

29. These criticisms, however, do not disturb the main point of Amar and Katyal's article, which is that there is a good structural argument for giving *presidents* temporary immunity from civil process. About that argument, this book is agnostic.

30. *See* 18 U.S.C. § 3144 (2000).

31. Kansas v. Hendricks, 521 U.S. 346, 361–65 (1997).

32. Bolton v. Martin, 1 U.S. (1 Dall.) 296, 304 (C.P. Phila. 1788).

33. *Id.* at 304–05.

34. *Id.* at 305.

35. *Compare* 1 William Blackstone, Commentaries on the Laws of England 160 (1st ed. photo. reprint 1979) (1765) (Privilege "includes not only privilege from illegal violence, but also from legal arrests, and seizures by process from the courts of law. To assault by violence a member of either house, or his menial servants, is a high contempt of parliament, and there punished with the utmost severity. It has likewise peculiar penalties annexed to it in the courts of law, by the statutes 5 Hen. IV. c. 6. and 11 Hen. VI. c. 11. Neither can any member of either house be arrested and taken into custody, nor served with any process of the courts of law; nor can his menial servants be arrested; nor can any entry be made on his lands; nor can his goods be distrained or seised; without a breach of the privilege of parliament."), *with* 1 William Blackstone, Commentaries on the Laws of England 164–65 (5th ed. Oxford, Clarendon Press 1773) (Privilege "included formerly not only privilege from illegal violence, but also from legal arrests, and seizures by process from the courts of law. And still, to assault by violence a member of either house, or his menial servants, is a high contempt of parliament, and there punished with the utmost severity. It has likewise peculiar penalties annexed to it in the courts of law, by the statutes 5 Hen. IV. c. 6. and 11 Hen. VI. c. 11. Neither can any member of either house be arrested

and taken into custody, without a breach of the privilege of parliament. BUT all other privileges, which derogate from the common law, are now at an end, save only as to the freedom of the member's person. . . . As to all other privileges, which obstruct the ordinary course of justice, they were restrained by the statutes 12 W. III. c. 3. 2 & 3 Ann. c. 18. and 11 Geo. III. c. 24. and are now totally abolished by the statute 10 Geo. III. c. 50. which enacts, that any suit may at any time be brought against any peer or member of parliament, their servants, or any other person intitled to privilege of parliament; which shall not be impeached or delayed by pretence of any such privilege; except that the person of a member of the house of commons shall not thereby be subjected to any arrest or imprisonment." (Internal footnotes omitted)). *See also* Fisher, *supra* note 2, at 234–35.

36. Judge Shippen is not the only one to make this mistake. *See, e.g.,* Miner v. Markham, 28 F. 387, 390–95 (C.C. Wis. 1886) (discussed *infra* text accompanying notes 47–49); Lyell v. Goodwin, 15 F. Cas. 1126, 1127–29 (C.C. Mich. 1845) (No. 8,616) (citing the 1700 Act, *Cassidy v. Steuart,* 133 Eng. Rep. 817; 2 Man. & G. 437 (C.P. 1841) (discussed in the previous chapter), and *Bolton,* among other precedents, but omitting mention of the 1770 act); Anderson v. Rountree, 1 Pin. 115, 118–24 (Wis. 1841) (citing *Martin,* as well as several British sources, all of them pre-1770); Doty v. Strong, 1 Pin. 84, 87–88 (Wis. 1840); Geyer's Lessee v. Irwin, 4 U.S. (4 Dall.) 107, 107 (Pa. 1790). *See also* Amar & Katyal, *supra* note 23, at 711 n.44 (citing *Bolton, Lyell, Anderson, Doty,* and *Geyer's Lessee* approvingly as examples of "the understanding of the Clause at the Founding," but nowhere mentioning the 1770 act (although Amar and Katyal do acknowledge that Shippen relied on an outdated version of Blackstone)).

37. United States v. Wise, 28 F. Cas. 742 (D.C. Crim. Ct. 1842) (No. 16,746a).

38. *Id.* at 743.

39. *Id.* On *Stockdale,* see chapters 1 and 3.

40. Kimberly v. Butler, 14 F. Cas. 498, 499–500 (C.C. Md. 1869) (No. 7,777).

41. Merrick v. Giddings, 11 D.C. (MacArth. & M.) 55 (1879).

42. *Id.* at 56–62.

43. *Id.* at 61.

44. *Id.*

45. *Id.* at 62–64.

46. *Id.* at 64.

47. Miner v. Markham, 28 F. 387, 393 (C.C. Wis. 1886).

48. *Id.* at 394.

49. *Id.*

50. Howard v. Citizens' Bank & Trust Co., 12 App. D.C. 222, 231–33 (D.C. Cir. 1898).

51. *Id.* at 233.

52. Williamson v. United States, 207 U.S. 425, 436–46 (1908).

53. *See* 3 Asher C. Hinds, Hinds' Precedents of the House of Representatives of the United States § 2673, at 1119–21 (1907).

54. Long v. Ansell, 293 U.S. 76, 82 (1934).

55. *Id.* at 83.

56. *Id.* at 82 & n.3. On *Bolton* and its kin, see *supra* note 36.

57. 3 Hinds, *supra* note 53, § 2676, at 1126.

Chapter Seven. Disputed Parliamentary Elections

1. It is thus worth noting that the Bill of Rights, which came at a time of transition from the Blackstonian to the Millian paradigm, specifically demands, "That election of members of parliament ought to be free." 1 Wm. & M., sess. 2, c. 2, art. 8 (1689). *See generally* Lois G. Schwoerer, The Declaration of Rights, 1689, at 78–81 (1981).

2. Charles Howard McIlwain, The High Court of Parliament and Its Supremacy 16 (1910). *See generally id.* at 14–39; 1 Frederick Pollock & Frederic William Maitland, The History of English Law Before the Time of Edward I, at 199–200 (2d ed. reprint Cambridge Univ. Press 1968) (1898).

3. John Glanville, Reports of Certain Cases, Determined and Adjudged by the Commons in Parliament, in the Twenty-first and Twenty-second Years of the Reign of King James the First, at xi (London, Baker & Leigh 1775).

4. *Id.* at xvi–xvii.

5. False Election Returns Act, 11 Hen. IV, c. 1 (1409).

6. Glanville, *supra* note 3, at xx–xxi.

7. 3 S. T. Bindoff, The History of Parliament: The House of Commons 1509–1558, at 28–29 (1982). *See also* F. W. Maitland, The Constitutional History of England 247 (H. A. L. Fisher ed., reprint Cambridge Univ. Press 1963) (1908).

8. 1 *Journals of the House of Commons* 117.

9. Simonds D'Ewes, The Journals of All the Parliaments During the Reign of Queen Elizabeth 281–82 (Paul Bowes ed., London, Starkey 1682).

10. *Id.* at 307–08.

11. *Id.* at 308.

12. Glanville, *supra* note 3, at xlii–xliii.

13. *Id.* at xliii–xliv.

14. D'Ewes, *supra* note 9, at 393.

15. *Id.* at 396.

16. *Id.*

17. *Id.*

18. *Id.* at 397.

19. 2 P. W. Hasler, The History of Parliament: The House of Commons 1558–1603, at 106–07 (1981).

20. *See generally* Goodwyn v. Fortescue, 2 State Tr. 91 (H.C. 1604).

21. Carl Wittke, The History of English Parliamentary Privilege 58 (photo. reprint 1970) (1921).

22. *Id.* at 58–59. *See also* 2 Hasler, *supra* note 19, at 148; George Petyt, Lex Parliamentaria: Or, A Treatise of the Law and Custom of the Parliaments of England 299–300 (London, Goodwin 1690).

23. 1 *Journals of the House of Commons* 151.

24. 1 *id.* at 156; Glanville, *supra* note 3, at lxxiv.

25. 1 *Journals of the House of Commons* 156.

26. *Id.*

27. 1 *id.* at 158.

28. Petyt, *supra* note 22, at 309; *see also* 1 *Journals of the House of Commons* 158.

29. 1 *Journals of the House of Commons* 162–65.

30. 1 *id.* at 168, 171.

31. Reprinted in Matthew Hale, The Original Institution, Power and Jurisdiction of Parliaments 206–40 (London, Tonson 1707).

32. *Id.* at 216.

33. Wittke, *supra* note 21, at 60.

34. Glanville, *supra* note 3, at lxxviii–lxxix.

35. Glanville's reports were not published until 1775, however. For a history of the manuscript, *see id.* at lxxxvii–lxxxviii. Wittke takes it for granted that Glanville himself wrote the Preface, which has been much cited above — *see* Wittke, *supra* note 21, at 55 n.1 — and, in the main, I see no reason to doubt that he did. Still, it is obvious that the anonymous editor made at least some contributions to the Preface — *see* Glanville, *supra* note 3, at i–ix, lxxxiv–lxxxviii.

36. Glanville, *supra* note 3, at 13–17.

37. *Id.* at 17–18.

38. *Id.* at 18.

39. *Id.* at 23–24.

40. *Id.* at 34.

41. *Id.* at 49.

42. *Id.* at 54–55.

43. *Id.* at 55.

44. *Id.* at 60.

45. Barnardiston v. Soame, 83 Eng. Rep. 475, 475; 2 Lev. 114, 114 (K.B. 1674). *See also* 6 State Tr. 1063, 1068 (K.B., Exch. & H.L. 1674).

46. *See Barnardiston*, 6 State Tr. at 1076.

47. *Barnardiston*, 83 Eng. Rep. at 475–76; 2 Lev. at 115 (emphasis added).

48. *Barnardiston*, 6 State Tr. at 1069–70.

49. *Id.* at 1098.

50. *Id.* at 1102.

51. *Id.* at 1073, 1078.

52. *Id.* at 1117.

53. 83 Eng. Rep. 561, 561; 3 Lev. 29, 30 (K.B. 1680). *See also* 86 Eng. Rep. 294; 2 Vent. 37 (K.B. 1680).

54. 7 & 8 Wm. & M., c. 7 (1696).

55. 91 Eng. Rep. 430; 2 Salk. 502 (K.B. 1703); 90 Eng. Rep. 1188; Holt K.B. 523 (K.B. 1703).

56. *Prideaux*, 91 Eng. Rep. at 430; 2 Salk. at 503.

57. *Id.*

58. Ashby v. White, 14 State Tr. 695, 780 n.† (H.L. 1704).

59. Ashby v. White, 92 Eng. Rep. 710, 712; 3 Ld. Raym. 320, 322–23 (Assize 1702).

60. Ashby v. White, 92 Eng. Rep. 126, 129; 2 Ld. Raym. 938, 941 (Q.B. 1703).

61. 92 Eng. Rep. at 129; 2 Ld. Raym. at 942.

62. 92 Eng. Rep. at 132; 2 Ld. Raym. at 947.

63. *See* 92 Eng. Rep. at 130; 2 Ld. Raym. at 944.

64. 92 Eng. Rep. at 136; 2 Ld. Raym. at 954.

65. 92 Eng. Rep. at 136; 2 Ld. Raym. at 953.

66. *Id.*

67. 92 Eng. Rep. at 137–38; 2 Ld. Raym. at 956.

68. 92 Eng. Rep. at 138; 2 Ld. Raym. at 956–57.

69. Ashby v. White, 14 State Tr. 695, 778–800 (H.L. 1704).

70. *Id.* at 787.

71. *Id.* at 794.

72. *Id.* at 792.

73. *See id.* at 705–75.

74. *Id.* at 764. *See also* Sergeant Hooper's comments at *id.* at 772.

75. *Id.* at 776.

76. *Id.* at 777.

77. *Id.* at 778.

78. *Id.* at 799.

79. *See* R. v. Paty, 92 Eng. Rep. 232; 2 Ld. Raym. 1105 (K.B. 1705); 90 Eng. Rep. 1189; Holt K.B. 526 (K.B. 1705).

80. *Ashby*, 14 State Tr. at 804–05.

81. *Id.* at 810.

82. *Id.* at 818, 820, 828.

83. *Id.* at 834, 864.

84. *See id.* at 863, 867, 870, 872, 888.

85. *Id.* at 878–79.

86. *See, e.g.,* 31 *Journals of the House of Commons* 211, 229, 279, 292–93.

87. Maitland, *supra* note 7, at 370.

88. Wittke, *supra* note 21, at 73. *See also* J. R. Pole, Political Representation in England and the Origins of the American Republic 458 (1966).

89. Wilkes' Case I, 19 State Tr. 981 (C.P. 1763); Wilkes' Case II, 19 State Tr. 1075 (K.B. & H.L. 1763–70); Wilkes v. Wood, 19 State Tr. 1153 (C.P. 1763); Wilkes v. Halifax, 19 State Tr. 1406 (C.P. 1769). *See also* Leach v. Money, 19 State Tr. 1001 (K.B. 1765).

90. *Wilkes' Case II*, 19 State Tr. at 1385. The King's speech and large portions of Wilkes' essay are reprinted in the addendum to *id.* at 1381–89.

91. *Wilkes' Case I*, 19 State Tr. at 981.

92. *Id.* at 989–90.

93. *Wilkes v. Wood*, 19 State Tr. at 1167–69; *Wilkes v. Halifax*, 19 State Tr. at 1406–07.

94. *Wilkes I*, 19 State Tr. at 993.

95. 15 William Cobbett, Parliamentary History of England 1346–47 (London, Hansard 1813). *See also* O.A. Sherrard, A Life of John Wilkes 121 (1930).

96. 15 Cobbett, *supra* note 95, at 1352.

97. *See* George Rudé, Wilkes and Liberty (1962); Sherrard, *supra* note 95, at 128. *See also* Wilkes' Case II, 19 State Tr. 1075, 1111–14 (K.B. 1763) (Lord Mansfield noting the public interest in and public pressure brought to bear upon the *Wilkes* case). For an indication of the continuing fascination of the *Wilkes* case, see, e.g., Arthur H. Cash, John Wilkes: The Scandalous Father of Civil Liberty (2006); Cynthia Crossen, *American Colonists Found Unlikely Hero in Salty British Author*, Wall St. J., Aug. 31, 2005, at B1.

98. *See* Sherrard, *supra* note 95, at 124–25; 1 Percy Fitzgerald, The Life and Times of John Wilkes, M.P. 218–40 (London, Ward & Downey 1888).

99. 29 *Journals of the House of Commons* 721–23; 15 Cobbett, *supra* note 95, at 1393.

100. Edmund Burke, *Thoughts on the Cause of the Present Discontents, in* 1 The Works of the Right Honorable Edmund Burke 500–01 (7th ed., Boston, Little, Brown 1881).

101. *See Wilkes' Case II*, 19 State Tr. at 1075–77.

102. *Id.* at 1077.

103. *Id.* at 1117.

104. *Id.* at 1124.

105. *Id.* at 1127.

106. 16 Cobbett, *supra* note 95, at 437, 532–46.

107. 16 *id.* at 437, 577–80.

108. 16 *id.* at 437, 580–82.

109. 16 *id.* at 437, 583–89; *see also* 18 *id.* at 358–60.

110. Wittke, *supra* note 21, at 120.

111. 1 Burke, *supra* note 100, at 507.

112. 1 *id.* at 503.

113. 18 Cobbett, *supra* note 95, at 367–68.

114. 18 *id.* at 358.

115. Sherrard, *supra* note 95, at 260–65; 2 Fitzgerald, *supra* note 98, at 205–33.

116. 22 Cobbett, *supra* note 95, at 1407–11.

117. William Blackstone, *The Case of the Late Election for the County of Middlesex, Considered on the Principles of the Constitution, and the Authorities of Law, in* An Interesting Appendix to Sir William Blackstone's Commentaries on the Laws of England 70–71 (Philadelphia, Bell 1773).

118. 10 Geo. III, c. 16 (1770).

119. 31 & 32 Vict., c. 125 (1868).

120. 42 & 43 Vict., c. 75 (1879). The same procedures were reenacted by the Representation of the People Act, c. 2, pt. III (1983).

121. Parliamentary Elections Act, 31 & 32 Vict., c. 125, § 26 (1868); reenacted in the Representation of the People Act, c. 2, § 157 (1983).

122. The Tamworth Case, 1 O'M. & H. 75 (C.P. 1869).

123. The Bolton Case, 2 O'M. & H. 138, 142 (C.P. 1874). *See* The Ballot Act, 35 & 36 Vict., c. 33 (1872).

124. *Bolton*, 2 O'M. & H. at 143.

125. *Compare* The Hackney Case, 31 *L. Times Repts.* 69 (C.P. 1874) (voiding the election), *and* Davies v. Lord Kensington, 9 L.R.-C.P. 720 (1874) (same), *with* Woodward v. Sarsons, 10 L.R.-C.P. 733 (1875) (upholding the election), *and* The East Clare Case, 4 O'M. & H. 162 (C.P. 1892) (same).

126. *In re* Parliamentary Election for Bristol South East, [1964] 2 Q.B. 257.

127. George Parker, *Lib Dems Storm Winchester With Big Majority*, Fin. Times, Nov. 21, 1997, at 1.

128. Attorney-General v. Jones, [2000] Q.B. 66.

129. *See* Bradlaugh v. Erskine, 31 Wkly. Rept'r 365 (Q.B. 1883); Bradlaugh v. Gossett, 12 Q.B.D. 271 (Q.B. 1884).

130. David McKittrick, *Sinn Fein MPs Take Up Offices in Westminster*, The Independent (London), Jan. 22, 2002, at 9.

Chapter Eight. Disputed Congressional Elections

1. U.S. Const. art. I, § 5, cl. 1. *See* 2 The Records of the Federal Convention of 1787, at 254 (Max Farrand ed., rev. ed. 1966) (Philadelphia Convention unanimously agreeing to the provision) [hereinafter Farrand's Records]. The provision was also uncontroversial in the states' ratifying conventions. *See* 1–5 The Debates in the Several State Conventions, On the Adoption of the Federal Constitution, as Recommended by the General Convention at Philadelphia, in 1787 (Jonathan Elliot ed., 2d ed. reprinted Philadelphia, J. B. Lippincott 1907) (1836) [hereinafter Elliot's Debates]. *But see* 4 The Complete Anti-Federalist 142 (Herbert J. Storing ed., 1981) ("Cornelius" complaining that the power to judge the qualifications of Members is "equal to that of a negative on elections in general") [hereinafter Anti-Federalist].

As noted in chapter 2, of the original thirteen states, eight had constitutional provisions giving legislative houses the power to judge the elections, returns, and qualifications of their Members. *See* Del. Const. of 1776, art. V; Md. Const. of 1776, arts. IX, XXI; Mass. Const. of 1780, pt. II, ch. 1, § 2, art. IV; *id.* pt. II, ch. 1, § 3, art. X; N.H. Const. of 1784, pt. II, Senate, para. 9; N.J. Const. of 1776, art. V; N.Y. Const. of 1777, art. IX; N.C. Const. of 1776, art. X; Pa. Const. of 1776, § 9.

2. U.S. Const. art. I, § 2, cl. 1.

3. 1 Farrand's Records, *supra* note 1, at 49.

4. *Id.*

5. 1 *id.* at 50.

6. 2 *id.* at 201.

7. 2 *id.* at 202.

8. 2 *id.* at 204.

9. 2 *id.* at 206.

10. 2 *id.* at 216. The exact wording—*see* 2 *id.* at 178—would undergo some minor revisions, but nothing substantive.

11. U.S. Const. art. I, § 2, cl. 4. *See* 2 Farrand's Records, *supra* note 1, at 231.

12. The Federalist No. 57, at 351 (James Madison) (Clinton Rossiter ed., Mentor 1961) [hereinafter all citations are to this edition].

13. 1 The Debate on the Constitution 105 (Bernard Bailyn ed., 1993) (Plain Truth's "Rebuttal to 'An Officer of the Late Continental Army'" (Nov. 10, 1787)) [hereinafter Bailyn's Debate].

14. U.S. Const. art. I, § 3, cl. 1.

15. 1 Farrand's Records, *supra* note 1, at 52.

16. 1 *id.* at 51.

17. *Id.*

18. 1 *id.* at 151.

19. 1 *id.* at 156.

20. 1 *id.* at 202.

21. *See, e.g.*, 1 *id.* at 405–06 (Wilson); 1 *id.* at 468 (Ellsworth).

22. *See* 1 *id.* at 482–84.

23. 1 *id.* at 516.

24. 1 *id.* at 549. The decision to give each state two senators was reached with relatively little debate. *See* 2 *id.* at 94.

25. U.S. Const. art. I, § 3, cl. 2.

26. 2 Farrand's Records, *supra* note 1, at 231.

27. U.S. Const. amdt. XVII, cl. 1.

28. *Id.* amdt. XVII, cl. 2.

29. Articles of Confederation arts. I–III.

30. *Id.* art. V, cl. 1–2, 4. Indeed, not only did states not benefit in terms of voting power by sending extra delegates to Congress, sending them actually had significant costs. Unlike the Constitution, which provides that the national government will pay legislative salaries — *see* U.S. Const. art. I, § 6, cl. 1 — the Articles of Confederation left that duty to the states. Articles of Confederation art. V, cl. 3.

31. Articles of Confederation art. V, cl. 1.

32. *See* United Nations Charter arts. 9, 18.

33. 2 Farrand's Records, *supra* note 1, at 94. In his antifederalist tract "The Genuine Information," Martin would write that, under the Constitution, "the senators are rendered totally and absolutely *independent* of their states, of *whom* they ought to be the representatives, without any *bond* or *tie* between them." Reprinted at 1 Elliot's Debates, *supra* note 1, at 361.

34. 2 Farrand's Records, *supra* note 1, at 95, 234.

35. 1 Bailyn's Debate, *supra* note 13, at 210 (Thomas Jefferson to James Madison (Dec. 20, 1787)).

36. Indeed, two states' ratifying conventions proposed amendments making senators recallable, but the proposed amendments were never taken up. *See* 1 Elliot's Debates, *supra* note 1, at 337 (Rhode Island); 2 *id.* at 545 (Pennsylvania). *See also* 2 *id.* at 289 (John Lansing proposing the same amendment in the New York Ratifying Convention, but it was not ultimately among those amendments submitted by that convention — *see* 1 *id.* at 327– 31).

37. U.S. Const. art. I, § 4, cl. 1.

38. 2 Farrand's Records, *supra* note 1, at 240–42.

39. *See* 2 Anti-Federalist, *supra* note 1, at 47, 124–25, 142, 159, 386; 3 *id.* at 94, 199–200; 4 *id.* at 42–43, 102–04, 142–43, 187–88, 218–19; 5 *id.* at 75, 168–70, 204, 225; 6 *id.* at 31–32, 115–16, 137.

40. U.S. Const. art. I, § 2, cl. 2.

41. *Id.* art. I, § 3, cl. 3.

42. 1 Farrand's Records, *supra* note 1, at 375.

43. *Id.*

44. *See* 1 *id.* at 375 (House), 217–18 (Senate).

45. 2 *id.* at 178–79.

46. 2 *id.* at 216.

47. *Id.*

48. 2 *id.* at 235.

49. *Id.*

50. *Id.* He did not actually recommend limiting membership to natives but said, "Were it not that many not natives of this Country had acquired great merit during the revolution," he would favor such a proposal.

51. 2 *id.* at 236.

52. *Id.*

53. 2 *id.* at 237.

54. 2 *id.* at 238–39.

55. 2 *id.* at 268.

56. 2 *id.* at 267–72.

57. *See* 2 *id.* at 216–19 (House), 239 (Senate).

58. 2 *id.* at 218.

59. 2 *id.* at 179. *See also* 1 *id.* at 428 (Mason's suggestion).

60. 2 *id.* at 248.

61. 2 *id.* at 249.

62. *Id.*

63. *Id.*

64. 2 *id.* at 249–50.

65. 2 *id.* at 250.

66. 2 *id.* at 251.

67. The Federalist No. 52, at 326 (James Madison).

68. Dionisopoulos argues that there are five, pointing to the provision that anyone who has been impeached and convicted can be disqualified from holding "any Office of honor, Trust or Profit under the United States," U.S. Const. art. I, § 3, cl. 7. *See* P. Allan Dionisopoulos, *A Commentary on the Constitutional Issues in the* Powell *and Related Cases*, 17 J. Pub. L. 103, 108 n.16, 111 (1968); *see also* Gerald T. McLaughlin, *Constitutional Self-Discipline: The Power to Expel, to Exclude and to Punish*, 41 Fordham L. Rev. 43, 55 (1972) (citing Dionisopoulos). This reading, however, is sloppy. As one of the other qualifications that Dionisopoulos himself points to—the disqualification of any person "holding any Office under the United States," U.S. Const. art. I, § 6, cl. 2—makes clear, the Constitution uses the phrase "Office . . . under the United States"—and its textual cousins, "Officers of the United States," *see, e.g., id.* art. II, § 2, cl. 2; *id.* art. II, § 3, "civil Officers of the United States," *see, e.g., id.* art. II, § 4, and "Office of Trust or Profit under the United States," *see, e.g., id.* art. II, § 1, cl. 2—as a term of art to refer to *executive and judicial positions only.* Indeed, the president is required to "Commission *all* the Officers of the United States," *id.* art. II, § 3 (emphasis added), but he does not commission Members of Congress. *See also* 1 Joseph Story, Commentaries on the Constitution of the United States § 792, at 577 (Melville M. Bigelow ed., Boston, Little, Brown rev. ed. 1891) ("[A]ll officers of the United States, therefore, who hold their appointments under the national government, *whether their duties are executive or judicial*, in the highest or the lowest departments of the government, with the exception of officers in the army and navy, are properly civil officers within the meaning of the Constitution, and liable to impeachment." Emphasis added. Note the pointed omission of *legislative* "duties"); 1 *id.* §§ 793–95, at 577–80 (noting that Members of Congress are not civil officers

of the United States and therefore not subject to impeachment). *See generally* Akhil Reed Amar & Vikram David Amar, *Is the Presidential Succession Law Constitutional?*, 48 Stan. L. Rev. 113, 114–16 (1995).

It is worth noting that a current Member of the House of Representatives, Florida's Alcee Hastings, was a federal judge who was impeached and convicted on bribery-related charges in 1989. He was first elected to the House in 1992. *See* William E. Gibson, *Alcee's D.C.*, Sun Sentinel (Fort Lauderdale, FL), Apr. 19, 1993, at 1D. However, the Senate only removed Hastings from office; it did not disqualify him from holding future "Office . . . under the United States." *See A History of Senate Impeachment Proceedings*, Associated Press, Jan. 5, 1999. The Hastings case is, therefore, evidence neither for nor against Dionisopoulos.

69. U.S. Const. art. I, § 6, cl. 2.

70. *Id.* art. IV, § 4.

71. *Id.* art. VI, cl. 3.

72. *Id.* amdt. XIV, § 3.

73. James Wilson, *Lectures on Law, Part Two: Of the Constitutions of the United States and of Pennsylvania—Of the Legislative Department, in* 1 The Works of James Wilson 402 (Robert Green McCloskey ed., 1967).

74. 1 *id.* at 406–07.

75. Alexis de Tocqueville, Democracy in America 198 (George Lawrence trans., J. P. Mayer ed., 13th ed. 1969) (1850). *See also id.* at 59–60.

76. *Id.* at 201.

77. *See* Vikram David Amar, *Indirect Effects of Direct Election: A Structural Examination of the Seventeenth Amendment*, 49 Vand. L. Rev. 1347, 1354–55 (1996).

78. Note, *The Power of a House of Congress to Judge the Qualifications of Its Members*, 81 Harv. L. Rev. 673, 681 (1968).

79. The Federalist No. 57, at 351 (James Madison).

80. 2 Farrand's Records, *supra* note 1, at 218.

81. The Federalist No. 60, at 371 (Alexander Hamilton). *See also* 1 Story, *supra* note 68, § 625, at 461 ("It would seem but fair reasoning, upon the plainest principles of interpretation, that when the Constitution established certain qualifications as necessary for office, it meant to exclude all others as prerequisites.").

82. McLaughlin, *supra* note 68, at 58.

83. Dionisopoulos, *supra* note 68, at 115 (citing U.S. Const. art. I, § 9, cl. 8 (Foreign Gifts Clause); *id.* art. III, § 3, cl. 2 (Punishment of Treason Clause)).

84. Dionisopoulos, *supra* note 68, at 116.

85. *See* U.S. Const. amdt. VIII.

86. Dionisopoulos also points to a law passed by the First Congress—An Act for the Punishment of Certain Crimes against the United States, 1 Stat. 112 (1790)—and to the Religious Tests Clause—U.S. Const. art. VI, cl. 3—as evidence that Congress had statutory authority to prescribe additional qualifications. *See* Dionisopoulos, *supra* note 68, at 116–121. Among other problems, both of these arguments rest upon the mistaken premise that the phrase "Office . . . under the United States" encompasses Members of Congress. As I have shown above, it does not. *See supra* note 68.

87. *See* U.S. Const. art. I, § 5, cl. 2.

88. *See* 2 Farrand's Records, *supra* note 1, at 254 (Madison: expulsion is "too important to be exercised by a bare majority of a quorum: and in emergencies of faction might be dangerously abused.").

89. *See* David P. Currie, The Constitution in Congress: The Jeffersonians, 1801–1829, at 74–75 (2001) ("The distinction [between exclusion and expulsion] thus seems to turn not on the time at which the motion is made but on the grounds on which it is based. A simple majority may determine at any time that a member is not qualified; expulsion of a duly elected member for any other reason requires stronger support. Unlike a purely temporal test, this distinction makes eminent sense. For unlike a decision that a member was not properly elected, denial of a seat for any other reason frustrates the people's choice; unlike a decision that he is unqualified, it reflects a policy decision of the House rather than of the people.").

90. *See* U.S. Term Limits v. Thornton, 514 U.S. 779 (1995) (states may not add qualifications); Powell v. McCormack, 395 U.S. 486, 550 (1969) (Congress may not add qualifications).

91. *See* McLaughlin, *supra* note 68, at 45–47 (suggesting procedural rules for *expulsion* proceedings); *id.* at 54 (suggesting that the same procedural rules should apply to *exclusion* proceedings).

92. *But see* C. H. Rammelkamp, *Contested Congressional Elections*, 20 Pol. Sci. Q. 421, 428–37 (1905) (noting periods of high levels of partisanship in the resolution of election and qualifications disputes).

93. Contested Elections Act, 1 Stat. 537 (1798).

94. Act to Continue in Force the Contested Elections Act, 2 Stat. 39 (1800).

95. Contested Elections Act, 9 Stat. 568 (1851).

96. Supplemental Act to the Contested Elections Act, 17 Stat. 408 (1873).

97. Supplemental Act to the Contested Elections Act, 18 Stat. 338 (1875); Appropriations Act, 20 Stat. 377, 400 (1879); Contested Elections Act, 24 Stat. 445 (1887).

98. Federal Contested Election Act, 83 Stat. 284 (1969).

99. Henry L. Dawes, *The Mode of Procedure in Cases of Contested Elections*, 2 J. Soc. Sci. 56, 63 (1870). *See also* Rammelkamp, *supra* note 92, at 427 (noting the same).

100. The Committee on Elections, established in 1789, was the first standing committee of the House of Representatives. Since 1946, it has been a standing subcommittee of the Committee on House Administration. *See* George B. Galloway, History of the House of Representatives 64 (1961).

101. Chester H. Rowell, A Historical and Legal Digest of All the Contested Election Cases in the House of Representatives of the United States from the First to the Fifty-sixth Congress, 1789–1901, at 37–38 (1901) (*Ramsay v. Smith*, First Congress).

102. *Id.* at 39–40 (*Jackson v. Wayne*, Second Congress).

103. *Id.* at 41 (*Lattimer v. Patton*, Third Congress).

104. Angie Welborn, House Contested Election Cases: 1933 to 2000, at 75 (2003) (*Lowe v. Thompson*, Ninety-first Congress).

105. Rowell, *supra* note 101, at 54 (*Spaulding v. Mead*, Ninth Congress).

106. *See also id.* at 123–24 (*Brockenbrough v. Cabell*, Twenty-ninth Congress).

107. *Id.* at 67–68 (*Porterfield v. McCoy*, Fourteenth Congress); *see also id.* at 60 (*Turner v. Baylies*, Eleventh Congress) (different spellings of the same name); *id.* at 313

(*Lee v. Rainey*, Forty-fourth Congress) (same); *id.* at 314 (*Fenn v. Bennett*, Forty-fourth Congress) (minor electoral irregularities); *id.* at 547–52 (*Yost v. Tucker*, Fifty-fourth Congress) ("The intention of the voter, if it can be clearly ascertained from the ballot, will generally be given effect to, and when it is not expressed according to the strict requirements of a statute, such requirements will often be regarded as merely directory, unless a failure to comply with them is declared to be fatal to the ballot. But where the statute itself provides that a certain thing shall be done by the voter or his vote shall not be counted, then there can be no question that a provision of that character is mandatory and that a failure to comply with it is fatal to the ballot."); Welborn, *supra* note 104, at 5–7 (*Chandler v. Burnham*, Seventy-third Congress) ("The rules prescribed by law for conducting an election are designed chiefly to accord an opportunity for the free and fair exercise of the elective franchise to prevent illegal voting, and to ascertain with certainty the result. A departure from the mode prescribed will not vitiate an election, if the irregularities do not deprive any legal voter of his vote, or admit illegal vote, or cast uncertainty on the result, and has not been occasioned by the agency of a party seeking to derive benefit from them.").

108. Rowell, *supra* note 101, at 111 (*New Jersey Case*, Twenty-sixth Congress).

109. *Id.*

110. *Id.* at 112.

111. *See id.* at 109–112.

112. Apportionment Act, 5 Stat. 491 (1842). *See* David P. Currie, The Constitution in Congress: Democrats and Whigs, 1829–1861, at 256–64 (2005).

113. Rowell, *supra* note 101, at 118 (*Members Elected by General Ticket*, Twenty-eighth Congress).

114. *Id.* at 119.

115. *Id.*

116. *Id.* at 117–20.

117. Richard D. Hupman, Senate Election, Expulsion and Censure Cases from 1789 to 1960, at 21–22 (1962) (*Harlan*, Thirty-fourth Congress).

118. *See* Cong. Globe, 34th Cong., 3rd Sess. 112–17, 238–70 (1856–57).

119. Hupman, *supra* note 117, at 22–24 (*Fitch and Bright*, Thirty-fourth Congress); *see also id.* at 79–80 (*Davidson v. Call*, Fifty-second Congress).

120. *Id.* at 38–39 (*Stockton*, Thirty-ninth Congress).

121. *Id.* at 84 (*Mantle*, Fifty-third Congress).

122. In fact, he first appointed Henry Clayton, who withdrew, and then he appointed Glass. *Id.* at 104 (*Glass*, Sixty-third Congress).

123. *Id.* at 106.

124. 1 Stat. 50 (1789) (reprinting and amending the 1787 act, which was promulgated under the Articles of Confederation).

125. Rowell, *supra* note 101, at 43 (*White*, Third Congress).

126. *Id.* at 49–50 (*Van Ness*, Seventh Congress).

127. Note that "no Person holding *any Office* under the United States" may simultaneously sit in Congress. U.S. Const. art. I, § 6, cl. 2 (emphasis added). In other places, such as the Impeachments Clause, the reference is to "all *civil* Officers of the United States." *Id.* art. II, § 4 (emphasis added). As Story notes, this latter formulation excludes

military positions. *See* 1 Story, *supra* note 68, § 792, at 577. The implication of the omission of the word "civil" in the disqualifying clause, then, is that military posts fall within the category of those prohibited to serving Members of Congress.

128. Rowell, *supra* note 101, at 56–57 (*Barney v. McCreery*, Tenth Congress).

129. *Id.* at 57.

130. *See, e.g., id.* at 141–42 (*Turney v. Marshall* and *Fouke v. Trumbull*, Thirty-fourth Congress); *id.* at 401–02 (*Wood v. Peters*, Forty-eighth Congress).

131. *Id.* at 70–73 (*Hammond v. Herrick*, Fifteenth Congress).

132. *Id.* at 583 (*Roberts*, Fifty-sixth Congress).

133. *Id.* at 590.

134. *Id.* at 591. *See also id.* at 592–95 (the minority's structural reasoning).

135. *Id.* at 596.

136. Welborn, *supra* note 104, at 8–9 (*Estep v. Ellenbogen*, Seventy-third Congress).

137. Hupman, *supra* note 117, at 1 (*Gallatin*, Third Congress).

138. *Id.* at 5 (*Griswold*, Eleventh Congress).

139. *Id.* at 21 (*Trumbull*, Thirty-fourth Congress). *See also* Cong. Globe, 34th Cong., 1st Sess. 579–84 (1856).

140. Hupman, *supra* note 117, at 97–98 (*Smoot*, Fifty-seventh, Fifty-eighth, and Fifty-ninth Congresses).

141. *Id.* at 135 (*Hatfield v. Holt*, Seventy-fourth Congress).

142. Rowell, *supra* note 101, at 42–43 (*Trigg v. Preston*, Third Congress).

143. *Id.* at 43.

144. M. St. Clair Clarke & David A. Hall, Cases of Contested Elections in Congress, from the Year 1789 to 1834, Inclusive 82–83 (Washington, Gales & Seaton 1834) (*Trigg v. Preston*, Third Congress). *See also* Edmund S. Morgan, Inventing the People: The Rise of Popular Sovereignty in England and America 183–89 (1988) (noting the drunkenness, debauchery, and brawling regularly attendant on eighteenth-century Southern elections, including the *Trigg* case).

145. Rowell, *supra* note 101, at 145 (*Reeder v. Whitfield*, Thirty-fourth Congress). *See also* the Kansas-Nebraska Act, 10 Stat. 277 (1854).

146. Rowell, *supra* note 101, at 146.

147. *Id.* at 146–47.

148. *Id.* at 149 (*Reeder v. Whitfield, II*, Thirty-fourth Congress) (emphasis added).

149. *Id.*

150. *Id.*

151. *Id.* at 150.

152. *Id.* at 156 (*Whyte v. Harris*, Thirty-fifth Congress).

153. *Id.* at 156–57.

154. *Id.* at 157.

155. *Id.* at 159.

156. *Id.* at 174 (*Clements*, Thirty-seventh Congress).

157. *Id.* at 175 (*Upton*, Thirty-seventh Congress).

158. *Id.* at 177 (*Beach*, Thirty-seventh Congress).

159. *Id.* at 181 (*Flanders and Hahn*, Thirty-seventh Congress).

160. *Id.* at 182.

161. *Id.*

162. *Id.* at 182 (*McCloud and Wing*, Thirty-seventh Congress).

163. *Id.* at 183.

164. *Id.*

165. *See also id.* at 183 (*McKenzie*, Thirty-seventh Congress) (presenting similar facts and a similar resolution); *id.* at 184 (*Grafflin*, Thirty-seventh Congress) (same); *id.* at 186–87 (*McKenzie v. Kitchen*, Thirty-eighth Congress) (same).

166. Oath of Office Act, 12 Stat. 502 (1862).

167. *See* Rowell, *supra* note 101, at 218 (*Kentucky Members*, Fortieth Congress) (four of the Kentucky Members-elect cleared); *id.* at 218 (*Symes v. Trimble*, Fortieth Congress) (fifth Kentucky Member-elect cleared). *See also id.* at 220–21 (*Smith v. Brown*, Fortieth Congress) (finding a Member-elect disloyal); *id.* at 222–24 (*McKee v. Young*, Fortieth Congress) (same).

168. *Id.* at 224 (*Butler*, Fortieth Congress).

169. Removal of Political Disabilities from Roderick R. Butler, 15 Stat. 360 (1868).

170. Rowell, *supra* note 101, at 241–42 (*Hunt v. Sheldon*, Forty-first Congress).

171. *Id.* at 242–43.

172. *See id.* at 243–44 (*Morey v. McCranie*, Forty-first Congress); *id.* at 244–45 (*Wallace v. Simpson*, Forty-first Congress); *id.* at 447–50 (*Mudd v. Compton*, Fifty-first Congress); *id.* at 452–54 (*Waddill v. Wise*, Fifty-first Congress).

173. *Id.* at 453 (*Waddill v. Wise*, Fifty-first Congress).

174. Reconstruction Act, 15 Stat. 73 (1868).

175. Merrill Moores, A Historical and Legal Digest of All the Contested Election Cases in the House of Representatives of the United States from the Fifty-seventh to and Including the Sixty-fourth Congress, 1901–1917, at 25 (1917) (*Dantzler v. Lever*, Fifty-eighth Congress).

176. *Id.* at 26.

177. *Id.*

178. Hupman, *supra* note 117, at 29 (*Willey and Carlile*, Thirty-seventh Congress).

179. *Id.* at 35 (*Fishback, Baxter, and Snow*, Thirty-eighth Congress).

180. *Id.* at 37 (*Cutler, Smith, and Hahn*, Thirty-eighth Congress).

181. *Id.* at 39 (*Patterson*, Thirty-ninth Congress).

182. Cong. Globe, 40th Cong., 2nd Sess. 321 (1868).

183. Sen. Jour., 40th Cong., 2nd Sess. 63–64 (1867).

184. Cong. Globe, 40th Cong., 2nd Sess. 322 (1868).

185. Hupman, *supra* note 117, at 40 (*Thomas*, Fortieth Congress).

186. Act Relating to the State of Georgia, 16 Stat. 363 (1870).

187. Resolution Prescribing the Oath to Be Taken by H. V. M. Miller, 16 Stat. 703 (1871); Hupman, *supra* note 117, at 42–43 (*Hill and Miller*, Fortieth and Forty-first Congresses).

188. Dred Scott v. Sandford, 60 U.S. (19 How.) 393 (1857).

189. Hupman, *supra* note 117, at 45–46 (*Revels*, Forty-first Congress).

190. 58 Cong. Rec. 8221–22 (1919).

191. 40 Stat. 217 (1917); Amendments to Espionage Act, 40 Stat. 553 (1918).

192. Berger v. United States, 255 U.S. 22 (1921).

193. 58 Cong. Rec. 8221 (1919).

194. 58 *id.* at 8223. *See also* 58 *id.* at 8240 (Joe Eagle of Texas, arguing the same).

195. 58 *id.* at 8223.

196. 58 *id.* at 8223–33.

197. 58 *id.* at 8232.

198. 58 *id.* at 8232.

199. 58 *id.* at 8259.

200. 58 *id.* at 8262–63.

201. *See* Zechariah Chafee Jr., Free Speech in the United States 250–52 (1942).

202. On a proper interpretation of the First Amendment, see Akhil Reed Amar, The Bill of Rights: Creation and Reconstruction 231–46 (1998); Chafee, *supra* note 201, at 257–61. On the interpretation of the First Amendment prevailing at the time, see, e.g., United States *ex rel.* Milwaukee Social Democratic Publishing Co. v. Burleson, 255 U.S. 407 (1921); Debs v. United States, 249 U.S. 211 (1919).

203. Rammelkamp, *supra* note 92, at 421.

204. 405 U.S. 15 (1972).

Chapter Nine. Breach of Privilege and Contempt of Parliament

1. Thomas Erskine May, Erskine May's Treatise on the Law, Privileges, Proceedings and Usage of Parliament 128 (William McKay ed., 23d ed. 2004).

2. Henry Elsynge, The Manner of Holding Parliaments in England 189 (London, Richardson & Clark rev. ed. 1768).

3. *Id.* at 190.

4. *Id.* at 190–91.

5. 11 Hen. 6, c. 11 (1433).

6. F. W. Maitland, The Constitutional History of England 244 (H. A. L. Fisher ed., reprint Cambridge Univ. Press 1963) (1908).

7. 1 John Hatsell, Precedents of Proceedings in the House of Commons 92–94 (rev. ed., London, Hansard 1818).

8. 1 William Cobbett, Parliamentary History of England 822–23 (London, Hansard 1806).

9. 1 *id.* at 823.

10. 1 *id.* at 825–26.

11. 1 *id.* at 826–27.

12. William Camden, The History of the Most Renowned and Victorious Princess Elizabeth, Late Queen of England 305–08 (London, Tonson 4th ed. 1688). *See also* 1 Cobbett, *supra* note 8, at 823.

13. Maitland, *supra* note 6, at 244 (Bland); Simonds D'Ewes, The Journals of All the Parliaments During the Reign of Queen Elizabeth 448–49 (Paul Bowes ed., London, Starkey 1682) (Drurie).

14. *See* Stockdale v. Hansard, 112 Eng. Rep. 1112; 9 Ad. & E. 1 (Q.B. 1839); Case of the Sheriff of Middlesex, 113 Eng. Rep. 419; 11 Ad. & E. 273 (Q.B. 1840). *See also* chapters 1 and 3 of this book.

15. 1 Hatsell, *supra* note 7, at 193–94.

16. *See, e.g.*, 1 *id.* at 194–96.

17. 65 *Journals of the House of Commons* 224, 228.

18. 65 *id.* at 252.

19. Carl Wittke, The History of English Parliamentary Privilege 128 (photo. reprint 1970) (1921).

20. 2 *Journals of the House of Commons* 220.

21. 2 *id.* at 500.

22. 11 *id.* at 193.

23. 20 *id.* at 99 (1722); 26 *id.* at 754 (1753); 29 *id.* at 206–07 (1762).

24. 11 *id.* at 439 (Card and Stokes); 11 *id.* at 710 (Dyer).

25. 12 *id.* at 48.

26. 14 *id.* at 269–70.

27. 21 *Journals of the House of Lords* 660, 667.

28. 21 *Journals of the House of Commons* 238.

29. 87 *id.* at 360.

30. Excerpt from the article reprinted at Madeline R. Robinton, *Parliamentary Privilege and Political Morality in Britain, 1939–1957*, 73 Pol. Sci. Q. 179, 183 (1958).

31. *See id.* at 188.

32. Geoffrey Marshall, *The House of Commons and Its Privileges, in* The House of Commons in the Twentieth Century 229 (S. A. Walkland ed., 1979) (citing H.C. 38 (1956–57)). *See also* Robinton, *supra* note 30, at 179–80.

33. 13 *Journals of the House of Commons* 732–34.

34. 13 *id.* at 734–35.

35. *See* Parliamentary Elections Act, 31 & 32 Vict., c. 125 (1868).

36. *See, e.g.*, 9 *Journals of the House of Commons* 24 (Member receiving a bribe); 11 *id.* at 236 (same); 11 *id.* at 274 (non-Member offering a bribe); 11 *id.* at 276–77 (same); 14 *id.* at 474 (same); 17 *id.* at 493–94, 498 (same). *See generally* Erskine May, *supra* note 1, at 132–36.

37. 11 *Journals of the House of Commons* 331.

38. 37 *id.* at 902.

39. Edward Coke, The Fourth Part of the Institutes of the Laws of England, Concerning the Jurisdiction of Courts 14 (London, Brooke 1797) (1644).

40. *See* Erskine May, *supra* note 1, at 129, 143–46, 148, 150–52.

41. *See* Anthony Summers & Stephen Dorril, Honeytrap (1988), for all the tawdry details, and Lord Alfred Denning, John Profumo and Christine Keeler (reprint 1999) (1963), for the report of the government inquiry into the matter.

42. *See* Wittke, *supra* note 19, at 38.

43. 9 *Journals of the House of Commons* 378.

44. Brass Crosby's Case, 95 Eng. Rep. 1005, 1006–07; 3 Wils. K.B. 188, 191–92 (C.P. 1771).

45. 95 Eng. Rep. at 1006–07, 1014; 3 Wils. K.B. at 191–92, 205.

46. Wason v. Walter, [1868] 4 Q.B. 73, 95.

47. *Id.* at 95–96.

48. 226 *Journals of the House of Commons* 548. *See also* 226 *id.* at 549 (The House will not consider it a contempt or breach of privilege to publish votes, questions, or

motions, or the expressed intention of a Member to vote, refrain from voting, or table a question or motion in advance of the official publications.).

49. Erskine May, *supra* note 1, at 139–42.

50. Robinton, *supra* note 30, at 190.

51. Colin R. Munro, Studies in Constitutional Law 232–33 (2d ed. 1999) (citing H.C. 27 (1956–57)).

52. 1 Committee on Standards in Public Life, First Report, 1995, Cmnd. 2850-I.

53. 1 *id.* at 42.

54. 1 *id.* at 43–44.

55. 1 *id.* at 42.

56. 251 *Journals of the House of Commons* 469–70. *See* Nick Allen, Sleaze-buster? The Evolution of the Office of the Parliamentary Commissioner for Standards, Paper Presented at the Annual Conference of the Political Studies Association (April 2005) (unpublished manuscript), for a history of the office to date. Allen concludes that the scheme "may fail to meet the demands of those seeking a fully independent public sleaze-buster, but it has strengthened parliamentary self-regulation." *Id.* at 1.

57. Maitland, *supra* note 6, at 244–45; Wittke, *supra* note 19, at 76–77; 3 *Journals of the House of Lords* 110–11, 113, 116, 124, 127, 132–34.

58. *See, e.g.,* 4 *Journals of the House of Lords* 138–39 (destruction of the Countess of Exeter's mill); 3 *Journals of the House of Commons* 65–66 (cutting down a Member's timber); 9 *id.* at 93 (stealing tin from a Member); 10 *id.* at 451 (trespassing in the mine of a Member); 23 *id.* at 505 (killing a Member's rabbits); 28 *id.* at 598 (killing a Member's fish). *See generally* Wittke, *supra* note 19, at 44–47.

59. Marshall, *supra* note 32, at 229–30.

60. Report from the Select Committee on Parliamentary Privilege, H.C. 34, at viii (1967). *See also* Munro, *supra* note 51, at 234.

Chapter Ten. Punishment by Congress

1. 2 The Records of the Federal Convention of 1787, at 140 (Max Farrand ed., rev. ed. 1966) [hereinafter Farrand's Records].

2. 2 *id.* at 156.

3. Del. Const. of 1776, art. V; Md. Const. of 1776, art. X; Pa. Const. of 1776, § 9.

4. 2 Farrand's Records, *supra* note 1, at 180.

5. 2 *id.* at 254.

6. *Id.*

7. *Id.*

8. U.S. Const. art. I, § 5, cl. 2.

9. In the states' ratifying conventions, see 1–5 The Debates in the Several State Conventions, On the Adoption of the Federal Constitution, as Recommended by the General Convention at Philadelphia, in 1787 (Jonathan Elliot ed., 2d ed. reprinted Philadelphia, J. B. Lippincott 1907) (1836). In the press, see The Federalist Papers (Clinton Rossiter ed., 1961); 1–2 The Debate on the Constitution (Bernard Bailyn ed., 1993); 1–7 The Complete Anti-Federalist (Herbert J. Storing ed., 1981).

10. 2 Farrand's Records, *supra* note 1, at 341.

11. James Wilson, *Lectures on Law, Part Two: Of the Constitutions of the United States and of Pennsylvania — Of the Legislative Department*, *in* 1 The Works of James Wilson 421 (Robert Green McCloskey ed., 1967).

12. *Id.*

13. 1 Joseph Story, Commentaries on the Constitution of the United States § 837, at 607 (Melville M. Bigelow ed., Boston, Little, Brown rev. ed. 1891).

14. *Id.*

15. 1 *id.* § 845, at 612–13.

16. 1 *id.* § 847, at 615.

17. 1 *id.* § 849, at 621.

18. *See* Gerald T. McLaughlin, *Congressional Self-Discipline: The Power to Expel, to Exclude and to Punish*, 41 Fordham L. Rev. 43, 60–62 (1972); Jack Maskell, Expulsion, Censure, Reprimand, and Fine: Legislative Discipline in the House of Representatives 2, Congressional Research Service Report for Congress RL31382 (2002).

19. McLaughlin, *supra* note 18, at 60; *see also* Maskell, *supra* note 18, at 17–18.

20. U.S. Const. art. V.

21. Maskell, *supra* note 18, at 3.

22. *See* Pauline Maier, *John Wilkes and American Disillusionment with Britain*, 20 Wm. & Mary Q. (3d ser.) 373 (1963).

23. *See* Dorian Bowman & Judith Farris Bowman, *Article I, Section 5: Congress' Power to Expel — An Exercise in Self-Restraint*, 29 Syracuse L. Rev. 1071, 1102–04 (1978); Maskell, *supra* note 18, at 6–8.

24. Bowman & Bowman, *supra* note 23, at 1104.

25. C. S. Potts, *Power of Legislative Bodies to Punish for Contempt (Continued)*, 74 U. Pa. L. Rev. 780, 780 (1926).

26. *See id.* at 828–29.

27. Allen B. Moreland, *Congressional Investigations and Private Persons*, 40 S. Cal. L. Rev. 189, 189 (1967).

28. *See id.* at 271.

29. Congressional Attendance of Witnesses Act, 11 Stat. 155 (1857).

30. 2 U.S.C. §§ 192–94 (2000). That change and a few other minor modifications were enacted by the Congressional Investigations Act, 49 Stat. 2041 (1936); Congressional Investigations Joint Resolution, 52 Stat. 942 (1938).

31. 11 Stat. at 156.

32. Act Amending the Congressional Attendance of Witnesses Act, 12 Stat. 333 (1862). For an example of the abuse possible under the previous law, see Cong. Globe, 37th Cong., 2d Sess. 428 (1862).

33. Counselman v. Hitchcock, 142 U.S. 547 (1892).

34. Compulsory Testimony Act, 68 Stat. 745 (1954). *See* Ullman v. United States, 350 U.S. 422 (1955) (upholding the act's immunity provisions as sufficient for Fifth Amendment purposes in a case arising out of a grand jury investigation).

35. Organized Crime Control Act, 84 Stat. 922, 927–28, 930 (1970).

36. 18 U.S.C. §§ 6001–05 (2000).

37. Robert L. Tienken, House of Representatives Exclusion, Censure and Expulsion Cases from 1789 to 1973, at 119 (1973) (*Lyon and Griswold*, Fifth Congress).

38. 2 Asher C. Hinds, Hinds' Precedents of the House of Representatives of the United States § 1642, at 1114–15 (1907).

39. Tienken, *supra* note 37, at 119 (*Lyon and Griswold*, Fifth Congress).

40. *Id.* at 120 (*Graves*, Twenty-fifth Congress).

41. *See generally* David P. Currie, The Constitution in Congress: Democrats and Whigs, 1829–1861, at 209–12 (2005).

42. Richard D. Hupman, Senate Election, Expulsion and Censure Cases from 1789 to 1960, at 15 (1962) (*Benton and Foote*, Thirty-first Congress).

43. 2 Hinds, *supra* note 38, § 1655, at 1129.

44. 2 *id.* § 1656, at 1134–35.

45. Cong. Globe, 34th Cong., 1st Sess. app. at 529–44 (1856).

46. *Id.* 34th Cong., 1st Sess. app. at 530 (1856).

47. *Id.* 34th Cong., 1st Sess. 1348 (1856).

48. For a fascinating history of Sumner's convalescence and the political consequences thereof, see Laura A. White, *Was Charles Sumner Shamming, 1856–1859?*, 33 New Eng. Q. 291 (1960).

49. Cong. Globe, 34th Cong., 1st Sess. 1348–49 (1856).

50. *Id.* 34th Cong., 1st Sess. 1348 (1856).

51. *Id.* 34th Cong., 1st Sess. 1349 (1856).

52. *Id.* 34th Cong., 1st Sess. 1628 (1856).

53. *Id.* 34th Cong., 1st Sess. app. at 831–33 (1856).

54. *Id.* 34th Cong., 1st Sess. 1863 (1856).

55. 2 Hinds, *supra* note 38, § 1245, at 797.

56. 2 *id.* § 1665, at 1138.

57. 2 *id.* § 1665, at 1141–42.

58. Hupman, *supra* note 42, at 94–97 (*McLaurin and Tillman*, Fifty-seventh Congress).

59. Cong. Globe, 39th Cong., 1st Sess. 2572 (1866).

60. *Id.* 39th Cong., 1st Sess. 2575 (1866).

61. 2 Hinds, *supra* note 38, § 1247, at 798.

62. 2 *id.* § 1251, at 802.

63. *Id.*

64. Hupman, *supra* note 42, at 149–50 (*McCarthy and Benton*, Eighty-second Congress).

65. *Id.* at 150–51.

66. *Id.* at 152–54 (*McCarthy*, Eighty-third Congress).

67. 2 Hinds, *supra* note 38, § 1263, at 813–15; Hupman, *supra* note 42, at 3 (*Blount*, Fifth Congress).

68. 2 Hinds, *supra* note 38, § 1263, at 814–15.

69. Hupman, *supra* note 42, at 3 (*Blount*, Fifth Congress).

70. 2 Hinds, *supra* note 38, § 1264, at 816.

71. *Id.*

72. 2 *id.* § 1264, at 817.

73. 2 *id.* § 1264, at 817–18.

74. 2 *id.* § 1264, at 820–21.

75. 2 *id.* § 1264, at 821.

76. 2 *id.* § 1264, at 822.

77. Cong. Globe, 27th Cong. 2d Sess. 168 (1842).

78. 2 Hinds, *supra* note 38, § 1255, at 805–07.

79. Hupman, *supra* note 42, at 11–13 (*Tappan*, Twenty-eighth Congress).

80. *Id.* at 27 (*Davis et al.*, Thirty-seventh Congress).

81. *Id.* at 28 (*Mason et al.*, Thirty-seventh Congress) (adherence to the Confederacy); *id.* at 29–30 (*Breckinridge*, Thirty-seventh Congress) (same); *id.* at 30 (*Bright*, Thirty-seventh Congress) (Confederate sympathies); *id.* at 30–31 (*Johnson*, Thirty-seventh Congress) (same); *id.* at 31 (*Polk*, Thirty-seventh Congress) (same).

82. Tienken, *supra* note 37, at 143 (*Clark*, Thirty-seventh Congress); *id.* (*Reid*, Thirty-seventh Congress); *id.* at 143–44 (*Burnett*, Thirty-seventh Congress).

83. 2 Hinds, *supra* note 38, § 1253, at 804 (Long); 2 *id.* § 1254, at 804–05 (Harris).

84. 2 *id.* § 1288, at 858–60.

85. Tienken, *supra* note 37, at 121 (*Lyon*, Fifth Congress).

86. 2 Hinds, *supra* note 38, § 1275, at 835.

87. 2 *id.* § 1285, at 850–51.

88. 2 *id.* § 1285, at 851.

89. 2 *id.* § 1285, at 851–52.

90. 2 *id.* § 1286, at 852–57.

91. 2 *id.* § 1281, at 844–45.

92. 2 *id.* § 1274, at 832–33.

93. 2 *id.* § 1279, at 839–44.

94. Anne M. Butler & Wendy Wolff, United States Senate Election, Expulsion and Censure Cases, 1793–1990, at 413–18 (1995) (*Dodd*, Ninetieth Congress).

95. *Id.* at 418.

96. *Id.* at 429 (*Talmadge*, Ninety-sixth Congress).

97. *Id.* at 431–32.

98. *Id.* at 432–33.

99. *See* Katherine Q. Seelye, *Packwood Says He is Quitting as Ethics Panel Gives Evidence*, N.Y. Times, Sept. 8, 1995, at A1 (Packwood); Steven V. Roberts, *House Censures Crane and Studds for Sexual Relations with Pages*, N.Y. Times, July 21, 1983, at A1 (Studds and Crane); Butler & Wolff, *supra* note 94, at 434–37 (*Williams*, Ninety-seventh Congress) (Abscam); John Kornacki, *Expulsion and Ethics in the House*, The Hill, May 29, 2002, at 7 (same); Richard L. Berke, *House, 408 to 18, Reprimands Rep. Frank for Ethics Violations*, N.Y. Times, July 27, 1990, at A1 (Frank).

100. *See* Alison Mitchell, *House Votes, with Lone Dissent from Condit, to Expel Traficant from Ranks*, N.Y. Times, July 25, 2002, at A1. *See also* David Grann, *Crimetown USA*, New Republic, July 10, 2000, at 23.

101. *See* Maskell, *supra* note 18, at 15–17.

102. 2 Hinds, *supra* note 38, § 1599, at 1048.

103. 2 *id.* § 1600–03, at 1048–52.

104. 2 *id.* § 1606, at 1058.

105. *Id.*

106. 2 *id.* § 1606, at 1059–60.

107. Anderson v. Dunn, 19 U.S. (6 Wheat.) 204, 224 (1821).

108. *Id.* at 228.

109. *Id.* at 230–31.

110. 2 Hinds, *supra* note 38, § 1616, at 1083.

111. *Id.*

112. *Id.*

113. 2 *id.* § 1617, at 1084.

114. 2 *id.* § 1618, at 1087.

115. 2 *id.* § 1619, at 1089.

116. 2 *id.* § 1625, at 1097.

117. 2 *id.* § 1626, at 1098.

118. 2 *id.* § 1627, at 1099–1100.

119. 2 *id.* § 1628, at 1100–01.

120. 2 *id.* § 1604, at 1052–54.

121. 2 *id.* § 1604, at 1055.

122. *See* 10 Annals of Congress 122–24 (1800).

123. 2 Hinds, *supra* note 38, § 1604, at 1056.

124. 2 *id.* § 1636, at 1109.

125. 2 *id.* § 1640, at 1110.

126. *Ex parte* Nugent, 18 F. Cas. 471, 481 (C.C.D.C. 1848) (No. 10,375).

127. 3 Hinds, *supra* note 38, § 2686, at 1133–34.

128. Marshall v. Gordon, 243 U.S. 521, 531–32 (1917).

129. *Id.* at 541.

130. *Id.*

131. *Id.* at 545–46.

132. 3 Hinds, *supra* note 38, § 1666, at 1.

133. 3 *id.* § 1666, at 2.

134. 3 *id.* § 1671, at 14.

135. 3 *id.* § 1671, at 15–16.

136. 3 *id.* § 1672, at 17–18.

137. 3 *id.* § 1722, at 74–75.

138. 3 *id.* § 1722, at 75.

139. 3 *id.* § 1722, at 76–77.

140. 3 *id.* § 1689, at 34–35.

141. Cong. Globe, 42nd Cong., 3rd Sess. 952–56 (1873). As a matter of law, the committee was quite right to conclude that the name of a client does not fall under the attorney-client privilege. *See* R. M. Weddle, Annotation, *Disclosure of Name, Identity, Address, Occupation, or Business of Client as Violation of Attorney-Client Privilege*, 16 A.L.R.3d. 1047, § 3 (2004).

142. 3 Hinds, *supra* note 38, § 1689, at 35–37.

143. 3 *id.* § 1690, at 37–38.

144. 3 *id.* § 1690, at 38.

145. 3 *id.* § 1690, at 38–43.
146. 3 *id.* § 1698, at 52–53.
147. 3 *id.* § 1698, at 53.
148. 3 *id.* § 1698, at 53–55.
149. 2 *id.* § 1608, at 1064.
150. 2 *id.* § 1609, at 1066.
151. 2 *id.* § 1609, at 1067.
152. 2 *id.* § 1609, at 1068–69.
153. 2 *id.* § 1610, at 1069–70.
154. Kilbourn v. Thompson, 103 U.S. 168, 190 (1881).
155. *Id.* at 192.
156. *Id.* at 196.
157. *Id.* at 196–200.
158. Potts, *supra* note 25, at 819.
159. 3 Hinds, *supra* note 38, § 1699, at 56–57.
160. 3 *id.* § 1699, at 57–58.
161. 3 *id.* § 1699, at 58–59.
162. 3 *id.* § 1700, at 59.
163. 2 *id.* § 1612, at 1073–74.
164. *In re* Chapman, 166 U.S. 661, 668 (1897).
165. *Id.* at 668–69.
166. *Id.* at 670.
167. *Id.* at 671–72.
168. 273 U.S. 135 (1927).
169. 294 U.S. 125 (1935).
170. *Id.* at 147.

171. *Id.* at 149–50. Although the Court does not use this language, the implication is clearly that the Houses of Congress have the power of criminal contempt as well as civil. On the difference between the two, see Dan B. Dobbs, *Contempt of Court: A Survey*, 56 Cornell L. Rev. 183, 235–39 (1971).

172. *Jurney*, 294 U.S. at 151–52.

173. United States v. Rumely, 345 U.S. 41 (1953).

174. *See* Tobin v. United States, 306 F.2d 270 (D.C. Cir. 1962), *cert. denied*, 371 U.S. 391 (1962); Brewster v. United States, 255 F.2d 899 (D.C. Cir. 1958), *cert. denied*, 358 U.S. 842 (1958); United States v. Lamont, 236 F.2d 312 (2d Cir. 1956); United States v. Cuesta, 208 F. Supp. 401 (D. Puerto Rico 1962).

175. 167 F.2d 241 (D.C. Cir. 1948), *cert. denied*, 334 U.S. 843 (1948).

176. *Id.* at 246–47.

177. Lawson v. United States, 176 F.2d 49 (D.C. Cir. 1949), *cert. denied*, 339 U.S. 934 (1950); United States v. Josephson, 165 F.2d 82 (2d Cir. 1947), *cert. denied*, 333 U.S. 858 (1948).

178. Barenblatt v. United States, 360 U.S. 109, 134 (1959).

179. Christoffel v. United States, 338 U.S. 84 (1949).

180. United States v. Bryan, 339 U.S. 323 (1950).

181. *Id.* at 332.

182. United States v. Moran, 194 F.2d 623 (2d Cir. 1952), *cert. denied*, 343 U.S. 965 (1952).

Conclusion

1. Carl Wittke, The History of English Parliamentary Privilege 206 (photo. reprint 1970) (1921).

Index

Schwartz, Morton, 103

secrecy issues: Congressional record, 51, 52–53, 59–61; parliamentary privilege, 80–81

seditious behavior: breach of privilege, 130, 197, 204; electoral disputes, 199; expulsion rights, 221; free speech privilege, 73, 74, 88, 156, 191, 197; Sedition Act of *1798*, 221, 263n127; writ of habeas corpus, 32

self-dealing, 18, 91

Senate: congressional privilege, 3; democratic principles, 169–70; election guidelines, 163–65; justiciability, 53–67; member qualifications and disqualifications, 166–68, 188–89. *See also* Congress

separation of powers, 19, 54, 57, 59, 90–91, 177–78

Seventeenth Amendment (U.S. Constitution), 164, 170, 176

Seward, George F., 230–31

Shaftesbury, Earl of, 33–34

Sheldon, Lionel, 186

Shepley, George, 183

sheriff appointments, 201

Sherman, Roger, 163

Shippen, Judge, 139, 140

Shirley, Sir Thomas, 29–30, 195–96

Shirley, Thomas, 30–31, 196

Shirley case, 29–30, 115, 119, 195–96

Shirley v. Fagg, 30–31, 195–96

Silverglate, Harvey, 90, 91, 92, 93

Simmons, James, 221

Sinn Fein, 161

Skewys, John, 28

Skewys v. Chamond, 28–29, 118

slavery, 15, 16

Smalley, Edward, 124–25

Smalley case, 124–25

Smith, George Otis, 58

Smith, John, 218, 220

Smith, Samuel, 181

Smoot, Reed, 179–80

Soame, Sir William, 150

Solon, 16

South Carolina, electoral disputes, 187

Southern Conference Education Fund, 97

Spaulding v. Mead, 174

Stanbery, William, 224

Stanhope, Sir Henry, 121, 130

Stanly, Edward, 216

state sovereignty, 13

Stephen, Justice, 40

Stepneth, Alban, 123

Stern, Michael, 84

Stewart, Joseph, 228

Stewart, Potter, 56

St. John, Mr., 154

Stockdale v. Hansard: free speech privilege, 77–78, 83, 96, 99, 110; *lex parliamenti* versus *lex terrae,* 39–40; parliamentary privilege, 139

Stokes, Jeremiah, 197

Storie, John, 194

Story, Joseph, 89–90, 103, 135–36, 209, 212

Strauss, George, 41

Strauss case, 41–42

Streater, John, 32–33

Streater case, 32–33

Strickland, Sir William, 154

Strickland, Walter, 71

Strode, Richard, 70

Strode's Act, 70, 73–74

Strowd, William, 121

Studds, Gerry, 222

suffrage. *See* voter eligibility

Sumner, Charles, 215–16, 227–28

Sundquist, Don, 104–5

Supreme Court: Arrest Clause, 141; bribery cases, 105–6; Congressional record, 60; contempt cases, 226, 229–34; free speech, 95–105; impeachment decisions, 62, 64; political questions doctrine, 55–56; punishment decisions, 223–24

Talmadge, Herman, 222

Tappan, Benjamin, 220

Wolcott, John, 227
women, exclusion of, 15, 16
Wood, Fernando, 217
Wood, Gordon, 11–12
Wood, Robert, 156
Woods, Patrick, 224
Wray, Bourchier, 123–24

writ of *capias ad satisfaciendum,* 131–32
writ of habeas corpus, 3, 31–36, 156

York, Duke of, 114
Young, Thomas, 70

Zenger, John Peter, 246n83